DWIGHT D. EISENHOWER

SOLDIER AND STATESMAN

DWIGHT D. EISENHOWER

SOLDIER AND STATESMAN

R. Alton Lee

Nelson-Hall nh Chicago

LIBRARY OF CONGRESS CATALOGING IN PUBLICATION DATA

Lee, R. Alton.
  Dwight D. Eisenhower, soldier and statesman.

  Bibliography: p.
  Includes index.
  1. Eisenhower, Dwight D. (Dwight David), 1890-
1969.   2. United States—Politics and government—
1953-1961.   3. Presidents—United States—Biography.
I. Title.
E836.L42   973.921'092'4 [B]   81-519
ISBN 0-88229-626-4 (cloth)   AACR2
ISBN 0-88229-786-6 (paper)

Manufactured in the United States of America

10   9   8   7   6   5   4   3   2   1

For Gilbert C. Fite
Scholar, Teacher, and Friend

Contents

Chronology ix

Preface xi

1. The Kansas Farm Boy 1

2. Training for Leadership 27

3. Commanding the Allies 67

4. The Cold War Unfolds 117

5. Fighting the Cold War 171

6. Pursuing the Middle Road 215

7. Hazards of the Middle Road 251

8. Working for Peace 293

9. Verdict of History 331

Notes 337

Selected Bibliography 359

Index 371

CHRONOLOGY

1890 Born October 14 in Denison, Texas

1891 Family moved to Abilene, Kansas

1909 Graduated from Abilene high school

1911 Entered West Point

1915 Graduated from West Point

1916 Promoted to first lieutenant; married Mamie Geneva Doud in Denver

1917 First son, Doud Dwight, born (died in 1921)

1918 Commander of Camp Colt, Gettysburg

1920 Promoted to major

1922 Second son, John S. D., born

1926 Graduated first in class, Command and General Staff School, Fort Leavenworth

1928 Graduated from Army War College; worked in France for Battle Monuments Commission

1933 Assistant to Chief of Staff General Douglas MacArthur

1935 Senior assistant to General Douglas MacArthur, military adviser to Commonwealth of the Philippines

1936 Promoted to lieutenant colonel

1939 Returned to active duty in United States Army

1941 Chief of staff of the Third Army; promoted to colonel (temporary); promoted to brigadier general (temporary)

1942 Promoted to major general (temporary); promoted to lieutenant general (temporary); commanded Allied invasion of North Africa

1943 Promoted to general (temporary); directed invasion of Italy; named supreme commander, Allied Expeditionary Forces

1944 Directed invasion of Normandy; appointed general of the army (temporary)

1945 Accepted surrender of Germany; became chief of staff

1946   Promoted to general of the army (permanent)
1948   Became president of Columbia University; published *Crusade in Europe*
1950   Appointed supreme commander of NATO
1952   Elected president of the United States
1953   Delivered "Atoms for Peace" speech to the United Nations
1955   Attended summit conference in Geneva; suffered heart attack
1956   Had ileitis operation; re-elected president of the United States
1957   Signed first civil rights act since Reconstruction; sent troops to Little Rock
1959   Visited eleven European, Asian, and African countries; voted "World's Most Admired Man" by American people
1960   Attended abortive summit conference in Paris
1961   Delivered Farewell Address; retired to Gettysburg farm
1963   Published *Mandate for Change*
1965   Published *Waging Peace*
1967   Published *At Ease*
1968   Suffered four heart attacks
1969   Died March 28 at Walter Reed Army Medical Center; buried at Eisenhower Center, Abilene, Kansas

Preface

Dwight D. Eisenhower best exemplifies the new breed of officer that emerged during and after World War II, the type that developed a distinct ability to move with ease from the military to the industrial to the governmental world, and back again. This biography traces the highlights of his military and public career and is intended to meet the need for a brief, scholarly narrative of the life of one who was so important to America and to the world. I have endeavored to appeal to those who enjoy the lively art of biography; for those concerned with scholarly apparatus, footnotes and a brief bibliography are included to indicate my sources and where more can be learned about the subject. The final chapter, "Verdict of History," is a short survey of Eisenhower historiography.

This is an appropriate time to examine Eisenhower's life and contributions because scholars are now modifying their previously critical interpretations of his presidency. I empathize quite easily with Eisenhower's boyhood life for my hometown is forty miles from Abilene and our socio-economic backgrounds were similar. But I came to maturity during the years when his administration was viewed most adversely by historians and political scientists—while he was president—and I have been influenced by these early writings. I have also been impressed, however, with the recent scholarship. I have, therefore, carefully weighed both viewpoints while keeping in mind that neither a conservative nor a liberal political philosophy is inherently good or evil. The result is an attempt to present Eisenhower's political and fiscal beliefs as objectively as possible. On the other hand, I have not hesitated to pass moral judgment on his actions, or inactions, when I believed it was deserved.

In writing a volume like this, one is indebted to a great number of previous writers. I have tried to indicate my conscious debts in the notes. My failure to cite those obligations of a subconscious nature will, I hope, be forgiven. Several scholars contributed their insights and knowledge to improve the book. Professor Robert L. Branyan of Central Michigan University shared ideas about the Eisenhower presidency. The late professor Cedric Cummins of the University of South Dakota and James T. Patterson of Brown University read parts of the manuscript and offered valuable comments. I am particularly indebted to Professor Thomas Buckley of the University of Tulsa and Dean Emeritus Herbert S. Schell of the University of South Dakota for reading and criticizing the biography in its entirety. These fellow historians saved me from numerous mistakes. Any errors of omission or commission, or other inadequacies in the book, are my responsibility.

A sabbatical from the University of South Dakota provided a block of time for concentrated work and a grant from the University of South Dakota Research Fund helped financially with the research. Dr. John Wickman and the staff at the Eisenhower Library, especially Judy Lanvin and James Leyerzapf, were most helpful. Robert Carmack and the staff at the University of South Dakota Library also aided in locating materials. As for the support of my wife, Marilyn, suffice it to say that this book would not have been written without her patience and understanding.

CHAPTER ONE

The
Kansas
Farm Boy

The four-year-old boy had never been so far away from home before. When his Aunt Minnie visited the family he found that he liked her so much that he wanted to repay the visit. So he rode back home one hundred miles on a train with the aunt to her farm north of Topeka. Although he was surrounded by relatives there, they were all older than he. The boy soon felt lonesome and homesick, and there was little with which to entertain himself. But he decided the farm would be an exciting place to explore and he determined to familiarize himself with the area and the animals. When he did, he came in conflict with one of the inhabitants.

There were a pair of geese in the farmyard and the male resented any intrusion into his domain. Whenever the youngster approached, the gander would stretch his long neck and, hissing menacingly, chase him with flapping wings and darting beak. This was too much for four-year-old courage. The boy would flee ignominiously to the safety of the kitchen, there to complain tearfully to his elders. Repeated encounters convinced his Uncle Luther that an adult needed to take a hand in the situation. He cut the straw off an old broom except for a knob at the end, to protect the goose in case the boy's strength was greater than he surmised, and taught the young fellow how to swing the weapon.

Thus armed, the boy again ventured into the farmyard with a good deal of trepidation. Sure enough, the gander soon appeared to defend his kingdom. This time the lad gathered his courage and, as the fowl approached, he let out a howl of defiance that was designed to reassure himself as much as to frighten his adversary and charged with his newly acquired confidence and weapon. This was a strange development for the gander, who had never before experienced difficulty in evicting young boys from his kingdom, and the bird decided that retreat was in order for the moment. As he turned to flee, the boy whacked him hard on the rear, producing a hearty squawk of outrage and pain. The youngster always remembered thereafter to carry his weapon with him on his forays into the farmyard; when the gander saw him approach with his club, he would emit his frightful hisses and threats only at a safe distance. This episode, Dwight D. Eisenhower later recalled, impressed upon his receptive young mind the lesson that he should never attempt "to negotiate with an adversary except from a position of strength."[1]

THE EISENHOWERS

Dwight Eisenhower's ancestors once lived in the Bavarian Palatinate. Family legend translates the name as "iron striker"; probably it meant "iron hewer" or one who made armor and weapons. Some philologists believe it meant "armoured knight." The medieval Eisenhowers, in any case, were fighting men. Then the Reformation brought a sharp turn away from this military tradition in the family.[2]

During the sixteenth century, the Eisenhowers came under the influence of preachers who were imbued with the ideas of Menno Simons. The teachings of Menno Simons included rejection of the concept of a divinely ordained priesthood and authority of the church. The Bible was to be the sole source of religious authority, according to Menno Simons, and he emphasized the importance of the individual conscience, along with a strict pacifism. The various protestant sects—the Eisenhowers eventually became members of the Brethren in Christ—suffered severe persecution during the Thirty Years War.

The first Eisenhowers migrated from Germany via Switzerland to Pennsylvania in the eighteenth century and settled with coreligionists along the Susquehanna River some fifty miles north of Gettysburg. This group of the Brethren in Christ subsequently became known as the "River Brethren" because of their location. Despite their pacifist views, several Eisenhauers, as the name was then spelled, took part in the Revolutionary War. By the time the first United States census was taken in 1790, the present spelling of the name was being used. Frederick Eisenhower, Dwight's great-grandfather, was born four years later in 1794. Among the River Brethren the acquisition of property was a mark of God's favor, and, as a weaver, Frederick received God's blessing rather abundantly. He added to his worldly goods by marrying Barbara Miller, also of German ancestry and of his religious views, who brought a substantial dowry to the union. They reared six children, one of whom, Jacob, was Dwight's grandfather.

Jacob Eisenhower was a bright boy who early evinced an interest in books. He became a minister in the River Brethren church and preached in both English and German.[3] He continued the Eisenhower prosperity by becoming a capable farmer during the weekdays. He married Rebecca Matter who shared his religious convictions and who also brought a sizeable dowry to her marriage. Of the

fourteen children born to this union, only six survived
their teens. One son, David, was born during the Civil
War, just three months after the battle of Gettysburg.

When, after the Civil War, the River Brethren decided
to move west, Jacob Eisenhower migrated with his pa-
rishioners to Kansas. Selling his property, he and his wife
and their four children made the three-day train trip to
Abilene, Kansas, in 1878 to begin a new life. They settled
on a farm twelve miles south of the town. The Eisenhowers continued to prosper in Kansas, and Jacob was
able to give each of his children, upon their marriage, a
quarter section of land and $2,000 cash.[4]

Young David, fifteen at the time of the family migra-
tion, never learned to like farming. He was a quiet boy
who spent much time in self-contemplation and was far
more interested in scholarly pursuits than in tilling the
soil. He early decided against farming as a career. Once
he made the decision, he pursued it stubbornly and his
father was unable to persuade him to accept an agrarian
life. The only thing David enjoyed about the farm was
repairing the machinery and other equipment. He had
an unusual combination of interest in books and
machines.

His mechanical inclinations led him to the decision to
attend college and become an engineer. Jacob agreed to
finance his education and he entered Lane University, a
college in Lecompton, Kansas, operated by the United
Brethren church. Lane, of course, was a religious institution, but the curriculum stressed a combination of liberal
education, vocational training, and religious instruction.
It was during his second year at Lane that David began
paying increasing attention to a vivacious and attractive
blonde-haired girl named Ida Stover.

The Stovers were a Brethren in Christ family that
came from Germany via Switzerland and settled in the
Shenandoah Valley near Staunton, Virginia. Ida was
born in May 1862 during the Civil War. The Shenandoah

Valley, the granary for Lee's Army of Virginia, became a strategic area for both the Union and Confederate armies and the victim of General Philip Sheridan's campaign in 1864. After his army marched through the valley, Sheridan reported that "a crow flying over it would have to carry his rations." Undoubtedly, growing up in this utter devastation in the war and postwar years strengthened the pacifist views Ida received from her religious instruction.

Ida's mother died when the girl was quite young, leaving the father with eleven children. Unable to cope with this large brood by himself, Mr. Stover parceled them out to various relatives, and Ida was reared by her maternal grandparents. Her grandfather became her legal guardian and the trustee of her small estate upon the death of her father. Two of her brothers migrated to Kansas in the 1870s, and Ida determined to follow them when she reached legal age. After she arrived in Kansas she used her inheritance to purchase an ebony piano and to enroll in Lane University to study music.[5] She was a popular girl, but in their second year of enrollment the dark-haired, handsome, quiet David Eisenhower defeated his numerous rivals and Ida agreed to marry him. This meant that both must terminate their education, but they agreed that their love was more important than their careers. The year was 1885.

Jacob's offer of a quarter section of land and $2,000 to each of his children was open to David, but he and Ida wanted no part of farm life. Instead, he persuaded his father to let him mortgage his 160 acres for $2,000 and use that cash and the dowry to open a general merchandise store with a partner named Milton Good. The young businessmen chose the nearby thriving little village of Hope for their enterprise. For the Eisenhowers it was to prove bitter that the town was christened Hope and the partner named Good.

For the next two years the young couple were quite

happy. They proved to be very compatible, and the store seemed to be prospering. Their first child, Arthur, was born in 1886 and in 1888 Ida was again pregnant. The Eisenhowers appeared to have successfully begun establishing a happy home. But 1888 was a bad year for Kansas farmers, with a terrible drought scourging the Great Plains. The business of the store was based upon credit; the farmers around Hope purchased on time and the businessmen replenished their stocks in like manner. When the farmers were unable to pay their bills, the businessmen went broke. One night Good absconded with the little cash the business still had. Crushed by this betrayal, David hired a lawyer to straighten out the business affairs and determine if anything could be salvaged financially while he fled south to seek work. He took a job as a railroad mechanic in Denison, Texas, to support his family. The lawyer completed David's financial ruin, contributing only a large legal fee to the balance sheets. The business went bankrupt, and the mortgage was foreclosed, which meant that the farm was also lost. Ida remained in Hope until their second son, Edgar, was born in January 1889. Then, leaving her precious ebony piano with an Abilene friend, she took a train to Texas with her two sons to join her husband. After this bitter episode, David never again trusted lawyers and never permitted any member of his family to purchase anything on credit. It also took him a long time to recover his self-confidence.

The Eisenhowers were never happy in Texas. They missed their friends and relatives in Kansas. The one bright spot in their Texas sojourn occurred when their third son, David Dwight (later changed to Dwight David), was born on October 14, 1890. Although they did not particularly need another mouth to feed on David's meager wages, this joy helped compensate for the news of the death of Rebecca Eisenhower the previous June. Jacob was now alone, and he began importuning David to return home. But, with three children to feed, how could he give up his job, small as the pay was, and return to unknown prospects in Dickinson County? The problem was solved by his brother-in-law, Chris Musser.

The River Brethren had built the Belle Springs creamery in their settlement. It soon developed into the most prosperous business in the county, and in 1889 they constructed a large, new plant beside the railroad tracks on the south side of Abilene. Chris Musser became foreman of the industry and Jacob turned to his son-in-law for help in getting David home. Chris offered David a job as plant engineer or mechanic and sent money to transport the family and household goods to Abilene. Encouraged by Ida, David accepted the offer.[6] In the spring of 1891, the family returned to Abilene. Here Roy was born in 1892, Paul was born in 1894 but died from diphtheria after a few months, and Earl arrived in 1898. The last son, Milton, was born in 1899. Jacob, the family patriarch, lived with David and his family until his death in 1906.

ABILENE BOYHOOD

Abilene was an ideal place in which to raise six healthy, energetic boys at the turn of the century. It was changing at that time from a western motif to a rural setting. Texas cowboys and western gunslingers had made quite a reputation for Abilene in the 1870s, when it served as end of the trail for the massive herds of longhorn cattle that were driven north to be shipped on the Kansas Pacific (later Union Pacific) Railroad to the eastern packing houses. But, when Dwight Eisenhower moved there in 1891, the village was losing its cowtown image and developing into a small, rural county seat of about four thousand people, although the frontier spirit still clung to it. The town boasted two railroads, a branch of the Union Pacific and a branch of the Santa Fe.

Abilene, about one hundred miles west of Topeka, lies

between fertile, hilly eastern Kansas and the semi-arid plains of the western part of the state. The surrounding countryside is a flat alluvial plain with sufficient annual rainfall for diversified farming, with wheat and livestock as the major crops. Subject to climatic extremes, the environment of Abilene broke the spirit of many settlers. The survivors were a hardworking, courageous, and optimistic people, impatient to "get on with it" while at the same time patiently accepting the results that a harsh environment offered them. The frontier tradition there bred in its people an instinctive, rather than a philosophical, sense of democracy.

Abilene at the turn of the century was still a rather primitive rural town, little different from scores of others dotting the prairies. The streets were unpaved until the first decade of the twentieth century, and a sewage and a water system were installed about the same time. The sidewalks were made of board with some stone walks existing for help in crossing the muddiest holes in the streets. The police force consisted of two marshals, one who shook the doors of businesses at night to make certain the proprietors had locked them, and one for the daytime hours to chase truant boys—a far cry from the days of Wild Bill Hickok who tamed the town just a quarter of a century earlier.[7]

Abilene was divided socially and economically by the railroad tracks. There were three schools, one elementary school for each side of town and a high school for the few boys and girls who continued beyond the eighth grade. There were numerous churches which nearly everyone in town attended each Sunday. The churches also served as the center of what little social life there was, hosting picnics and various other "church socials." Nineteenth century Victorian mores still prevailed in Abilene; it is significant that Dwight did not know anyone from a divorced family until he went to West Point.

The house into which the Eisenhowers finally moved

was on South Fourth Street on the outskirts of town and is now preserved as the Eisenhower home. Set on three acres of land, there was room to grow alfalfa and corn for the livestock. There was also a big vegetable garden, a small vineyard, and a fruit orchard. A large barn on the property enabled the Eisenhowers to keep a flock of chickens, ducks, Belgian hares, pigs, milch cows, and a horse for pulling the family wagon and buggy. The huge barn loft stored several tons of prairie hay and alfalfa for the animals.

These assets made the Eisenhower family nearly self-sufficient, and David could raise his six sons on his modest salary. The boys were always dressed in neat, clean clothes, although they were often hand-me-downs, provided the older boys did not wear them out, and they had plenty of plain, wholesome food to eat. They were not conscious of being "poor." Shoes were the most precious commodity. The boys endured the usual amount of teasing from schoolmates about their shabby clothes, especially from the more affluent north side children. This could have turned them inward, causing them to be moody and bitter; instead, they tended to fight the taunting, literally with fists, and Edgar and Dwight particularly gained reputations for being "tough" south side kids.

The Eisenhower day usually began at sunrise during the summer and before sunup in the winter. With no girls in the house to share household duties, all chores, inside and outside, were divided among the boys and rotated weekly. In the summer there was also plenty of work for all in the garden and cornfield. David Eisenhower was concerned that the children have some money to spend as they pleased, especially for athletic equipment. Each, therefore, had a small plot in the garden, from which he sold the produce. Dwight usually raised sweet corn and cucumbers, as these were in the greatest demand. The boys learned both industry and frugality. As they grew older they had part-time jobs at the Belle Springs creamery, at other Abilene businesses, or on nearby farms. There was time for play, but that time had to be earned by doing the assigned chores properly and thoroughly. David rigidly enforced family discipline.

Family life centered around the father. He normally worked a twelve-hour shift, six days per week, at the creamery and either he came home for lunch or one of the boys delivered it to him so that he could have a hot noonday meal. One day when Dwight was about eight years old, he and Edgar were sent to the creamery with their father's lunch. Spring rains had flooded the Smoky Hill River and Mud Creek and the two boys found a deserted boat floating in the flood waters. They captured it, got in, and soon accumulated a boatload of boys to help in their explorations. Some time later, dripping wet, they were stopped by a neighbor who informed them their mother was looking for them. Guiltily they looked at each other and rushed home. Mrs. Eisenhower got them out of their wet and muddy clothing and gave them one of the worst whippings they ever had with a maple switch. Forgetting to deliver the family breadwinner's meal was almost sacrilegious in that household. They never again forgot.

David and Ida maintained an ideal partnership in raising their sons. Dwight later declared he never heard a cross word pass between them. David seemed to rely on Ida and to draw strength from her. She managed the household, but David was "breadwinner, supreme court, and lord high executioner."[8] Mother Eisenhower dispensed the minor discipline and Father handled the serious breaches of the family code. With six lusty, growing sons, strict discipline was undoubtedly necessary. David was of the traditional mold where the German father was an absolute authoritarian who did not believe in sparing the rod. David and Ida agreed on the verities of life and the best way to raise boys in accordance with those tenets. Their sons learned respect for elders and for authority; self-respect; that no matter how poor they were, opportunities existed for those willing to work; and the virtues of prayer, honesty, and self-reliance. Both parents were deeply religious and devout pacifists. Both were opposed to fighting, although with young sons who had reputations as "scrappers," this was not an absolute.

Dwight's father was fluent in German and conversed with his father in that language. After Jacob died, however, he spoke only in English because he wanted his sons to speak perfect English.[9] It was David who led the family in prayer at each meal and read and explained Scriptures to the children in the evenings. Following this Bible study, the boys had to do their homework while David read further in the Scriptures from his Greek Bible, the translation he loved best, as Ida sewed and mended clothes. In short, David was a quiet, retiring, contemplative man who worked hard, was stern with his children, and they in turn greatly respected and admired him.

It was probably Ida Eisenhower who had the greatest influence on Dwight. She always called him Dwight instead of by his first name to avoid the confusion of having two Davids in the house. Also she greatly disliked nicknames and was afraid David would be shortened to Dave at school. Years later when asked about her famous son, she would reply, "Ike? Who's Ike?" When he enrolled at West Point he reversed his name, making it officially Dwight David Eisenhower. Ida was a pretty, blonde-haired, blue-eyed woman who was a lively conversationalist, in contrast to her reserved husband, and she had a vivacious manner about her. It is a real tribute to her managerial ability and her psychological acumen that she took care of a father-in-law and a husband and raised six sons to maturity in a house of that size and on David's wages. Years later, Dwight recalled his father with respect and devotion and his mother with love and reverence. Friends noted that when he spoke of his parents he always talked more of his mother.[10] He received his physical characteristics from her, for he inherited her blonde hair, high forehead, firm chin, and a direct, searching expression in his blue eyes.

DWIGHT AND EDGAR

The Eisenhowers were a tightly knit family and no one boy seemed to stand out as a prominent individual. Edgar and Dwight, who were quite close in age, attended school together and were almost constant companions, both in work and play. There was nothing unusual about Dwight's early years.[11] He was of average size for his age, an active, aggressive boy who was just beginning to develop the grin for which he would later become famous worldwide. He did demonstrate rather early that he had a bad temper.

When he was ten years old, his mother gave Arthur and Edgar permission to go "trick or treating" on Halloween, but she told Dwight he was too young for such activities and he must stay home. This command was too much for Dwight, who considered himself the equal of Edgar, his constant playmate, and a crying spree resulted that culminated in hysterics. His father had to grab him by the shoulders and shake him back to consciousness. At that point Dwight discovered that he had been standing before an apple tree beating the trunk in rage with bleeding fists. He received a whipping for this temper tantrum and was sent to bed. His mother soon joined him in the bedroom and put salve on his torn hands. As she worked, she quoted a passage from the Bible, "He that conquereth his own soul is greater than he who taketh a city," adding that, of all her precious boys, Dwight had the most to achieve in this category. This episode made a deep impression on the young boy's mind. Out of this eventually developed the habit of not hating anyone or mentioning in public the name of anyone with whom he strongly disagreed.[12]

Ida, like David, was not fond of the boys fighting, but she always permitted her sons to settle their arguments physically, if necessary. She believed that this was the best way for them to clear their differences and that they would get along better together afterwards. She was quite aware of Dwight's nasty temper, and perhaps this accounts for her never interfering with any of the numerous fights Edgar had with him. Edgar's superior size and strength always permitted him to whip his younger brother. Possibly, Ida had decided that Dwight, forced to yield physically to Edgar in their boyhood battles, might learn self-control from it.[13]

However much they fought with each other, Dwight and Edgar were the best of friends and, being so close in age, were inseparable. They were the most mischievous of the six boys, forever daring and encouraging each other to attempt new things. There were few adventures so dangerous as to discourage them. Repeated whippings did not deter them from seeking new thrills.

When Dwight was six years old, he entered first grade at Lincoln School, located just one block north of his home. Here he left the familiarity of the family and ventured into the world of strangers for six hours per day. It was a two-story brick building with a cellar that contained a coal burning furnace. There was no plumbing and no lighting so the pupils used an outdoor privy and there were no evening or nighttime activities. On a cloudy, snowy winter day, the rooms were quite dark for reading.

Each room contained two classes. The girls usually jumped rope or played with jacks at recess time while the boys engaged in rougher play called shinny. This was their ground version of ice hockey with rules made up on the spot and promptly ignored. They used sticks or whatever they could find for clubs and the puck was a battered tin can. Dwight excelled at this dangerous game and could always be found where the action was the roughest.

When the puck finally knocked four or five front teeth from a boy, the principal put an end to the game.[14] The students were called to order from recess by a drum or triangle. The lower grades used slates to write on; the upper grades graduated to paper. After completing the sixth grade, Dwight entered Garfield School on the north side of town to finish his elementary education.

It was at Garfield that the traditional rivalry between north and south side students usually broke out. If no personal rivalry developed between two boys, the crowds would help initiate some. Dwight was chosen in his seventh grade year as the south side champion to meet the north's challenger, Wesley Merrifield. With repeated attempts after school, the crowd finally succeeded in forcing the two to fight one afternoon. Neither boy was very skillful in fisticuffs, but both had endurance. Finally, over an hour later, both were near exhaustion, barely able to lift their arms to slam each other, but neither would yield. At that point Wes said, "I can't lick you, Ike." Dwight replied that he could not whip Wes either, and the fight ended in a draw.[15] It was in grade school that Dwight got the nickname "Ike." Most of the Eisenhower boys were nicknamed Ike at one time or another. Edgar was known in school as "Big Ike," and Dwight was called "Little Ike." But of all the boys, it was Dwight to whom the nickname stuck for the rest of his life.

Dwight was only an average student in grade school. His interests in those years were far more physical than mental. He enjoyed all sports as a youngster and especially enjoyed baseball and football. His love for athletics is demonstrated by a story, undoubtedly exaggerated, that both he and Edgar told of one of his childhood illnesses. One day, while running and playing with a group of friends, he fell on a boardwalk and skinned a knee, seriously damaging, he thought, only a good pair of trousers. Two evenings later he did not feel well and lay down on the sofa in the living room. He dropped off into a restless sleep that turned into a delirium. The doctor was summoned. His diagnosis, particularly frightening in those days before antibiotics, was blood poisoning. Soon Dwight's leg was swollen as large as his body with an angry red line running up it. The doctor painted strips of carbolic acid around the leg, hoping the poisoning would not reach the groin; if it did, the boy would die. As he grew worse, the doctor recommended amputation. Dwight grimly refused. "I won't be a cripple," he said. "I'd rather die." His was an uncompromising will and the fortitude necessary to endure what might come. He got Edgar to promise not to let anyone cut off his leg if he were to lose consciousness.

While Edgar slept on a blanket spread across the doorway, the fever mounted higher and higher. The parents refused to let the doctor operate despite his insistence. Dwight was old enough to make his own decisions and this was one he had to make. Miraculously the infection stopped spreading and the fever subsided. Three weeks later he was up and walking around.[16] A school chum remembers this episode and insists that both the duration and the danger of the illness have been greatly exaggerated.[17] Even though it became distorted in childhood memories, the story is indicative of Dwight's attitudes and reactions. He had saved his leg, but he had missed so many days of school that year that he had to repeat the grade. Because Edgar later dropped out of school for two years to work, he and Dwight attended high school together and graduated in the same class.

Dwight and Edgar were the cooks for the family on Sundays. The family always attended the Brethren in Christ church in the morning. Later David and Ida became interested in the teachings of the Jehovah's Witnesses and the meetings were held in the Eisenhower home. But after the services, the boys prepared the noon meal to let their mother rest for the day. Dwight never lost his enjoyment for cooking, and in later years it was one of his favorite forms of therapy. When the gang of boys went camping, this chore usually fell to him as he was the best at it. This training stood him and the family in good stead the year Milton contracted scarlet fever.

It was a terrible blow to the family when this disease struck the youngest boy. The doctor announced that the family and the house would have to be quarantined. The boys would miss school but, more importantly, David, the breadwinner, would have to miss work for several weeks. How could the family survive this financial shock? The doctor finally agreed that Milton could be quarantined in his room along with Earl, who shared his room and thus had been directly exposed, and the mother who would try to nurse him back to health.

The following six weeks were a nightmare for all. Milton hovered near death for days, with Ida bathing him in cold packs. If he survived, there was the danger that the high fever would cause brain damage. Earl could not make even the normal amount of play noise. Ida dosed Earl constantly with sulfur and molasses and washed his skin and hair with formaldehyde to prevent him from contracting the disease. She called instructions through the door to Dwight, who cooked meals for the family accordingly. The door was opened only long enough to shove food through it and to empty the chamber pot. Finally Milton recovered and the family returned to normal. Neither Earl nor anyone else in the family caught the disease.[18]

Bob Davis was Dwight's great boyhood hero. He was in his fifties when Dwight was in his teens. Bob was an illiterate who had done many things in his travels. He fished for a living in the summer and trapped mink and muskrat in the winter. He taught Dwight much about the woods—how to handle a rowboat, how to fish and set fishnets, how to trap, how to hunt with a shotgun, how to avoid acquiring warts when handling toads. Most important, he taught the boy poker, continually stressing the importance of percentages in a deck of cards. Dwight was an eager pupil and became a good player. He continued to play poker until he was about forty, when he discovered that a number of fellow officers were losing more money than they could afford and he quit.[19] The heroes in American history that Dwight came to admire most were Washington, for his fortitude and capacity for self-sacrifice; Lincoln, for his perseverance; Lee, because he was "a perfect character, a person of sensitivity and kindness, a gentleman through and through;" and Franklin, for his ability to get people together for cooperation.[20]

HIGH SCHOOL DAYS

At the turn of the century, high school dropouts were numerous. Most boys had to go to work as soon as possible and girls sometimes married at an early age. Most of the students attending high school were girls. Arthur quit school after the eighth grade to go to Kansas City to seek his fortune. Edgar and Dwight were able to attend high school because they got part-time jobs, working after school hours, on Saturdays, and during the summer months. Usually one boy or the other or both had a job at the Belle Springs creamery. At one time, they jointly held down a full time job there, working alternate nights as night foreman. The work was not time-consuming. About every hour the fires had to be stoked, clinkers raked out, and fresh coal shoveled in. It permitted them to doze frequently between the hourly checks on the fires and also to study occasionally by the light of a naked electric lightbulb.

In their spare time, Dwight and Edgar also participated in high school athletics, especially football and baseball. Edgar was the better athlete of the two, but in his senior year Dwight had surpassed Edgar in size and gained enough weight to play in the line on the football team. At that time athletics were extracurricular activi-

orted by school boards. No funds were appro-
their support; someone volunteered to coach
without pay, and each player was responsible
ng his own uniform and equipment.

with these bleak financial prospects during
last year in high school, the students organized
ne High School Athletic Association and elected
sident. The association raised funds by contribu-
timulated student support for the teams during
s, and, directed by Dwight's energy and enthusi-
romoted a successful sports season that year.

ght somehow found time for dating. He was shy
d girls, possibly because he had no sisters, and this
ulness took the external form of acting indifferent
rd them; many girls found this fascinating. Dwight
seems to have taken pride in his "south side tough-
," and, when he became a football hero, the girls
nd him all the more attractive. Girls he dated later
alled that he was careless in dress and appearance,
th his hair seldom combed. He had a normally sunny
sposition and was engagingly extroverted, but his fiery
mper occasionally flared out of control.[21] Because of his
amily background, he would always remain shy around
women and prefer the company of men, with whom he
empathized and whom he really understood.

During his first two years in high school, the academic
environment was not the most conducive to scholarly
endeavors. Classes were held in the old city hall, a brick
monstrosity of arches and turrets of the style so popular
in municipal buildings at the turn of the century. There
was a room on the north side of the building which dou-
bled as a classroom and for the city council chambers in
the evenings. The city fire equipment was housed on the
south side. A large bell tower capped the edifice, and
hen a fire broke out in town the bell was rung lustily to
mmon assistance. Then all the high school boys and the
-bodied businessmen would become Abilene's volun-

teer fire department. Academic pursuits could be inter-
rupted at any time by a blaze or a false alarm, and the
boys then dragged out the hose cart and raced with it to
the fire, pursued by cheering girls, barking dogs, and
puffing middle-aged businessmen. As one biographer of
Eisenhower has noted, it was a school system that Tom
Sawyer would have enjoyed.[22] Dwight's last two years
in public school were spent in the newly constructed
Abilene High School.

The curriculum offered few choices; only Latin and
German were offered as foreign languages, and Dwight
chose Latin. As in elementary school, he was an average
student (no mean accomplishment considering the part-
time jobs he held). Like his father, Dwight was interested
in solving practical physical problems, and he enjoyed
plane geometry. He was quick to perceive errors of fact
or reasoning and seemed to delight in tormenting one
young teacher who was not as well prepared in his subject
as he should have been. Dwight relentlessly extracted the
last ounce of information possible from the poor fellow
and cruelly embarrassed him before the class on different occasions by trapping him in errors or lack of
information.[23]

The study of history, especially ancient history, was
Dwight's favorite subject even before he entered high
school, and he received his highest grades in this course.
Unfortunately, history as studied at that time was primarily a collection of facts concerning wars, treaties,
inventions, and explorations. Nothing was done to try to
train the student to shape a philosophy of history or to
discern trends or processes. Dwight's skill in this subject
undoubtedly stemmed from his marvelous memory that
was a storehouse of facts and dates, but he did not learn to
ask the whys and hows of history, and, unlike mathematics and physics, history did not really pique his curiosity.
The *Helianthus*, his high school yearbook, described him
as "our best historian and mathematician," and the class

prophecy predicted that Edgar would be elected president of the United States twice while Dwight would become "a professor of history at Yale."[24]

Joe Howe, a young bachelor who published a weekly newspaper, the *Dickinson County News,* had a considerable amount of contact with Dwight in those years. The star high school baseball pitcher, "Six" MacDonald, set type for Howe, and the newspaper office became one of the hangouts for the gang of high school athletes that included Edgar and Dwight. Howe was interested in the boys and was a member of the school board. When Joe occasionally helped with homework assignments, he found Dwight to be an average student who could compose a good speech, memorize it easily, and, if he forgot a line, extemporaneously fill in until he picked up the thread again later. He was quite good at writing themes but tended to procrastinate on them until the last possible moment for completing them. His themes were articulate, logically organized, and accurate, rather than original or inspired.[25] The exchange newspapers Dwight read in Joe's office further stimulated his interest in history— here was history in the making!

In May 1909, Dwight graduated from high school in a class of thirty-one, only nine of them boys. The commencement speaker was Henry J. Allen, editor of the *Wichita* (Kansas) *Beacon* and later governor and United States senator from Kansas. His major admonishment to the graduates was that he "would sooner begin life again with one arm cut off than attempt to struggle without a college education." Dwight's parents had constantly emphasized the importance of an education and thus had already planted the seed of the idea so this "emphatic pronouncement was iron in the spine of purpose" to the boy.[26]

Both Dwight and Edgar wanted to go on to college, but for financial reasons, only one could go at a time. They agreed to rotate, one working and one going to college, and in eight years they would both be finished. They flipped a coin to see which one would go first. Edgar won and left home to enroll at the University of Michigan Law School; Dwight got a full-time job at the creamery and sent Edgar money in order for him to remain in school.

By the time he graduated from high school Dwight had almost fully developed physically, and his mature personality and character had emerged. He was five feet, eleven inches tall, 145 pounds, with a rangy but solid body. The hard work he had done made his torso powerful and his hands rough. He was industrious and determined to succeed. He had a good native intelligence and, when properly stimulated and he concentrated, could absorb a mass of material quickly and organize it in a sensible manner. He was socially mature, for he had grown up with the constant realization that other members of the family were as important as he. As a younger son, he did not feel compelled to be the pacesetter; nor did he have a number of older brothers that he would feel impelled to emulate to exceed. He was aggressive and confident, but he was also cautious in never underestimating the opposition. He was completely unpretentious, and he had a pleasant personality and an engaging grin that he would cultivate in later years. He also had a dogmatic will and an explosive temper that he was learning to keep under control.

MAKING A DECISION

Dwight worked in the ice room and the boiler room of the creamery for a year after high school graduation. Then he was promoted to night engineer, working eighty-four hours a week, fifty-two weeks a year. The pay was an impressive $90 per month, and he was able to send Edgar some money. That and adding a year's physical growth and maturity was about all that he had achieved. A year after high school he was still undetermined about a permanent career except that he was sure he wanted to go to college. This aimlessness was changed by his friend Everett E. Hazlett, Jr.

"Swede" Hazlett, as Dwight nicknamed him, was the son of an Abilene physician. He had early determined on a military career, and three years at a military prep school failed to dampen this desire, much to his father's dismay. Swede asked his congressman for an appointment to West Point, but this did not materialize. As few Kansas farm boys were interested in the sea, however, appointment to Annapolis offered less competition, and Hazlett was offered an appointment to the naval academy instead. Hazlett accepted it, and in early May went to Annapolis where he attended a prep school to cram for the entrance exams in June. Much to his chagrin, he was deficient in mathematics and he failed the examination. But this experience generated in him a tremendous enthusiasm for the naval academy, and the congressman, upon request, kindly reappointed him for the next year. In the meantime, Swede returned to Abilene to study for a year to make certain he passed the examination the second time. He got a not very time-consuming job managing the office of a small business in Abilene, and this allowed him to devote many of his working hours to studying.

Although Swede and Dwight were about the same age, they did not know each other very well because Swede had gone to a military prep school; but he was one of the fellows who began to stop in and visit while Dwight worked his night shift. That year Dwight was working as night foreman, and, although he had only two men working under him, this was a responsible job for a nineteen-year-old boy. Swede was not only impressed with his position, but he also liked Dwight's personality. The two played penny ante poker, a game at which Dwight was becoming increasingly adept, and they occasionally raided the creamery's stock of ice cream or eggs and chickens which they cooked over the boiler fires on a well-scrubbed shovel. Swede came to like Dwight for his "candor, honesty, horse-sense and a keen sense of humor."[27] He also discovered that Dwight had a mind that seemed to be wasted in the Belle Springs creamery. The two developed a friendship that was to last their lifetimes; in later years, Dwight, in his letters, "opened up" and confided more to Swede than to any of his other correspondents.

Swede, of course, was full of enthusiasm that year for Annapolis, and the academy was often the topic of his conversations. During the course of their discussions one night, Swede suddenly said, "Why don't you come with me? We could have a swell time together and it would be a way for you to get a college education and you don't have to pay for it."[28] The latter point was the most impressive of Swede's argument. The same thought had been going through Dwight's mind but he was not really interested in the sea and a military career at that time seemed to lead to a dead end. Yet Swede's voicing what he had been thinking led him to review his current situation. What could he lose? He could always return to the creamery job, or a better one. He was dissatisfied with the last aimless year and this would be a way to get a free college education. But there was one problem: Swede had the only appointment their congressman could give. "Sure," said Swede, "but senators can make appointments too."

Once Dwight made up his mind to try for Annapolis, he pursued his course with vigor. Although he did not know anyone with "political pull," he was the unwitting beneficiary of the political liberalism that had swept the Kansas prairies during the two previous decades. In 1908, Joseph L. Bristow, a Progressive, became the first United States senator to be elected under the state's new primary law. Previously, politics sometimes played a role in academy appointments, particularly the coveted West Point ones, and they were often made on the basis of patronage or personal whim. But Bristow began the practice of giving competitive examinations and then appointing the most qualified boys. Dwight asked Abilene's leading citizens, including Charles Harger and Philip Heath, editors of the *Abilene Reflector* and *Abilene Chronicle,* respectively, to write letters supporting his request that Senator Bristow appoint him to Annapolis. Over a dozen letters were sent from Abilene, all glowing with praise for David Eisenhower and his family in general and for the industrious, dependable Dwight in particular. The merchants and solid citizens of Abilene were eager to help a bright, hardworking boy get ahead and would undoubtedly lobby even harder for one from the south side of town who they believed might not have had all the opportunities a north side boy had.

Some weeks later, Senator Bristow informed Dwight that appointments were available for both Annapolis and West Point and that he should appear at the office of the state superintendent of public instruction in Topeka on October 4 to take the examinations. Dwight was pleased; his parents were not. His mother especially abhorred war, considering it sinful, and here one of her sons was thinking of choosing a military life for a career. Yet the choice must be his. To decide for him would be to violate the principle that the individual must follow the dictates of his conscience and make decisions for himself. Besides, David remembered how his father had tried to make a farmer out of him, and Ida recalled elders trying to prevent her from coming west to Kansas to be with her brothers or to enroll in Lane University at a time when few girls sought a college education.

Swede and Dwight immediately began a crash program to prepare Dwight for the Topeka exams. Swede had the advantage of having gone to the Maryland prep school, and he also had West Point and Annapolis example tests with which to study. Every afternoon, for three hours or more, they worked in Swede's office, continuing their studies at night while Dwight worked at the creamery.

His intellectual ability was high, especially when he applied himself, and by October Swede pronounced him ready. Off to Topeka he went on the train to compete with eight other boys. They were told they could try for either academy or for both. For insurance, Dwight asked to compete for both Annapolis and West Point.

He was quite elated when a letter arrived announcing that he had scored highest for those wanting to go to Annapolis and second highest for West Point. But, in discussing the news and their future together, he and Swede discovered they had overlooked an important point. To be eligible for Annapolis one had to be between ages seventeen and twenty; this meant the boy could not be twenty when the class assembled at the academy. The Annapolis entrance exams were scheduled for next June. Classes then began that summer and Dwight would be twenty-one that following October. This seemed to dash all his rosy dreams. But the boy who placed first for West Point failed his physical examination, and Senator Bristow wrote Dwight that he could have the army appointment if he wanted it, as he was next on the list. West Point's age limit for entry was twenty-two.

He wanted it. The concept of getting a free college education had firmly taken root. Now the next problem was preparing for the West Point entry examination to be given the following January. This was only two months away and the cost of a cram school was out of the question. Dwight found the answer by returning to Abilene High School as a postgraduate student. His former teachers were eager to help and allowed him to attend classes and brush up on chemistry, mathematics, and the other courses that would be covered by the examinations. This also gave him a chance to play on the high school football team for one more season, there being no rules governing eligibility at that time. Years later he could not recall when he slept during these months—working a twelve-hour shift at night, going to school during the daytime, and practicing football in his spare moments.[29]

The time finally arrived for him to take the train to Jefferson Barracks, just outside St. Louis, Missouri, to take the West Point examinations. St. Louis was the largest city he had ever visited, and while there he did a foolish thing that could have jeopardized his chances for entrance into the academy. He and a friend decided one night to go see the sights of the big city. They wandered the streets for a while and then got on a streetcar. Soon they found themselves at the end of the line in East St. Louis. It was late at night and no more cars were running back across the Mississippi River. Frantically, they followed the tracks in a heavy fog until they came to a turn-off. At this point they did not know which branch to follow, but saw a light in a building. They went over and knocked on the door to ask directions. The door was opened by a man holding a revolver. When he finally determined that they presented no danger, the man lowered the gun and gave them directions for catching the last car for Jefferson Barracks that left St. Louis at 1:00 A.M. They raced to catch it, but they still faced the problem of getting back into their barracks undetected. They had been ordered to return to their rooms by taps and the guard at the gate would surely halt them. How would this breach of the rules affect their possible admission to West Point? Arriving at the barracks, they solved the problem by climbing over the wall at a deserted point. Fortunately for them, military security was lax, and they made it to their beds without being apprehended.[30]

After returning to Abilene, the long wait began for the results of the examinations to arrive. Dwight knew he had passed the physical test but the scholastic examinations were harder than he had expected. At last the news came. He had made an average score and was accepted. He was to report to the United States Military Academy on June 14. He entered West Point with the class of 1915, while his good friend Swede entered Annapolis that same summer.

CHAPTER TWO

Training
for
Leadership

When Dwight D. Eisenhower left the plains of Kansas in 1911 for the wooded granite bluffs of the Hudson, he entered a completely new life. At the same time, his country was entering a new era. The United States was ready to step onto the world stage and play an ever increasing role in world affairs. Dwight Eisenhower learned and grew with his nation so that at midcentury, when America assumed leadership of the "Free World," he was prepared to lead his country. His choice of a military career and his successes in it had an impact upon world history.

Dwight decided to take a week to make the journey to West Point. He stopped in Chicago and spent two days with Ruby Norman, who was studying at the Chicago Conservatory of Music. He had dated Ruby in his last two years in Abilene and enjoyed seeing her again. Then he visited Edgar in Ann Arbor for two days. Edgar was just finishing his semester exams at the University of Michigan, and Dwight toured the campus during the days. The last evening, they rented a canoe and took two girls for a moonlight ride on the river. Ike was so impressed that he nearly decided he had made a mistake in choosing West Point instead of enrolling at the University of Michigan.[1]

One can be certain that while he was riding on the train through the rolling green hills of Pennsylvania, Dwight thought of his father and the boyhood he had enjoyed there. He changed trains in New York City and took the West Shore Railroad north to West Point. The car he rode in was filled with Academy appointees. They unloaded at the station and made the long climb up the hill to the Plain.

WEST POINT

The boys registered at the administration building. They turned all their money over to the treasurer and were told from then on they would pay everything by check from the account containing their meager cadet salary. Any cadet caught with money on his person would be dismissed. Civilian suitcases and clothing were stored until the first furlough. Finally, they received a physical examination; Dwight's five feet, eleven inch height put him in the tallest company, for cadets were assigned according to height. When these preliminaries were concluded, the nervous, green cadets were then thrown into bedlam.

They entered into Beast Barracks with a number of Third Classmen descending upon them, yelling and barking out orders. The older boys were the Beast Detail, assigned to take charge of the Fourth Classmen who would be known as Beasts until after summer camp was ended. The Beasts were informed that they were a disgrace to the Academy and the human race and were ordered to "pull that gut in" and "wipe that smile off your face, mister." From now on, everywhere they went—to the barbershop, to get their issue of clothing, up to their rooms—it would be at double time—even on the stairs.

This introduction to West Point discipline was deliberately staged. It was calculated confusion designed to instill in the cadets a sense of absolute and unquestioning obedience as the complement to command. But it was bewildering to the uninitiated, and it continued for the remainder of the afternoon. As Dwight later recalled, if anyone had been given time to think, he would have left the academy immediately. But he constantly kept in mind "Where else could you get a college education without cost?" That evening the cadets were massed together and sworn into the service. This simple ceremony of taking the oath had a significant impact on Eisenhower and henceforth the flag and the term "The United States of America" would have a more profound meaning for him than it ever had before.[2]

Dwight took the harassment in stride. He was determined to adjust and to enjoy life while outwardly conforming to regulations. While external smiles were forbidden, he could grin inwardly and accept the system for what it was. His age and physical toughness stood him in good stead during the June heat and the required tempo of movement. This initiation was particularly difficult for some of the younger, inexperienced boys who had led more protected lives. But in his work experience Ike had met many tough bosses, and upperclassmen posed no threat to his inward serenity. West Point, in a sense, was Abilene all over again, only on a larger scale. Here, too, he was the boy from "the wrong side of the tracks," competing with fellows generally from upper-middle-class origins, many with Southern accents, and he would eventually win the respect of his peers with his engaging personality and athletic prowess.[3]

Beast Period ended after three weeks and the cadets were permitted to choose a permanent roommate. Dwight had noticed a tall, well-built, friendly looking fellow and, although they had never spoken to each other, they seemed to find a mutual attraction. Eisenhower walked over and introduced himself. He discovered that his new friend, Paul Hodgson (better known as P.A.), was a fellow Kansan and also loved sports. He asked him to be his

roommate and, in cadet slang, P.A. agreed to become
Ike's "wife" for the rest of their cadet days. P.A. was a fine
athlete and a good scholar. The two got along tremen-
dously well and formed a friendship that lasted until
P.A.'s death in 1955.[4]

The new cadets quickly discovered that the West Point
mold, with its emphasis on "Duty, Honor, Country," was
rigid. The purpose of the academy was to train instru-
ments, not molders, of national policy. Emphasis was
placed upon building character, and the curriculum
stressed the study of science to the neglect of the liberal
arts. Fourth-year cadets took a one-year course in
English and modern European history. This single combined course, plus one in a modern foreign language (Ike
took Spanish), were the only concessions the curriculum
made to the humanities.[5] This is probably the curriculum
Dwight would have chosen, though, if he had been permitted an elective system. It coincided with his analytical
ability, his logical thinking, and his extraordinary memory. His scholarship at the Point was similar to that of his
high school days, merely adequate. He had no desire to
shine academically; he was more interested in athletics.
His basic character was set when he arrived at West
Point. The military academy merely added a high polish
to it.

Playing football proved to be one of Ike's primary interests. Although he weighed only 152 pounds in his fourth
year, he and Hodgson were able to make the Cullom Hall
(plebe) team and the upperclassmen expected the two to
make the varsity team the next year. Participating in
athletics had an additional compensation; athletes were
"recognized" (spoken to) by upperclassmen and permitted
to eat meals with the athletic squads. During the next
summer, Dwight practiced running, fast starts, and gym-
nastics. He indulged his appetite and, by the time football
season opened in 1912, he weighed 174 pounds and was in
excellent physical shape. He made the varsity team as a

speedy halfback and played enough to win his letter. Eastern newspaper sports writers suggested the possibility that he might make the All-American team that year. But in the Tufts game, he was tackled and held by his foot. When he tried to twist loose, a sharp pain came from his knee. The joint quickly swelled up and became inflamed. He was hospitalized for a few days and then discharged with instructions to be careful in his movements.

A short time later he participated in riding drill under the eye of an instructor who was something of a martinet. When Dwight failed to go through all the exercises of mounting and dismounting, the instructor accused him of malingering. Instead of explaining his physical situation, this challenge acted as a personal affront to his code of honor and a spark to his temper. He ignored P.A.'s whispered pleas to disobey the orders and instead complied with the drill instructions. All afternoon Dwight mounted and dismounted while the pain in his knee increased with each jolt. He would not give up. Finally, the knee crumpled under him as the strain tore the ligaments loose. He was carried off to the hospital.

A half-century later, this injury would be regarded as a normal result of playing football and an immediate operation would be in order. At that time, though, with the development of antibiotics far in the future, doctors operated on the knee only when absolutely necessary because infection could result in a permanently stiff knee.[6] For four days doctors worked to straighten his knee. He stayed in the hospital for a month. The knee mended but the loose cartilage remained and ended Ike's athletic career. For the rest of his life he would have to be careful of that trick knee. He found an outlet for his energy during his last two years by becoming a cheerleader. He also worked out regularly on the horizontal and parallel bars and developed powerful arm and shoulder muscles. When he was at the Point, he could chin himself five times with his right arm and three times with his left. It was during this time that Dwight designed the black and gold capes the cadets still wear at athletic contests and which, when massed in proper formation in a football stadium, spell out "Army." He enjoyed helping coach the Cullom Hall football team in his first year. But the end of his playing career was a bitter blow, and he "took it pretty hard."[7]

Dwight adhered strictly to the Point's code of honor but viewed the remainder of the regulations with amused tolerance and a challenge to his ingenuity. P.A. was often terrified at the chances Ike took in risking disciplinary action. But Eisenhower once told P.A. rather nonchalantly that, if he were ever dismissed, he would "go to South America and help open up the country."[8] In the tradition of his boyhood, he continued to court danger for the thrill of it, while his roommate took the rules far more seriously. P.A. was especially horrified at the delight Ike and a classmate, Tommy Atkins, took in bedeviling upperclassmen who took themselves too seriously. One day, after being caught in a minor infraction of the rules, they were ordered to report to an upperclassman's room after tattoo in "full dress coats," a cutaway with long tails in back and cut straight across the waist in front. They obeyed the order literally and appeared at the appointed time without any other stitch of clothing. They saluted and solemnly declared, "Sir, Cadets Eisenhower and Atkins report as ordered." The upperclassman let loose an involuntary scream of outrage which quickly drew a large crowd of cadets. Some were greatly amused and others highly indignant. The two cadets considered their subsequent punishment worth the pleasure they had received from discomfiting an upperclassman.

One Eisenhower escapade led to a change in the wording of the punishment code at West Point. At a dance he and a professor's daughter were whirling more than was considered proper. He was admonished not to dance that vigorously in the future. Some time later he attended another dance and met the same girl, with whom he repeated the earlier performance. The commandant demoted him from sergeant to private and gave him a "month on the area." This confined him to the barracks area or the gymnasium and he had to walk punishment tours. But he had to spend that month in the hospital with his injured knee and could not walk the tours. From then on, punishments of that type were worded so that the cadet would be confined and, at an unspecified time, walk the punishment tours.[9]

With the end of his football career, it might be expected he would concentrate more on scholarship. This was not the case; the reverse was true. His grades dropped and, at the end of his second year, he stood 81 in a class of 177, compared to 57 the previous year. He also learned to smoke cigarettes, a violation of the rules. He accumulated numerous entries on his "skin sheets," the record of demerits, with many offenses for tardiness and using improper language. A number of his infractions were self-reported for, although he was not a strict disciplinarian, he subscribed completely to the honor code. He willingly walked off the "slugs" he earned. This entailed hours of marching ramrod straight with the rifle properly on the shoulder. But he ranked 125 in conduct in a graduating class of 164.

Dwight continued his interest in poker while at West Point and established a reputation as a good player. In his later cadet years he usually played poker during the Academy dances, attending only those "hops" that had "boodle" (cadet slang for forbidden food). Because use of money was forbidden, accounts were kept on the poker losses and were to be paid after the cadets graduated and were commissioned. For some time after graduation, checks poured in to Eisenhower from Army posts all over the world, paying the poker debts from cadet days.

Ike's reputation for writing with ease was early established at the Point. P.A. noted in a letter he wrote home that Dwight had "naturally a very direct and pleasing style of writing." Themes were due on Mondays at 2:00 P.M. Hodgson agonized over his for days. In contrast, when they returned to their room after lunch on Mondays, Ike would take a nap, leaving instructions to wake him at 1:30. P.A. would then enviously watch Eisenhower scribble out an excellent three hundred-word theme in half an hour.[10] Dwight ranked tenth in his class in English.

At the end of the second year, cadets were given a two-and-a-half month furlough, a respite almost as welcome as graduation itself. This was the first time Dwight was able to visit home. No doubt he strutted a little before his brothers and boyhood friends in Abilene and was persuaded once to don his full-dress uniform for display. It was wonderful to see his parents again that summer as well as Earl and Milton, who worshipped their big brother.

An event occurred during this furlough that revealed something of Ike's basic personality. He was asked to umpire a baseball game at Chapman and, before the game, he decided to amuse himself at a shooting gallery. As he picked up a rifle, he heard a man offer to bet another person that the "soldier boy" could shoot better than he could. This caught Dwight completely by surprise, for he was a stranger in Chapman and was not wearing any cadet clothing. The episode so astonished him that "a fit of trembling" struck him; with shaking hands, he laid down the rifle and walked away without speaking. Never before or after did he experience that feeling.[11] The surprise of being identified without wearing his cadet uniform must have been great for him to pay for shells and then not use them. Not only was this contrary to his nature, but that summer he did not have sufficient funds to spend money foolishly. The vacation time passed all too swiftly, and soon it was time to say goodbye. This farewell was not as difficult as his first one, but it would be two more years before he would see them again.

It was much easier to fit back into the system this time. He was popular with his fellow cadets, and life continued as it had when he was a plebe and a Third Classman. His academic record improved the last two years and he moved up to 65 in a class of 170. His graduation rank academically was 61 in a class of 164, a good, but not outstanding, record.

In June 1914, the Archduke Francis Ferdinand of Austria-Hungary and his wife were assassinated in Sarajevo, and soon Europe was engulfed in war. Although West Point was not closed to the outside world, the developments of this terrible struggle impressed the busy cadets only indirectly. But to Dwight, this was an opportunity to observe and to learn at a distance, and he and P.A. traced the movements of the war with pins on a map of Europe. From this study he learned a most significant point. The machine gun had completely changed the science of warfare by giving the defense a three-to-one advantage over the offense. It was obvious to Dwight that new answers must be devised to meet the problem. As a result, he became one of the earliest and most ardent supporters of the tank and airplane as military weapons.

In the spring of 1915, just weeks after the sinking of the *Lusitania,* Ike was ready to be graduated. As the Annapolis graduation was earlier, Swede Hazlett came up to West Point to see him. It did not surprise him to find that Dwight was universally liked and respected by his fellow cadets. One of Ike's superiors at West Point evaluated him thus: "We saw in Eisenhower a not uncommon type, a man who would thoroughly enjoy his army life, giving both to duty and recreation their fair values [but] we did not see in him a man who would throw himself into his job so completely that nothing else would matter."[12]

Eisenhower wrote in the *Howitzer* (yearbook) of a class-mate, Omar Bradley: "Brad's most important characteristic is getting there, and if he keeps up the clip he's started some of us will someday be bragging that, 'Sure, General Bradley was a classmate of mine.' " The Class of 1915 was "The Class the Stars Fell On." Out of 164 cadets, 59 became generals. Among them, Bradley and Eisenhower became five-star generals, while James Van Fleet and Joseph McNarney became full (four-star) generals.[13]

Dwight's graduation was never in doubt, but his commission was. The head of West Point's medical staff called him in and told him that because of his knee it might be necessary to recommend that he be denied his commission. The regular army was only 120,000 strong at that time, and the military academy graduated more than enough second lieutenants. Officials were careful not to commission someone who would have to retire early and draw a disability pension. This news did not particularly upset Ike. He had achieved his major purpose of acquiring a free education. There was a sum of money awaiting him out of the compulsory savings made for all cadets and from which they purchased their uniforms. His response to this bad news was that he had always been interested in Argentina, and perhaps he might go there for a while.

A few days later the medical official sent for him again and said he would recommend him for a commission in the coast artillery. This had no appeal to an adventurer from the plains of Kansas, so Eisenhower refused. He was called in for a third interview and informed that, because his injury had been aggravated by a riding accident, the officer would recommend him for a commission if he did not request the mounted service. Dwight had no interest in the cavalry and agreed to this condition; on his preference card he put infantry first, infantry second, and infantry third.[14]

Graduation ceremonies were held in June. For the last time, as a cadet, Dwight heard the choir sing the West

Point hymn to Duty, Honor, Country, one stanza of which is particularly stirring:

> The long grey line of us stretches
> Through the years of a century told,
> And the last man feels to his marrow
> the grip of your far-off hold.

Again, as on that first day at the academy, in taking the oath to the United States, an overpowering feeling of dedication came over him. Surely, those of that long grey line would live forever.

Dwight did not receive his commission and assignment until September 1915. In the meantime he took an extended vacation in Abilene. He had applied for duty in the Philippine Islands and was certain he would receive his choice because that country had a low priority for service preference. Ike used his equipment fund to purchase tropical uniforms—khaki for the field and white for dress. He was given the remainder of his equipment fund in cash, and, because his tropical uniforms were far below the average cost of the olive-drabs and dress blues, this amounted to several hundred dollars which financed an enjoyable summer at home. Much to his surprise, he received orders to report to Fort Sam Houston, Texas, and had to borrow money to purchase the regular uniforms. He was now prepared to begin serving his country and acquiring the experience that would be vital for participation in the global conflict of midcentury.

Fort Sam Houston and World War I

United States relations with Mexico were in turmoil following the 1911 revolution against Porfirio Diaz and the counterrevolution against Francisco Madero in 1913 that brought Victoriano Huerta to power. President Woodrow Wilson refused to recognize Huerta as the law-

ful ruler, for he had come to power by murder; Venusti-
ano Carranza, with the aid of arms purchased in the
United States, replaced him in 1914. Other revolutionar-
ies, such as Pancho Villa, were waiting for the opportunity to depose the American-supported Carranza, and
meddling in their domestic affairs by the United States
was resented in many quarters in Mexico. This created a
tense situation along the border. The conflict culminated
in the frustrating Pershing expedition of 1916–1917
wherein the American Army sought in vain to capture
Villa after his raid on Columbus, New Mexico. Eisenhower and a number of young officers were assigned to aug-
ment the strength of the border forces.

Ike's reputation as a good fellow and as something of a
daredevil preceded him to Fort Sam Houston, and, while
there, he added to it. The young Second Lieutenants on
the post were forced to create their own amusements,
except for those occasional times when they could afford
an evening in San Antonio. One evening a group of them
were standing near the post flagpole which was supported against the Great Plains winds with strong cables
fastened to the pole some fifty or sixty feet high. Dwight
casually mentioned that he thought he could climb one of
the cables by using only his hands. A companion
expressed skepticism over the idea and produced a five-
dollar bill, which was promptly matched by Ike. A time
limit was set, Dwight stripped off his blues, and started
"overhanding" his way to the top. As he approached his
goal, he heard a call from below. "Who is that up on that
cable?" shouted colonel Millard Waltz, the commanding
officer. "Come down at once." Trying to save his bet, Ike
explained the situation while dangling from the cable,
and asked permission to continue to the top. He promised
he would then descend immediately. "DO AS I SAY AND DO
IT RIGHT NOW. GET DOWN HERE," bellowed the colonel. He
gave Dwight a few suggestions for self-improvement and
stalked off. The bettor then asked for his winnings, but

Ike claimed he had won, for everyone could see he was just about to succeed when the colonel appeared. The argument waxed hotter until Eisenhower suggested they settle it behind the barracks with fists. The thought of what the colonel, in his present mood, would say if he caught them fighting served to cool off tempers and the bet was off.[15] Ike also built up his reputation as a poker player at Fort Sam Houston.

The month following his arrival at the fort, Eisenhower met his future wife. One Sunday afternoon, when he was officer of the day, he began an inspection of the guard posts. As he passed a group of people, Mrs. Hunter Harris, a popular woman on the post, called to him to come over and meet some people. He responded that he was on duty and was busy. Mrs. Harris turned to an attractive young lady and said that he was "the woman hater of the post." This caught the girl's attention and she said something in reply to Mrs. Harris who again called to Dwight that he did not need to stay, but only to be introduced to some friends. He came over and met Mr. and Mrs. John Sheldon Doud and their daughter Mamie Geneva. Mamie was an attractive girl—pictures of her at the time show a striking resemblance to the actress Lillian Gish—with dark brown hair cut in bangs and blue, almost violet, eyes.[16]

Ike was immediately intrigued with her and asked if she would care to walk with him on his inspection tour. Although she disliked walking, she agreed and as they strolled they began to get acquainted. He told her of his background and learned something of hers. Her father, John Doud, had moved from Chicago to Boone, Iowa, where he established a very successful meat-packing plant. He married a Boone girl, Elvira Carlson, and they had a family of four girls, two of whom died in their teens. The Douds eventually settled in Denver, and every year they drove south to San Antonio in the family's big Winston Six to spend the winter months. Mamie's background seemed far more affluent than his, but they found they had much in common. Mamie, in turn, was attracted by his athletic appearance, his handsome features, his West Point polish, and his infectious grin.

Dwight became certain she was, in West Point parlance, his "one and only" and he began an arduous courtship of Mamie and of her family. Although Mamie was one of the most popular girls on the post, her other beaux soon discovered Dwight had the inside track. He was a persistent suitor and she accepted his West Point ring as an engagement ring on Valentine's Day 1916.

At this time, Dwight was becoming more and more convinced of the increasing importance of the airplane and the tank in modern warfare. He applied for transfer to the new aviation section of the army because he was enthusiastic about learning to fly and because men in the aviation section received a 50 percent increase in pay. The latter was an important item to a young man in debt who was thinking of marriage. He happily reported to the Doud family one night the news that his transfer had been accepted. The announcement was greeted with stony silence. The Douds liked him, but flying was a dangerous experiment. If he were going to be so foolish as to go into this branch of service when he was thinking of marriage, Mr. and Mrs. Doud would have to withdraw their consent. This was cold water dashed on Ike's high hopes and he left the house to think about this turn of events. Two days later he announced his agreement with the Doud's decision, to the relief of Mamie's family. This episode made Eisenhower think through his ambitions thoroughly and from this he determined to become the best officer he could regardless of the branch in which he served.[17]

Ike's reputation as a football coach and player preceded him to Texas. Soon after he arrived at Fort Sam Houston, Peacock Military Academy in San Antonio asked him to coach their football team. Although he needed the extra money, Dwight declined, feeling this would be inconsistent with his dignity as an army officer. His commander, General Frederick Funston, a friend of Mr. Peacock, thought differently. He briefly discussed the matter with Ike who then accepted the position. The Doud family became football enthusiasts that fall and came out each week to cheer on "Ike's boys." During these weeks and months, Dwight was completely accepted into the Doud family. He thoroughly enjoyed Mamie's father and mother, and they reciprocated the feeling. Having a home life was important to him, and he made their house a second home.[18] Mamie later recalled that he especially captured her mother's affections, and she learned that when she and Ike had a quarrel, she could usually expect her mother to take his side in the argument.

They planned initially to get married in November 1916, when Mamie would be twenty. But with the tense situation on the Mexican border, plus the uncertainties with the European war and congressional debates on Wilson's Preparedness Program, they accelerated their schedule. Ike wrangled a ten-day leave, and they were married in a Presbyterian church in Denver on July 1, 1916. The bride wore a white lace gown, and the groom wore his white dress uniform. That same day he was promoted to First Lieutenant with an increase in pay to $151.67 per month. After a brief honeymoon, they took a train to Abilene to visit the Eisenhower family.

From the beginning there was mutual affection between Mamie and the Eisenhowers. The Doud and Eisenhower families, far apart in social and economic status, accepted the same basic values. Mamie learned a great deal from Ida Eisenhower about the Eisenhower men in general and Dwight in particular. The boys had been taught that the husband was to be head of the family, she was told, and they were strong willed. A confrontation of wills by a wife could only end in defeat for her. Dwight soon found, though, that Mamie had a mind of her own. He went to Joner Callahan's cafe one afternoon and got into a poker game. He did not return home for supper and Mamie was furious. Ida tried to soothe her but, when he had not returned by dark, Mamie called him on the telephone. In reply to her order to "come home this instant" or not at all, Dwight said he never left a poker game when he was behind and he hung up. When he came home at 2:00 A.M. with his winnings, the storm broke. Both learned a great deal about each other from this episode; Mamie discovered what Ida meant by a conflict in wills, and Ike, in turn, recognized Mamie's spirit and how deeply he had hurt her with his thoughtlessness. In her own way, Mamie could be as determined as Dwight. This experience matured him a great deal.[19]

Mamie quickly learned about her new husband and his profession. Soon after their marriage, Ike came home early one afternoon and, without saying anything, began packing his bedroll. "You're not going to leave me this soon after our wedding day, are you?" she wailed. He hugged her and gently said, "Mamie, there is something you must understand. My country comes first and always will; you come second." This revelation was quite a shock to the young bride. Another episode involved a small hoard of money she had saved from a wedding gift. One day for emphasis in an argument, she slapped the back of Dwight's hand which was resting on a table. Her ring struck his West Point ring and broke the amethyst. "He looked at it sadly for a moment," she reported, "then said quietly: 'Young lady, for that fit of temper, you will buy me a new amethyst with your own money.' And I did—although parting with those dollars almost killed me."[20] But they soon adjusted to each other and had a good marital relationship. Mamie quickly learned the rules of army etiquette and made a good home for Ike—wherever they were stationed—in the next five decades. She was vivacious, and Dwight had an easy charm, so they were a popular couple at every post. Most important, Eisenhower quickly matured in his marriage, and, while he retained his pleasant and engaging personality, he shed his rule-breaking, devil-may-care attitude of cadet days and began taking life more seriously.

It was well that he did, for the situation in Europe was rapidly becoming critical for the United States. With stalemate on the Western Front and Russia withdrawing from the war on the Eastern Front, Germany decided upon a calculated risk in early 1917. In January of that year, Germany sought through official channels to take advantage of the strained Mexican-American relations by persuading Mexico to wage war on the United States. At the same time, the Kaiser announced that Germany would begin a policy of unrestricted submarine warfare on February 1, 1917. These events would undoubtedly bring the United States into the war on the side of the Allies, but, with Russia out of the fighting and with extensive use of the submarine, Germany expected to win on the Western Front before America could make any significant contribution to the Allied war effort. With the sinking of four American ships in March 1917, President Wilson asked Congress to declare war. This was done on April 6. Now Mamie's worst fears were realized; Dwight might have to go to war. What if he had to go before the baby was born in September or October? Ike, like other West Pointers, sought duty where the fighting was as the best way to fulfill the purpose for which he had been trained.

He was to be disappointed in his quest for overseas duty. To build an army quickly, cadres of officers and men were split off to form new regiments of recruits. Dwight was transferred from the Nineteenth Infantry to the Fifty-Seventh Infantry as supply officer. The new unit was based at Camp Wilson, some twenty miles from San Antonio. These were hectic weeks of work, especially with the keen competition for supplies and equipment, and Mamie resented this forced separation. Eisenhower had Sundays off but lacked transportation. One Sunday Mamie decided to take matters into her own hands. She called her husband to tell him she was coming out and asked him to meet her at the camp gate. John Doud had given the Eisenhowers a used roadster but Mamie had never driven it. She got an enlisted man to show her how to start the motor and put it in gear. Then she started off. As she approached Camp Wilson, Dwight could hear her crying, "Ike, get on, get on quickly—I don't know how to stop this thing." Ike jumped on the running board and turned off the ignition. Part of the day was then spent in teaching Mamie how to drive so she could reach home safely.[21]

Dwight's career looked promising in 1917. On June 1 he was promoted to Captain and the Fifty-Seventh Infantry was getting ready to go overseas. He hoped they would remain in Texas until the baby was born. On September 20, he received the disheartening news that he was to report to Fort Oglethorpe, Georgia, to instruct officer candidates. The baby, named Doud Dwight, was born in San Antonio four days after Ike arrived in Georgia. More disappointing orders soon arrived. He was transferred to Fort Leavenworth, Kansas, as an instructor of provisional officers. He was just too good at training men![22] Soon thereafter he received better news. He was to report to Fort Meade, Maryland, to help organize the 301st Tank Battalion which would then go overseas with Dwight in command. Instead, in the following weeks his commander was so impressed with his organizational ability that Ike was ordered to take command of Camp Colt near Gettysburg—the only tank training center in the United States.

This was an important position for a twenty-seven-year-old captain—to command a camp training six thousand men. Swallowing his disappointment at again being thwarted in obtaining European service, Ike threw all his energy into his new responsibility. This command meant

Mamie could now join him, which she did, bringing along little "Icky" as they nicknamed their boy. They lived in a rented house in Gettysburg.

Camp Colt only had one tank, a small Renault. The factory at Dayton, Ohio, was supposed to be turning out American tanks, but none arrived at Camp Colt until after the war was over. As camp commander, the former rule breaker now became a strict disciplinarian. At the same time he was "most human, considerate" of his men. He was always available to discuss either personal or military problems and he "shied at publicity, preferring to remain in the background."[23] Promotions came rapidly; he was promoted to major (temporary) and then, on his twenty-eighth birthday, made lieutenant colonel (temporary). The men he trained for tank warfare (without tanks) performed so well in France that, in 1922, Dwight received the Distinguished Service Cross for his "unusual zeal, foresight and administrative ability" while at Camp Colt.

Ike finally persuaded his commander to let him take the next contingent of troops overseas. His orders were to embark from Fort Dix, New Jersey, on November 18, 1918. The Armistice was signed on November 11, though, and Eisenhower never saw combat in the "war to end all wars." This was to be a serious drawback for him a quarter century later. But the Treaty of Versailles had set the stage for a later conflict, and he would have another chance for action. Dwight emerged from his World War I experiences with a self-confidence born of his achievements in commanding men. Now he would spend much of the next twenty years of his life studying the techniques of warfare from a command and staff position.[24]

Fox Conner Inspires

At the end of the war, Dwight had an opportunity to participate in an adventure that he never forgot. With the automobile and truck assuming an increasingly important role in American life, numerous people and groups were promoting the idea of building a transcontinental highway. Experiences in World War I demonstrated that army dependence upon the horse and mule would soon be displaced by motor transportation. With a view toward promoting highway construction and also to test the capabilities of different types of vehicles, in 1919 the Department of War sponsored a coast-to-coast convoy of various kinds of trucks and cars, and even a small Renault tank. Officials wanted observers from the different branches of the army to accompany the convoy, and so when the request came for two tank officers, Ike volunteered and was accepted.

The trip began at the White House on July 7 and ended on September 6 in San Francisco. Considering the primitive equipment they drove and the equally crude roads they had to use, this average of about fifty miles per day was actually quite good. Not only did they endure all kinds of mechanical breakdowns, but they were further delayed by being routed through all the major towns and cities along the way. Because publicity constituted a principal reason for the trip, they naturally wanted to be seen by as much of the populace as possible. By participating in this convoy, Ike saw many communities for the first time and increased his knowledge of the country. More importantly, he became impressed with the need for a good highway system. This experience, plus the realization he attained a quarter of a century later about the importance of modern *autobahns* to the military power of Germany, led Eisenhower, as president, to emphasize successfully the need for a good interstate highway network for the United States.[25]

Following this trip, Ike was transferred again to Camp Meade which had been converted into the army tank school. His disappointment and frustration in not seeing combat during the war, plus the remote possibility of another war in his lifetime, made him wonder during the idle months of demobilization if he had not made a mistake after all in choosing the army for a career. But at Camp Meade, as commander of the Heavy Tank Brigade, Dwight was happier because Mamie and Icky could join him and his job seemed to have a purpose. It was at Meade also that he met one of the most interesting men in the United States Army at that time, George S. Patton, Jr.

Patton, the son of a well-to-do Virginia family, became a dashing, flamboyant officer. He carried two ivory-handled Colt .45 revolvers on his hips, in violation of regulations, and it was rumored they were not purely ornamental. He had commanded the American Tank Brigade at Langres, France, where Ike's students from Camp Colt were shipped for final training. Some of the men at Camp Meade who had served under Patton in France swore they had seen him riding into battle *astride* a tank and waving a sword. He gloried in the military and, by the end of the war, was well on his way to becoming a legend. He and Dwight shared a mutual interest in tanks.

Both Patton and Eisenhower were convinced the tank would play a prominent role in future warfare, and they pioneered together in developing its use and doctrine. During World War I, the slow-moving tank had been used primarily to precede an infantry attack by destroying machine gun nests. Ike and George were convinced they should be made speedier and used for surprise attacks and in mass. For a year they worked with tanks and terrain and then described in detail the type of tank they wanted—one with speed and firepower and armor that could withstand machine guns and light field guns, without sacrificing maneuverability.

They experimented with a light Renault that bogged down too easily in rough terrain and also with the powerful, slow, American-made Mark VIII. They used the

heavy tanks to tow the light ones with strong steel cables.
One day out in the field they hitched three light tanks to
a Mark VIII to pull up a hill. Patton and Ike were out in
front observing when suddenly they saw the cables parting. The front part came whistling at them with the speed
of a bullet, snapping off saplings as if they were twigs.
The two came within inches of death. On another occasion they took a .30 calibre Browning water-cooled
machine gun out into the field for target practice and
experimentation. While Patton fired the gun, Eisenhower observed the results through field glasses. After
firing an especially long burst of ammunition they decided to take a closer look. As they approached the target,
the over-heated weapon commenced firing at them. They
were forced to race out of the line of fire and back to the
gun to twist the ammunition belt so it would stop feeding
into the gun.[26] These experiments and developments
were to prove invaluable some twenty years later. More
importantly for Ike, George Patton introduced him to
General Fox Conner.

Fox Conner was one of the outstanding officers of his
time. He had attended the Leavenworth Command and
General Staff School and the Army War College. During
World War I, he served as operations officer at general
headquarters under Pershing in France. When Conner
visited Camp Meade in the fall of 1919, he accepted a
dinner invitation from the Pattons who also invited the
Eisenhowers. George had told Conner about the work he
and Ike were doing, and, after dinner, Conner asked them
to take him down to their shops and discuss their work.
Because he had already talked to Patton about his ideas,
Conner directed most of his questions at Ike, and they
spent much of the afternoon discussing these new concepts. Conner did not say anything except that their ideas
were interesting and Dwight thought that was the end of
it. He was impressed with Conner and apparently this
was mutual. He was to hear from the general a short time
later.[27]

Ike began coaching football again at Camp Meade and enjoyed a fuller home life than ever before. Icky was in the height of his glory now. The three-year-old was the camp mascot, complete with a tank uniform the men bought for him. Watching the football team scrimmage, or watching a parade, or riding in a tank (the early tanks were extremely noisy) was thrilling, and he enjoyed being the center of attention. By this time, the Eisenhowers were out of debt and thought they could afford a hired girl to help Mamie. They did not know it, but the girl was not completely recovered from a bout with scarlet fever when she came to work for them. Little Icky got the disease. They did all they could to help him. Mamie was also sick at this time, and Dwight haunted the hospital by himself, hoping and praying. They brought in a specialist from Johns Hopkins Medical School. It was to no avail. The boy died the week following Christmas of 1920. This was a blow from which Ike and Mamie never recovered. Almost a half century later Dwight described this as "the greatest disappointment and disaster" of his life, and even at that late date, the "keenness" of his loss was as "fresh and terrible" as when it happened.[28] This disaster produced the first real conflict between Ike and Mamie. They blamed themselves for hiring the maid, for perhaps not doing everything they possibly could to save the boy and, to an extent, these reproaches were turned against each other. Their previous enviable marital relationship was not restored until they had another child.[29]

Soon after this tragedy, Dwight accepted orders to report to the Panama Canal Zone to become Fox Conner's chief of staff. Not only was it a rare opportunity to serve under this man, but it proved to be a welcome change of scenery for the mourning parents. They arrived at Camp Gaillard, a jungle post in the center of the Zone, early in 1922. Their quarters were distressing. Mamie described the house as a "shanty." Built by the French years earlier, it stood on stilts on a hillside, with a porch running entirely around it. It had no panes or shutters for the windows. The numerous bats were the worst problem. The French had imported them to help control the mosquitoes, and it was still against the law to kill them. No rooms on the base had cooling systems.

General Conner had the task of reorganizing and modernizing the defenses of the Canal Zone in the light of military experiences of World War I. To help with this task, he needed a chief of staff who would enforce discipline in the languid tropical climate. Dwight went to work with a will, making certain the grounds were kept trimmed and that all regulations were obeyed. The junior officers viewed Conner as a hard driver and soon came to evaluate Ike in the same way, despite his good natured personality.[30] The Eisenhower house became the social center for the camp, and Ike began here to perfect his bridge game. Mamie became pregnant and happily sailed to the United States (without Dwight) in the summer of 1922 to give birth to her child in Denver. A boy was born on August 3 and was named John Sheldon Doud after Mamie's father. When he was three months old, Mamie brought him to Panama. While John could never replace their first-born son, raising a healthy, happy baby did much to take their minds off the loss of Icky and to restore their earlier marital bliss.

The way Dwight handled his assignments vindicated Conner's judgment of him, and the older man soon came to look upon him as a valued protege. During their conversations, he discovered Ike had lost interest in military history because of the way it was taught at West Point— as an exercise in memorizing the names of commanders and their battle stations, with no attempt to explain the whys or the results of battles. Fox Conner had a good library and was especially fascinated with military history, an interest that he managed to instill in Eisenhower. First he had him read some good novels. After he got him interested in the military history of the period of the novels' settings, he then had him read some good military books.

Ike's reading was followed by close examination on the part of the General to make sure he really understood what he was reading. Dwight explored the memoirs of Grant and Sherman and read *Steele's Campaigns,* which Conner thought was the best summary of the military history of the Civil War. He read Clausewitz's *On War* three times. Ike and Conner were out on reconnaissance a good deal of the time, and the evening hours before bedtime were long in this area close to the Equator. They used this time in front of a campfire to hold their discussions about the Civil War battles or Napoleon's strategy. Conner was somewhat of a philosopher and had a considerable knowledge of history. He induced Ike to read Plato, Tacitus, modern historians, and philosophers such as Nietzsche. Gone were Dwight's carefree days when he studied only as much as was necessary to get by. He now read and studied carefully for he was well motivated and knew he would be questioned closely. The three years Eisenhower served under Conner turned out to be, he discovered later, "a sort of graduate school in military affairs and the humanities."[31]

While Ike was in Panama, the Washington Conference treaties were signed (1922) and the world was lulled into a sense of security and a feeling that war was outmoded. Fox Conner knew better. He was convinced that the Treaty of Versailles had built-in causes for a second world war and that the Washington Conference pacts merely hastened the coming of that conflict. Conner especially saw Japan as a menace in the Pacific and was certain that, although both the United States and Japan agreed in the 1922 treaties not to build further fortifications in the Pacific, America would live up to that promise but Japan would not. Discussing geopolitics with Eisenhower, he noted that, with China an uncertain giant and Russia torn up internally in attempting to establish communism, maintenance of world peace was left to the other five great powers—the United States, Great Britain, France, Germany, and Japan. Japan and Germany would become more aggressive. Another war was coming, he predicted. When? Soon. Fifteen years, perhaps, twenty at the most.[32]

Ike must begin now to prepare himself. He and his generation of officers would be in command. Conner told Dwight about George C. Marshall—a master of logistics. This was the first Ike had heard of him. Marshall would be an important commander in the next war. Dwight must prepare himself for a general's stars in order to be ready also. "You and Marshall are a lot alike," Conner told him. "I've noticed time and again that you attack problems in the same way."[33] This was high praise. Conner's discussions and "bull sessions" made a deep impression on Eisenhower's thinking and he admitted he owed the general "an incalculable debt."[34]

The next step, of course, was for Dwight to attend his service school in order to qualify for the Leavenworth Command and General Staff School. Graduation from Leavenworth was a necessity for advancement, and the order of graduation in terms of achievement was important. Superiors kept their eyes on those who ranked high at this school.

Despite his rewarding experience with Fox Conner, three years in Panama were enough and when Ike heard through the military grapevine that he was to be transferred, he was relieved. In September 1924 he was given the rank of major (permanent) and ordered to report to Camp Meade. He was greatly disappointed when he found himself back in the rut of coaching a football team. At the end of the football season, he was ordered to Fort Benning, Georgia, to command a tank battalion. But he wanted—and needed—desperately to go to Infantry Command School. He discussed his problem with the chief of infantry. The chief, for some reason, refused to listen to his request. But Fox Conner was able to pull other strings for him, because Conner's mentor, John Pershing, was then chief of staff and Conner was his assistant.

One day Ike received a cryptic telegram: NO MATTER WHAT ORDERS YOU RECEIVE FROM THE WAR DEPARTMENT MAKE NO PROTEST ACCEPT THEM WITHOUT QUESTION SIGNED CONNER. A few days later he was further confused when he received orders to report to Fort Logan, outside Denver, as a recruiting officer. He trusted Conner and made no protest. Then a letter came from Conner. He had arranged through the Department of War to have Dwight transferred temporarily to the adjutant general's office, which also had charge of recruiting. A few days later his final orders came. He had been selected as part of the adjutant general's quota to attend the Command School at Leavenworth. He was to report there in August 1925.[35]

He asked Conner what he needed to do to prepare himself for the Leavenworth school and was told that, because of the reading and studying he had done in Panama, he was as trained and prepared as anyone could be. The next few months of recruiting in the Denver area were pleasant because the Eisenhowers could spend a lot of time with the Douds at their large house. But Ike did not waste this time. He got copies of problems assigned at Leavenworth in the past and studied them. Also, while riding in Panama, he had occasionally had a severe ache in his lower abdomen. The doctors diagnosed it as chronic appendicitis; it might never bother him again or it might flare up at any time. (It did recur several times, and in the 1950s was diagnosed as ileitis.) To make certain he did not have another attack while at Leavenworth, he went to Fitzsimmons Army Hospital in Denver and had his appendix removed. When August came, he was prepared mentally and physically for officer school.

The officer-students at the Command and General

Staff School at Leavenworth pushed themselves to the limit. Some broke under the strain. It was rumored that there were suicides. The course of study involved medical, ordnance, quartermaster, and signal services, as well as logistics and strategy. There were no examinations except a final. Instruction was through the case method. The student was given data on an imaginary enemy and a mission for his forces. He decided what actions should be taken. If he were incorrect, he would be given the correct decisions and then asked for plans and dispositions to carry out the strategy.

Ike soon established a routine in his studies. Most of the officers joined groups in order to study together. Dwight, instead, decided he would study only two and a half hours each evening, get a good night's sleep, and be fresh and alert in class the next day. Fortunately, an old friend from his Fort Sam Houston days, Leonard T. Gerow, was also attending the school. He agreed with Ike's approach, so they studied together. They took a room on the third floor of the Eisenhower quarters and converted it into a command post. There were bookshelves and a worktable, and the walls were covered with maps. The room was "off limits" to everyone except Dwight and Gerow. In plotting tactical maneuvers, one would read instructions and the other would mark maps.[36]

It was a hard nine months. Then came the final examination. Ike and Gerow planned a celebration in Kansas City with Arthur Eisenhower. The fact that they finished the school was something to celebrate. When the rankings were posted, Dwight had even more reason to rejoice. Out of 275 of the best minds in the army, he was ranked first and Gerow second! His name was now placed on the general staff list. He was marked for advancement. Fox Conner wrote his congratulations and George Patton, now an instructor at Leavenworth, told Ike, "Major, some day I'll be working for you."[37]

That summer the Eisenhowers had a family reunion in Abilene. This was the first time all the boys were together since Arthur left home to make his way in Kansas City; it was also the last time. What a family of boys! There were six of them, and each had taken a different path to success. Arthur was a banker in Kansas City; Edgar, in Tacoma, was rapidly becoming a prominent West Coast lawyer; Dwight was a major in the army; Earl was an engineer in Pennsylvania; Roy was a pharmacist who owned a drug store in Junction City, Kansas; and Milton was a journalist currently serving as an assistant to the secretary of agriculture (he would later become a university president). During this three-day visit they brought each other up-to-date on their careers and lives. Childhood memories were revived and family values were re-affirmed and strengthened. After this, each brother would date family events from the memorable reunion of 1926.

WASHINGTON AND THE PHILIPPINES

After leaving Leavenworth, Ike was ordered to report to Fort Benning where he coached a football team that fall. During the winter of 1926, he received an unusual request. Would he be interested in working on a booklet for the Battle Monuments Commission? He was not particularly intrigued, but his current assignment was not very stimulating, and he accepted. He reported to the commission, under the direction of General John Pershing, in January 1927. At the time he was unaware that this assignment would be another one of those turning points in his life.

Ever since the end of the war the commission had been gathering maps, photographs, reminiscences, and all types of materials on battles in which Americans had participated in World War I. It was Ike's job to sift this mountain of information and condense it into a readable

guidebook. Eisenhower digested the mass and completed
the book within the six months deadline. As a result of
this experience, he had more detailed knowledge of the
role of the American Expeditionary Force in World War I,
in terms of strategy and logistics, than anyone, including
the commander himself. In addition, he did this work
under the approving eye of that commander who wrote to
Dwight's superior:

> In the discharge of his duties, which were most dif-
> ficult, and which were rendered even more difficult
> by reason of the short time available for their com-
> pletion, he has shown superior ability not only in
> visualizing his work as a whole but in executing its
> many details in an efficient and timely manner.
> What he had done was accomplished only by the
> exercise of unusual intelligence and constant devo-
> tion to duty.[38]

From now on, General Pershing would be one of Eisenhower's supporters.

When he completed the guidebook, Dwight was chosen
to attend the Army War College in Washington, D.C.
This was somewhat of a "gentlemen's graduate school"
for officers. The course covered problems in national policy and objectives, including political, budgetary, interservice, and foreign policy. Ike graduated from the Army
War College on June 30, 1928, again at the head of his
class.

One of the side benefits Eisenhower derived from being stationed in Washington, D.C., was the opportunity
of becoming reacquainted with Milton, his youngest
brother. Milton had attended Kansas State College, taking a degree in journalism. William Jardine, the college
president, was impressed with Milton and persuaded him
to remain at Kansas State as an instructor. When President Calvin Coolidge appointed Jardine secretary of
agriculture in 1925, he took Milton along with him as an

assistant. Milton and his wife's closest friends, Mr. and Mrs. Harry Butcher, were included in Dwight and Mamie's close social circle. Milton had met Harry Butcher when the latter was editor of *The Fertilizer Review*. Butcher had just opened WJSV, Columbia Broadcasting's new Washington radio station, when Ike met him, and he was rapidly on his way to becoming a CBS vice president. Butcher and Ike found many common interests, including communications, news events, and writing.[39] Butcher was handsome, congenial, and capable, and Dwight later selected him as his naval aide in World War II.

Upon graduation from the Army War College, Eisenhower was asked to return to the Battle Monuments Commission to revise his booklet. When he discovered this meant touring the battlefields of France, he and Mamie were both eager to go. They moved to Paris, and John entered school at Macjannette's. Ike toured the roads and fields of France, always with an eye on the terrain and the feasibility of tank operations. He and Mamie also took a leave and toured Belgium, Germany, Switzerland, and Italy. He was seeing a region in which he would later direct the movements of millions of men.

When his tour with the Battle Monuments Commission was completed, Dwight decided to stay in Washington and work for the assistant secretary of war. His new task was to prepare plans for mobilizing the nation's economy in the event of war. The pressures and power of the military-industrial complex that Dwight would warn the nation of three decades later were the reverse in 1930. It was difficult for him to get manufacturers interested in plans for conversion to war production. Bernard Baruch, head of the War Industries Board during World War I, was one of the few persons who was willing to talk about these problems. Baruch was a firm believer in the necessity of freezing wages and prices as soon as hostilities commenced, in order to prevent an inflation that the nation had experienced in all its wars. He was so convincing that Ike incorporated many of his views into the plans he drafted.[40] Dwight also played an important part in founding the Army Industrial College at this time. The college offered officers lectures by leading industrialists about the problems of war production.

When Herbert Hoover lost the election of 1932 to Franklin D. Roosevelt, Eisenhower's boss was replaced. Prior to this, however, Ike had agreed to assist General Douglas MacArthur, the current chief of staff of the army. His job was primarily as a writer, drafting statements, reports, and letters for MacArthur's signature. As a result, MacArthur received much acclaim for his speeches, and his reports as chief of staff were considered classics of their type.[41]

Eisenhower and MacArthur were a study in contrasts. Both were physically attractive in different ways. Where Ike was indifferent in his dress, Mac was as flashy in appearance as was possible in an army uniform. Dwight's speech and writing style was terse, direct, and clear, while MacArthur's was flamboyant and majestic. Eisenhower was practical and down-to-earth and extremely likeable; MacArthur believed he was born to greatness and acted the part. MacArthur had the imperious habit of referring to himself as "MacArthur." Years later, as the relations between the two became strained, MacArthur would refer to Eisenhower as "the best clerk" he ever had, and Ike would admit to having profited from studying "theatrics" under MacArthur. This is not to say that Eisenhower had no respect for MacArthur; quite the contrary, he merely knew him quite well after serving under him for several years. He later recalled that Mac-Arthur had "a hell of an intellect. My God, but he was smart. He had a brain."[42] But Eisenhower was always conscious of the line of separation between civilian (political) and military affairs and discussed the former only when off duty and among friends. If MacArthur was ever aware of the existence of such a distinction, he studiously ignored it.[43]

The "Bonus Army March," a political issue, developed soon after Eisenhower joined MacArthur's staff. This problem had its roots in the demand of World War I veterans that they receive a bonus for their military service. The American Legion had lobbied unsuccessfully for this until 1924 when Congress enacted the Adjusted Compensation Act over President Coolidge's veto. This law gave each veteran an endowment policy that would mature in twenty years, the face value being determined primarily by the number of days in service and the time spent in overseas duty. When the Great Depression engulfed the country, veterans began demanding that they receive this bonus at once rather than in 1944. Congress voted in 1930 to give them half the amount.

As the Depression worsened and an increasing number of veterans became unemployed, they began insisting that Congress give them the other half of their bonus at once. To demonstrate their plight, some twenty thousand of these jobless veterans, many with their wives and children, marched on Washington in the spring and summer of 1932. The "Bonus Expeditionary Force," as they were called, lived in vacant buildings or wherever they could find shelter. Most of them ended up in the tent and tar-paper shack camp on Anacostia Flats within sight of the Capitol. The House of Representatives compassionately agreed to pay them the remainder of their bonus but, to the veteran's dismay, the Senate, under pressure from President Hoover, refused to pass the bill. Congress did agree, though, to pay their transportation home and deduct this expense from their bonus.

The veterans were orderly and well disciplined, but many of them had no homes to which to return. When they did not leave Washington after Congress refused their request, government officials began to panic. Many erroneously believed that Communists were taking control of the marchers and that rioting and revolution would soon erupt. When the "squatter" marchers refused the demand of officials to vacate the empty government buildings that were going to be torn down, General MacArthur was ordered to send in troops to remove them by force. To Eisenhower's surprise, MacArthur decided to lead the troops in person. Ike protested that the chief of staff should not dignify the disorder by his presence but was informed that this was a serious test of strength for the national government and that Dwight was going to accompany him.

The army fulfilled its instructions to evacuate the men from the buildings and the veterans moved across the Anacostia Bridge to the Flats. Orders then came from President Hoover through Secretary of War Patrick Hurley that the army was not to pursue them further. These instructions were first delivered by the secretary of the general staff and then, when they were ignored, repeated by the assistant secretary of war. When Ike called MacArthur's attention to the directives, the reply was, "I don't want to hear them, and I don't want to see them."[44] The troops proceeded on to Anacostia Flats with tanks and tear gas and completely routed the marchers. During the rout, fires were started and the camp was burned. This episode left a bad blot on the records of all officials responsible for it—President Hoover, Secretary Hurley, and General MacArthur.

It was a valuable experience for Ike to be in Washington and to see the New Deal alter government policy. In 1933, the nation's power center shifted from Wall Street to Pennsylvania Avenue where it has remained ever since. The New Deal "went to war" against the Depression, and deficit spending and pump priming replaced economizing and balanced budgets. The concept of work relief replaced that of the dole or direct relief. Bureaucracy burgeoned and Eisenhower was a witness to it all;

he disapproved of much of it. The army was required to play a role in this change by operating the Civilian Conservation Corps, a program of work relief for young men who worked on conservation programs. Also the armed services benefited from the Public Works Administration. When the armed forces were increased slightly in 1935, the PWA built barracks and provided additional airplanes and aircraft carriers. With this military expansion, Ike was promoted to lieutenant colonel in 1936.

Eisenhower's reputation as a writer had extended beyond the army by this time, and a newspaper chain offered him a job as military editor at a high salary. His future in the army looked bleak; at his age, the best he could hope for would be promotion to colonel after he reached fifty and then retirement. Despite this, Ike declined the offer.[45] It was well he did, for soon thereafter he reached another turning point in his military career.

There was to be a New Deal for the Philippine Islands as well as for the United States. The Filipinos had long wanted their independence, and, as their vegetable oils and other agricultural products presented severe competition to American farmers during the Great Depression, Congress acceded to their demands. The Filipinos were to receive independence in 1946; meanwhile they were making plans and preparations for self-rule. The president-elect, Manuel Quezon, looking apprehensively northward at Japan, asked Douglas MacArthur to become military adviser for his nation. MacArthur accepted the position and was granted leave from the United States Army. He wanted to take his staff, including Eisenhower, along with him.

MacArthur's high impression of Ike was indicated in his letter of appraisal:

> You were retained by the secretary of war and later
> by myself on critically important duties in the

department long past the duration of ordinary staff duties, solely because of your success in performing difficult tasks whose accomplishment required a comprehensive grasp of the military profession in all its principal phases, as well as analytical thought and forceful expression. Through all these years I have been impressed by the cheerful and efficient devotion of your best efforts to confining, difficult and often strenuous duties, in spite of the fact that your own personal desires involved a return to troop command and other physically active phases of army life, for which your characteristics so well qualify you.

In this connection, I should like to point out to you that your unusual experience in the Department will be of no less future value as a commander than as a staff officer, since all problems presented to you were necessarily solved from the viewpoint of the High Command. . . . The numbers of personal requests for your services brought to me by heads of many of the army's principal activities during the past few years furnish convincing proof of the reputation you have established as an outstanding soldier. I can say no more than that this reputation coincided exactly with my own judgment.[46]

MacArthur wanted to take such a man with him to the Philippines, but Dwight demurred. MacArthur then made the request a command, and Ike was forced to consent.

When Dwight sailed in September 1935, Mamie stayed in Washington to allow John to finish junior high school. They joined him a year later and John then attended school in Baguio. Eisenhower now entered a military world in which politics played a major role. He had done some preparatory work before he sailed and soon after landing presented a plan for Philippine military defenses. It called for an absolutely minimum budget of $8 million annually. This would provide for a barely sufficient defense system for the Filipinos within these financial limitations.

It was necessary to create at least a token air force for the Philippines, and, in the process of developing one, Ike learned to fly. One of the American instructors, Lieutenant William Lee, taught him. He soon had enough experience to qualify him for the pilot's test. Because he would be soloing in a two-seat training plane, Ike and the trainer put a bag of sand in the rear seat for ballast. They neglected to take out the dual control, however, and as Eisenhower dropped the nose down to land, the bag fell against the rear control stick. He could not force the tail low enough to land! On the third attempt, he managed by brute strength to force the front stick back far enough to permit a landing. The instructor came running, ready to chew him out for poor flying. They then discovered the sandbag.[47] Ike went back up and passed his test. He got his license and eventually logged 350 flying hours. He never lost his delight in flying and for years would occasionally go forward and take over the co-pilot's seat to relieve the boredom of a long flight.

Dwight and Manuel Quezon became good friends. Quezon gave him an office in his Malacanan Palace and frequently asked his advice on matters. Gradually these conversations broadened into topics other than military defenses. In addition, Quezon was an ardent bridge player and enjoyed Ike's ability in this game. It was in the Philippines that Eisenhower began to acquire his reputation for diplomacy. He gave no hint of the white supremacy attitude Filipinos had discovered in some Americans. Dwight liked and trusted the Filipinos, and they reciprocated. Quezon came to appreciate Eisenhower's candor and frankness in stating his opinion or offering his advice. Quezon was truly sorry when Ike decided to return to the United States. He handed Dwight a signed contract to remain and told him to fill in the salary. It was refused. He offered him a $100,000 annuity policy as a gift of appreciation. Ike declined it. He did accept the Distinguished Service Star of the Philippine Islands which Mamie proudly pinned on him as President Quezon looked on approvingly.

At this time he also received another interesting overture. He was offered a salary of $60,000 a year, plus expenses, for a minimum of five years, to seek havens in different countries for Jews who were being victimized by the anti-Semitic policies of Nazi Germany. He declined this fabulous proposal and remained in the army; he was obviously not burning with a desire to be rich.[48]

By 1939 Dwight was determined to return to the United States. It appeared that Fox Conner's prediction about another world war would come true at any moment. World conditions were rapidly deteriorating. Adolf Hitler had come to power in Germany in January 1933, two months before the New Deal was inaugurated. He brought his country out of depression by giving the German people both guns and butter. He and his fellow-fascist dictator, Benito Mussolini of Italy, went on a rampage of conquests in the 1930s. In 1935 Italy attacked Ethiopia. In early 1938 Hitler absorbed Austria in violation of the Treaty of Versailles. In September 1938 the major European powers sought to appease Hitler at Munich by letting Germany acquire the German Sudetenland that had been given to Czechoslovakia by the treaty of Versailles. In early 1939 Hitler took the remainder of Czechoslovakia by force, while Mussolini attacked Albania. In September 1939 Hitler launched a "blitzkrieg" against Poland. England and France then declared war on the Fascists, touching off World War II. In the meantime, Japan, ally of Germany and Italy, was attempting to conquer China.

In the spring of 1940, Hitler launched another "blitzkrieg," quickly overrunning Denmark and Norway in April and attacking France through the Low Countries in May. The fall of France in June 1940 shook Americans out of their complacency. Great Britain was now the sole democracy still standing against the Fascist powers. In September 1940, after a heated debate, the United States Congress enacted its first peacetime draft in history. Germany, Italy, and Japan signed a Tripartite Treaty that month by which they agreed to defend each other against attack from any other nation not then at war. This was obviously directed at the United States. The following month Ike became Chief of Staff of the Third Division at Fort Lewis, Washington. His superior staff work here earned him a promotion to chief of staff of the Ninth Army Corps at Fort Lewis in March 1941 and promotion to colonel (temporary). With draftees pouring into the army at a rapid rate, Eisenhower hoped perhaps to achieve his ambition and receive command of a tank regiment. But the results of the forthcoming Louisiana maneuvers were to open up far broader horizons for his career.

Chief of Staff George Marshall and Lieutenant General Leslie McNair, chief of general headquarters, agreed with Lieutenant General Ben Lear, commander of the Second Army, that practical maneuvers, simulating war conditions, would be good practice for the developing army. It would also help in the search for good officer material to command the burgeoning numbers of draftees. Plans were made to have the Third Army, under Lieutenant General Walter Kreuger, fight Lear's Second Army in "war games" in Louisiana. McNair's deputy chief of staff, Wayne Mark Clark, had been traveling the country searching for officer talent. When asked who would make a good choice for Kreuger's chief of staff, Clark unhesitatingly recommended Dwight Eisenhower. The Eisenhowers returned to San Antonio in the summer of 1941 for their twenty-fifth wedding anniversary and Ike became chief of staff of an army of almost 250,000 men that August.

The Second Army of about 200,000 men was given most

of the tanks, many of which were trucks with signs saying "tank" on them; the Third Army was assigned the task of developing strategy against the "tanks." There were two phases of the war. Kreuger attacked in the first part and Lear was on the offensive in the second. The first stage ended in victory for the Third Army and the press gave Colonel Eisenhower credit for this. In the second phase, Eisenhower seemed able to anticipate Second Army strategy before they maneuvered. Much to the disgust of George Patton, commanding the Second Armored (Division), the Second Army was unable to take advantage of its tank superiority. Patton made a forced night march and, when the reports came in the next morning, Eisenhower declared Patton could not be where he was reported; it was logistically impossible. It was soon discovered that Patton had made prior arrangements for filling stations along the way to provide gas for his tanks, which he paid for out of his own pocket. The umpires ruled Patton out of the action and the Third Army won a decisive victory. Again reporters gave Eisenhower credit for his brilliant planning.[49] Marshall and McNair made a point of talking to Ike about maneuvers. They also talked to each other about him. A short time later Dwight received his first star and, in celebration, the Third Army marched in parade for him.

On December 7, 1941, the Japanese made a surprise attack on the United States armed forces at Pearl Harbor. Congress declared war the next day. On December 14, Ike received a call from Washington. General Marshall wanted him to come at once. The hard work and training of the last two decades were now going to be put to use. It seems almost as if Fate had directed his career thus far, for all his experiences and positions since graduation from West Point helped prepare him for his mission in World War II. He was now on the road that would lead to Berlin four years later.

CHAPTER THREE

Commanding
the
Allies

Even Dwight was wrong about the way in which the United States would become involved in World War II. Many people believed the passage of the Lend-Lease Act in March 1941, by which the United States became the "Arsenal of Democracy," and the convoying of these goods across the Atlantic, would eventually lead to war with Germany.[1] During the fall and winter of 1941, the United States did become involved in an undeclared naval war with German submarines in the Atlantic, but it was in the Pacific that the real blow came.

When Hitler overran the Netherlands in May 1940 and defeated France the following month, he in effect made orphans of the oil-rich Dutch East Indies and of French Indo-China. This was of assistance to Japanese plans of conquest. One year later the pro-Nazi Vichy government of unoccupied France permitted Japan to acquire French Indo-China, thus helping Japan to encircle and to strangle China proper. The United States responded to this aggression by freezing Japanese financial assets in this country. American opposition helped bring General Hideki Tojo, a militarist and an expansionist, to power as premier of Japan.

Tojo agreed, under pressure from the emperor and business groups who hoped to avoid war, to allow Saburo Kurusu, a special envoy to the United States, to make final attempts to persuade President Roosevelt to permit Japan a free hand in China. But Tojo gave Kurusu a deadline. When that date passed without Japanese success in the diplomatic arena, Tojo ordered the imperial fleet to sail on November 26 for a surprise attack. United States experts had broken the Japanese diplomatic code and thus were aware of an impending attack. The puzzler for American military officials, however, was the location. Most expected the attack in the Dutch East Indies; few thought the Japanese would be so foolish as to make a direct hit on the Philippine Islands. Instead, the Japanese made a colossal blunder in attacking Pearl Harbor on December 7, 1941. This was diplomatically a stupendous mistake, for it united the American people as few other events could have done. But, in the immediate weeks after the strike, the assault proved itself tactically sound, for it crippled the American Navy and permitted a rapid conquest of the Pacific islands in the Japanese march on the Philippines and on Australia.

Preparing to Command

When Ike arrived in Washington, he immediately reported to the chief of staff, General George C. Marshall. He was assigned to the War Plans Division under General Leonard Gerow, his old friend from Fort Sam Houston and the Leavenworth school. Marshall wanted Eisenhower's expertise to work on the Far East problem, for Ike knew more about defending the Philippine Islands than anyone else in the country. Marshall also hoped Ike's presence as Far East expert would mollify and probably flatter MacArthur, who was most impatient with the decision to make the war in Europe the primary Allied effort. To MacArthur, the secondary importance of the war in the Pacific appeared a serious tactical error, for he believed Asia was the more important for the future.[2]

When Ike reported for duty, Marshall gave him a brief summary of the current situation in the Far East. He then asked what the United States should do there. Dwight hesitated a moment, then said, "give me a few hours," to which Marshall agreed. Eisenhower realized that Marshall was only testing him; the chief of staff had already decided upon his strategy. Even before the United States entered World War II, the Department of War had adopted a plan called "Rainbow Five," which was to be followed in the event the country became involved in the war. "Rainbow Five" was rooted in the idea that the European theatre was more important than the Pacific.[3] Military efforts, therefore, would be basically offensive in Europe and defensive in the Pacific until the European enemies could be defeated. This was a strategic decision based on the proximity of Europe in terms of shipping and on the fact that the huge and potentially powerful Russia was fighting the Axis powers, along with England, and it was vital to keep the Russian bear draining German strength. In addition, "Rainbow Five" resulted from the foreign policy decision that Europe was paramount to United States interests while Asia was of secondary importance. The United States never altered this basic premise during the first three-quarters of the twentieth century.

Ike's strategy for the Far East had to be based on "Rainbow Five." He studied the problem carefully and then reported to Marshall. He insisted that, for morale purposes, the Filipinos must never think they were being abandoned. The United States had to make every effort to reinforce MacArthur and the American garrison there. Because this could not be done until the fleet was partially rebuilt, the immediate necessity was to build a base of operations in Australia for supplies and personnel. This would tell the Filipinos and other Asian peoples they were not being abandoned. Meanwhile, every effort should be made to help them with supplies through submarine and air support and to keep lines of communications open to Australia, both from the United States and through the chain of islands running north to the Philippines. Marshall listened carefully and then simply replied, "I agree with you. Do your best to save them."[4] Eisenhower had passed his first test!

He soon passed others under the watchful eye of Marshall. The chief of staff insisted upon subordinates making decisions on their own and then informing him later what they had done. Marshall was a cold, aloof man; everyone was afraid of him. His staff tended to analyze problems thoroughly and then take them to him for final solution. But Eisenhower was not afraid of responsibility. At one point he needed transportation to Australia for a division of men. The British ship *Queen Mary* was available, but there was no escort at hand. Dwight loaded 15,000 men on the *Queen Mary* and sent her off alone without asking Marshall. A few tense weeks followed. Too large to pass through the Panama Canal, the ship had to put in at a Brazilian port for fuel on her way around South America. Ike was horrified when a radio intercept was made on an Italian broadcast in Rio who reported the presence of the ship to his government. The *Queen Mary* would have to pass through the submarine-infested South Atlantic and the Straits of Magellan and then cross the South Pacific unescorted, easy prey for a sub. A week later the welcome news came that the division had landed safely in Australia. Ike then told Marshall the story; the chief smiled and said he had seen the intercept. "I was hoping you might not see it," he said, "and so I said nothing to you until I knew the outcome."[5] Marshall appreciated the fact that Eisenhower could make his own decisions and thus relieve some of the burdens from himself.

Ike soon became Marshall's protege. He worked for the

chief for four years and never once disappointed the older man on a major development. A sort of father-son relationship emerged. Yet Marshall never openly displayed his affection; in all that time he called Ike by his nickname only once and then, to make up for the slip, said "Eisenhower" five times in the next sentence.[6] One day Marshall discussed his attitude toward promotions. He said advancements would go to the field officers and not to the staff officers as had been the case in World War I. Then he informed Ike that the latter was going to stay where he was. "While this may seem a sacrifice to you," he said, "that's the way it must be." Dwight had already reached a rank he had never expected, but he was still frustrated over not having seen combat. Impulsively he blurted out: "General, I'm interested in what you say, but I want you to know that I don't give a damn about your promotion plans as far as I'm concerned. I came into this office from the field and I am trying to do my duty. I expect to do so as long as you want me here. If that locks me to a desk for the rest of the war, so be it!" He then marched stiff-backed to the door, turned around and saw Marshall watching him intently. Feeling sheepish over his outburst, Ike turned on his grin; Marshall replied with a tiny smile in the corners of his mouth. A few days later Marshall recommended Dwight for his second star.[7] Marshall and Eisenhower developed into a tremendous team over the years. Marshall was the theoretician who functioned at the highest levels of policy and strategy. Eisenhower, the operator, was the perfect man to translate Marshall's concepts into actuality.[8]

Ike spent long hours during the winter of 1941–1942 doing what he had been trained to do—fight a war. He was so proficient that in March 1942 he became chief of operations division (OPD), the War Plans Division renamed. It was during this busy hectic period that news arrived of his father's death. Dwight was unable to attend the funeral, but on that day he shut himself in his office for a half-hour in memoriam. He noted in his diary that he loved his father and that his only regret was that he had been unable fully to communicate his great affection.

Shortly after Dwight became chief of OPD, Marshall put him to another test, ordering him to prepare invasion plans for a future cross-channel attack on France. Ike believed it was vital to keep Russia in the war. Josef Stalin, the Russian premier, was insisting that the Allies open up a second front in the West. Eisenhower believed the attack should take place in northern France and he convinced Marshall of this strategy. Marshall, in turn, sold Roosevelt on the idea. The next step would be to choose the commander of the invasion forces so he could proceed with the planning.

In December 1941, immediately after Pearl Harbor, Prime Minister Winston Churchill of Great Britain and a number of his military staff came to Washington for strategy talks. The most important result of this meeting was the reaffirmation of "Rainbow Five"—to make the Pacific war primarily a defensive one and to go on the offensive in Europe. Eisenhower met both Roosevelt and Churchill for the first time during these meetings. The British were impressed with Ike and let it be known they would like to have him in London. In May 1942 Marshall sent him to England so the British could get to know him better. Churchill was "extravagant" in his praise of Ike, and Marshall was certain he had found his man.[9]

Marshall told Dwight, upon his return to the United States, to prepare draft plans for a commanding general of American forces in the European Theatre of Operations (ETO). Ike submitted the document on June 8 with the comment that Marshall would probably want to read it carefully for it might become an important position. "I certainly do want to read it," Marshall replied. "You may be the man who executes it." Three days later Marshall told Ike he would be the commander of ETO and for him to make plans to leave again for England.[10] Eisenhower was suddenly jumped ahead of 365 other officers who had seniority over him.

The necessary buildup for ROUNDUP (code name for the crosschannel invasion) would not be completed until 1943. In the meantime, Roosevelt insisted upon an invasion somewhere in 1942—he was not concerned about where—in order to get American troops in action for morale purposes, both in the military and on the home front, and also for diplomatic reasons. There were a number of possibilities. An invasion of Norway was suggested; the British recommended that American reinforcements be sent to the British army then fighting Field Marshal Erwin Rommel in Egypt; an invasion of French Northwest Africa, then under the control of Vichy France, was also proposed. Marshall flew to England in July for a series of conferences to decide on the location of the invasion.

Ike thought all the alternatives were wrong and held out for ROUNDUP. But pressure from the Allies, and from Roosevelt for action in 1942, forced him and Marshall to accept the most feasible of the other proposals. The Allies finally decided upon TORCH, the invasion of North Africa. This action, of course, would necessarily delay the buildup for ROUNDUP, which was the reason for the opposition of Eisenhower and Marshall. The strategy would free the Mediterranean for Allied shipping but it would also delay significantly the dealing of a direct blow against Germany on the Continent.

Ike's next step was to build a staff and to prepare plans for TORCH. When he went to London, he took General Mark Clark with him. He also made an unusual request for a major general: he asked for a naval aide, specifically his old friend Lieutenant Commander Harry Butcher. The request was granted. (While the men were overseas, Mamie and Ruth Butcher occupied apartments across the hall from each other in Washington's Wardman Park

Hotel.) Eisenhower said he wanted Butcher along because he had to have someone with whom he could relax. "Someone I can trust absolutely. Someone who isn't subservient. Someone who'll talk back."[11] Ike chose General Walter Bedel Smith as his chief of staff. Where Butcher was handsome, suave, and adept at handling public relations, Smith was tough, giving the appearance of a hard-bitten, Prussian-type professional soldier. His considerable talent for saying "no" made him an ideal chief of staff. Smith and Butcher remained with Dwight throughout the war and became indispensable—Butcher for his companionship and Smith for his brilliant staff work.

Next Eisenhower had to build a staff approach. His work in football influenced him here; he insisted on a team effort where everyone would think and plan war every waking hour. Also, because this was an Allied effort, he insisted on the complete integration of the forces serving him, not only between the two national-ities, but also among the services—land, air, and sea.

Soon British officers joined Americans for a morning coffee break and American officers joined the British in their afternoon tea. One day it was reported to Eisen-hower that an American, while drinking, had boasted that the Yanks would show the Limeys how to fight. Ike "went white with rage" when he heard this. "I'll make the son-of-a-bitch swim back to America," he vowed, and or-dered the man sent home. On another occasion he heard of a fracas between a British and an American officer and ordered the latter reduced in rank and sent to the United States. The British officer protested that he had only been called a son-of-a-bitch and he understood this was an American colloquialism of endearment. "I am informed that he called you a British son-of-a-bitch," Dwight replied. "That is quite different. My ruling stands."[12] This approach paid off, for Eisenhower was able to build the first truly cooperative Allied command in history. It was also of immeasurable assistance that he and Churchill admired and respected each other. Ike dined with Churchill once a week during these months, in addition to attending frequent staff meetings with him, and the two became very close. As Eisenhower later recalled, "In countless ways he could have made my task a harder one had he been anything less than big, and I shall always owe him an immeasurable debt of gratitude for his unfailing courtesy and zealous support, regardless of his dislike of some important decisions."[13]

In order to have some time of his own away from headquarters, Dwight's aides found Telegraph Cottage, a house on the outskirts of London. He could get away here sometimes on weekends and unwind with Butcher or play bridge with visitors. When his staff discovered he wanted a dog, they got a black Scottie for him. Ike thought it was symbolic that the pup, which he named Telek, had a British father and an American mother. Dwight refused to read newspapers or serious books when he was at Telegraph Cottage, for he went there to relax. Kay Summersby, one of his British drivers and a close friend, thought it terrible that one of the most important men in the world read trashy magazines, but he told her he read Westerns for relaxation because with them he did not "have to think."[14]

Rumors flew through army circles that Ike and Kay Summersby were having a love affair. Some of these reports reached Mamie, who naturally was upset. The rumors continued to arise after the war and, in a book published in 1973, *Plain Speaking,* Merle Miller quoted Harry Truman as saying that at the end of the war Eisenhower wanted to divorce Mamie and marry Kay. General Marshall, according to Truman, wrote Ike that if he did, Marshall promised to "bust" him out of the army. No evidence exists to support this story. Summersby, in her posthumously published memoir, *Past Forgetting: My Love Affair with Dwight D. Eisenhower,* claimed that they were in love but the romance was unconsummated because Ike was impotent with her. White House aides, though, when Ike was president, circulated a version that during the war it was Mamie who wanted the divorce, but Marshall urged her "to stick with Eisenhower in the interests of her country if for no other reason." John Eisenhower later edited a book of letters Ike wrote Mamie during the war that demonstrated that Eisenhower never contemplated divorce, so the true relationship "remains something of an enigma."[15]

Eisenhower made a point of visiting every unit under his command. Instead of formal reviews, though, he preferred to mingle with the men and visit with them informally. He became extremely popular with the enlisted men and found it gratifying to hear them shout "Ike! Ike!" when he drove up in a jeep. They loved him for his frequent derogatory remarks about the "big shots," as though he were just one of the fellows instead of the highest of the brass.

Meanwhile, Ike's staff completed plans for TORCH. Libya was under Axis control and Rommel had pushed the British Army under General Bernard Montgomery eastward to within sixty-five miles of Alexandria, Egypt. Morocco, Algeria, and Tunisia were neutral, under the control of Vichy France. It was decided to land troops at Casablanca on the west under the command of General George Patton while a second force, under General Lloyd Fredendall, would attack Oran. A third group, under General Charles Ryder, would simultaneously invade Tunis. When these three linked up, they would then hit the Germans and Italians in Tunisia on the western side while Montgomery pushed westward from Egypt toward Libya and northward toward Tunisia. This would drive the Axis from North Africa. The three invasions were to be as completely American as possible because of the antagonistic attitude of Vichy France toward the English.

The reaction of French North Africa would be crucial to success. If the French would welcome the Americans as allies and resist a German and Italian move into Tunisia, this would greatly accelerate the Allied timetable. But to achieve this accord, the Allies needed a Frenchman around whom North Africans could rally.[16] It proved exceedingly difficult to find such a man because of the nature of politics in France and French North Africa at that time.

When Vichy France, under Marshal Henri Philippe Petain, signed the armistice that permitted Germany to occupy northern France, General Charles de Gaulle fled to England. He became the leader of the Free French, a group dedicated to the defeat of the Axis and who considered the Vichyites to be traitors. De Gaulle would not be the one that North African Frenchmen, who supported Vichy, would obey or follow. Besides, President Roosevelt and the Department of State disliked and distrusted de Gaulle. Roosevelt and Secretary of State Cordell Hull believed they could work with Vichy France, and they resented de Gaulle's constant denunciations of United States policy toward Vichy.

The United States representative to North Africa, Robert Murphy, tried to find the proper man. Unfortunately, his closest French contacts and advisers were reactionary businessmen and political leaders. Thus, while there was a latent French resistance to the Axis in North Africa, it was de Gaullist and so Murphy ignored it. Instead, he chose General Henri Giraud, a World War I hero living in Vichy France who, Murphy was told, could rally the support of the French military if he could be smuggled out of France. Giraud arrived at Gibraltar shortly before the invasion. Meanwhile, with the plans all set, Ike flew to Gibraltar in early November to set up his headquarters for the launching of TORCH.

NORTH AFRICAN CAMPAIGN

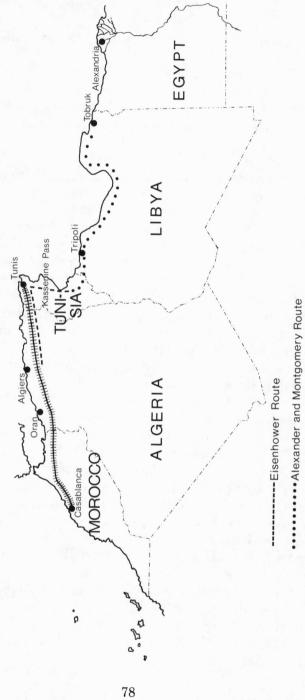

——— Eisenhower Route

••••••• Alexander and Montgomery Route

NORTH AFRICA

When he arrived at Gibraltar, Eisenhower met with Sir Andrew Cunningham, the British admiral in command of the invading fleets, to check last-minute details. This was the beginning of a close professional friendship, for Cunningham continued to be one of Ike's warmest supporters throughout the war. Headquarters at Gibraltar were reached by subterranean tunnels deep in the rock and were, Dwight later recalled, "the most dismal setting we occupied during the war."[17] Perhaps part of his bad memories of Gibraltar stemmed from his meeting there with Giraud.

General Giraud arrived at Gibraltar the night before the North African landings were to take place. When he landed, he was taken immediately to Ike's headquarters where he grandly announced, "Giraud is ready to take command." He mistakenly believed he was to command the Allied expedition. Furthermore, he had decided that the invasion must take place in southern France, not in North Africa. It took all of Eisenhower's tact and powers of persuasion, and most of the night, to convince Giraud that the destination of the greatest amphibious force in history could not be changed that quickly and easily and that the Allies had agreed upon Eisenhower, not Giraud, as commander. Finally, Giraud yielded, but with two demands: (1) he must be recognized as the military and civil head of North Africa; and (2) the Americans must help him to raise and to equip a French Army to invade southern France at a later date. Wearily, Ike agreed to see what he could do so that he could get on with the business of invading North Africa.[18]

By noon, November 8, 1942, Dwight had fairly clear reports on operations. The French at Casablanca, under General Auguste Nogues, were putting up stiff resistance. The landing at Oran was also being contested. The Allies had been completely misinformed about Giraud. His appeal to the French Army had absolutely no effect, and, in fact, he had to go into hiding temporarily at Algiers. But the Allies had an unbelievable stroke of luck: Admiral Jean Francois Darlan, the commander of the French military establishment and second only to Petain in power in Vichy, happened to be in Algiers visiting his son who had polio. The Allies were able to capture him. Eisenhower immediately sent General Mark Clark to Algiers to talk to him. Clark put heavy pressure on Darlan who finally ordered a cease-fire on November 9, 1942. That night Ike had the best night's sleep, he reported to Marshall, that he had had in fourteen weeks.[19]

When North Africa was invaded, Hitler immediately put pressure on Petain who ordered Darlan to rescind his cease-fire order. Clark told Darlan he would throw him in prison if he tried to cancel the agree-upon armistice. The Allied problem was solved, fortunately, on November 11 when Hitler moved in and occupied Vichy France. Darlan then announced that this freed him from Petain's control and he ordered the French Army to resist the Germans who were landing in Tunisia. When Ike arrived in Algiers on November 13, the American armies had control of Casablanca, Oran, and Algiers. He met with Darlan and quickly confirmed the pact he had ordered Clark to make with the French Admiral. This deal made Darlan, not Giraud, head of the civil government in North Africa. In turn, Darlan promised to keep the French fleet from falling into the hands of Germany and to support the Allied effort to drive the Axis out of Tunisia. Darlan and Giraud then worked out an agreement by which Giraud took command of the French military while Darlan headed the civil government.

When news of the Darlan agreement reached England and the United States, a storm broke over Ike's head. Liberals everywhere viewed Darlan as a collaborationist and a Fascist. To work with him seemed the antithesis of all

for which the Allies were fighting. Darlan was especially
repugnant to the followers of de Gaulle and these forces
proved reluctant to fight the Germans in North Africa for
the perpetuation of a French Fascist regime. The public
outcry seemed to drown out Eisenhower's military reasoning. The Allies had expected eighteen thousand casualties in the North African landings and, because of
Darlan's cooperation, these had been held to eighteen
hundred, or one-tenth. This was Eisenhower's first introduction to international politics and he was deeply hurt
by the criticism. As late as the summer of 1944, he said in
private conversation that:

> The liberals crucified me in North Africa. All this
> talk about my "betraying the common people"—
> it's absurd. I'm a common man myself, more so
> than most of the people who are always talking
> about the proletariat. I've worked with my hands
> at about every kind of job there is. The liberals
> didn't try to understand that I had to protect my
> communications, that by securing French coopera-
> tion we almost got Tunis for nothing. They didn't try
> to realize that you can't do everything at once, that
> the world moves forward in little steps [20]

The worst result of the Darlan deal was that Fascist policies, such as suppression of the Jews and denial of civil
and political rights, were continued in North Africa.
After a week, Eisenhower was able to relinquish sole
responsibility when Roosevelt and Churchill concurred in
the arrangements. The Darlan problem was finally
resolved when a young Frenchman, Fernand de la Cha-
pelle, assassinated him on December 24, 1942, and
Giraud was named to succeed him as head of the civil
government. But, because of this confused French political situation, the conquest of Tunisia was vitally delayed.
Gradually, de Gaulle's influence increased until he finally dominated the political scene in North Africa.

Because Ike had never led soldiers in combat he, like the inexperienced troops he commanded, had much to learn. Tunisia was to prove a valuable training ground for the Americans. By Christmas 1942 it was clear that the Allies had lost the race to occupy Tunisia. Winter rains had set in and the Allied forces occupied only muddy airfields while the Germans had good, hard-surfaced airstrips in Sicily, Sardinia, and Tunisia from which to operate. Also, Eisenhower's troops had to be supplied by a single thousand mile railroad that ran from Casablanca through Algeria to Tunisia, and it could run only nine trains per day. As a result, equipment and supplies were in constant demand for the Tunisian fighting.

Roosevelt and Churchill decided to meet in Casablanca in January 1943, so Eisenhower had to make the necessary military arrangements for this conference. Several important results came from this meeting. De Gaulle and Giraud met, and though they were unfriendly to each other, Roosevelt persuaded them to shake hands for the benefit of the press photographers. Several changes were made in the military organization. At this point, the British First Army was fighting in northern Tunisia and the Americans in the south, while the French Army operated in the mountainous central area. The British Eighth Army, under generals Sir Harold Alexander and Bernard Montgomery, was in Libya. The Combined Chiefs of Staff were favorably impressed with the way Ike and his headquarters were functioning; beginning February 1, they decided, Eisenhower would become supreme allied commander of all these forces. When Alexander and Montgomery reached eastern Tunisia, they would come under his command. Cunningham would remain in charge of naval operations while Air Marshal Sir Arthur Tedder would command the Mediterranean air forces. Tedder and Eisenhower hit it off immediately; Tedder, who would remain under Ike's command for the remainder of the war, was a great admirer of the American and came to have more influence upon him than any other Englishman.

This was a significant elevation for Ike to be placed in command of Britain's senior generals. Sir Alan Brooke, the British Chief of Staff, explained his nation's reasoning for this move.

> We were pushing Eisenhower up into the stratosphere and rarefied atmosphere of a Supreme Commander, where he would be free to devote his time to the political and interallied problems, whilst we inserted under him one of our own commanders [Alexander] to deal with the military situations and to restore the necessary drive and co-ordination which had been so seriously lacking.[21]

The problem of rank was partially offset on February 15, 1943, when Eisenhower received his fourth star.

Grand strategy was also discussed at Casablanca. It was here that Roosevelt and Churchill made the decision to insist upon unconditional surrender of the Axis. This demand would become a serious liability to Ike, both in Italy and in Germany, for it meant the Axis leaders would prolong the war much longer than if they were given the opportunity to negotiate.[22] Also, it was decided that, after the conquest of North Africa, the Mediterranean area would be cleared of Axis forces by invading Sicily and Italy. This meant the cross-channel attack would have to be postponed until some time in 1944. This was a serious blow to Marshall. While Eisenhower would have been just as disappointed as his chief if that decision had been made six months earlier, he now agreed with this strategy. The Allied forces in North Africa were too great to remain idle until ROUNDUP was ready, and he agreed that these troops should be deployed where they could best be used, even though this would delay the cross-channel invasion of France.[23]

Dwight spent one day in Casablanca at this meeting, making reports, then returned to his headquarters. Rommel had strategically retreated to southern Tunisia to make his stand and, according to Allied intelligence, was preparing to attack in force. General Juergen von Armin commanded the German-Italian forces in the north. Rommel hoped to break through the Allied forces in the south and prevent the British Eighth Army under Montgomery from joining the Allies from the east. Ike decided to tour the front to make certain the instructions he had made for defenses had been carried out. He was annoyed to find a number of things wrong. Complacency was a major problem. When the Germans decided on a defensive position, they had the area mined and machine guns emplaced within two hours. Due to lack of training and inexperience, the Americans tended to procrastinate and, in this case, had made few defensive preparations for Rommel's attack. Also, Ike found the First Armored Division, a part of the II Corps under Fredendall's command, was not properly deployed to operate as a unit. Finally, faulty Allied intelligence reported the German attack would come through Fondouk, which the First Armored Division was defending, not Faid, which helped account for this misplaced complacency.

Eisenhower ordered changes, but it was too late. When he arrived at Tebessa, news came of a German attack at Sidi bou Zid in the Faid area. By the time he had reached Constantine, he received word of the American disaster: half of First Armored had been lost. Ike told General Sir Kenneth Anderson to pull back from the Eastern Dorsale (mountain range) of the Atlas Mountains but to hold fast on the Western Dorsale; if the Germans broke through there, they would reach the supply center at Tebessa and the main Allied depots at Le Kef. In the meantime, he began rushing reinforcements, materials, and supplies in from Algeria. The Germans soon reached the Kasserine Pass in their drive; if they broke through here, Tebessa and Le Kef were theirs.

By this time Ike had completely lost confidence in Fredendall's ability. He brought in General Ernest Harmon and, to avoid relieving a commander in the middle of battle, kept Fredendall in command but put Harmon in charge of directing the fighting. That day Rommel saw he could not defeat the Allies and began to withdraw in force from the Kasserine Pass. Sensing this, Eisenhower ordered an immediate offensive. But Anderson and Fredendall hesitated too long, and Harmon, new to the situation, was uncertain whether or not to attack. As a result, Rommel was permitted to escape to his strongly fortified Mareth Line. The Battle of Kasserine Pass restored some self-confidence in the Americans, but Ike had had enough of Fredendall. He replaced him with Patton and sent him home. Eisenhower also got a new intelligence officer and he promised himself that, until the war was won, American troops, including those on the front lines, would never stop training.[24] Dwight was also receiving a good initiation and apprenticeship into diplomacy and European politics.

At this point the Allied buildup was sufficient for the final push to drive the Germans out of North Africa. Ike wanted the American troops to participate in this effort but Alexander, who had taken combat command of the Allied troops just before Kasserine Pass, was unimpressed by the fighting ability of the Yanks. Eisenhower ordered Patton to rehabilitate the troops and restore their morale, which he did in a short time. Dwight also put his old classmate, General Omar Bradley, in command of the II Corps. Then he ordered Alexander to include American troops in his final drive. Reluctantly, Alexander agreed and, much to his surprise, the Americans performed well. After the Battle of Kasserine Pass, the American and British troops fought well together.

When they broke the German power at Bizerte-Tunis, the end was in sight. The battle for Hill 609 that overlooked the city of Tunis, one of the most bitterly fought struggles in the North African campaign, came on April 30. The Thirty-Fourth Division, in Bradley's II Corps, performed valiantly here and vindicated Ike's faith in the fighting abilities of his countrymen. By mid-May the Axis forces were driven across the Mediterranean.

Meanwhile the local political situation had stabilized under de Gaulle. He had refused to come to Algiers until Giraud dismissed all the Vichy people from office. Giraud, on the other hand, wanted stability, and this meant keeping competent, experienced officials in office and suppressing radicalism. De Gaulle came to Algiers on May 30 to begin discussions. Out of these talks emerged the French Committee of National Liberation with de Gaulle and Giraud as co-presidents. The committee would govern until France was liberated and elections could be held. Slowly de Gaulle came to dominate this committee so that when the Allies invaded France in 1944, he had emerged as the single leader of France. This settlement of French North African politics helped the immediate military situation, for now Eisenhower did not have to worry about using troops to occupy his rear while he invaded Sicily and Italy.

The campaign of North Africa was an important preparation for Dwight and the Americans. Both gained combat experience and thus confidence. Ike demonstrated his ability, not only in command, but also in tactics and strategy. He revealed his willingness to relieve an ineffective subordinate. Besides learning to emphasize training constantly, he also learned a bitter lesson—never to allow units to be divided as Fredendall had done before the Kasserine Pass. Most important of all, the Allies had successfully cooperated in fighting a major campaign. TORCH demonstrated that an effective, unified Allied command was feasible and possible.

SICILY AND ITALY

The planning for HUSKY, the invasion of Sicily, had been going on since February 1943. It had caused endless debate, not along nationalistic lines but over strategy. The island is mountainous, with the largest city, Messina, located at the northeastern tip, just across the Straits of Messina from the toe of Italy. The Axis had a reported force of 350,000 men on the island. If Messina could be taken quickly, these troops and their equipment could be cut off and captured. But the city was heavily fortified and well protected by antiaircraft guns. The Allies finally decided to hit Sicily on the relatively unprotected southern and southeastern coasts and then move against Messina as quickly as possible.

By this time there was much speculation about where the Allies would strike the fascist powers next. War correspondents quickly acquired a knack for gathering bits and pieces of information and piecing them together into fairly accurate predictions. To forestall accurate guesses and to attempt to keep the Axis off-guard, Eisenhower took an unprecedented step: he called a news conference and stunned the reporters by announcing that "our next objective is Sicily." It was most disconcerting to the newsmen to be put on their honor this way, but it was successful. No one wrote "think" pieces suggesting the invasion of Sicily. In fact, it had a permanent effect in curing many correspondents of, or at least making them much more cautious about, writing such stories for the remainder of the war. Ike was as open as possible with reporters, confiding in them when possible, and they reciprocated his friendship. He was able to develop the best relationship with the press that any American, other than Franklin Roosevelt, at that time had.[25] This, of course, enhanced his popularity even more.

The Axis would have the air power advantage in defending Sicily. This disturbed Eisenhower, for by now

Tedder had convinced him (if he ever needed convincing) of the importance of air support to ground and naval operations. He immediately realized the necessity of first taking Pantelleria and other straits islands between North Africa and Sicily for use as bases. Pantelleria was called the Gibraltar of the central Mediterranean because it was believed to be unassailable. Ike's plan was opposed almost unanimously by his staff because of the projected high cost in lives. Assured by the air forces that they could reduce the islands in two weeks, however, Eisenhower gave the go-ahead over the objections of his staff. Two weeks later he was proved correct; the islands surrendered three-quarters of an hour before the invasion forces landed. Dwight now had his air bases.[26] Plans for Sicily could proceed.

Eisenhower was the supreme commander, but Alexander was to command the ground forces, Cunningham the naval, and Tedder the air support. There were two armies, the American Seventh under Patton and the British Eighth under Montgomery. Between these two armies were a Canadian infantry division and an armored brigade under General Guy Simons. The landings would be made primarily with LSTs (large landing craft) and DUKWs (amphibious vehicles). Ike described the latter as one of the most valuable pieces of equipment in World War II, along with the bulldozer, the jeep, the two-and-a-half-ton truck, and the C-47 airplane. He found it interesting that none of these, except the DUKW, was designed specifically for military purposes.[27]

There were three thousand vessels to land these armies, making HUSKY a larger amphibious operation than TORCH. On D-Day minus two there was nothing further for the supreme commander to do but go to Malta, set up headquarters, and wait. On D-Day minus one the weather turned bad. Marshall wired, asking if the invasion would progress as scheduled. Eisenhower checked with the meteorologist, then went outside to check the wind. He decided it would subside before launching time, prayed for success, rubbed his three lucky coins (an American silver dollar, a British five guinea gold piece, and a French franc), and went inside to cable Marshall that everything would proceed according to schedule.

The invasion came off as planned. The wind was so high during the previous night that the Fascists did not expect an attack anywhere in the Mediterranean on July 10, so the Allies had surprise on their side. Patton took Gela and Licata that day while Montgomery captured Syracuse. In order to gain time, the Axis pulled their forces out of western Sicily and concentrated them on the Catania Plain near Mount Etna, the mountain that guards the approach to Messina.

Unfortunately, Montgomery did not push hard enough to reach Messina immediately. But neither did Alexander press him, and, instead of visiting the British Army to see what was happening, Ike visited Patton in the west on July 12. The Axis forces were able to hold Montgomery on the Catania Plain while Patton quickly dashed around the southwestern part of Sicily and rapidly took the northwestern side. He believed he could have taken Messina easily, but Montgomery persuaded Alexander to let him move around Mount Etna to the left while Patton and the Seventh Army guarded his rear. Alexander, remembering the poor showing the Americans made at the Battle of Kasserine Pass, thought Montgomery should have the opportunity of taking Messina, so he restricted American operations to central Sicily. But the Axis continued to hold Montgomery. Patton was able to capture Messina eventually by moving around the northwestern coast of the island, taking the city on August 17. This was too late, however, for by that time the Axis had managed to escape to Italy with most of their supplies and equipment.

It was during this campaign that the famous incident occurred in which Patton slapped a soldier. The general

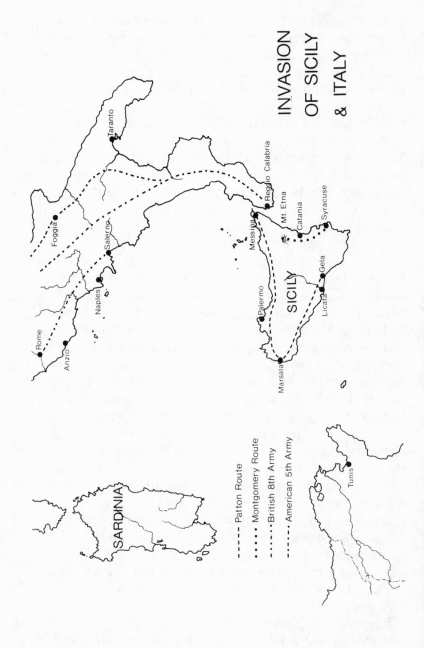

INVASION
OF SICILY
& ITALY

Taranto

Reggio Calabria

Foggia

Salerno

Mt. Etna
Messina
Catania
Syracuse

Naples

Palermo
Gela
SICILY
Licata

Rome
Anzio

Marsala

SARDINIA

----- Patton Route
••••• Montgomery Route
••••• British 8th Army
----- American 5th Army

Tunis

was visiting the wounded in a forward hospital when he encountered a shell-shocked enlisted man. He asked what wound he had and the young fellow said it was his nerves. This was the second such case Patton had encountered at the hospital and his patience snapped, for he believed battle fatigue was cowardice. "Your nerves, hell," he shouted. "You're just a goddamn coward, you yellow son-of-a-bitch," and he struck the soldier. The doctors who were present sent a report of the incident to Eisenhower's surgeon general. This was certainly grounds for a court martial, but Ike believed Patton was the best pursuit general in the Allied forces, and he was determined not to lose him if possible. After an investigation, he ordered Patton to apologize to the two soldiers and the medical staff of the hospital and to make a public apology to all the men serving under him; Patton complied. Meanwhile, the press uncovered the story. A news conference was called and Eisenhower explained everything, including Patton's punishment. The correspondents sympathized with Ike's desire to keep "Georgie," and they did not print the story.[28] Several months later, however, the columnist Drew Pearson stumbled on the incident and publicized it. With the revelation coming at that late date, it erroneously appeared that Ike had forcibly censored the episode.

Almost everyone, even Axis officers after the war, agreed the Sicilian campaign was poorly conducted. The Allies should have landed closer to Messina, or at least at Catania. Many agreed that Montgomery had moved too cautiously. The main significance of this campaign lay in the lessons learned. Ike was reinforced in his favorable impression of Patton and Bradley, and amphibious techniques were developed that became standard for the remainder of the war.[29] Dwight also learned not to send airborne troops in waves during an invasion, but to move them all in at once. If they were not landed in force behind enemy lines, they were too easily subdued in the smaller groups, and the later units were more reluctant to jump in.[30]

Meanwhile, the Allies had begun bombing selected targets in Rome on July 19, and a week later Mussolini was forced out of office. King Victor Emmanuel III then appointed Field Marshal Pietro Badoglio as premier. Badoglio announced that Italy would continue in the war, but it was obvious the country would attempt a separate surrender. Realizing that if this occurred, the German troops in Italy would be cut off, Hitler began to move more troops into Italy and to occupy the country. Strategically this was sound, for Italy would be relatively easy to defend. Soon he had twenty-five divisions there. When Mussolini fell, Ike wanted to invade Italy immediately rather than wait until Sicily was conquered. But the lack of shipping prevented this.

From a military viewpoint, Eisenhower wanted an early surrender of Italy before the German buildup became too great. Thus, to him, it was as simple as the North African problem; he was willing to work with whatever government could control Italy and bring the country over to the Allied side. This would save Allied lives, permit a faster buildup for ROUNDUP, and provide the Allies with Italian air bases from which to bomb German industry with long-range bombers. But Eisenhower was thwarted in his hopes because Roosevelt and Churchill refused to yield on the terms of unconditional surrender. Negotiations were conducted with Badoglio over a period of time, involving a secret and dangerous trip to Rome by General Maxwell Taylor. They came to terms and it was agreed that Eisenhower and Badoglio would simultaneously broadcast news of the Italian surrender on September 8, 1943. At the last minute, justifiably fearful of German reprisals, Badoglio refused. Ike told the Italian premier that he was going to announce it anyway, and Badoglio had no choice but to fulfill his bargain. But these negotiations and the delay involved permitted the

German buildup in Italy that would prove terribly costly to destroy. They also made Eisenhower wary of accepting Germany's surrender in 1945. The twenty-month battle for Italy continued.

While Ike was negotiating the Italian surrender, the Allied Forces began invading Italy at three points: across the Straits of Messina with the British Eighth moving up the east coast of the toe and the American Seventh advancing on the west; the Fifth Army under Mark Clark landing at Salerno; and a British division invading at Taranto. The fighting in the boot of Italy was quite different from that in Sicily for here the Allies faced crack German soldiers, not Italians and poorly trained and equipped Nazi troops. Following fierce fighting, Foggia fell on September 27 and Naples was captured on October 1, giving the Allies an outstanding port with the latter and a good air base at the former. The conquest of Foggia not only deprived the Germans of a strategic base, but gave the Allies one that permitted the bombing of German targets too distant to be reached from British air bases. There now began a long, hard march on Rome. Meanwhile, Ike recommended that the Italian government should be retained and strengthened, provided they declared war on Germany: this was done in mid-October 1943.[31]

The area between the Volturno River and Rome is ideal for defensive operations, for it is criss-crossed by mountains and streams that run from east to west. To speed the Allied advance, Eisenhower asked the Combined Chiefs of Staff to leave a number of landing craft in his theatre until January 1944, several weeks after they were to have departed for England for the ROUNDUP campaign. When they assented on November 8, Ike tentatively approved plans to use them for an amphibious operation at Anzio, twenty miles south of Rome. But before this disastrous invasion took place, Eisenhower left for Washington on the last day of 1943 for a new assignment.

Roosevelt and Churchill had held another joint meeting in Cairo in November 1943. Ike went to Oran on November 19 to meet Roosevelt, who was on his way to Cairo, and they spent some time together before the conference. During their conversation, Roosevelt mentioned that it was time to choose a commander of OVERLORD, as the 1944 cross-channel invasion was now called. This was the most important appointment of the war—perhaps the most prestigious command in military history—and thus was much coveted. Roosevelt did not hint as to his choice, although it would obviously be Marshall or Eisenhower, but he mentioned that he dreaded the thought of Marshall leaving Washington and noted that "it is dangerous to monkey with a winning team."[32]   The British chief of staff, Alan Brooke, was a possibility for the appointment but, because the United States would have the major commitment in the operation, it was decided that the command would have to go to an American and Churchill so informed Brooke. Churchill and most others assumed that Marshall would be chosen and that Ike would return to Washington as chief of staff. Dwight thought so, too, and had sadly reconciled himself to the idea of returning to a desk job. At the Cairo meeting, though, Roosevelt told Churchill he would not permit Marshall to leave Washington and asked if the British would accept Eisenhower as the commander instead. Churchill replied that the British had "the warmest regard for General Eisenhower, and would trust our fortunes to his direction with hearty good will."[33] When the Big Three met at Teheran a few days later, Stalin wanted to know the name of the commander of OVERLORD. He was fighting three hundred German divisions and wanted the Allies to speed up plans for the cross-channel invasion. Roosevelt had not definitely made up his mind at that point but a few days later he notified Stalin that Ike was the man. On his return to Washington, Roosevelt stopped in Tunis and informed Eisenhower that he was appointed commander of OVER-

LORD. This was one of the "wisest decisions" Roosevelt made during the war.[34] It was a disappointment for Marshall, but he accepted it in good grace, for it seemed to be the best decision for his country.

Ike began immediately to drain some of the best men from the Mediterranean to build a new staff. He insisted that Smith go with him, as well as Tedder. He also wanted Patton and Bradley as Army commanders and was forced to take Montgomery whether he wanted him or not. All these transfers were agreed to by the Combined Chiefs of Staff. Leaving General Maitland Wilson as commander of the Allied Forces in the Mediterranean, Dwight departed with Butcher on New Year's Day 1944 for a well-deserved furlough in the United States before he went to London to begin the most important assignment of World War II.

It was wonderful to see Mamie again, even though their travel was restricted, for Ike had to move everywhere in secrecy. The two took a train to West Point, where the car was parked on a siding, to see John. There were important meetings in Washington, too, but Ike managed to take time to fly out to Manhattan, Kansas, where Milton was President of Kansas State College, for a family reunion. David Eisenhower had died in 1942, as had Roy, but Ida was in good enough health to come to see her boys. It was the first family reunion since 1926 and Dwight's brothers were struck by the differences they saw in him since last they met. Although Dwight was much like he had been, his brothers now noticed a new, quiet self-confidence that gave him an air of serenity. He had faced and met successfully many great challenges and was now sure he could meet any difficult circumstances the future might hold. When he left for London on January 13, Mamie kissed him goodbye and cried, "Don't come back until it's over, Ike. I couldn't bear to lose you again."[35]

OVERLORD

Eisenhower set up headquarters outside London for Supreme Headquarters, Allied Expeditionary Forces (shortened to SHAEF) to plan OVERLORD. The planning for the invasion had been going on for some time, of course, so Dwight had to evaluate what had been done and then complete the work. The British General, Sir Frederick Morgan, had been in charge of the preliminary study. Ike was convinced Morgan's decision to invade with three divisions was inadequate. To assure success, the original assault must be widened, he insisted, to at least five divisions. But there would not be sufficient landing craft available for such a force. There were several alternatives. Many suggested abandoning the Anzio landing, which Dwight agreed should be dropped, but Churchill remained adamant that it must be undertaken. ANVIL, the plan for invading southern France simultaneously with OVERLORD, thus catching the Germans in a pincers in Normandy, could be cancelled, but Eisenhower refused to do this and Marshall agreed with him. Finally, to obtain the necessary shipping, Ike agreed to postpone ANVIL and to move the OVERLORD invasion date from May to June, dependent, of course, upon favorable weather.[36]

The location of the landing was extremely important. Proximity to England was a necessity, but the better potential the site had, of course, the greater the German fortifications. It was finally decided to invade the Normandy beaches closest to southeastern England, where there were no fortified ports; artificial harbors would be manufactured and towed to France. Fantastic as this idea sounded, it worked. At the start of the invasion ships would be sunk to build breakwaters called "gooseberries." Then concrete caissons, called "mulberries," made in England in sections and towed to France, would be fitted together between the gooseberry and the beach to make docks. In addition, a constant and huge supply of gasoline would be vital to sustain operations once beach-heads were established. Vast quantities of flexible, four-inch pipe were manufactured in England and, after the invasion, were laid across the Channel and then on the surface of the ground, following the advancing armies. Gasoline was pumped from England through these lines at the rate of one million gallons per day.[37]

Eisenhower's attention was occasionally diverted from this planning by other incidents, including another touchy episode involving Patton. Eisenhower had warned Patton to avoid press conferences and the flamboyant general really tried to follow this advice for he knew his weakness for making outlandish statements for shock effect. But he attended a meeting where he was asked to say a few words about Allied unity. Believing no report-ers were present, he observed, among other things, that this was an important topic for, after the war, America and Britain would have to rule the world together. Another storm broke in the press and Ike was ready to relieve Patton of his command this time if public opinion seemed to demand it. As usual, Marshall let Eisenhower make the decision. After agonizing over the problem for several days, Ike called Patton in and informed him he was keeping him in command of the Third Army. He could not imagine facing Rommel and the Germans with-out George. Patton burst into tears in gratitude, for he wanted nothing more than to finish the war in glory, but Eisenhower brushed off his abject apologies with the statement that "You owe us some victories; pay off and the world will deem me a wise man."[38]

Dwight was also busy visiting the troops and watching training maneuvers. He tried to visit as many units as possible and became very popular with the enlisted men. His grin, his regard for their well-being, and his outgoing manner won them all. His occasional reference to Chur-chill and Roosevelt as "the big shots," his sincere interest and concern over their problems and the fact that he could swear like a sergeant, made the men feel he was one of them. Few commanders were so popular with their men.

Final plans called for several weeks of massive air attacks to prepare for the landings. Invasions would then take place at three points: the British Second Army would land opposite Caen, an operation called GOLD; the American Fifth Corps at the eastern base of the Cotentin Peninsula at a place called "Omaha Beach;" and the American Seventh Corps on the eastern side of the Cotentin Peninsula at a point labeled "Utah Beach." A huge buildup would follow the establishment of these beachheads, which would permit a breakthrough. Then the Allies would advance on a broad front, with emphasis on the left flank in the north.

Ike received divided counsel on the use of air support. The objective was to get the men on the beaches and to make certain they remained; the question was how could the superior Allied air power best be utilized to assist them? The commander of the American air forces, General Carl Spaatz, believed that strategic bombing would win the war—by itself if necessary—and argued for an all-out attack on German petroleum production. The British RAF commander, General Trafford Leigh-Mallory, however, was opposed to this "Oil Plan" as it was called. The Englishman supported instead what was labeled the "Transportation Plan." This called for sustained attacks on all types of railroad facilities, including locomotives and rolling stock, which would prevent the Germans from rushing up reinforcements to the beaches. But the Transportation Plan ran far greater risks of incurring heavy French civilian casualties. After prolonged argument Eisenhower decided the Allies must risk the civilian casualties because the Transportation Plan held the greater assurance for the success of OVER-LORD. He was proved correct, for this turned out to be the decisive factor in his victory in Normandy, and the civil-

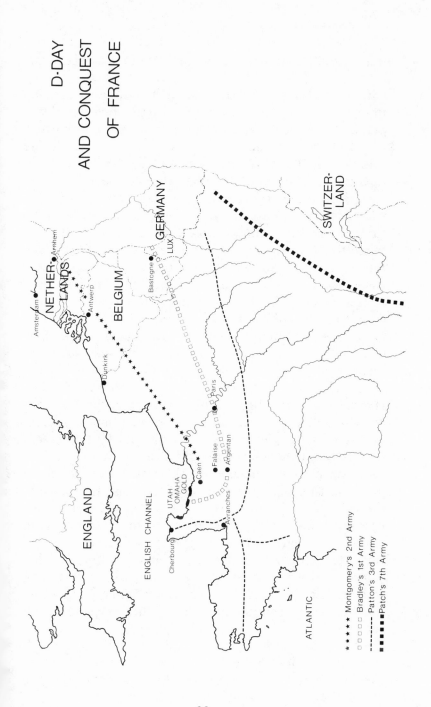

D-DAY
AND CONQUEST
OF FRANCE

SWITZER-LAND

GERMANY

NETHER-LANDS

Arnhem

Amsterdam

Antwerp

BELGIUM

LUX

Bastogne

Dunkirk

ENGLAND

Paris

Caen

Falaise

Argentan

UTAH
OMAHA
GOLD

Avranches

ENGLISH CHANNEL

Cherbourg

ATLANTIC

★ ★ ★ ★ ★ Montgomery's 2nd Army
▫ ▫ ▫ ▫ ▫ Bradley's 1st Army
‑ ‑ ‑ ‑ ‑ Patton's 3rd Army
■ ■ ■ ■ ■ Patch's 7th Army

99

ian casualties fortunately proved to be relatively light.[39]

Dwight also was forced to make a significant decision in regard to the use of paratroopers in the invasion. It was planned to drop several airborne units behind the German lines so they could prevent the enemy from rushing reinforcements to the beaches to repel the Allied landings. At the last minute Leigh-Mallory became most concerned over the reported German buildup in the areas where the drops were planned. He excitedly informed Ike that casualties would run as high as 70 percent. Yet, cancelling these attacks would mean calling off the Utah Beach invasion and endangering the entire operation. Eisenhower finally concluded that Leigh-Mallory was wrong in his estimates and ordered the airdrops to proceed. Again events proved him correct and Leigh-Mallory later expressed his regrets for having added to the burdens of the supreme commander at such a tense moment.[40]

Churchill had never been enthusiastic about OVERLORD. He preferred the Allies to concentrate in southern Europe and the Balkans, and he had little expectations of success in France where the enemy was strongest. He told Eisenhower that, if by winter Dwight had his thirty-six divisions securely established on the Continent, he would proclaim the operation "as one of the most successful of the war." Then he added that, if Ike also had secured the port of LeHavre by that time and freed Paris, he would "assert the victory to be the greatest of modern times." But after a final review of the plans was held in May before all the commanders, with Churchill and the king of England also present, the prime minister admitted that he was becoming convinced the enterprise would succeed.[41]

By May 1944, southern England looked like a vast military camp. Men and equipment were ready and plans were finalized. All that remained was to determine the attack time. It was decided to strike early in the morning at low tide so the German mines would be exposed and could be avoided. It would also be necessary to have a full moon the night before in order to have sufficient light to make successful air drops. Meteorologists informed the planners that the necessary combination of correct moon and tide would occur in that area in the first few days of May, the first week in June, and then again in the third week in June. The date of June 5 was then set for D-Day. Postponement for two weeks would endanger the secrecy of the plans. One million men, eleven thousand planes and five thousand ships were involved—the mightiest armada the world had ever seen. With D-Day set, the final launching would be postponed only by adverse weather conditions. In early June, Ike and the staff began meeting twice daily (at 9:30 P.M. and 4:00 A.M.) with the meteorologists for weather reports.

On June 3, a low pressure system started moving in. Bad weather then came on June 4 with high winds and hard, driving rain. The huge waves would capsize the smaller ships hauling troops and the waves pounding the beaches would prevent landings. Also, the Allies would be unable to utilize their superior air power to soften up the German defenses preliminary to the landings. Eisenhower cancelled the launching and ordered the ships already at sea to return and refuel so they would be ready to leave the next day.

That night at 9:30, the chief meteorologist predicted the bad weather would move out, and the order was given for the first ships to set sail again. The next morning at 4:30, the wind was at hurricane proportions and the rain was coming almost horizontally. The meteorologist noted that this was the bad weather he had predicted for June 5 but continued to insist that it would clear by June 6. This was the last moment for calling back the ships if the invasion were to be postponed. Ike could either take a chance that the weather prediction was right and give the go-ahead or wait two weeks and hope the conditions would then be right. The decision was his alone. He weighed all the alternatives briefly and then at 4:45 A.M. said, "O.K., let's go." Everyone rushed for their command posts and Dwight was alone in seconds. A minute earlier he was all-powerful; now, as over five thousand ships began moving toward France, there was nothing more he could do. He spent the day with the paratroopers who would take off that night, for he was deeply concerned that Leigh-Mallory might be right about their casualties. The next morning, June 6, an aide coming to report that the air drop was a success and the troops were going ashore, found the supreme commander, Allied Expeditionary Forces, sitting up in bed, smoking a cigarette, and reading a Western novel.[42]

OVERLORD went as planned. The Allies had the advantage of surprise, for the Germans were not expecting an attack in such foul weather. In fact, Rommel had gone to Berlin to confer with Hitler. The troops at Omaha ran into trouble, for they encountered a German division that G-2 (Intelligence) had not reported. But, on June 7, Ike toured the invasion areas in a British ship and found all the lodgements were secure. He spent a week holding press conferences, acknowledging messages of congratulations, and trying to secure de Gaulle's cooperation in the liberation of France. Then, on June 12, Marshall and the chiefs of staff joined Eisenhower in crossing the Channel and they spent the day touring the battlefronts. A week later, after the success of the invasion was assured, the weather proved Dwight had been right in deciding to attack when he did. On June 19 a terrible storm struck the coast of Normandy and destroyed one of the two artificial harbors and severely damaged the other. If Ike had postponed D-Day until after June 6, the invasion would have been scheduled for a time when the worst weather in twenty years hit the English Channel.[43]

The Normandy invasion came just in time, for on June 12 the Germans began launching V-1 rockets at England from the coast of France. These were small, pilotless airplanes loaded with explosives. When the motors shut off at a prearranged time, they crashed and exploded. In August, the Nazis began launching the V-2s. Rockets loaded with TNT, they were fired to great heights and then fell silently at great speed. The first warning of their approach was the explosion upon impact. These new weapons were additionally nerve-wracking to the British people, for they were nondiscriminating in selecting their targets. Fortunately, the conquest of the French coast eliminated the Germans from the launching areas.

After initial success, Allied progress in Normandy slowed down. Terrain constituted part of the problem, for Normandy was hedgerow country, divided into small fields bounded by bases of earth three or four feet high upon which trees and shrubs grew. These served both as boundary markers and as barriers to the Channel winds and proved to be excellent natural fortifications. As tanks tipped up to climb them, the less heavily armored undersides were exposed to fire while their own guns were pointed helplessly skyward. Finally, one of Bradley's men hit upon the idea of welding steel shafts to the front of tanks. As the tank approached the barrier, the shafts would penetrate, keep the machine level and the tank could then bulldoze its way through, tearing out trees and earth. Offensive operations subsequently speeded up when the tanks were equipped in this manner.

Also, Montgomery, the commander of Allied ground forces, disagreed with Ike over strategy. Eisenhower and the Americans favored constant attack and the direct approach. Dwight was concerned over logistics and insisted on assuring a constant flow of mass-produced goods from the factory to the battlefield. The British general, on the other hand, was cautious to a fault. He was careful with his resources and preferred to have the enemy commit himself on a broad front while he would attack at a narrow front. He would then cut through the enemy lines and rush on to his objective.[44]

Bradley soon captured Cherbourg, giving the Allies a good port, and the Americans moved southward. Montgomery, on the left, had the strongest of the Allied Forces and his primary objective was to capture Caen the first day. But he failed to move rapidly enough, and the Germans were able to strengthen Caen before he could take the city. Finally, he made an all-out attack in early July. After capturing half of the city to the Orne River, he failed to secure any bridgeheads and called off the attack. Then he pleased Ike by announcing a new major offensive called GOODWOOD. The massive attack came off and Montgomery captured the remainder of Caen, but with such terrific losses that four days later he halted the offensive. Eisenhower was outraged. It had taken seven thousand tons of bombs for Montgomery to capture seven miles of territory.[45] Montgomery's strategy, or what his critics called his refusal to be aggressive, eventually paid off, for in strengthening the area around Caen the Germans thus weakened their forces in the south. The strategy permitted Bradley and Patton to break through rapidly, although it necessitated a change in Allied plans.

By late July, Patton's Third Army became operational and the Americans were ready for a major offensive. On July 25, 1944, Patton made an important breakthrough and two days later captured Avranches at the base of the Brittany Peninsula. The Germans then withdrew some of their troops from the Caen sector and moved them toward Avranches in a counterattack. Bradley decided to go on the defensive at Avranches while sending Patton eastward against Argentan. Because the Canadian Army was coming south toward Falaise, Bradley ordered Patton to hold at Argentan in order that the two Allied armies would not collide. Unfortunately this left a twenty-five mile gap between them, and the Canadians, instead of closing the gap, held at Falaise, permitting the German Army to escape the trap.

But the way was now open to Paris and, as a symbolic gesture, if nothing else, it was important to liberate the capital city. Ike made an agreement with de Gaulle in

late 1943 for a French division to participate in OVER-
LORD. The Second French Armored Division under General Philippe Leclerc, brought to France with Patton's
Third Army, was given the honor of liberating Paris. The
evening of August 25, 1944, de Gaulle made his triumphal entry, and the next day he led a victory parade down
the Champs Elysees. To establish firm control of his government, de Gaulle asked Eisenhower for the use of two
divisions. These could not be spared from the pursuit of
the Germans but Ike marched two divisions through the
city, instead of around it, on their way to the front so
de Gaulle could review them. This gave the Frenchman a
show of strength and support from the Americans. A seg-
ment of the British press misunderstood the purpose of
this and complained of American love for parades, charging that the Yanks were seeking to monopolize the glory
of liberating Paris.[46]

The planners of OVERLORD had predicted that the Germans would try to hold their line at the Seine River.
Instead, as the Allies found themselves pushing ahead
rapidly all along the front, Eisenhower decided to continue the momentum right across the Seine. At the same
time he announced he was taking personal command of
the ground forces, a decision Montgomery tried to persuade him to reverse throughout the remainder of the
war. The British compensated for this "demotion" of
Montgomery by promoting him to field marshal, whereby he would outrank Ike, a four-star general. At this
time, ANVIL, renamed DRAGOON, was launched; on August
15 the Seventh Army under General Alexander Patch
landed in southern France in an amphibious operation
even larger than OVERLORD. The strategy was for Patch to
take the port of Marseilles and then march northward to
join Bradley and Patton, thus cutting France in two,
while Montgomery moved northeast to Antwerp and
thence to the Ruhr. Antwerp was badly needed as a port
to supply the rapidly moving Allied armies.

It was at this point that Montgomery asked Eisenhower for full supply support. With this, he promised to break through the German lines, rush to Berlin, and end the war quickly. It has been argued that the war could have been ended in September 1944 if this strategy had been followed. The Germans were near collapse, and a major push would have finished them, or thus the proponents of this debate suggest.[47] But this does not sufficiently take into account the ultimatum of unconditional surrender which persuaded Hitler to hold out to the bitter end nor the fact that the Allies were already outrunning their sources of supplies, especially gasoline. By mid-September, the Allied drive was slowing down, thereby permitting the Germans to begin regrouping their forces. Eisenhower decided to continue his broad front approach. Montgomery, though, persisted with his argument. He believed the broad front strategy was being pursued because 1944 was an election year in the United States and it was politically desirable for the Democrats to prolong the war.[48] He further believed there were insufficient supplies for all the Allied armies to arrive at the Rhine simultaneously. So he proposed MARKET-GARDEN, a daring plan to get airborne and armored divisions across the Lower Rhine and into the Netherlands. He persuaded Ike to slow down the advance of Patton in the south and divert Patton's gasoline supplies northward.

This meant deferring the rehabilitation and utilization of the port of Antwerp. That city had been captured in early September but it was necessary to clear out the heavily defended fifty mile stretch of the Schelde Estuary that approached the port before it could be used. Although he badly needed Antwerp with winter coming on, Eisenhower agreed to try Montgomery's strategy. This was Eisenhower's gravest error of the war.[49] The Allies desperately needed this port if they were to crush the Germans in 1944. Instead of ordering an all-out assault for the purpose of opening Antwerp for use, Ike approved a delay in order to carry out Montgomery's fruitless attempt to cross the Rhine at an early date.

On September 17, 1944, paratroopers were dropped into Arnhem, but bad weather set in, and in one week Montgomery had advanced only sixty-five miles into the Netherlands and failed to cross the Rhine, all at a loss of twelve thousand men. Of the eight thousand men dropped at Arnhem, there were six thousand casualties. Eisenhower then ordered Montgomery to abandon this campaign and to clear out the Schelde. By the time the port of Antwerp was made operational, bad weather had set in and the possibility of ending the war in 1944 was gone.

Dogged German resistance combined with adverse weather to slow the Allied advance in October and November. During this time Ike traveled constantly, visiting troops and checking conditions. Supplies remained scarce until Antwerp was functioning, which was early 1945. SHAEF plans called for a major offensive in early 1945 north of the Ardennes by Montgomery while Bradley would move against the Saar in the south. In the Ardennes region itself, things were quiet and the Allies were stretched quite thin. Four divisions were holding a seventy-five mile front, an area that normally would require ten divisions. Eisenhower questioned Bradley about this but was assured that if the Germans attacked there, they could be promptly counterattacked on either flank and stopped.[50]

On December 16, two German armies of twenty-four divisions suddenly struck the three American divisions in the Ardennes, smashing through and crushing two of these divisions. The following battle, known as the Battle of the Bulge, was the last German effort. Although they did not have enough gasoline to go fifty miles, Hitler believed his armored divisions could cut through Allied lines quickly, capture American supplies of gasoline, and race on to Antwerp. Eisenhower had two divisions in reserve which he committed to the defense of Bastogne with orders for them to hold out. He then ordered Patton to turn northward to Bastogne and hit the German flank. Fighting men were so desperately needed that Ike offered military pardons to anyone serving prison sentences of fifteen or more years if they would shoulder a rifle. He also invited blacks, who were serving in segregated service units, to volunteer for combat duty. Walter Bedell Smith, his chief of staff, was alarmed over this violation of War Department policy. To take such an unorthodox step as this, he warned, would mean to the American people that the Battle of the Bulge was causing the supreme commander to panic. Ike, no social revolutionary, retracted his invitation, but thousands of blacks had already volunteered. They were trained for combat and later served as segregated combat units.[51]

This German thrust cut the American forces in two, severing their communications; thus on December 20, Eisenhower decided to give Montgomery temporary command of the American troops on the north flank of the Germans and to keep Bradley in command of those on the south. The height of the German attack came on December 22. The Germans demanded the surrender of Bastogne. To this the American commander, General Anthony McAuliffe, gave the legendary reply, "Nuts," an expression the implications of which were not in the German commander's English vocabulary. The "Embattled Bastards of Bastogne" held their ground. Eisenhower ordered Montgomery and Bradley to counterattack by January 1, cut off the Bulge, and trap the Germans. Montgomery would not move until January 3, and Eisenhower was ready to send him home. (Ike relieved his tensions and controlled his temper when dealing with Allied generals like Montgomery by keeping his hands hidden under his desk while he shredded cloth handkerchiefs. It was reported that he demolished three handkerchiefs the day he heard Montgomery could not move for several days.)[52] January 3 was too late, and the Germans escaped the trap by fighting their way out of the Bulge.

By February 7, 1945, the Allied line was restored to the position it had held before the German counteroffensive. In the meantime, Montgomery called a press conference on January 7 to describe the Battle of the Bulge. He depicted it in terms of his British troops having to come to the rescue of the Americans, an explanation which was extremely unfair to Bradley. This threatened the Allied unity Ike had worked so hard for, especially when the British press began suggesting Montgomery be restored to complete ground command. Bradley declared he would quit before he would serve under Montgomery, but Eisenhower and Churchill were able to smooth out the issue and prevent the single ground commander-in-chief concept from being carried out.[53]

It was a remarkable coincidence that, on the day of the German breakout, Ike received a tremendous promotion. Congress authorized a new five-star rank, general of the army, and Eisenhower, along with Marshall, MacArthur, and H. H. (Hap) Arnold (who represented the air force on the Joint Chiefs of Staff) became the first named to this rank.

The Third Reich Collapses

Hitler had committed his last major reserves to the Ardennes offensive, and, when the German collapse came, it was swift. By early 1945, the Russians were moving rapidly on the Eastern Front. Soon the Allied Forces would be in danger of coming together, and it was necessary to have plans for coordination. This was particularly true of aerial missions. Ike sent Tedder to Moscow to hold preliminary discussions. Then the combined chiefs of staff authorized Eisenhower to communicate directly with Stalin on matters that were strictly military so the two fronts could come together with a minimum of mistakes and incidents.[54]

On February 15, the Russian armies reached the Oder-Niesse River line, thirty-five miles from Berlin, and secured bridgeheads. The Americans were two hundred and fifty miles from Berlin, for they were still west of the Rhine at this point. By March 1, the Germans were rapidly retreating across the Rhine and destroying all bridges as they moved. On March 7, Eisenhower was having dinner at his Reims headquarters when Bradley called with the exciting news that General Courtney Hodges' First Army had captured the Ludendorf Bridge at Remagen before the Germans could destroy it. Ike ordered him to get everything he could across the Rhine before the Nazis could drive the Americans back or before they destroyed the bridge. Later that month Patton's Third Army crossed the Rhine on the run. With the Allied armies across the Rhine in strength, Eisenhower developed the strategy that would end the war.

He ordered Montgomery and Bradley to encircle the Ruhr, the great industrial heart of German military power. Because it was vital to the Nazis, it would be strongly defended. As Walter Bedell Smith put it, "to destroy the Ruhr would be to destroy a sizeable part of the German army."[55] Montgomery told Ike that, after he had the Ruhr surrounded, he intended to move toward the Elbe, meaning he wanted to take Berlin. Thus was born what would become the most acrimonious and controversial issue of World War II: Why did Eisenhower not try to capture Berlin before the Russians arrived there?

Although Ike agreed with Clausewitz that war is a continuation of politics by military means, he saw his own role primarily as military, not political. The capture of Berlin would undoubtedly have political significance, but that was a situation to be dealt with by the political leaders. In fact, Roosevelt, Churchill, and Stalin had already agreed at the Yalta meeting in February 1945 that postwar Germany would be occupied; they had also agreed upon the zones each country would have. Berlin, also to be divided and occupied, would be completely within the Russian zone, while the British and American zones would be two hundred miles to the west of Berlin. Eisenhower was opposed to this division and wanted the Allies to occupy Germany as an entity, but was unable to persuade Roosevelt to accept his concept.[56] Dwight accepted the zone approach because his civilian superior had decided upon it.

Regardless of what army captured which part of Germany, the occupation forces of each country would be shifted to the agreed-upon zones when Germany surrendered. Also, for Montgomery to reach Berlin ahead of the Russians, the remaining Allied forces would have to go on the defensive at the Rhine while pouring all the available supplies into the Englishman's two-hundred-mile race to the German capital. When asked, Bradley estimated that capturing Berlin would require 100,000 casualties. If Montgomery's strategy were adopted, would not the Russians, who were only thirty-five miles from Berlin, cease their "mopping up" operations in eastern Europe and dash to the German capital first? Obviously the Soviets would win the race for an objective that was meaningless except as a symbol. As events turned out, the Russians battered their way into Berlin at a cost in lives probably in excess of Bradley's estimate and then gave their Western allies half the city to occupy; three decades later the West still held half the city that they acquired with no loss in lives.[57]

Eisenhower viewed the conquest of Germany from a military viewpoint. After the Yalta decision, Berlin was not a military objective for him. His orders were to defeat the Nazi power. There were rumors that, with the imminent collapse of the capital city, Hitler intended to make a desperate stand in the National Redoubt, the easily

DIVISION AND OCCUPATION OF GERMANY

Berlin

EAST GERMANY

●Bonn

WEST GERMANY

defended mountainous area of southern Bavaria, western Austria, and northern Italy. Ike's staff believed the Fuhrer would withdraw the cream of the German forces, which were fanatically devoted to him, and fortify the area, which could probably not be taken without great cost in lives and time. Eisenhower decided, therefore, the best strategy would be for Bradley to thrust hard through the center of Germany, meet the Russians at the Elbe, and thus cut German forces in two. In the meantime, the northern flank under Montgomery would cut off Denmark while the southern flank under Patton would race for the National Redoubt. Ike communicated these plans to Stalin, the commander of the Russian military forces, on March 28, as the combined chiefs of staff had previously authorized him to do. Churchill was furious over the Allied commander's direct correspondence with Stalin, whereby Ike announced what Churchill considered a political decision to a political leader.[58] The prime minister did his utmost, therefore, to change these plans, but to no avail.

Eisenhower continued to adhere to his decision to stop at the Elbe. On April 11, Allied troops reached that objective and then turned north and south to "mop up" the remaining German troops. The Russian army met the Allies at the Elbe on April 25. Germany was now cut in two. With no unified command and all hope lost, the German soldiers began surrendering by the tens of thousands. Fearful of the Russians, most Germans sought to surrender to the Western Allies in hope of kinder treatment. Hitler committed suicide on April 30, and German officials made overtures to surrender to the British and Americans and thus split the Allies. Eisenhower refused to listen. He kept the Russian commanders apprised of developments, insisting that Germany surrender on both fronts simultaneously. The Germans had no choice; on May 7, General Alfred Jodl signed a surrender document at Reims with the Western Allies and a similar one in

Berlin on May 8 with the Russians. Ike's staff wondered what flowery language the supreme commander would use in his message to the combined chiefs of staff informing them of the defeat of the Third Reich. They all tried their hands at writing eloquently worded drafts, but Dwight rejected their efforts. His message was simply, "The mission of this Allied force was fulfilled at 0241, local time, May 7, 1945." In June, the Allies began moving troops to the agreed-upon zones of occupation and the Americans began shifting armies to the Pacific theatre: With this buildup, plus use of the terrifying atomic bomb on Japanese cities in early August and the Russian declaration of war on August 8, Japan surrendered to the Allies on August 14, 1945, bringing World War II to an end.

Ike felt deeply obligated to Marshall for his success in Europe. Through crisis after crisis, Marshall had firmly supported him, and he was truly grateful. The knowledge that Marshall stood behind them "had a tremendous effect on my staff and principal subordinate commanders," he wrote the chief of staff. Marshall replied:

> You have completed your mission with the greatest victory in the history of warfare. You have commanded with outstanding success the most powerful military force that has ever been assembled. You have met and successfully disposed of every conceivable difficulty incident to varied national interests and international political problems of unprecedented complications. Through all of this, since the day of your arrival in England three years ago, you have been selfless in your actions, always sound and tolerant in your judgments and altogether admirable in the courage and wisdom of your military decisions. You have made history, great history for the good of mankind and you have stood for all we hope for and admire in an officer of the United States Army. These are my tributes and my personal thanks.[59]

Ike could ask for no higher praise.

Dwight went to England to receive further accolades. He was made an honorary citizen of London where he gave a moving speech at the Guildhall. Then he came home for a short visit and received a hero's welcome from his countrymen. Mamie, Marshall, and thirty thousand people met him in Washington, D.C., chanting "Ike, Ike, Ike!" The next day four million Americans cheered him in the streets of New York City. Three days later he came home; the Union Pacific took him across the plains of Kansas as it had done fifty-three years previously when he was a little over one year old. This time thirty thousand people greeted his arrival in Abilene. He told the crowd that never, in all the years and in all his travels, had his memories of Abilene left him.

> Here are the people that are life-long friends of my mother and my late father—the truly great individuals of the Eisenhower family. They raised six boys and they made sure that each had an upbringing at home and an education that equipped him to gain a respectable place in his own profession. My brothers and I, with our families, are the products of the loving care, the labor and work of my father and mother—just another average Abilene family. All of us are practically choked with emotion. Good luck and God bless every one of you.[60]

With that, he grinned and waved goodbye.

Men usually react to great power in one of two ways: with arrogance or humility. Eisenhower displayed an amazing humility. Unlike MacArthur, who believed he was born to greatness, Eisenhower could never believe the good luck that brought him to his position. Ike had been open, honest, and sincere in working with the Allies, and he made the coalition succeed as no other general, English or American, could have. He was successful as supreme commander because of his chief characteristic— his trustworthiness. The Allies, from Churchill and de Gaulle to the lowest mudslogging infantryman, trusted him and subsequently performed for him as they would for no other.

It is generally believed that Eisenhower was a great political general during the war, that he served as sort of chairman of the board. There is much truth in this. He learned a great deal about diplomacy and European politics. His major contribution to the war was to make the Allied military operation work with generals as diverse as Montgomery and Patton. His innate political ability made him the ideal commander to mediate the conflicting views of the Allies and persuade them to work for the common cause. But Eisenhower contributed more than this to the war effort; a great tactician in his own right, he made numerous military decisions during the war, some of them against all the expert advice, and events usually proved him correct. This was true in the field as well as at staff headquarters. Yet he never tried to claim credit for his successes. News reports always came from "Allied headquarters," not "General Eisenhower's headquarters." When he discussed military successes, he always talked of Walter Bedell Smith and Omar Bradley and George Marshall, not of himself. George Marshall and this fundamentally peaceable man deserve the credit for leading the Allies to victory in Europe in World War II. Marshall was the global strategist and Eisenhower carried out the plans. Now they could begin the work of making the peace equally successful.

CHAPTER FOUR

The Cold War Unfolds

Eisenhower emerged from the war a world hero. He was greatly admired in the Soviet Union, and Marshal Georgi Zhukov, his Soviet counterpart, awarded him the Russian Order of Victory, a decoration not previously given a foreigner. In those early weeks following V-E Day, when the victors were establishing their occupation governments in Germany, Dwight found Zhukov and his subordinates to be extremely friendly and cooperative. So he was quite pleased when Washington permitted him to accept an invitation from Premier Josef Stalin to visit Russia in August 1945. General Lucius Clay, his deputy commander for the American zone of occupation in Germany, accompanied him as did his son John, now a lieutenant in the United States Army.

During his trip Eisenhower visited the scene of Russia's heroic defense at Stalingrad and was given a tour of the ancient national capital in the Kremlin. But the highlight of the visit proved to be the annual sports parade in Red Square in Moscow. Thousands of athletes from all over the Soviet Union participated in this event, performing for five hours for the benefit of a few hundred invited guests. Because there were no seating arrangements, everyone had to stand. But soon after the ceremonies began, Stalin invited Dwight to join him atop Lenin's Tomb, an honor never before accorded a foreigner. During the show, the two men conversed intermittently through an interpreter. The Soviet premier repeatedly emphasized that Russia and the United States must remain on friendly terms.[1]

This wartime harmony dissipated, however, and the two superpowers rapidly grew apart in a rift sparked by mutual suspicion and hostile actions. Even while Eisenhower was visiting in Russia, the world was dividing into the two armed camps that would carry on what became known as the cold war. During Eisenhower's visit to Russia, he and Zhukov debated the relative merits of their respective economic and political systems, and these arguments indicated the larger disagreements of the two nations. Zhukov adhered to the communist doctrine just as wholeheartedly as Ike defended the principles of free enterprise and personal liberty. Thus, while the two generals respected each other, they were never able to convince each other of the merits of their respective governmental systems. Each man was passionately devoted to his country. Both nations, in pursuing their national interests, quickly found their policies inimical to the goals of the other.

Chief of Staff

After a subsequent leave in the United States, Dwight returned to Germany in time to help prepare for the meeting of the Big Three at Potsdam in July 1945. Because Franklin Roosevelt had died in April, before Germany surrendered, the new president, Harry S Truman, was having his first opportunity to meet Stalin. Churchill, bitterly disappointed that the English electorate had turned him out of office at this point, was replaced at the conference by Clement Attlee, head of the new Labour government.

Ike met Truman and Secretary of State James Byrnes at Antwerp and escorted them to Potsdam. This gave him an opportunity to discuss military problems with the president. He urged that a civilian government take over the American zone of Germany from the military authorities as soon as possible. He further recommended that, with the collapse of Japan imminent, the United States should not encourage Russia to enter the war in Asia.[2] He was unaware that a positive decision on the question of the Soviets fighting Japan had already been made at Yalta the previous February.

It was at Potsdam that Truman received word of the successful testing of an atomic device at Alamogordo, New Mexico. Although the British had been kept apprised of this development, the Russians had not. According to General Leslie Groves, the director of the Manhattan Project, "Russia was our enemy and . . . the project was conducted on that basis."[3] Fundamentally, United States policymakers viewed the Soviet Union as a temporary ally; American opposition to communism and fear of the emerging strength of Russia had meant that assistance was granted in World War II only because nazism presented a much more immediate menace. Truman told Stalin at Potsdam that he had a new weapon of tremendous potential, but the Russian dictator appeared uninterested.[4] The president failed to realize until later that Stalin already knew a good deal about the atomic bomb.

The "Big Three" issued an ultimatum to Japan from Potsdam, vigorously asserting that "the alternative to unconditional surrender is prompt and utter destruction." When Japan made no direct overtures to surrender, President Truman ordered the first atomic bomb delivered. It was dropped on Hiroshima on August 6, 1945, killing and wounding hundreds of thousands of civilians. When Japan did not respond overtly to this destruction, Truman ordered a second bomb dropped on Nagasaki on

August 9. Russia had declared war on Japan the previous day. These developments prompted Japan to surrender on August 14, 1945. The immediate effect of the bombs is clear, but they left a legacy of unanswered questions. Should their destructive power have been demonstrated instead on uninhabited areas? Was their use (especially the second time) justified? Was their awesome destructiveness a necessary deterrent to even more tragic atomic warfare in the future? Eisenhower was not a party to the decision to drop the bombs but, in principle, he opposed their use at the time.[5] Later, at least in theory, he would approve their potential employment.

Eisenhower hoped to retire soon after the close of the war. But his plans were postponed in late 1945 when Truman asked General George Marshall to go to China with the mission of bringing Nationalist Chiang Kai-shek together with the Communist Mao Tse-tung to end that country's civil war. This left the president without a chief of staff. Ike's expressed desires by this time were to settle down on a ranch in Texas or a small town in the Midwest, or better yet to attach himself to a small college where he could informally pass on to students some of his vast experience and knowledge of the world. But Truman persuaded him to replace Marshall as chief of staff of the army, a post he reluctantly assumed on November 19. In this position, he presided over the demobilization of the United States Army after V-J Day.

Americans had been basically a nonmilitaristic people, at least until the cold war. Their suspicion of standing armies dates from the colonial period, and they have traditionally relied upon a strong militia or national guard, with the raising of a civilian army when the need arose. Then, at the conclusion of each war, there has been a rush to disassemble this temporary war machine. The experience after World War II proved no exception to this tendency. Recalling the demobilization problems after World War I, General Marshall had wisely begun planning for the end of World War II as early as 1942. In September 1944, the Department of War announced it would use an "adjusted service card," or point system, to determine priorities for discharge of military personnel. Two days after V-E Day, the system for granting credits was clarified: servicemen would receive a certain number of points for time in service, overseas duty, dependents, and decorations. Those with the highest number would be discharged first; those with the lowest would perform occupation duty or be shipped to the Pacific theatre until Japan was defeated.

Demobilization after the war was a massive problem compared to previous wars, for in May 1945 there were almost 12.5 million men and women in the armed forces, some 7.5 million of them being stationed overseas. Pentagon plans required a postwar army of 1.5 million. The remaining personnel were to be discharged according to their points, the critical score being set at eighty after V-J Day. But the pace proved to be too slow, for the GIs wanted to come home immediately and the general public talked in terms of having the boys home at least by Christmas. Servicemen's wives organized "Bring Back Daddy" clubs and inundated congressmen with baby shoes that had cards attached pleading "Please bring back my daddy." Because lack of shipping facilities constituted one deterrent to rapid demobilization, soldiers overseas organized a "No Boats, No Votes" campaign. They deluged congressmen with messages threatening retaliation in the elections of 1946 if the demobilization rate was not accelerated. Nervous congressmen, in turn, put pressure on the White House and the Pentagon. The critical score was accordingly lowered to seventy, then on November 1 to sixty, and to fifty-five on December 1. By Christmas, 5 million personnel had been discharged.

Meanwhile, inductees into the army for overseas replacements were not as numerous as expected, thus creating a serious problem. If the goal of 1.5 million soldiers by July 1, 1946, was to be met, the demobilization rate would have to be reduced. In early January 1946, the Department of War subsequently announced a curtailed schedule for discharges. This resulted in a series of spontaneous riots in military posts throughout the world. Beginning in Manila, when several thousand soldiers marched against their headquarters in a protest demonstration, the idea spread rapidly among the enlisted men to bring direct pressure to bear on the authorities to accelerate the discharge rate. Eisenhower, as chief of staff, investigated these uprisings and reported that the major cause was "acute homesickness aggravated by the termination of hostilities"; these men "were not inherently challenging discipline or authority." He recommended that no mass disciplinary action be taken against the rioters even though, technically speaking, they were committing mutiny. Dwight also appeared before alarmed congressmen on January 15 to explain the army's new demobilization system. He informed Congress that he had banned further demonstrations but promised that every man overseas who was not needed would be brought home immediately. He deplored such rapid dismantling of American military power, but the administration, faced with powerful political pressure, found no viable alternative. This ended the controversy and demobilization continued at a rapid pace.[6]

As army chief of staff, Eisenhower also became deeply involved in the postwar reorganization of the armed forces. The attack on Pearl Harbor and the subsequent military confusion and lack of coordination or communication between the civilian and military branches demonstrated that the system needed revamping. Then, too, experiences of World War II indicated a need to rethink the military posture and approach. This problem became closely entwined with two other related issues—universal military training (UMT) and control of atomic energy.

There were numerous suggestions on what to do with the secret of atomic energy. Some wished to destroy knowledge of it while others insisted that the Soviet Union would soon be able to develop an atomic bomb anyhow. Many people, therefore, supported those military authorities who wanted to guard the monopoly position of the United States and stockpile an atomic arsenal. Others emphasized further experiments and the development of peaceful uses. In October 1945 President Truman made his decision. The United States would seek agreement with other nations to share scientific information on atomic energy and would renounce the use of the bomb for military purposes. He appointed a committee, chaired by Undersecretary of State Dean Acheson, to prepare a plan to implement this decision. Before the proposal was completed, Truman appointed Bernard Baruch as ambassador to the United Nations Atomic Energy Commission. Baruch modified the committee's tentative proposal and presented it to the United Nations for consideration. It called for U.N. inspection of countries working on atomic energy, a gradual relinquishing of information, and penalties for violations. Most importantly, it advocated a waiver of Security Council vetoes on actions pertaining to this issue. Ike warned Baruch at this time that "If we enter too hurriedly into an international agreement to abolish all atomic weapons, we may find ourselves in the position of having no restraining means in the world capable of effective action if a greater power violates the agreement."[7] In other words, the United States must have adequate safeguards before abandoning its monopoly. Baruch's proposal took cognizance of this warning.

The Soviets counterproposed that the United States cease bomb production and destroy existing atomic weapons. They would then be willing to discuss inspection and controls. This resulted in stalemate, causing President Truman and Congress to decide that America should proceed to develop atomic energy. Therefore, on August 1,

1946, the president signed into law the Atomic Energy Act. This statute maintained the constitutional principle of civilian control over the military by permitting only the president of the United States to authorize use of atomic weaponry for military purposes. It further established a five-man Atomic Energy Commission empowered to control and to direct atomic research.

UMT and military reorganization also created headaches for Eisenhower. The American experience in World War II and the subsequent unfolding of the cold war led military planners to explore the concept of a different type of "citizens army"—one commanded by professional soldiers with young men conscripted for a short period of service to fill the ranks. Such an army could be quickly mobilized in time of war and would require relatively little training. Truman asked Congress for a conscription program as a major part of his military reorganization plans. He wanted to require one year of military service for all men when they reached the age of eighteen or finished high school, whichever came last. A committee of the House of Representatives began hearings on this proposal in June 1945. Ike, who was on duty in Europe at the time, sent his views, upon request, to the committee in writing. He endorsed this approach over the alternative of a large standing army because it would be less expensive and because it would also be a good experience for the boys.[8] But the concept of UMT was too antithetical to American traditions and Congress never approved it. Instead, a peacetime draft, with all its inequities, was continued.

In September 1945, Eisenhower wrote Marshall that, whenever he had an opportunity to speak before groups, he stressed three main themes: the need for universal training; unification of the military services; and the necessity of international cooperation. In regard to the last, he would soon change his mind and become a staunch cold warrior. On the second point, success was achieved, although not in the form Dwight sought. His experiences as supreme commander in World War II made him more aware than any man that modern warfare had become triphibious. "The closest possible kind of association" among the three services, therefore, was "mandatory," he believed. Marshall agreed with him and was also "unshakably committed to the thesis of a single civilian secretary with a single military chief of staff."[9]

Yet, many other military personnel disagreed, for when President Truman presented a military unification plan to Congress, he touched off a major battle among the rival services. The army spokesmen favored complete unification, for it was believed they would thus receive a greater share of the defense budget than if they had to compete with the more glamorous air force and navy. The air force agreed basically with the army, for Truman's proposal would make that branch an independent unit. But the navy fought unification bitterly, as the officers of that service were certain the army would dominate any single department. The result was an eighteen-month struggle in Congress with the various services lobbying to achieve their goals.

Ike believed so strongly in unification that he went so far as to advocate a single uniform for all military personnel. When he appeared before a Senate committee to testify for a bill that would provide for a single department, he assured his listeners that his experience in World War II demonstrated a need for unitary organization. In addition, he "emphatically" supported the idea of a single civilian head for the department. When some senators expressed skepticism, he used the recent Battle of Pantellaria as an illustration of the need for a single person to make final decisions. There had been "more desk hammering" in planning that battle than any other one in Europe during the war, and Eisenhower finally had arbitrarily decided to invade the island. In time of war, he argued, even a "bum" decision is sometimes better than none, and a single secretary was the only answer. When one senator expressed concern that the proposed secretary might become too powerful, Ike warned prophetically that, with experience "you are going to find you want him to do more," not less.[10]

The efforts of Marshall and Eisenhower bore fruit when Congress enacted the Military Security Act in July 1947. This law established a National Security Council, the Central Intelligence Agency (CIA), and a National Security Resources Board, all separate from the military establishment. The first was to be composed of the president, vice president, certain key cabinet officials and such other members as the president wished to appoint. They would constitute an advisory body, designed to integrate diplomatic and military policies vital to the nation's security. The CIA was an espionage agency, directed to gather information world-wide for the president and the National Security Council for planning purposes. The last agency was to coordinate the military sector of the economy for mobilization purposes. In addition, a representative from each branch of service— army, navy, air force, and marines—would comprise a Joint Chiefs of Staff.

On the military side, the law abolished the departments of war and navy and created a new cabinet position called the National Military Establishment, headed by a civilian whom some bureaucratic genius fortuitously labeled the secretary of defense. Funds would be far more easily forthcoming from Congress for "defense" than for "war." This secretary was to direct the civilian secretaries of army, navy, and air force and the Joint Chiefs of Staff. James Forrestal, the former secretary of the navy who had fought complete unification so desperately, became the first secretary of defense.

It was one thing to achieve unification of the armed forces on paper and quite another to do this in actuality. Following establishment of the new military organization, there ensued what reporters called the "Battle of the Pentagon," with each service fighting for a larger share of the defense budget. True to Ike's warning, the secretary of defense was given inadequate powers and, in trying to achieve genuine unity, Forrestal's state of mental health deteriorated to the point that he had to resign in 1949. Soon thereafter he committed suicide in a siege of depression, which shocked Congress into belated action.

Congress, therefore, amended the law in 1949, changing the National Military Establishment to the Department of Defense and giving the secretary greater authority over the three service secretaries. In addition, a chairman was added to the four Joint Chiefs of Staff, and this officer would also serve as military adviser to the President. In 1950, Truman called George Marshall out of retirement to serve as defense secretary and he did much to achieve genuine unification of the armed forces. Meanwhile, Eisenhower, who never liked desk jobs, became bored with his tasks as chief of staff and resigned from the army in early 1948. In addition, he had become exceedingly restive over the severe budget cuts for military purposes during his tenure in the Pentagon. The postwar world was too dangerous, he thought, for the United States to remain unprepared to defend itself.

POLITICS BECKONS

Although his work in Washington had been less exciting than his wartime activities, this period had to be a significant one for Ike. While working in the Pentagon and appearing before congressional committees, he became acquainted with the nation's leading political figures and learned much about the political process. Furthermore, he met some of the country's most powerful industrialists and business leaders. During these years he began golfing and playing bridge with a number of influential men. Among them were Thomas Watson, Jr., of IBM and a member of the Columbia University trustees; Clarence Dillon, a member of a Wall Street firm;

Douglas Black, president of the Doubleday publishing company; Roy Roberts, publisher of the *Kansas City Star;* Paul Hoffman of the Studebaker corporation; and John Hay Whitney, publisher of the *New York Herald Tribune.* Clifford Roberts, a New York investment banker, became his financial adviser. Close friendship was begun with Sid Richardson, a Texas oil multimillionaire who persuaded him to join a successful venture in off-shore oil drilling. When Ike moved to New York City in 1948, political supporters who wanted to groom him for the presidency began holding a carefully orchestrated series of luncheons and dinners for him around the country to let the nation's financial leaders inspect him and begin to get acquainted.[11] Eisenhower soon found himself moving in these circles with ease. He was a long way, literally and figuratively, from the streets of Abilene when he joined the prestigious Blind Brook Golf Club in New York City. He enjoyed these new acquaintances and contacts very much for, like many military men, he was greatly impressed with financial success even though he was not intensely concerned with amassing great wealth for himself.

Despite his disclaimers to the contrary, Eisenhower was apparently interested in the presidency. When queried about this interest, Harry Butcher replied, "Want it! He wants it so bad he can taste it!"[12] But to achieve that goal, he would have to hide carefully his desire and yet not discourage too effectively the interest that politicians expressed in his candidacy. His exploits in World War II made him a universally admired hero and thus the subject of pursuit for the presidential nomination by both major political parties. Even during the war he was mentioned as presidential material, to which he would reply "baloney," and disclaim any interest in politics. When he met Truman at the Potsdam conference, the latter was still awed by his new responsibilities in the White House and, like most Americans, deeply impressed with Ike's successes as supreme commander. Truman stunned him by impulsively declaring, "General, there is nothing that you may want that I won't try to help you get. That definitely and specifically includes the presidency in 1948." Momentarily taken aback, Dwight treated the remark as a joke and replied, "Mr. President, I don't know who will be your opponent for the presidency, but it will not be I."[13] His response should have alerted a careful Eisenhower student to his political party preference.

Reconversion problems and bitter partisan battles between the White House and Congress marked Truman's first administration. As vice president, Truman had been kept unaware of many of the administration's activities and policies. Thus when he was suddenly thrust into the "splendid misery" of the presidency, particularly at one of the most crucial periods in American history, he was awed by his new position and its responsibilities. In the beginning, the citizenry sympathized with him and public opinion polls indicated that 87 percent of the people supported him—a figure higher than that ever achieved by the very popular Franklin D. Roosevelt. But, during the reconversion period, Truman faced the weighty problems of demobilization, a significant inflation which stimulated waves of strikes, and a severe housing shortage, to name a few of his concerns. Even the politically shrewd Roosevelt would have had difficulty surmounting these national issues; Truman, far less astute, was soon in serious difficulties. Public frustration over these continuing problems found a target in the White House. Truman's popularity declined correspondingly and when the congressional elections were held in 1946, a poll indicated he retained the support of only 30 percent of the people. The Republicans exploited this public distrust of Truman by capturing control of Congress for the first time since 1930.[14]

The Eightieth Congress, assembling in January 1947, was as admittedly partisan as was Truman. Generally, it supported the president's foreign policy of containment of communism. But on domestic affairs, the Republican leaders believed they were representing the desires of a majority of the American voters and they confidently looked forward to capturing control of the White House in 1948. Even before that year, both major parties were seeking out Eisenhower as their candidate, for he had not yet publicly expressed a party preference.

During his Abilene homecoming back in 1945, Eisenhower had been queried about the possibility of his entering politics. "In the strongest language you can command," he had responded vehemently, "you can state that I have no political ambitions at all. Make it even stronger than that if you can. I would like to go even further than Sherman in expressing myself on this subject."[15] Then came the frustrating two years as chief of staff in Washington when he became convinced the country was erring, both in its unilateral disarmament and also in expanding the role and activities of the national government in domestic affairs. By 1948, he was beginning to question seriously his previously adamant attitude about a political future.

There were many responsible people during these years clamoring for Ike to run for the presidency and it was sometimes difficult not to listen. They appealed to his patriotism. Did he have the "right" to withdraw himself from politics? Did he not have a "duty" to serve his country in any capacity that he was asked? Because most politicians were convinced that he could win, there were many who sought, for selfish or altruistic reasons, to convince him there was a public demand for him to be in the White House. Such disparate groups as Southern Democrats, Northern big city bosses, and the liberal Americans for Democratic Action wanted him as the Democratic candidate. When a Gallup Poll in December 1947 showed Eisenhower leading all presidential contenders, both parties began seriously to woo him. Truman even offered to take the second spot on an Eisenhower-Truman ticket, which Ike declined.[16] This was an interesting offer, especially in the light of evidence that at least some administration officials knew that Ike was a Republican. He had confessed to this privately at the Army and Navy Club.[17] Eisenhower endorsed Republican principles, and he believed 1948 would be a Republican year, but he was not yet ready to "plunge into presidential waters." He would wait and see what befell Dewey, the titular head of the Republican party. This sound strategy called for continued public disclaimers of interest in politics while awaiting developments of the next four years. Within this framework, Dwight made a public statement on January 23, 1948, in response to a request from a New Hampshire newspaper publisher that he run in that state's primary.

He noted that he had previously withdrawn his name from politics quite emphatically but that he had apparently failed "to convince thoughtful and earnest men" of his sincerity. He had not flatly stated he would refuse a nomination because that "would smack of effrontery" but, more importantly, he did not want to appear to violate "that concept of duty which calls upon every good citizen to place no limitations upon his readiness to serve in any designated capacity." Dwight was convinced that "the necessary and wise subordination of the military to civil power will best be sustained, and our people will have greater confidence that it is so sustained, when life-long professional soldiers, in the absence of some obvious and overriding reason, abstain from seeking high public office." Then he carefully added that "politics is a profession; a serious, complicated and, in its true sense, a noble one." But he could see no compelling reason in the current situation that commanded his nomination.[18]

This statement probably ended all doubt that the Republicans would again nominate Thomas E. Dewey as their standard-bearer in 1948. But some Democrats refused to give up on Eisenhower. Left-wing Democrats had despaired of Truman and organized the Progressive party with Henry A. Wallace as their candidate. Southern Democrats, fearful that Truman might advocate a strong civil rights program, later bolted the Democratic convention, organized the Dixiecrat party, and named J. Strom Thurmond for the presidency. The remaining center core of Democrats, convinced by convention time that Truman could not win, began a drive to "dump Truman" and nominate Ike. Many Democratic politicians became enthusiastic over this possibility when a public opinion poll, taken in June 1948, showed only 26 percent support for Truman compared to 53 percent in favor of Eisenhower. One week before the Democrats convened, though, Ike reiterated his firm decision not to be considered as a candidate and the movement collapsed.

Winston Churchill wrote Dwight that he thought he had made the right choice in 1948. Running for the Democrats would make it appear he was rescuing a party in difficulty, while accepting the Republican nomination would mean repudiating the party he had been serving for the previous three years. Besides, Churchill noted, "luckily, there is plenty of time" to run later.[19] Contrary to Dwight's expectations, this proved to be a Democratic year and in one of the greatest upsets in history Truman defeated Dewey, winning by 24 million votes to his opponent's 22 million. While this campaign and election were taking place, Ike assumed his new duties as a university president.

At the end of the war, Dwight had received numerous offers of positions in civilian life, mostly of a commercial nature. These he rejected out of hand for he believed, rightly so, that the firms were only trying to exploit his name and he was not interested solely in making money. He had suggested that he would like to find a small college with which he could become associated, but, instead, he was approached by the trustees of a great university,

Columbia, to become its president. Ike disliked the uncertainties of life in large cities and Columbia was in the nation's largest metropolis; he always carried his service revolver when he had to walk the streets of New York City alone at night. He was also apprehensive over a position that called for experience so different from his own. But the trustees assured him they wanted "an organizer and a leader, not a professor," so he accepted the position.[20]

Before he moved to New York City he wrote his memoir of World War II, *Crusade in Europe.* Though he had earlier spurned many offers to publish his memoirs, Douglas Black of Doubleday and William Robinson of the *New York Herald Tribune* approached him with a new argument. Historians use as primary sources contemporary accounts by participants in events. Often these are written too hurriedly, they argued, and are replete with inaccuracies; therefore, Eisenhower owed it to himself and to history to write his own accurate version. He finally agreed, if Black and Robinson would arrange a package deal to purchase the manuscript. They cleared it with the Internal Revenue Service and bought his manuscript with all the relevant rights. Eisenhower, as a nonprofessional writer, sold the book as a piece of property; this sale was regarded, legally, as a transfer of a capital asset. He kept the manuscript six months after its completion so that it would become a long term capital gain, thereby avoiding a much higher income tax of $400,000 on royalties. Thus he paid only $158,000 and the book netted him about a half-million dollars after taxes.[21]

He did not begin the writing until after leaving office as chief of staff. Over the years he had periodically dictated memoranda on current activities, so he had much material readily available on his war experiences. Using these files, plus his official correspondence, Ike dictated the first draft which a researcher then documented from the records. Dwight then rewrote this draft and it was retyped until he was satisfied with it. Unlike many books of this kind, his was not ghostwritten. Working sixteen hours a day in this manner, Eisenhower was able to complete the 200,000-word manuscript in an incredible seven weeks. It became a best-seller and the purchasers reassured him that he had not cheated them.

Crusade in Europe was published in the fall of 1948, soon after he joined Columbia University. Written in his solid, straight-forward style, it received good reviews for being a sound, factual account. Although it is a superior war memoir, Ike was typically reluctant to admit errors, and he was careful in concealing his inner thoughts. He also refrained from dealing in personalities, and the reader has trouble, for instance, in determining his true feelings about Field Marshal Montgomery.

The publication of this book came at a propitious time for his academic career. Yet Eisenhower was never particularly well-received by a majority of the Columbia faculty even though he made a number of important innovations while he was president. He went there under the erroneous assumption that he could work at a slower pace than previously. Indeed, he might have been able to relax somewhat if Secretary of Defense Forrestal had not asked him to serve part-time as an informal chairman of the Joint Chiefs of Staff during those hectic early months when attempts were being made to make the National Military Establishment operational. So he commuted one or two days a week to Washington. Holding down two jobs took its toll, and in March 1949 Ike fell quite ill from an attack of disease that, in 1956, would be diagnosed as ileitis. After several days in the hospital, he was transferred to Key West, Florida, to recuperate. His doctor strongly recommended a significant reduction in the four packages of cigarettes that he had smoked daily throughout his adult years. Having just gone ten days without a cigarette, Dwight decided he could break the smoking habit, so he quit entirely, another example of his strong will and determination.[22]

Performing at two jobs, plus the very nature of the work involved in the administration of a large university, thwarted Dwight in achieving his goal of intimate association with the students and faculty. Instead, he found himself extremely busy representing the university at functions, raising money, and coordinating the work of his subordinates. During his presidency he managed to establish the American Assembly, a "think tank" where experts in many fields exchanged ideas concerning contemporary problems. In addition, the Institute for the Study of Peace and War was begun at Columbia. Also, thinking of future retirement, Ike and Mamie began to search for a permanent home. In 1950, with the assistance of good friends, the George Allens who owned a home in Pennsylvania, the Eisenhowers purchased a small farm near Gettysburg. In the 1950s they built a home there to which they would retire in 1961.

It was while at Columbia that Eisenhower taught himself to paint and he enjoyed spending many hours at this recreation. By this time, too, his family was growing. His son John, on postwar occupation duty in Austria, had met and married another Army "brat," Barbara Jean Thompson, in 1947. Their first child, Ike's namesake, Dwight David Eisenhower II, was born in 1948. He was soon followed by three sisters: Barbara Anne, Susan, and Mary Jean. Ike and Mamie now became doting grandparents, enjoying the company of the children whenever possible. During the White House years, this would include almost every weekend and holiday.

Disliking the large city, and never really enjoying the president's mansion at Morningside Heights or his role as university administrator, Ike felt increasingly frustrated at Columbia. This feeling seemed to be reciprocated by the faculty. He was criticized for his inaccessibility to faculty and students. In addition, the academic community became more and more irritated by his speeches, which were becoming increasingly to sound like those of a Republican campaigning for the presidency. At one time he declared that if all that Americans want is security "they can go to prison." On another occasion he deplored America's increasing demands for "caviar and champagne when we should be eating hot dogs and beer."[23] He particularly spoke out against big government, noting that there was a tendency among young people to think that "hard work on the part of the individual was no longer the key to his own social and financial betterment." Thus, when a new call to duty beckoned, Eisenhower was ready to respond.

FOREIGN PROBLEMS AND NATO

By the time Eisenhower became president of Columbia, the cold war had enveloped the world. By 1948, relations between the United States and Russia were exceedingly tense. With the defeat of the Axis powers, the United States became increasingly anticommunist, and the Soviet Union viewed this hostility as proof of the evil intentions of the Americans to destroy the Soviet Union. The United States viewed atheistic communism as a monolithic structure bent on imposing its system on the world by force, and the Soviet Union was convinced that capitalist imperialists were determined to encircle and destroy Russia. Each side began to adopt policies which the other viewed as a threat to its own security and to world peace. Inevitably, the tougher one side acted, the greater the other side reacted. Eisenhower changed his views toward Russia as his country did. Under the tutelage of Admiral Forrestal, who was zealously anticommunist, Ike moved from a position of seeking cooperation with Russia in 1946 to a firm posture as a militant cold warrior in 1948.

The Nazi armies had wreaked tremendous devastation on Russia during the war. Their invasion and subsequent repulsion had cost Russia a fantastic number of lives— some 20 million soldiers and civilians—and the destruction of fifteen large cities plus thousands of towns and villages. When Eisenhower flew to Moscow in 1945, from the Russian border to the capital he did not see a building standing. Surviving this traumatic experience, the Russians were determined such a catastrophe should never happen again. To prevent such a recurrence, the Russians believed they must make the governments of eastern European countries either subservient or at least extremely friendly to the Soviet Union. Stalin took steps at once to achieve this "cordon sanitaire" to protect Russia. It was imperative for him to establish Russian hegemony there to maintain the balance of power.

The United States, in turn, began to lay the foundations for the policy of containment. This included the Truman Doctrine of aid to Greece and Turkey, the Marshall Plan of assistance to West Europe, and the creation of an autonomous West Germany to contain the further expansion of communism. The most comprehensive effort to contain Russian and communistic influence in West Europe came in April 1948 when a Senate resolution requested the President to negotiate a defense agreement with Western Europe. In April 1949, therefore, the United States and Canada and ten (later thirteen) European nations signed a pact creating the North Atlantic Treaty Organization. Article Five of this pact declared that "the parties agree that an armed attack against one or more of them shall be considered an attack against them all." For the first time since the Revolutionary period, the United States again formally became a part of the European balance of power system by entering into a peacetime military alliance. The "Free World" now had European communism ringed by military force, although it took a year for the signatory nations to agree upon how to implement the pact.

The Korean War marked a turning point in the development of NATO. At first the alliance was conceived as a political commitment. Then, with the communist in-

vasion of South Korea, the Western allies saw a need for
something more concrete. In September 1950, they
agreed to establish an international military organization to implement the original intent of the treaty. In
December 1950, while enroute to Denver for a Christmas
visit, Ike learned that President Truman was trying to
reach him. Upon making a telephone connection with the
White House, Truman informed Eisenhower that the
NATO countries unanimously requested that he command the new military force. Eisenhower, by now an avid
cold warrior and a firm believer in the containment
policy, accepted out of a sense of duty. Fortunately, for
him, this tour of service helped prevent his drive for the
Republican presidential nomination from cresting too
early. Europeans admired Ike, particularly for his
"civilian-mindedness." He, like they, was concerned with
building defenses to prevent war. His primary task was to
convince the member nations of the need for a NATO
army and to persuade each to contribute its share. In January 1951, he made a quick tour of Europe, talking to the
various heads of state. He discovered all were willing to
cooperate, some more than others, but they also wanted a
strong commitment from the United States in terms of
American troops stationed in Europe. When he returned
home, President Truman asked Eisenhower to tell Congress, and later the nation through a radio broadcast,
what he had learned on his trip. In these speeches,
Dwight emphasized the need for the United States to participate fully in NATO in order to preserve American
freedom. He was able to return to Europe with assurances
of support from both the president and the Congress.

Eisenhower's main work consisted in establishing a
command for NATO, a job he found to be more difficult
than producing Allied unity in World War II. Headquarters for SHAPE (Supreme Headquarters, Allied Powers,
Europe) was set up outside Paris, and Ike and Mamie
moved into a villa a few miles away in the Parc de

Marnes. There were three other houses there: one occupied by General Alfred Gruenther and his wife; another by General Howard Snyder, the medical officer, and his wife; and the third by aides. Actually, the Eisenhowers lived not so much in a foreign country as on an American army post set in the middle of another nation.

Ike soon surrounded himself with familiar faces. In addition to Gruenther, his staff included Kevin McCann; Paul "Pete" Carroll, who had been with him in the Pentagon (both Carroll and McCann also served with him at Columbia); Major Wilton B. "Jerry" Persons; and an English soldier who was on his staff in World War II, Colonel James Gault. Field Marshal Montgomery was his deputy commander; in this tour of duty, the two worked together much better than they had in World War II.

The military force was rather quickly and efficiently organized, with nearly two-thirds of the officers at SHAPE being American or British. Some eighteen months after he accepted the assignment, when NATO had reached the point of development where Ike believed someone else could effectively continue the work, he resigned as commander and came home. This experience and these months in Europe gave him a thorough knowledge and a deep understanding of European affairs and politics. He had been quite impressed with French Foreign Minister Jean Monnet, who was the chief advocate of a United States of Europe, and he believed the Schuman Plan to establish the European coal and steel community constituted "real progress toward unity in Europe."[24]

Meanwhile, back in the United States, foreign affairs were impelling the American people through the traumatic experience that became known as McCarthyism. The year 1949 brought a series of shocks for Americans.[25] Generalissimo Chiang Kai-shek, fighting a losing battle against Mao Tse-tung's Communists in China's civil war, was forced to yield the mainland and Mao proclaimed the People's Republic of China that August. In December,

Chiang retreated to Formosa (now Taiwan) with his remaining followers. The United States refused to recognize Mao's regime as legitimate.

Americans were further startled when President Truman announced on September 23, 1949 that Russia had exploded an atomic device. This was years ahead of schedule, for American scientists had predicted 1952, and some even 1955, as the earliest possible date for the Soviet Union to become a nuclear power. Ominously, the United States had now lost its nuclear monopoly and its most powerful potential enemy would, in five more years, have the military capability of delivering an armed attack on an equal basis. Truman responded to this challenge by ordering a crash program to develop a hydrogen bomb. Also, the National Security Council produced, in 1950, a paper labeled NSC/68. This blueprint for an accelerated defense program suggested that an annual expenditure of as much as 20 percent of the Gross National Product (GNP) for military purposes would be possible and feasible.[26]

Soviet emergence as a nuclear power was soon followed by the perjury trial of Alger Hiss who was accused of being a Soviet agent and the trial and conviction of a number of Americans for atomic espionage, including Judith Coplon (her conviction was reversed in 1952), Julius and Ethel Rosenberg, and Karl Fuchs, a British scientist. These revelations convinced many Americans that the United States was being betrayed from within. All these developments, coming so closely after each other, helped create an anticommunist hysteria that swept the nation after 1949. Senator Joseph R. McCarthy of Wisconsin was the most effective politician to exploit this madness, and McCarthyism was the label applied to this frenzy.

Although he was not up for reelection until 1952, McCarthy decided to campaign in 1950 for some of his Republican colleagues. He chose the theme of Communists in government as his campaign issue. In a speech in

February 1950, he made national headlines when he announced he had a list of 205 "known Communists" in the State Department. When proof was demanded, he responded with further unsubstantiated charges. Continuing this technique, McCarthy cleverly exploited public frustration during the big Red Scare and became the most successful demagogue in American history.[27] His chief target was the State Department and especially secretaries George Marshall and his successor Dean Acheson, who were most closely associated with the loss of China. McCarthy once described Marshall as being part of "a conspiracy so immense, an infamy so black, as to dwarf any in the history of man"—a plot to betray the United States to communism.

American foreign policy since World War II usually attracted bipartisan support in Congress. This was certainly true in the early years of the cold war under the leadership of Senator Arthur Vandenberg of Michigan, the leading internationalist Republican in the Senate. But, increasingly, there was a deepening split in the ranks of Republicans over foreign policy, especially after Vandenberg's death. The events of World War II and the Cold War persuaded many Republicans to become internationalists and to support America's role as leader of the "Free World." But as the Cold War progressed, with the United States becoming increasingly involved in world affairs, and with subsequent setbacks, particularly in 1949, growing numbers of citizens were reverting to isolationism, or to a position of unilateralism, believing the United States should "go it alone" in fighting the Cold War. They deplored the increased involvement with foreign nations and were especially apprehensive over the march of communism in Asia. In the eyes of many of these new isolationists, the Truman administration had closed the door to communism in Europe only to leave the back door open in Asia. These "Asia Firsters," who believed Asia to be more important than Europe to American interests, became increasingly vocal with the rise of McCarthyism. Then the Korean War strengthened their position.

North Korean troops crossed the 38th parallel on June 25, 1950, determined to unite all of the country under communist rule. President Truman, recalling the piece-meal aggressions that had led to World War II, decided to institute collective security. While Korea was not vital to American safety, he determined that such overt aggression must be met with force in order to defend containment. Receiving United Nations support, he committed United States troops to action there, and troops were quickly shipped out under the command of General Douglas MacArthur. Unfortunately, Truman sought only unofficial approval from Congress for his action, leaving himself open to later Republican criticism. In one week he committed the United States to a major war without a congressional declaration of war, demonstrating how greatly executive power had grown since 1945. Eisenhower agreed, though, that this decision to intervene in Korea "was wise and necessary."[28]

The United States quickly mobilized its economy and troops, and soon had sufficient military forces in Korea to permit MacArthur to recapture South Korea. Then in late September, Truman made a fateful decision. Yielding to the traditional American desire to defeat the enemy totally, he abandoned containment and ordered MacArthur to establish control over all of Korea. At this point, Chou En-lai, foreign minister of the People's Republic of China, announced that his country would never allow any capitalist imperialists to overrun a neighbor. Concerned over possible communist Chinese intervention in North Korea, Truman flew to Wake Island in mid-October to confer with MacArthur. The latter assured him that China would not intervene and, if it did, its military forces would be disposed of easily. Based upon this assurance, Truman ordered the U.N. troop's progress northward to be continued. As the United Nations forces approached the Yalu River (the boundary between Korea and Manchuria), more and more Chinese troops were encountered. Then on November 26, 1950, the U.N. forces were attacked by 200,000 to 300,000 Chinese troops and quickly driven back to the 38th parallel.

The Western Allies and the United Nations promptly repudiated further widening of the war effort. The Truman administration therefore returned to the policy of containment and ordered MacArthur to confine his actions to the defense of the Republic of South Korea. This Korean "police action," as Truman ineptly described it, with its limited objective of containing communism, was frustrating to those conservatives, or unilateralists, who wanted the United States to use its vast military power decisively, and they agreed with General Mac-Arthur that there was "no substitute for victory." MacArthur chafed under Truman's restrictions and began advocating an aggressive military policy in Asia. He urged a naval blockade of China, and aerial bombardment of Chinese industry, communications, and supply networks, and an "unleashing" of Chiang Kai-shek on the mainland—in other words, he wanted to destroy China's military capability before it became too powerful and while the opportunity existed to do so.

The Joint Chiefs of Staff rejected MacArthur's strategy, however, with their chairman, Omar Bradley, observing that it would involve the United States in "the wrong war, at the wrong time, with the wrong enemy." The administration still believed the Korean activity was merely a communist feint to persuade the United States to abandon Europe and concentrate its military power in Asia. When MacArthur failed to convince the administration that his strategy was sound, he began issuing unauthorized statements deploring the restrictions placed upon him. This placed President Truman, the general's constitutional commander-in-chief, in an intolerable position. Finally, on April 11, 1951, Truman took one of the most courageous actions of his presidency and relieved MacArthur of his command, replacing him with General Matthew B. Ridgeway.[29]

Undoubtedly, the dismissal of MacArthur came as no surprise to Eisenhower. Reporters caught his reaction splendidly. A photo of Ike's face showed an almost mockingly quizzical expression when he was told the news. He responded, "When you put on a uniform, there are certain inhibitions you accept." He had learned long ago to accept them, while MacArthur never did.

The fighting continued in Korea on a limited scale. Finally, in June 1951, both sides agreed to armistice negotiations which began at Panmunjom. These discussions broke down in October 1952, just prior to the presidential election, however, and the fighting was resumed. Meanwhile, MacArthur made a triumphal tour of the United States, appealing to the growing number of conservatives who were becoming alienated from the United States policy of emphasis on the importance of Europe.

Increasingly, the Republican Senator from Ohio, Robert A. Taft (labeled "Mr. Republican" by friend and foe alike) was emerging as the chief spokesman for this type of thinking. A fiscal conservative, he had been a contender for the Republican presidential nomination since 1940 and during the Korean War appeared to be his party's probable nominee for 1952. As a senator, Taft had opposed NATO, and his views on Asia had been inconsistent. Like most Americans, he supported Truman's decision to intervene in Korea and also the decision to invade across the 38th parallel. The Chinese intervention forced him back to his isolationist position of wanting to withdraw American troops from the Asian mainland, but when MacArthur was fired, Taft supported his strategy of widening the war is Asia. In addition, Taft, for partisan purposes, supported McCarthy in his attacks upon the Democrats. To prepare for the presidential campaign of 1952, Taft published his views in November 1951 in a book entitled *A Foreign Policy for Americans*. First, he advocated a campaign of propaganda and infiltration of communist countries by secret agents, a policy that, within a few months, became known as "Liberation." Secondly, he advocated support of Europe with a limited number of troops for NATO and principal reliance upon a powerful air force—a concept that would later be labelled "massive retaliation."[30]

THE FIRST CAMPAIGN

Eisenhower grew alarmed when he saw that Taft and the isolationists were rapidly gaining control of the Republican party, for he feared they would dismantle the policy of containment. Ike was a cold warrior who firmly supported the concept of collective security for Western Europe. Before leaving for Paris to assume the NATO command, he had a long discussion with Senator Taft in his Pentagon office. Dwight later said he wrote a strong statement that he planned to make public after the visit, which would irrevocably remove him from the political arena. But when Taft refused to endorse firmly a bipartisan support of collective security and worried instead about whether he would agree to sending one American division, or six, to NATO, Ike said he tore up his statement, and, while in Paris, he had W. Averell Harriman keep him posted on Taft's voting record in foreign affairs.[31]

Eisenhower's tremendous popularity insured that both political parties would continue to woo him until, finally, his sense of duty would permit him to succumb when he believed there was a sincere demand for his candidacy and a probability he could win. His old wartime comrade, Winston Churchill, knew him well. When asked if he thought Dwight would be a presidential candidate in 1952, Churchill grinned broadly and replied, "Ike has not only to be wooed but raped."[32] Eisenhower would yield, but he obviously preferred being drafted. He naturally desired the presidency, but he was also aware that the American voter prefers the candidate to be a reluctant aspirant.

Both parties again sought him as their candidate in 1952. The Democrats needed a popular standard-bearer like him for, in addition to their troubles defending Truman's foreign policy, the years 1951 and 1952 had brought out the revelations of the Truman scandals. Critics had unearthed irregularities in the Reconstruction Finance Corporation and revealed that a number of Truman associates, including his close friend General Harry Vaughan, had accepted mink coats and deep freezes in return for political favors. Several officials resigned or were fired from the Internal Revenue Service when irregularities were discovered in that politically sensitive agency. Truman compounded the problem by failing to act quickly and thoroughly to cleanse his administration of corruption.

Believing the Republicans would wage an effective campaign and wanting victory for his party, Truman again solicited Ike to run on the Democratic ticket. Dwight came to Washington in November 1951, ostensibly to discuss NATO affairs, and during the course of their conversation Truman offered the Democratic presidential nomination to him. Again he refused, explaining he was opposed to many Democratic domestic policies, especially Truman's pro-labor position in regard to the Taft-Hartley Act. When the columnist Arthur Krock published this story, both Truman and Eisenhower hotly denied even discussing politics at their meeting.[33] By that time there was a stream of political visitors passing through Ike's Paris office, each trying to sound him out and get a commitment, all to no avail.

Thomas Dewey had declared for Eisenhower as early as 1950 and he and his supporters began to organize to obtain his nomination. Included were Dewey's top advisers: James Hagerty; Herbert Brownell, Jr.; and senators

James Duff of Pennsylvania, Frank Carlson of Kansas, and Henry Cabot Lodge of Massachusetts. The group acquired a significant addition in September 1951 when Governor Sherman Adams of New Hampshire announced Ike's name would be placed on the ballot in his state's primary the following March. A turning point came in Eisenhower's thinking in September 1951 when Lodge visited him in Paris. Lodge stressed the developments of the previous twenty years, especially the predominance of one party, and Dwight agreed that maintenance of the two-party system was vital. Eisenhower further agreed with Lodge's denunciation of the burgeoning bueaucracy in Washington, the increasing centralization in government, and the rapidity with which the American dollar was losing its value. Most importantly, Lodge hammered away on the theme that Ike was really the only Republican who stood a chance of being elected. Dwight promised Lodge he would "think the matter over."[34] From this point on Ike was apparently a candidate, at least subconsciously.

Because public knowledge of his communications with professional politicians could damage his image of being above politics, Dwight had his wartime colleague, Lucius Clay, now president of the Continental Can Company, serve as an intermediary. When Clay informed Eisenhower supporters that Ike was truly a Republican, Lodge announced this fact in January and his name was entered in the New Hampshire primary on that ticket. The liberal, internationalist wing of the party, "the Eastern Establishment," now had a candidate who would accept a draft; but to overcome the strength of Taft and the conservative isolationists they had to convince their man that he must come home and make a fight for the nomination.

To impress the professionals of his political appeal and to help convince the candidate himself to work actively and openly, the Eisenhower forces held a political meeting at midnight in Madison Square Garden, following a prize fight. Fifteen thousand supporters enthusiastically joined the rally, which was filmed. Well-known aviatrix Jacqueline Cochran flew the film to Paris and showed it to Ike and Mamie who were quite impressed.[35] Then, in New Hampshire, a state that was thought to be rather strongly isolationist, Dwight defeated Taft in the primary by 46,661 votes to 35,838, while Harold Stassen picked up 6,574. Eight days later, Eisenhower made an even more impressive showing in Minnesota, Stassen's home state. Local efforts to put Ike on the ballot had failed, so supporters staged a last-minute effort for a write-in campaign. As a result, he lost to Stassen, but by a narrow vote of 129,076 to 108,692, while Taft, with an organized write-in campaign, only garnered 24,093 votes.

Clay now reported that, with these victories, Eisenhower was more enthusiastic about fighting for the nomination. But, by this time, the Eisenhowers were also getting a direct taste of politics. The Taft supporters, concerned over Ike's growing political strength, were beginning to distribute scurrilous pamphlets describing Mamie as a dipsomaniac, suggesting that Ike planned to divorce her and marry Kay Summersby, his wartime chauffeur, that he kept a mistress in Europe during World War II, that he was a Jew, a Catholic, a Soviet agent, and in ill health.[36] The Eisenhowers detested this ugly side of politics, but knew it had to be endured. Convinced by now that he should make a fight of it, Dwight asked Truman to relieve him of his NATO command on June 1 so that he would be free to campaign. The White House announced his retirement the same day Truman declared he would not be a candidate for the Democratic nomination.

The events of Ike's kick-off campaign could hardly be called auspicious. He chose a homecoming to Abilene on June 4 to make his maiden political speech. A heavy rain

Dwight Eisenhower, second from left, front row, the only boy in his fifth grade class wearing overalls.

Left to right: Milton, David, Dwight at twenty years of age, Ida, Earl, Flip in foreground.

Dwight and Mamie on their wedding day.

Eisenhower reunion in 1926. Front row: David, Milton, Ida. Back row: Dwight, Edgar, Earl, Arthur, Roy.

General Eisenhower with General Marshall during World War II.

Eisenhower talks to paratroopers prior to D-Day.

President Eisenhower taking practice shots at Newport in 1957.

Chief Justice Vinson administers the oath of office at the 1953 Inaugural.

President Eisenhower at a press conference in 1957. Hagerty is at his immediate left.

President Eisenhower and Mamie at their Gettysburg home in 1957.

President Eisenhower meets Premier Krushchev at Camp David in 1959.

A meeting with legislative leaders in 1959. Left to right: Charles Halleck, Allen Dulles, Everett Dirksen, Christian Herter, Sam Rayburn, Neil McElroy, President Eisenhower, Lyndon Johnson, Richard Nixon.

The last Christmas in the White House.

The oldest president in history meets the youngest to be elected to
that office.

(known in Kansas parlance as a "gully washer") held the
crowd far below the expected 50,000. His listeners stood
in mud and water while Eisenhower gave his speech during a lull in the downpour. His theme was

> in spite of the difficulties of the problems we have, I
> ask you this one question: If each of us in his own
> mind would dwell more upon those simple virtues—
> integrity, courage, self-confidence, an unshakeable
> belief in the Bible—would not some of these prob-
> lems tend to simplify themselves?

Ike's conservatism in domestic policy was basically
attuned to nineteenth century, small-town values. He
would reiterate the philosophy many times over the next
several years. He offered basically the same bland counsel to a national audience that evening. The next day at a
news conference he answered questions at length without
clarifying anything, a performance that he would develop
to a high art in the next several years. This poor start
depressed his admirers, for by this time Taft had about
five hundred pledged delegates and was campaigning
vigorously.

One of the first items of business for the 1952 Republican convention was to draw up a platform. The document
called for "sound tax and monetary policies," any necessary amendments needed in the Taft-Hartley Act, state
exploitation of off-shore oil deposits, and a mild civil
rights program.[37] The foreign policy planks were largely
the work of John Foster Dulles, the Republicans' leading
diplomatic expert. Dulles had just successfully negotiated
the final peace treaty with Japan in 1951 and, when the
Senate ratified it, he resigned from public service in order
to write and to speak on foreign policy.

In May 1952, Dulles published an article in *Life* that
advocated, and elaborated upon, two views Taft had
expressed earlier in his book—massive retaliation and

liberation. Lucius Clay was impressed and sent a copy of
the article to Ike, who then asked Dulles to come to Paris
to talk. Although Eisenhower did not accept Dulles's
views completely, especially on Massive Retaliation or
the use of force in Liberation, they found each other's
views on foreign policy were "satisfactory." Most Republicans by that time believed that either Taft or Eisenhower would choose Dulles as secretary of state, and both
contenders agreed he should advise the platform committee on foreign policy.[38] The platform was intensely partisan, declaring the Yalta and Potsdam agreements to be
blunders and charging the Democrats with waging war
in Korea with no hope for victory. It promised to "repudiate all commitments contained in secret understandings
such as those at Yalta which aid communist enslave-
ment" and to replace the negative and futile policy of containment with a positive one of Liberation of enslaved
peoples.

The Republican primaries in the South proved to be
the key to the nominating and balloting that followed
approval of the platform. Contested delegates, especially
from Texas, became a cause celebre, and it was this issue
that proved Taft's undoing. In Texas, as in Louisiana and
Georgia, the party was dominated by professionals who
existed primarily for patronage. In 1952, these politicians
were pro-Taft. When meetings were held to select convention delegates, the pro-Eisenhower amateurs, many of
them actually "Democrats for Eisenhower," swarmed in,
dominated the gatherings and selected delegates pledged
to the general. The pros left the meetings in disgust, held
their own gatherings, and chose delegates pledged to the
senator. Thus each of these states sent two slates of delegates, both claiming to be the true representatives. With
the two candidates running evenly in delegates, these
contested slates proved crucial.

The Eisenhower forces faced a difficult battle here, for
the Taft supporters controlled the party machinery and

thus, presumably, the convention. So, when the Credentials Committee accepted the Taft compromise of dividing the Texas delegates twenty-two for him and sixteen for Ike, Lodge, representing the Eisenhower faction, gambled and said, "No deal." Instead, he was able to persuade the delegates, who made the ultimate decision, to accept the "Fair Play" rule. This forbade the contested delegates from voting on seating other contested delegates and was adopted by the convention 658 to 548. As a result, Ike received approximately 80 percent of the contested delegates to 20 percent for Taft. Eisenhower was able to remain aloof from this, allowing his managers to carry the fight.

With this victory, the rest was rather anticlimactic. On the first roll call, before states began switching, Ike secured 595 votes to Taft's 500, with Governor Earl Warren of California receiving 81, Stassen 20, and MacArthur 10. Minnesota then shifted its nineteen votes to Eisenhower, giving him the victory and beginning a bandwagon that ended only when Taft's manager, John Bricker, asked the convention to make Ike's nomination unanimous. This was done, although most reluctantly by Taft's Midwest supporters. There now remained the choice of a running mate. The Dewey forces discussed a number of possibilities, including Taft and Taft's choice, Everett Dirksen of Illinois. They finally chose thirty-nine-year-old Richard Nixon of California, long known as a crusading anticommunist who was also an internationalist in foreign affairs. This gave the ticket geographical and age balance, and Nixon's presence on the ticket would help heal the breach between the liberal and conservative factions of the party. Dwight then addressed the convention, accepting the nomination with a pledge to lead a "crusade" against the waste and corruption in Washington, vowing to carry out a program of "progressive policies."

When Truman withdrew himself from the Democratic

race, Senator Estes Kefauver of Tennessee plunged down the primary trail, along with senators Robert Kerr of Oklahoma and Richard Russell of Georgia. Truman opposed the candidacies of these men, however, and endorsed Governor Adlai Stevenson of Illinois who declined the honor, saying he had not yet completed his program in his statehouse. Truman then backed his "Veep," Alben Barkley of Kentucky. Labor leaders opposed Barkley, though, because of his advanced age, and the convention ended up drafting Stevenson, along with Senator John Sparkman of Alabama for the second spot. The platform, written by the administration, endorsed the New Deal-Fair Deal policies and defended the Truman foreign policies.[39]

Stevenson fully accepted the Fair Deal foreign policies but disagreed with Truman's complete rejection of the Taft-Hartley Act. Also, because Truman, not Stevenson, became the target of the Republican attack, the Illinois candidate was forced to disassociate his candidacy from the White House as much as possible. He moved the Democratic national headquarters from Washington to Springfield, Illinois, and acquired his own campaign staff. His speechwriters included journalist John Bartlow Martin and Harvard economist John Kenneth Galbraith, and was headed by Pulitzer-Prize-winning historian Arthur Schlesinger, Jr. Early in the campaign, Stevenson blundered by referring to the "mess in Washington" which, of course, hurt Truman's feelings. The latter invited Stevenson to attend a cabinet meeting and to be briefed by CIA head Walter Bedell Smith. At this meeting, Truman agreed to give only a Labor Day campaign speech; he promised to refrain from any further campaigning except when Stevenson requested it. When the Republicans argued that this meeting proved Stevenson was a captive of the administration, Truman invited Ike to be briefed also by the CIA. Dwight testily declined, erroneously observing this would not permit him to remain free to criticize administration policy. His reply angered Truman who insisted Ike had let "a bunch of screwballs" come between them.[40]

Stevenson's campaign style contrasted sharply with Eisenhower's. The nation was treated to his superb wit that sparkled in his speeches. "If the Republicans stop telling lies about us," he quipped, "we will stop telling the truth about them." When Ike took him to task for treating serious matters so lightly, Stevenson responded that the GOP stood for "Grouchy Old Pessimists." The nation's intellectuals were so taken with Stevenson that the columnist Stewart Alsop commented that he had captured the complete support of the "Eggheads." But the voters were not so taken with Stevenson, for, as Eisenhower rightly guessed, inflation, corruption, and the prolonged conflict in Korea were not laughing matters to the average citizen.

In the conduct of his campaign, Dwight proved to be a natural politician. The professionals had no cause to worry about his lack of political experience. One of his first decisions was to persuade Sherman Adams, a seasoned, tough politician, to become his campaign chief of staff. His speechwriting team was composed of C. D. Jackson, a *Time* editor, and Emmet John Hughes, a writer for *Life,* who wrote the speeches in New York City, usually two days before delivery. They were then sent to the campaign train where they were rewritten by Gabriel Hauge, a young economist, into the language favored by the candidate. Ike then polished the address, trying always, as Hughes put it, "to reduce all issues to some bare essence starkly seen and graphically stated."[41] His speeches, therefore, rather than entertaining listeners, appealed to the voters' common sense. He also early established his campaign plan. He wanted to make a whirlwind effort, but he was also aware of the error of letting his drive climax too early. Taking this and his physical energy into account, he decided he would become active September 1 and that he and Adams, not the national committee, would determine his schedule and activities.[42] This led the Scripps-Howard chain of newspapers to lament in late August that Eisenhower was "running like a dry creek."

Ike responded to this criticism of his lack of activity with a speech on foreign policy before the American Legion convention. In this address, he espoused the Taft-Dulles theme of Liberation in one of his few speeches larded with purple rhetoric. "We must tell the Kremlin," he announced with a flourish, "that we shall never desist in our aid to every man and woman of those shackled lands who seek refuge with us, any man who keeps burning among his own people the flame of freedom or who is dedicated to the liberation of his fellows." The next day Dulles elaborated on this theme and outlined the steps that should be taken: first, Voice of America would stir the people to rebel; then the United States would air-drop them supplies with which to destroy the Communists. Europeans were aghast at this type of thinking. Eisenhower was concerned over this European reaction and made another major foreign policy speech in which he emphasized that his campaign of Liberation would be carried on through "peaceful means," and definitely not through war. Dulles henceforth faded from the campaign scene as Ike turned more and more to Jackson and Hughes for foreign policy ideas.[43]

Eisenhower knew full well he had to have the support of Taft and his followers to win. In addition, he viewed unification of the party as one of his major obligations. As a result, he invited Taft to his Morningside Heights home where they had a long discussion. Dwight read and made only minor changes in a statement Taft had prepared and which he released after their talk. Taft said the two were one hundred percent in agreement on domestic policies and that their differences over foreign policy were only "a matter of degree." This was not completely true, for

Eisenhower was more conservative than Taft on many domestic matters, but Taft and his followers nevertheless took up the campaign vigorously. Although the Democrats called this the "Surrender at Morningside Heights," the conservative and liberal wings of the Republican party were now united as they had not been since the New Deal.

The main issues in this campaign, Senator Karl Mundt of South Dakota believed, were Korea, communism, and corruption in government, which he reduced to the formula K_1C_2. His prediction proved true. Ike accepted the New Deal domestic programs of Social Security, minimum wages, unemployment compensation, farm subsidies, and housing. Instead, he stressed the need to curb the trend toward centralization, the need for "fiscal responsibility," and Democratic mistakes in foreign policy. He generally kept to the high road, hitting communism and corruption merely by referring to the "mess in Washington," and letting his running mate take the low road. Nixon was especially adept at this type of campaigning for he had a particular knack for political vilification of his opponents.

The Republican campaign nearly came apart in September when the *New York Post* headlined an expose with the words "Secret Nixon Fund." Wealthy California businessmen had collected some $18,000 for a slush fund for Nixon's use. Critics were quick to point out how his votes in the Senate in turn had benefitted these same special interests. When news of the fund reached Ike, he was thunderstruck. How could he continue his crusade to clean up the mess in Washington when he had a mess in his own political family? A chorus of demands arose from Republicans in every part of the country to dismiss Nixon from the ticket; he must be dropped if he refused to resign.

Characteristically, Ike refused to rush into a decision. Keeping Nixon could be a great liability, but dropping him perfunctorily could mean disaster. The presidential candidate informed newsmen that Nixon must be "clean as a hound's tooth" and the Republican National Committee purchased a half-hour of evening prime time on television to give Nixon an opportunity to explain. Five days later Nixon faced the largest television audience ever assembled to that time. He carefully explained that the fund was used solely to take care of political expenses and that neither he nor his family benefitted personally from it; he also carefully detailed his personal assets and liabilities. Then he concluded with a powerful emotional appeal. Regardless of what happened to his career, he proclaimed, he refused to return Checkers, a cocker spaniel given to his daughters by a Texas admirer, because they loved the dog too much and Nixon refused to hurt his children. This performance would always be remembered as the "Checkers speech."[44]

Ike watched Nixon's speech carefully while waiting to give his own address in the Cleveland auditorium that night. An observer, watching Ike with his pencil and yellow pad, noticed he became agitated on two occasions. In laying bare his financial condition, Nixon demanded the other candidates do likewise. (Ike's pencil jabbed the pad. He preferred the public did not know about the special tax concession he received when he sold *Crusade in Europe* and now he would have to make a financial disclosure.) Then, at the end of his speech, Nixon asked the viewers to notify the Republican national headquarters, not Eisenhower, if they thought he should remain on the ticket. (Ike's pencil jabbed the pad even harder. The old general knew at once that he had been outmaneuvered for, by doing this, Nixon took the decision of his future out of the hands of the presidential candidate and the Eastern Establishment.) After this duel, according to the writer Garry Wills, Nixon and Eisenhower never again trusted each other.[45]

Nixon's performance was a smashing success. Letters, telegrams, and calls swamped the Republican leadership throughout the nation, all favorable to his continuing on the ticket. Ike told the Cleveland crowd that he had always admired courage and he had seen a good example of it in Nixon's performance. But he did not say whether or not Nixon would be kept on the ticket. The vice presidential candidate believed he had vindicated himself and was angry at Ike's refusal to endorse him at once. "There comes a time in politics," he told Dwight over the phone, "when you have to [expletive deleted] or get off the pot," and he wrote out his resignation. His political adviser, Murray Chotiner, however, tore it up instead of mailing it.[46] The next day Eisenhower met his running mate at Wheeling, West Virginia, where he embraced him and called him "my boy." It is ironical that Nixon came through this crisis even stronger than he was before, because the episode undoubtedly garnered many votes for the Republicans. Eisenhower and his advisers were able to turn disaster into an asset, for the American voter loves to see the candidate reveal himself as human, as Nixon had done in his "Checkers speech."

From here on Ike's campaign gathered momentum and from mid-September to mid-October he maintained a grueling schedule. Everywhere he went, the crowds turned out to see their hero. His nickname lent itself naturally to the politically appealing slogan "I like Ike," which was plastered on signs everywhere at each stop. As his train "whistle-stopped" through the countryside, he would appear on the rear platform and give a short, homey address, replete with points on local issues. Then, with his bald pate shining and his face split with his wonderful grin, he would raise his arms in a final huge "V for victory" and the crowd would roar its approval. Then off the train sped to its next stop. It was good that he had such great physical stamina.

In all these speeches, he never really laid out a program of what he would do as president. He promised to cut taxes and spending, clean up corruption, and find a solution to the Korean problem, but he did not give any solid indications of his philosophy of government or his views on the major social and economic issues of the day.

Ike lost his tremendous affability at least twice during the campaign when he had to work with McCarthyites. It pained him deeply to cooperate with some of them; Joe McCarthy and Indiana Senator William Jenner, for example, had referred to Eisenhower's father figure, George Marshall, at various times as "a living lie" and "a front man for traitors." But, when he was introduced in Indianapolis by Jenner, he felt compelled by the exigencies of politics to ask the voters to elect a Republican slate, although he never referred to Jenner by name. At the end of the speech, while the crowd cheered, Jenner rushed up and embraced him. Ike endured it with a grimace but later told a confidant that he "felt dirty from the touch of the man."

Joseph McCarthy caused him even greater discomfort. Eisenhower had never referred directly to McCarthy or McCarthyism in his campaign speeches, although he detested the demagogue's techniques. McCarthy accompanied Ike on his campaign train through Wisconsin. Knowing that Eisenhower was planning to deliver a speech in Milwaukee rebuking McCarthy and defending Marshall, the senator asked him not to make any reference to Marshall while in Wisconsin. They had a heated discussion and Dwight refused to yield. Then Wisconsin Governor Walter Kohler, also up for re-election, pleaded with Sherman Adams to strike out the offending passage on the grounds that it seemed out of context with the rest of the message and was unduly provocative. In discussing the matter with Eisenhower, Adams agreed with Kohler, insisting that the wishes of the host of the state be observed. Ike left the meeting "purple with anger," but the offending paragraph was stricken. He subsequently told Wisconsin audiences that he and McCarthy agreed upon objectives of weeding out subversives and the

disloyal; they were at odds only on methods. "My opponent has been worried about my funnybone," Stevenson
remarked upon hearing of the incident. "I'm worrying
about his backbone."[47] He was right, for Ike should have
exerted his authority here and stood by his principles.
This is another instance where he believed he was at the
mercy of the "experts" on his staff. He appeased the
Red-baiters and won the support of the right-wing
Republicans, although with enduring damage to his
reputation.

Meanwhile, the Democratic effort was faltering badly,
and when Truman received a very favorable response to
his Labor Day speech, the Stevenson forces asked him to
campaign actively. Truman then began a repeat of his
1948 "give 'em hell" campaign with significant results.
Among other things, he launched a personal attack upon
Eisenhower that was unprecedented for an incumbent
President. Truman, the politician, could forget and for-
give after the campaign oratory was over, but Dwight
could not, and an animosity between them rankled for
years. The President's successful attacks led the Republican leadership to exploit public disgust over the Korean
War.

Peace talks at Panmunjom were stymied by the refusal
of thousands of North Korean and Chinese prisoners to be
repatriated to their homelands and the unwillingness of
the United States to force them. The Communists, on the
other hand, would not sign an armistice without an
agreement that these men would be returned. The talks
broke down and the fighting continued, although it was
desultory and there were few casualties. But as popular
discontent with the stalemate mounted, Ike began
demanding that American troops be replaced by Koreans,
which delighted Taft. Truman accused Eisenhower of
"making a political football" out of Korea and insisted
that he and "his snolly-goster foreign state advisers" tell
the nation how the conflict could be ended.[48]

Dwight gave his answer on October 24: "I shall go to Korea." This promise was the turning point, according to some experts. After the 1948 surprise, most pollsters were warily predicting a close outcome for the election. Now many politicians believed Dwight had clinched the race, and thus it was. "Ike in a landslide," reported the headlines on election day and, in retrospect, it seems obvious that the public was far more concerned with Korea than most politicians had been aware.

Stevenson received three million more votes than Truman did four years previously, but he was overwhelmed by the popular Eisenhower. An amazing number of voters who usually stayed at home went out to vote for their hero and Dwight carried thirty-nine states with thirty-three million popular votes to Stevenson's twenty-seven million. The Michigan Survey Center concluded that one-quarter of Ike's votes came from people who had supported Truman in 1948.[49] This number alone was enough for his margin of victory. In addition, Eisenhower captured Florida, Tennessee, Texas, and Virginia, making him the first Republican to crack the Solid South since Hoover in 1928. This election was a vote for Eisenhower, not for the GOP, however, as the Republicans emerged with only half the Senate (forty-eight seats) and controlled the House by a bare majority of nine. Yet the vote was not only in support of Ike, but also a protest against Truman and the frustration of Korea. The American voters had decided that Eisenhower, experienced in foreign affairs, was the more able of the two candidates to straighten out the "mess" in which the United States was then floundering in Asia. But the Korean problem was not the sole issue in this campaign. Eisenhower had surely been correct in stressing the "mess" in Washington, for the voters were also quite concerned over this.

The election proved Ike to be an instinctive and shrewd politician. He managed to unite the various factions of his party into a cohesive unit. "Hiding his cleverness from public view, he let Herbert Brownell and Sherman Adams gain the plaudits," a recent student of this election has observed, "and Richard Nixon and John Foster Dulles take the responsibility of any mistakes."[50] He successfully portrayed himself to the public as being above office, with the position seeking him, not the reverse. He would now have an opportunity to put his words into deeds. Would he be able to transform the Republicans into the majority party? Would he be able to bring peace to the nation? Time would prove he could do the latter but fail in the former.

CHAPTER FIVE

Fighting
the
Cold War

Many critics, liberals in particular, were certain that Eisenhower's personality changed once he entered the White House. They soon became convinced that, as President, he was indecisive, he was naive, he was lazy.[1] But he was the opposite of these, just as he had been all his life. His careful weighing of alternatives before making a decision gave the impression that he was vacillating. Many perceptive writers believed Eisenhower to be naive, especially in political matters and procedures, and he contributed mightily to the misconception that he was nonpolitical, the military hero above politics. But one did not survive the army of the period between the wars and then rise from lieutenant-colonel to five-star general of the army in a little over three years without possessing an extraordinary amount of political ability. He did not lose this capability in the White House; in fact, it was honed to a sharper edge.[2] He made one important personal change when he became president: he joined a church because he believed it important for the president to be affiliated with an organized faith. He chose Mamie's religion, the Presbyterian church. Mamie made an alteration in the White House sleeping arrangements; she had a large double bed installed for her and Eisenhower, rather than using separate bedrooms as the two previous presidents had done.

The concept that Eisenhower was a lazy president arose from several sources. His tempo of activity was patterned after a lifetime in the army, where short bursts of intense activity interrupt relatively long periods of repose. "Eisenhower drove himself without respite during a crisis," one perceptive writer noted, "but he was bored by the routine tasks of the presidency and took refuge in golf, bridge, painting and hunting, preferably under conditions that involved extended travel."[3] Like many presidents, he found the White House to be a prison from which he needed to escape periodically, and he particularly used the game of golf for relaxation. He had a short driving range installed behind a cover of trees on the south lawn of the White House where he could go for a half-hour of exercise in the afternoons. He also took many golfing vacations in Atlanta or at the Cherry Hills club in Denver. He preferred this over sailing and had the presidential yacht *Williamsburg* put in drydock to cut expenses.

He continued to use the presidential retreat in the Catoctin mountains of Maryland that Roosevelt had named Shangri-la. Eisenhower, being less romantic, renamed it Camp David in honor of his grandson. Liberals, overlooking the fact that their favorite, FDR, annually spent as many as fourteen straight weekends (running, in the later years, from Thursday to Tuesday) at Hyde Park during the hot Washington summers, in addition to frequent yacht trips, an occasional sail aboard a Navy cruiser, plus a month or two each year at Warm Springs, were less lenient with Eisenhower.[4] Reporters seemed to take delight in counting the number of days Eisenhower spent on the golf course with his wealthy industrialist friends.

Eisenhower's use of the staff system in the White House gave the appearance he was not working hard, an illusion that was much more apparent than real. The motto on the president's desk in the Oval Office, "suaviter in modo fortiter in re" ("gentle in manner, strong in deed"), is a good saying to keep in mind as one surveys his presidential years. He believed that presidents Roosevelt and Truman had been far too aggressive in their attempts to dominate the national government. In contrast, he had a Whiggish concept of the presidency, picturing the president as the nation's leader, but with Congress a co-equal partner; he believed that teamwork would achieve greater results than laying on with the presidential whip. "I am not one of the desk-pounding types that likes to stick out his jaw and look like he is bossing the show," he once told reporters. "I don't think it is the function of the president of the United States to punish anybody for voting as he likes."

BUILDING THE TEAM

To the surprise of his political opponents and the consternation of his supporters, Eisenhower actually made plans immediately after the election to visit Korea. Critics believed this had been a campaign promise made solely to win votes and his admirers thought the dangers involved in the trip far outweighed the advantages. But, Eisenhower viewed this as a definite commitment; besides, he wanted to see the military situation firsthand. He landed in Korea on December 2, toured the front, received briefings, and met with Syngman Rhee, the president of the Republic of Korea. As he had expected, Rhee, who was insisting on unification of all Korea under himself, presented a most difficult problem. But the president-elect managed to crowd his schedule to the point where he could have only two discussions with Rhee for a total of about one hour of talks.

His visit to the front, together with Mark Clark's briefings, convinced Eisenhower that the war must be ended.

"It was obvious," he concluded from his tour, "that any frontal attack would present great difficulties," and yet, "we could not stand forever on a static front and continue to accept casualties without any visible results."[5] Broadening United States efforts would only cause the Communists to escalate their own activities. Moreover the election of 1952 had just demonstrated that the public tolerance level had been reached on continued fighting in the peninsula. The stalemate must be ended.

Eisenhower left Korea on December 5 and flew to Wake Island, where he was joined by some of his cabinet-designates. As they sailed to Hawaii aboard the U.S.S. *Helena*, they discussed plans for assuming the burdens of government. The cabinet, chosen for him by Lucius Clay and Herbert Brownell, was a collection of wealthy businessmen, a development deplored by Robert Taft, who did not consider success in business to mean also success in governing people. Despite Eisenhower's promise in the campaign of 1952 to make use of "the best brains" in the country in his administration, the members of his cabinet were unusually devoid of new ideas. In fact, many observers soon noted that the two most influential members, John Foster Dulles and George Humphrey, were downright hostile to new concepts.

George Humphrey, of the M. A. Hanna Company of Cleveland, was to play a key role as secretary of the treasury. Just as Dulles was convinced "he knew how to stem the tide of Red power," Humphrey was "confident that he could staunch the flow of red ink."[6] When they first met, Eisenhower greeted him with "Well, George, I see you part your hair the same way I do," and the two immediately hit it off. Born in the same year, both men were quite conservative in fiscal matters and, in Humphrey, Eisenhower found the perfect agent for living up to one of the key Republican promises of 1952—balance the budget and reinstitute "fiscal responsibility" in the national government. Humphrey accepted the post after he was promised that if anyone wanted money from the president he would have "to see George first." Over the years, Eisenhower became closer to him than to any other cabinet officer.

Charles Wilson, president of General Motors and known as "Engine Charlie" (to distinguish him from "Electric Charlie" Wilson of General Electric who had occasionally served Truman), became secretary of defense. It was reported that, while at General Motors, Wilson had developed the automatic transmission so that he would always have one foot free to put in his mouth, but it seemed that he got into the most trouble when he took his foot out. He was forever a source of embarrassment to the administration, beginning with his Senate confirmation hearings. He could see no conflict of interest in his owning over $2 million in General Motors stock, plus several hundred thousand dollars he would receive from the company in bonuses in the next four years, and the fact that General Motors was one of the defense department's largest contractors. "I always thought what was good for the country was good for General Motors and vice versa," he complained to his senatorial inquisitors. He was promptly misquoted by the press as saying "what's good for General Motors is good for the United States." Only after he reluctantly agreed to sell his stock would the Senate confirm him.

Herbert Brownell, Jr., Dewey's former campaign manager, became attorney general and played an important role in the rapidly developing civil rights conflict. He also was instrumental in recommending people for Eisenhower's judicial appointments. Arthur E. Summerfield, Eisenhower's campaign manager, received the traditional reward of Postmaster General and sought, unsuccessfully, to put his department on sound financial footing. The department of the interior post went to Douglas McKay, an Oregon General Motors distributor, until he was replaced by Fred Seaton of Nebraska in 1956.

Ezra Taft Benson, a distant cousin of Senator Taft and one of the twelve apostles (ruling elders) of the Mormon church, became secretary of agriculture. Benson, like Eisenhower, was convinced the nation's farmers wanted an end to controls and a return to the operation of a free market in agricultural products. He was correct in his diagnosis that they did not like the regimentation but wrong in assuming they would relinquish subsidies on their crops to gain this freedom; consequently he became increasingly unpopular in the rural areas. Benson persuaded Eisenhower to open each cabinet meeting with a silent prayer which they consistently did except for one occasion. When a note reminded him of the omission, the President spontaneously burst out, "Oh, goddammit, we forgot the silent prayer," and the oversight was corrected.[7]

Sinclair Weeks, a New England industrialist, headed up the commerce department. Weeks was a moderate conservative who was willing to make some concessions to the welfare state in order to thwart any trend toward socialism.

Eisenhower made an interesting appointment to the Department of Labor. Convinced that organized labor should have its spokesman as long as that person pulled with the team, he chose Martin Durkin, president of the United Association of Plumbers and Steamfitters. When news of this selection reached Taft, he called it "incredible," for not only had Durkin supported Stevenson in 1952, but the labor leader viewed his appointment as approval for drastically revising the Taft-Hartley Act. When the president proved intractable on the latter, Durkin resigned in anger in August 1952. Durkin believed he was representing labor and was bargaining in the cabinet for his constituents. Eisenhower failed to convince him he was an "adviser" to the team, not a "bargainer," and noted this was the only instance where he and a principal subordinate failed to have "a meeting of the minds."[8] Durkin's place was taken by James Mitchell, who proved more willing to work with the team.

When Congress approved Eisenhower's request for a Department of Health, Education and Welfare in April 1953, he appointed his seventh millionaire to the cabinet, Oveta Culp Hobby, a Texas "Democrat for Eisenhower" and a newspaper publisher. (Benson, Durkin, and Dulles were the only members of the original team who were not millionaires.) John Foster Dulles, secretary of state, was the most important person in the cabinet, but more of him later.

Under Eisenhower, the cabinet met regularly once a week. An agenda was prepared ahead of time and adhered to unless an emergency arose. Henry Cabot Lodge, Sherman Adams, and Robert Cutler, who had cabinet-level appointments, also attended these meetings. Eisenhower asked each member for the opinion of that department on all questions and an attempt was made to arrive at a consensus. Then the president made his decision. Eisenhower viewed the cabinet both as "a co-ordinating mechanism to resolve interdepartmental disputes at the highest level" and also as a "direct communication between the president and his lieutenants of government—between the supreme commander and his theatre commanders—with no palace guard coming between them."[9] Each cabinet member could always plan on expressing his opinion at these meetings, even if he had difficulty in otherwise breaking into the president's appointment schedule.

Eisenhower's long military experience convinced him that the White House staff must be organized on a staff basis. During World War II, "Beetle" Smith had served as his chief of staff and had been outstanding as, in army parlance, his "son-of-a-bitch." Now, for the White House, Eisenhower found an excellent replacement for Smith in Sherman Adams, whom he appointed as assistant to the president. The position was not new, for Truman had attempted the same thing with John R. Steelman, but the latter had never made the position so powerful as did Adams. Eisenhower never did define Adams's responsibilities "or outline their limits." He expected his lieutenant to run the staff, keep everyone and everything that was of secondary interest and importance away from the president's office, and expedite the business that needed his personal attention.[10] He also handled patronage, which Eisenhower disliked intensely, and in general said no for the president. Adams became quite powerful, therefore, as he determined who and what Eisenhower saw. The importance of his role was exaggerated by the press, but he undoubtedly lightened the president's load a great deal. The staff system, on the other hand, meant Eisenhower was embarassingly deficient in knowledge of details on occasion when he should have been fully cognizant of important issues.[11] A man in Adams's position was bound to make many enemies and become extremely unpopular. Adams's nature and personality made this even more inevitable.

The "governor," as he was known, worked Saturdays, holidays, and on Sundays after church. His normal workday was eleven hours, from 7:30 A.M. to 6:30 P.M., and he expected a similar commitment from his assistants. A dour, taciturn New Englander, Adams was as sparing in his words and time as the stereotypical native of that region. His telephone manners were particularly discourteous and account for much of his reputation for gruffness. He was so busy and conscious of people wasting his time that he seldom said "hello" or "goodbye": he merely stated his business and hung up when he was finished. Perhaps he could be partially excused for this abruptness as he averaged about two hundred and fifty phone calls per day, in addition to his other activities.[12] The governor was particularly adept at handling complainers. He would stare coldly at the caller without saying a word throughout the interview. After several minutes of answering his own questions and carrying both sides of the conversation, the visitor would become discouraged and leave, without obtaining any satisfaction. Adams would dismiss him with a "come in and see me anytime." Whenever Eisenhower was absent from Washington because of illness, vacations, or other business—and this was about 20 percent of the time—Adams was particularly important in serving as a link and keeping the White House functioning on a "business as usual" basis.

In keeping with the operation of a military staff, Eisenhower insisted the White House staff carefully prepare plans and drafts of papers before bringing them to him for consideration. His staff soon discovered that he preferred, even insisted upon, reports and papers not being over one page in length if possible. As George Marshall had done with him, and as he himself had done in World War II, Eisenhower was quite willing as president to delegate authority; his subordinates were each permitted one serious mistake. He expected his staff to accept this responsibility and not bother him with details, and he became quite annoyed with Charles Wilson, for example, when the secretary worried him with particulars about running the defense department. He believed his staff was doing a good job when he was consulted on a problem only as it reached the decision-making point.

Eisenhower continued the office of congressional liaison and placed his old friend, General Wilton "Jerry" Persons, in charge of it. Persons had for several years performed this function for the Pentagon and was quite effective on Capitol Hill. At first the president considered abolishing the Council of Economic Advisers, but Taft persuaded him of its value; instead, he appointed Dr. Arthur Burns, a Columbia University economist, as its chairman. Burns soon became an important adviser. Henry Cabot Lodge, as ambassador to the United Nations, was also influential, as well as the president's brother, Milton, who had a direct telephone line from his presidential office at Pennsylvania State University to the White House. Milton also had an office in the Old State Department building and used it almost every weekend. The president had absolute confidence in his brother and used him as his principal confidant, knowing he could express his feelings and convictions freely and Milton would never betray that privacy.[13] "Beetle" Smith, as undersecretary of state, continued to have influence with Eisenhower.

The post of press secretary was filled for eight years by James Hagerty and it can be said that under him this position reached maturity. Hagerty was a genius at image-making, particularly in this period when television was beginning to play a dominant role in political life. Eisenhower had always had wonderful relations with the press during his military career in Europe, for he had treated them as part of his "team." As president, however, he resented the fact that most reporters had favored Stevenson and were quite willing to criticize the commander. But he permitted Hagerty to dissuade him from suspending the traditional press conferences and he became the first president to allow them to be televised, although they were edited before being released.

Eisenhower's complexion, under the TV lights, made him appear pasty white and sallow, and the glare of the lights on his horn-rimmed glasses was also distracting. But he came through on the "tube" as honest and sincere, and the public loved him. Through Hagerty's adroit manipulations, Eisenhower was able to continue his image of being above politics, a patient man who tried to convince rather than coerce his opponents. The liberal intellectual journals took great delight in calling their readers' attention to his lack of political sophistication, his confessions of ignorance on some of the problems raised by reporters, and his tangled syntax. But Eisenhower knew he was popular with the masses and could afford to ignore his liberal critics. "If you want to know how people feel about things," he once told Sherman Adams, "read the papers, but not the New York or Washington papers."[14]

Eisenhower's critics failed to note that syntax has a greater tendency to become tangled when speaking than it does in writing and that, in part, the president was putting on a performance before the cameras. "Don't worry, Jim," he told Hagerty on one occasion when the latter voiced concern about reporters quizzing the president on a certain foreign policy issue, "if that question comes up, I'll just confuse them."[15] It is a testimony to his ability that not once in eight years of press conferences and public addresses did he commit a significant political blunder. He was very perceptive of the public mood and, in addition, as one subordinate put it, "if there was any president better informed, I don't know who it could have been."[16] Eisenhower's confessions of ignorance on some of the public issues reporters raised were the spontaneous admissions of a president vitally concerned with foreign affairs and somewhat indifferent to domestic concerns, not of a figurehead shielded from the nation's woes by a diligent staff. These concessions of ignorance came only on domestic questions and never on foreign policy, where he was intimately knowledgeable.

Hagerty himself held two informal press conferences daily and kept a flow of favorable news going to eager reporters. He was thus able, to a remarkable degree, to transfer the blame for mistakes to other government agencies and to appropriate the maximum credit possible for achievements to the White House. He was especially adept in releasing big, favorable stories to blanket the bad news.[17] He also perfected the device known as "woodworking," so called because he would say, "Boy, I sure had to dig into the woodwork for that one." This was a contrived device of having the president announce vital statistics, grants, conferences, and similar matters.

In addition to these men, Eisenhower created several posts of special assistant to the president and brought in capable specialists to advise him. Gabriel Hauge was one of the most prominent of these figures, giving the president advice on economic matters (as did Arthur Burns) and occasionally writing speeches. One of the most important innovations in the White House staff came when Eisenhower transformed the National Security Council from the "loose framework" that Truman devised, "into a highly structured system."[18] He appointed Robert Cutler as special assistant to the president for national security affairs and used the NSC as a planning board to discuss foreign affairs issues and propose alternatives that were then discussed in the Oval Office. The council usually met weekly and considered an agenda made up weeks or months previously. Eisenhower used his staff system to delegate an unprecedented amount of work and authority over domestic matters and administrative details to Sherman Adams, thereby leaving himself more time for his primary interest—foreign policy. He used the National Security Council to help him define foreign policy matters to be brought before the cabinet for final determination.

The New Military Look

The budgetary problem was one of the first important items the president and the cabinet took up in 1953. Determined to balance the budget while cutting taxes and expenditures, Eisenhower and his advisers discovered with dismay that to do this would endanger the national security, which they could not do. They found that over 70 percent of the budget went for national security matters and that the remainder was largely committed to vital domestic programs. Eisenhower announced the bad news that there could be no budget cut at a White House conference with legislative leaders on April 30, 1953. When Senator Taft heard that military expenditures could not be reduced, he shouted at Eisenhower that he was taking them "down the same path that Truman traveled" and that "with a program like this, we'll never elect a Republican Congress in 1954."[19] (Taft died just three months later, and this outburst may have been partially caused by his uncontrollable pain.) The president calmly replied that they could not be cut without revamping the military posture and this would have to be worked out primarily with Secretary of State Dulles and Secretary of Defense Wilson.

When considering the performance of the secretary of state under Eisenhower, it is well to keep in mind the fate of Truman and Dean Acheson in foreign policy, as Dulles certainly did. Based upon the experience endured by his Democratic predecessor, Dulles was determined to remain popular domestically by presenting the public image of a staunch, dynamic fighter of communism. He was a lawyer by training and a diplomat by inheritance, for his maternal grandfather, John W. Foster, was secretary of state under Benjamin Harrison and an uncle, Robert Lansing, was Woodrow Wilson's secretary of state. Dulles spent his entire adult life in diplomatic work. Beginning as secretary for the Second Hague Peace Conference in 1907 at age nineteen, he served in every subsequent Democratic and Republican administration. He was a devout Christian and a Wilsonian who believed fanatically that communism was the world's worst evil and that the "Free World" should adamantly refuse to yield to it, either through force or compromise. So he had two principal objectives as secretary of state: stay in the good graces of Congress (unlike Acheson who was overbearing with what he considered to be inferior, questioning congressmen) in order to get the necessary supporting legislation for foreign policy; and retain Eisenhower's confidence so that there would be no doubt in the national government about who was running the state department.

It is widely believed that Dulles completely dominated American foreign policy in the 1950s. This is incorrect. Foreign policy was controlled by the president, just as the president made the ultimate decisions on domestic policy. It is true, though, that Eisenhower trusted his secretary of state more than most modern presidents have and gave him "wide responsibility" in shaping policy.[20] Eisenhower once remarked that Dulles knew more about foreign affairs than anyone else. "In fact, I'll be modest," the president observed, "and say that there's only one man who has seen more of the world and talked with more people and *knows* more than he does—and that's *me*."[21]

Both Eisenhower and Dulles were steadfast cold warriors whose major difference lay in approach. Where Dulles saw every gain by one side as a loss to the other, Eisenhower's experience convinced him that differences could be resolved to a mutual advantage. Dulles was the only cabinet member who could walk into the president's office at any time without an appointment. But, it is significant that he cleared with Eisenhower every speech he made before he delivered it. In a sense, he served the same function in foreign policy that Adams served in domestic affairs or Richard Nixon did in the political arena—he was unpopular and thus served as a lightning rod to draw the bolts away from the president. It was Dulles, not Eisenhower, who was popularly associated with such bellicose terms as "liberation" or "massive retaliation" or "brinkmanship."

The Truman administration left its successor a paper, NSC/141, that proposed an increase in military spending by 1954, even over that of Korean War levels, for by that time the Soviet Union would be capable of delivering devastating nuclear attacks against the United States.

Eisenhower thought this goal ignored fiscal responsibility. Furthermore, such a policy would result in stockpiling weapons that would quickly become obsolete and would make the United States a garrison state. He emphasized, therefore, a new concept, the "long haul," which would create a production base capable of expanding and contracting upon need.

Before preparing the 1955 budget, Eisenhower ordered investigations made of current policies and proposals, such as containment and liberation. He also asked the Joint Chiefs of Staff for estimates of defense needs by 1957. These studies resulted in a new defense posture. In formulating the "New Look," and also in his subsequent foreign policies, Eisenhower was guided by two precepts. First, he would avoid, if at all possible, committing American troops in any future local wars like Korea; and second, the United States must not fall heir to the mantle of the old colonialist powers.

The Joint Chiefs of Staff could find no area in which to cut expenditures and still maintain sufficient forces ready to fight conventional warfare like World War II or the Korean War. Eisenhower changed this. The new strategy was basically laid out in NSC 162/2 in October 1953. The United States reduced ground forces used for fighting brush wars and conventional warfare and the military was assured it could use nuclear weapons if the need arose. The United States would support indigenous forces to fight local communist aggressions. Major communist aggression would be countered by air and naval forces capable of retaliating instantly with nuclear weapons.

Unfortunately, when Dulles first described the new defense posture, he emphasized that the United States would use its massive nuclear capacity "to retaliate, instantly, by means and at places of our choosing" to any Soviet aggression; he scarcely mentioned the increased reliance upon indigenous forces.[22] Thus, the new policy became known popularly as "Massive Retaliation." The United States would warn the Communists ahead of time that any aggressive move on their part could lead to their destruction with nuclear weapons. "More bang for the buck," Secretary Wilson called the strategy. The "New Look" required an expansion of the Strategic Air Command, a long-range bomber force that would keep jet bombers loaded with atomic weapons in the air around the clock, and increased research and development of ballistic missiles and rockets by all of the military branches of service. In addition, the Defense Early Warning (DEW) system was installed, composed of a string of radar stations above the Arctic Circle from Alaska to the Baffin Islands. This would alert the military forces of an impending Soviet air strike.

In 1956 this "new look" of the military was reexamined. By that time the Soviet Union had almost achieved parity in military capability. Admiral Arthur Radford, chairman of the Joint Chiefs of Staff, wanted to continue the current level of spending but emphasize nuclear weaponry at the expense of conventional forces. The Democrats, then in control of Congress, wanted to increase significantly the air force appropriations. The president said no to both; he believed sufficiency in national defense was enough and he continued the current appropriations. His defense budgets were maintained in the $35 to $40 billion range, an amount he considered to be noninflationary and yet adequate for military purposes.[23] Two of his army chiefs of staff, Matthew Ridgeway and Maxwell Taylor, resigned in protest over the "New Look" cutting of conventional forces. Taylor was to see his views triumph under Eisenhower's successor in the White House.

The new approach that the press labelled "massive retaliation" was first used to end the Korean conflict. Some believe the death of Stalin on March 5, 1953, and the decreased intransigence of the new Soviet leaders led to a communist interest in reopening armistice negotiations. Others were convinced that the new "tough" military stance made the difference, for, on February 3, 1953, Eisenhower announced the "unleashing" of Chiang Kaishek by removing the Seventh Fleet from the Formosan Straits. Chiang could not invade mainland China without significant United States assistance, of course, but this was viewed as a threat that such help could come momentarily. In May, Dulles informed Jawaharlal Nehru of India (knowing the Indian ambassador to Peking, K. M. Pannikkar, would pass the word along) that the United States would very definitely consider using nuclear weapons if Red China sought to achieve further military advantages in Korea. On May 10 and May 11, United States bombers attacked the hydroelectric plants on the Yalu River. On May 13, American bombers hit five irrigation dams in North Korea, used to store water for rice production—an act that had been stigmatized as a war crime by the Nuremberg Tribunal. The truce talks then proceeded at a rapid pace.[24]

The efforts of the Truman administration to conclude the peace talks at Panmunjom had floundered on the question of repatriation of war prisoners. The U.N. forces had some forty-six thousand Chinese and North Korean prisoners who wanted to remain in South Korea (there were a dozen Americans in North Korea who refused repatriation) and the United States did not want to force them to go while the Communists were insisting upon their return. South Korea President Syngman Rhee, demanding unification of all Korea under his control, began to boycott the truce meetings on May 25 when he saw his goal would not be achieved. Then in early June the negotiators agreed on the issue of repatriation. The question would be turned over to an international tribunal which would determine what prisoners would be repatriated. When it appeared the truce talks would succeed, Rhee suddenly freed some twenty-seven thousand prisoners on June 18 and they immediately scattered throughout the countryside of South Korea. Eisenhower described this action as "so foolish as to be fantastic." Then on June 20 Rhee threatened to withdraw his Korean troops from the front lines. All to no avail. The final armistice was signed on July 27, 1953. The truce line was drawn where the front then existed, thus giving both countries some territory on the other side of the 38th parallel. While this was a truce that only a Republican president could have made in the political climate of McCarthyism, Rhee's actions demonstrated the limitations of massive retaliation; the United States "could hardly threaten to drop nuclear bombs on the Chinese" because the South Korean president had freed the prisoners.[25]

Eisenhower made an attempt soon after this to ease the threat of nuclear holocaust for the world. With the change in Washington administrations, Churchill, prime minister once again, sought to establish the same rapport with his old wartime comrade that he had enjoyed with President Roosevelt. Under Churchill's prodding, Eisenhower agreed to meet with him and the French prime minister, Georges Bidault, at Bermuda in December 1953. At this summit, Eisenhower tried, unsuccessfully, to obtain French ratification of the European Defense Community (EDC); France, still fearful of Germany, was most reluctant to support this agreement which Eisenhower believed was vital to the success of NATO. When the French Assembly refused to accept EDC, Dulles warned his European allies that failure of the plan would mean the United States would have to make an "agonizing reappraisal" of its West European policy. This harsh phrase spread consternation among the allies, but the new British prime minister, Anthony Eden, submitted an alternative proposal. As a result, by May 1955 the United States and its European allies had formed the Western European Union with all the signatory countries, including the now autonomous West Germany, supplying troops for a NATO army. Also, while at Bermuda, Eisenhower revealed to Churchill the gist of a plan he was going to present to the United Nations. He wanted to take advantage of the less belligerent attitude of the new Russian leaders and use the opportunity to promote world peace.

On the flight back from Bermuda, the president stopped in New York City and addressed the U.N. delegates. This speech, which the press labeled "Atoms for Peace," was a smashing success. Eisenhower recommended that the atomic bomb be taken "out of the hands of the soldiers" and put in the hands of those who would use it for peace. He suggested that the United States and the Soviet Union each donate a certain amount of fissionable material to the United Nations. This sounded wonderfully generous but Eisenhower, always playing the percentages, later admitted that he had been assured "the United States could afford to reduce its atomic stockpile by two or three times the amount the Russians might contribute and still improve our relative position."[26] The Communists could also count the odds, however, and they quickly refused to cooperate in the plan. But, the president had won a significant propaganda victory, for much of the world hailed this as a generous offer to ease world tensions.

CHECKING THE REDS

Elsewhere around the globe, President Eisenhower was containing communism, first in the Middle East where he thought he saw the Red specter rising in Iran. That country, having long been dominated by Great Britain, was seething with a desire for economic independence after winning its political independence. In fact, by the 1950s, the entire Arab Middle East was in turmoil, in part over the rise of Israel. In 1947 Jewish leaders established the independent nation of Israel. The surrounding Arab nations were determined to destroy the Israelis, and the United States was caught in the middle of this conflict. On the one hand, American politicians had to tread very carefully to avoid antagonizing well-organized Jewish constituents, but at the same time the Arab nations of the Middle East controlled some 65 percent of the world's known oil reserves. This petroleum was vital to the NATO powers and the communist bloc would exploit any possibility of extending its influence in the area. By 1953 the status of Iran became crucial.

In 1951, Iranians nationalized the Anglo-Iranian Oil Company and drove the British out of their country. In 1952, in an attempt to extend American influence over this important source of petroleum, Eisenhower's close friend, W. Alton "Pete" Jones of Cities Service Oil Company, traveled to Iran and concluded an agreement with the Iranian premier, Mohammed Mossadegh, to operate the industry under an Iranian board of directors.[27] But Mossadegh subsequently alienated powerful Iranians by promising to institute reforms, and to this end he began to ally himself with the Iranian Communist party, the Tudeh. To the United States, it was essential that Iran, with its thousand mile border along the Soviet Union, retain a stable and friendly government. The CIA therefore found an "alternative" to Mossadegh in General Fazollah Zahedi.

Under the guidance of Allen Dulles, brother of Secretary of State John Foster Dulles, the CIA took on an expanded role in the Eisenhower years. The agency enlarged its activities from its original charge of merely gathering intelligence to a more active one of implementing foreign policy. This was first evident in Iran when, in 1953, the CIA sent in Kermit "Kim" Roosevelt, Theodore Roosevelt's son, to help install Zahedi in power. On August 13, 1953, Shah Mohammed Reza Pahlavi dismissed Mossadegh from office and appointed Zahedi as premier. Mossadegh had great popular support and rioting immediately broke out in protest over his dismissal, forcing the Shah and his queen to flee to Bagdad for safety. Meanwhile, Roosevelt had been busily recruiting supporters and on August 19 he ordered his agents to get everyone they could into the streets. Between the mob in Teheran, the capital, and the army, which had now switched its support to the Shah, the necessary momentum was provided. Zahedi took over, Mossadegh surrendered, and the Shah returned to Teheran.[28] General Zahedi immediately suppressed all opposition to the regime and destroyed the Tudeh and its members. In 1954, Iran reached an agreement with an international consortium in which United States oil companies participated to sell its petroleum, and Eisenhower reported that Iran was "quiet—and still free."[29] Other trouble spots on the globe, however, were less easily managed. One of these problem areas was Indo-China.

In 1945, Japanese rule was ended in Indo-China, and the French reestablished their empire. The Vietnamese people, however, wanted independence, and they soon found a leader in Ho Chi Minh, head of the Vietminh, a communist-nationalist party. Ho wrote eight letters in August and September 1945 pleading with the Truman administration to help his country achieve the same status as the Philippines which was undergoing a period of tutelage pending complete independence. The letters went unanswered.[30] The United States was sympathetic to anticolonial movements, but France was an important ally who did not want to relinquish its world possessions. Ho then engaged in a successful guerrilla warfare that constituted a significant drain on French resources. As NATO commander, Eisenhower constantly urged the French to promise independence to Vietnam and make this move part of the cold war effort against communism. France, however, refused to give up this rich prize and Ho, appealing to Vietnamese nationalism, rapidly gained support with his guerrilla warfare. By the time Eisenhower entered the White House, Ho controlled the northern half of Vietnam. In analyzing the situation in Southeast Asia on April 7, 1954, Eisenhower likened it to a row of dominoes—if Vietnam fell, the other countries in the area would soon topple also. At this point the first domino was about to go over.

In an effort to thwart Ho's guerrilla warfare tactics and to draw the Vietminh out into the open, the French decided to concentrate their best troops in the fort of Dien Bien Phu, an isolated spot surrounded by high ground north of Hanoi. Eisenhower was horrified at this strategy. "The French know military history," he said. "They are smart enough to know the outcome of becoming firmly emplaced and then besieged in an open position with poor means of supply and reinforcements."[31] He was soon proved correct in his analysis of the military situation. The Vietminh came into the open, brought up their heavy artillery, and the French found themselves in an untenable position. They asked the United States for direct assistance.

The United States had been indirectly helping the French in the form of significant military equipment and supplies. But Eisenhower did not want to intervene directly without allies and without adequate indigenous forces to carry the major burden of warfare—a basic policy to which he continually adhered.[32] No supporting allies were to be found, for even Great Britain refused to help. The joint chiefs' chairman, Admiral Radford, wanted to test the "new look" and stage an air strike to relieve the garrison. But, although he had the support of Dulles on his proposal, Radford was the only member of the Joint Chiefs of Staff to advocate this action. A team sent by army Chief of Staff Matthew Ridgeway to survey the situation filed a chilling report: at least five divisions, and probably as many as ten, would be necessary to clear the enemy out, if backed by fifty-five engineering battalions and enormous construction expenditures. Radford's air strike was contingent upon seizure of Red China's island of Hainan which guards the Gulf of Tonkin. If this island were taken, the prospects were certain the war would be immediately enlarged.[33] Eisenhower decided against the strike. His extensive experience with bombing operations convinced him an air strike "would not only be futile" but would be an act of war and a "risk of having intervened and lost."[34] Dien Bien Phu fell to the Vietminh on May 7, 1954. In a celebrated article published in *Life* magazine in January 1956, Dulles admitted that three times in Asia—Korea, Vietnam, and the Formosan Straits—the United States had gone "to the brink of war," thus bringing another new term into the cold war rhetoric, "brinkmanship."

The French decided to withdraw completely from Vietnam, and a meeting was called in Geneva to settle the dispute. Dulles attended the conference when it opened but departed in two weeks, leaving Bedell Smith to act as an American "observer." While at Geneva, Dulles created a scene that amused some people and irritated others. When the Chinese foreign minister, Chou En-lai, saw Dulles, he immediately approached the secretary of state with outstretched hand. With visions of Roosevelt being photographed in cozy camaraderie with Stalin at Yalta, Dulles quickly turned and hurried the other way.

The participating powers agreed to place the Vietnamese situation in the political sphere where it belonged. On July 20–21, the Geneva Accords were signed which temporarily divided the country at the 17th parallel. Neither side could join a military alliance, and there would be a supervised election within two years to unify the nation under one power or the other. At this point, desperate to save something, Dulles, Radford, and Air Force Chief Nathan Twining worked out an invasion plan for a march on Hanoi. Again Ridgeway was in opposition and again, fortunately, the president refused to act.[35]

The United States and the South Vietnamese premier, Ngo Dinh Diem, refused to accept the Geneva agreements. The Accords limited foreign military personnel in South Vietnam to 342 men. Already, in June 1954, the United States had sent in a military team, the Saigon Military Mission (SMM), under the command of the CIA agent Colonel Edward Lansdale, their best counter-guerrilla warfare expert. The SMM just barely got the maximum of 342 men in before the deadline of August 11. The team then engaged in sabotage and various "psywar" activities. Diem, supported by the United States, refused to hold the agreed-upon elections in 1956 and, instead, held an election between himself and the emperor, Bao Dai. Diem won "too resoundingly," in the words of the *Pentagon Papers,* with 98.2 percent of the vote, and proclaimed himself president. In May 1956, in violation of the Geneva Accords, the United States sent an additional 350 military men to South Vietnam and continued to aid the Diem regime throughout the remainder of the Eisenhower presidency.[36]

The United States, in effect, created the Republic of South Vietnam and helped its creature, Diem, to retain control of the country. This policy would bear bitter fruit in the next decade under less cautious presidents. The formation of the Southeast Asia Treaty Organization (SEATO) in September 1954 was a direct result of the Vietnam conflict. Dulles persuaded Australia, Britain, France, the Philippines, Thailand, and New Zealand to join the United States in SEATO, in which the parties agreed to consult each other if any signatory power felt threatened.

Dulles was in Manila collecting these signatures when a crisis occured in the Formosan Straits over the offshore islands there. The large Pescadores islands in the straits, about one hundred miles from the mainland, had traditionally belonged to Formosa. But mainland China had always maintained control of the small islands, Quemoy and Matsu, about two miles off the coast. When he fled the mainland to Formosa, Chiang retained control of these two islands. Then, when Eisenhower "unleashed" Chiang in 1953, the Nationalists began staging nuisance raids on the mainland. Finally, in January 1955, Red China responded to this harassment by heavy shelling of Quemoy and Matsu. Shelling had actually been going on intermittently since September 3, 1954, but the increased bombardment in January 1955 appeared to be a preparation for invasion.

Fearful of losing the islands to the Communists, Eisenhower was in a dilemma; if he waited until the Red Chinese acted directly before he asked Congress for authority to respond, it might be too late. So, on January 24, he asked Congress for a blank check. This was just what the Asia firsters wanted. The Democratic-controlled Congress promptly responded with the Formosa Resolution by the overwhelming vote of 403 to 3 in the House and 85 to 3 in the Senate. This resolution took the unprecedented step of authorizing the president of the United States to use armed force "as he deems necessary" to protect the region from aggression. A major war scare ensued when Eisenhower sent arms into the area and had the Seventh Fleet begin convoying nationalist troops when they were moved about. The administration also considered using nuclear weapons on the mainland. "At no other time in the Cold War," claims one authority, "did the United States come so close to launching a preventative war."[37] Fortunately for chances of peace, American ships stayed out of mainland territorial waters and no American ships were hit, so when the Communists ceased shelling the islands, the crisis eased temporarily. The Asia firsters were thus frustrated in their efforts to unleash Chiang and to free mainland China.

Closer to home, the administration was taking direct action to halt the spread of communism in the Western Hemisphere. Guatemala is a beautiful Central American country that an American company, United Fruit, came to consider as its fiefdom. The company dominated the country economically while the dictator, General Jorge Ubeco, controlled the nation politically. Ubeco was overthrown in 1944 and a subsequent election brought Juan José Arevalo to power. He began reforms (labeled by some as communistic) such as raising the minimum wage to twenty-six cents per day. In 1951, Jacob Arbenz Guzman was swept into office and he accelerated the reform movement. The Guatemalan Congress approved a law providing for nationalization of idle lands and in March 1953 the Arbenz government expropriated 234,000 acres of unused lands owned by United Fruit. The government offered an idemnity of $600,000, an amount based upon the value set upon the land by the company itself for tax purposes. The company indignantly refused the offer.

A number of Americans were concerned for United Fruit. John Foster Dulles had been counsel for the company; his brother, Allen, head of the CIA, had formerly been the company president; Undersecretary of State Walter Bedell Smith later became a member of the company's board of directors when he retired from government service; and the husband of the president's secretary, Ann Whitman, was the company's public relations director. In any case, the Department of State watched Guatemalan developments quite closely. When the Arbenz government announced its intention to expropriate an additional 173,000 acres of United Fruit lands, this was the last straw. Something had to be done to stop what United Fruit considered to be the "march of communism," so plans were laid to organize a revolution.[38]

The CIA found Colonel Carlos Castillo Armas to head up a group of mercenaries being trained by the CIA in neighboring Honduras. The plot had the support of Nicaragua and the CIA was using Managua International Airport for its P47 Thunderbolts and C47 transport planes, piloted by Americans, to be used in the invasion. On June 18, 1954, Castillo and his "army of liberation" crossed the border from Honduras. Taking no chances of encountering force, he stopped six miles inside Guatemala and waited for the "air force" to topple Arbenz. Unfortunately, by this time the CIA had lost too many airplanes, and Allen Dulles was forced to ask Eisenhower for replacements.[39] What, the president asked, were Castillo's chances of success if he did not get the planes? They were about zero. What if the United States supplied the aircraft? About 20 percent, Allen Dulles replied.[40] The airplanes were supplied, their attacks were successful, and by June 30 Castillo was safely installed in Guatemala City. All of the recent reforms were rescinded, the expropriated lands returned, and all illiterates were disenfranchised. In a subsequent election, Castillo received a 99.9 percent majority vote to become president of the "republic" of Guatemala. The Eisenhower administration had successfully repelled what it considered to be the threat of communism. Meanwhile, Eisenhower's conduct of foreign policy was being hampered by conservative members of his party.

THE RIGHT WING

The elections of 1952 barely gave control of Congress to the Republicans. The Senate was divided among forty-seven Democrats, forty-eight Republicans, and Wayne Morse who remained independent until he became a Democrat in 1955. Republicans controlled the house 221 to 211, with one independent. To enact a program, Eisenhower needed full congressional support, but his party was sharply divided, and conservative Republicans and right-wing Asia firsters opposed much of his foreign policy. It was particularly important that the congressional leadership fell to conservatives, for Taft became senate majority leader and Joseph Martin of Massachusetts became house speaker. Taft supported the administration's policies but, when he had to relinquish his leadership position in six months due to ill health, Eisenhower refused to intervene in the choice of his successor and William Knowland of California was chosen. His colleagues referred to Knowland, not too jokingly, as the "senator from Formosa" because of his fervent Asia first position. This conservative wing of the party immediately pressed for enactment of the "captive peoples" resolution.

The Republican platform of 1952, in a direct slap at Franklin Roosevelt and the Yalta Agreement, called for a repudiation of "all commitments contained in secret understandings" which had helped the Communists to "enslave" people. The more conservative Republicans wanted to implement this resolution at once. Eisenhower and Dulles worked out a statement that rejected "any interpretations or applications" of these agreements that led to enslavements—a meaningless statement supporting the Republican suggestions about "liberation." Democrats were amenable to this innocuous declaration, but the Republican leadership was appalled. Here was the opportunity for which they had long awaited, to denounce Roosevelt for Yalta and Truman for Potsdam, and their leader wanted to deny them this satisfaction. It was useless for Eisenhower to point out that any stronger language might endanger American allies and put the United States in an embarrassing position in regard to Berlin and Vienna, then jointly occupied by the World War II victors as agreed at Yalta and Potsdam.

The Senate Foreign Relations Committee, with Taft joining the majority, amended the administration resolution so the statement read that it would "not constitute any determination by Congress as to the validity or invalidity of any provisions" of these agreements. This set the stage for a showdown as the Democratic Senate Policy Committee formally supported the president's position rather than the stronger one denouncing former Democratic leaders. Democratic opponents pointed out the obvious—if the Yalta and Potsdam agreements had no validity, how could one charge the Soviet Union with violating them? This put the conservative Republicans on the defensive. The death of Stalin at this point prevented a possible intraparty rupture. Most senators agreed the resolution was now in bad taste and also might, if approved, uselessly disrupt Soviet-American relations during the delicate transition period in the USSR. Senator Taft had the resolution killed in committee, and the struggle was then abandoned.[41]

In addition to this issue, Senator John Bricker of Ohio, a spokesman for right-wing Republicans, seized the opportunity of his party's control of Congress to introduce a constitutional amendment that would limit presidential power in foreign affairs. Conservatives had long worried over a 1920 Supreme Court decision that interpreted the all-encompassing treaty-making power. The opinion declared that any legislation designed to carry out treaty provisions was constitutional. Conservative fears that this ruling would lead to unknown innovations, such as agreeing by treaty to enact social reform laws contrary to the Tenth Amendment, never materialized, but the possibility existed. Also, many presidents, most notably Franklin Roosevelt, had circumvented the need for Senate approval of treaties by concluding executive agreements. Strict constructionists of the Constitution were particularly incensed over FDR's 1940 destroyer deal, whereby, by executive agreement, he traded Churchill fifty destroyers for the lease of eight naval bases in the Atlantic.

Senator Bricker had sought to curtail this activity through a constitutional amendment he introduced in 1951. It provided that any treaty would be void if it conflicted with the Constitution and that the provisions of a treaty would be effective internally in the United States only if the legislation carrying out the provisions would be constitutional without the treaty. It further proposed giving Congress the power to regulate executive agreements in the same manner that the Senate ratifies treaties. Democratic control of Congress prevented his amendment from acquiring the necessary support but Bricker confidently reintroduced it in January 1953.

At first Eisenhower saw nothing in the provisions of the Bricker amendment with which to disagree. It had the support of the Daughters of the American Revolution, the American Legion, and sundry other powerful conservative organizations and, to him, any reasonable attempt to curtail the rapidly proliferating power of the executive branch in the cold war period seemed meritorious. It appeared that, without outside interference, the Senate would approve the measure and there would be even less trouble getting it through the House of Representatives. But, after warnings from Dulles and the State Department counsel, Herman Phleger, that the amendment would put the president in a diplomatic straitjacket, Eisenhower made an exhaustive study of the proposal and eventually took a firm stance in opposition to it. Rejecting Dulles's advice that it should be opposed because it would subordinate the president to Congress, Eisenhower more correctly argued that it must be rejected because the amendment would take away presidential maneuvering room so necessary in the conduct of foreign affairs. He believed ratification of the amendment would return the United States to the situation that existed during the Confederation period when a national treaty could not override state laws, an intolerable circumstance that helped lead to the writing of a new Constitution in 1787.[42]

The administration then sought to substitute a proposal of Senate Majority Leader Knowland that would require the "internal legislation" only if the Senate so stipulated when the treaty was ratified. Bricker refused to budge, though, and the fight dragged on into 1954, consuming time that could have been better spent on other, more pressing, matters. When it came to a Senate vote in February 1954, the President threw all his personal prestige against it and the proposal was defeated by the narrow vote of sixty to thirty-one—one vote short of the necessary two-thirds. It failed primarily because of Eisenhower's prestige and because his staff did an outstanding job fighting the amendment and convincing a sufficient number of senators to ensure its defeat.[43]

While the "captive peoples" resolution and the Bricker Amendment were being debated, conservative Republicans also challenged an important Eisenhower nomination. The president named Charles E. "Chip" Bohlen, a career diplomat and one of the top U.S. experts of Kremlinology, as Ambassador to the Soviet Union. In the eyes of right-wingers, Bohlen had a decided blot on his record, for he had attended the Yalta meeting as an interpreter for Roosevelt. Asia firsters decided he had done more than merely interpret, and Joseph McCarthy, Republican Styles Bridges of New Hampshire, and others promptly denounced the nomination. Pat McCarran, the avid anticommunist Democrat from Nevada, charged that Dulles was concealing evidence on Bohlen and, when this was denied, McCarthy insisted the secretary of state submit to a lie-detector test. The situation was rapidly getting out of hand for, even if Bohlen was confirmed, the bitter debate would largely destroy his effectiveness. Taft intervened at this point and his prestige saved the day. He firmly opposed McCarthy's suggestion and, instead, the Senate appointed Taft and a Democrat, John Sparkman of Alabama, to inspect the FBI files on Bohlen. They reported to the Senate there was nothing in the files to suggest Bohlen was not dedicated to American interests and he was confirmed seventy-four to thirteen. "No more Bohlens," though, Taft warned the White House after the battle was over.[44] It was two days after this vote that

McCarthy announced he had negotiated with Greek ship-
owners to stop trade with communist China and North
Korea.

It was widely assumed that, with the Republican electoral success of 1952, McCarthy would cease his charges
of treason and communist infiltration in the executive
branch. This was not to be, though, for a demagogue such
as McCarthy thrives only upon opposition. When the new
Senate committee assignments were announced, Taft
was quite pleased with himself. He had placed William
Jenner of Indiana rather than McCarthy on the subcommittee on Internal Security, the Senate counterpart of
the House Un-American Activities Committee (HUAC).
"We've got McCarthy where he can't do any harm," the
Senate leader chortled.[45] But the junior senator from
Wisconsin quickly indicated this little maneuver would
not silence him. He accepted the chairmanship of the
Committee on Government Operations, appointed himself chairman of the Subcommittee on Investigations, and
hired two young lawyers, Roy Cohn and David Schine,
and a large staff which included Robert Kennedy.

He soon decided Dulles needed help in cleaning subversives out of the State Department and particularly
focused on that department's Voice of America program.
Then Cohn and Schine made a whirlwind tour of the overseas libraries of the International Information Administration in a farcical "investigation." This resulted in the
requested resignation of Theodore Kaghan, an official in
the United States high commission in Germany (well-
known in central Europe for his anticommunist propaganda activities) who had flirted with communism in his
younger days. There was also a "book-burning purge." A
number of books by such authors as Emerson, Thoreau,
and even Foster Rhea Dulles, a cousin of the secretary of
state, were removed from library shelves.[46]

Although these attacks completely disrupted the Foreign Service for a time, the president still refused to chal-

lenge McCarthy or, as he put it, "to get into the gutter with that fellow." His reticence was due to the belief that if the administrative branch assaulted McCarthy, the Senate would close ranks and rally around a member attacked from the outside. Eisenhower undoubtedly was overcautious in this assessment, for by this time McCarthy was one of the most detested and feared men in the Senate. Soon after the library purge, however, Eisenhower was at Dartmouth College to give a speech. On the platform with him were the Canadian secretary of state, Lester Pearson, who was to give the main address; Judge Joseph Proskauer of New York; and a friend, John J. McCloy, all of whom made no attempt to conceal their contempt for the book burnings. Obviously influenced by their conversation, the president felt constrained to make the following extemporaneous remarks to the graduating class: "Don't join the book burners," he advised. "Don't think you are going to conceal faults by concealing evidence that they ever existed. Don't be afraid to go to your library and read every book, as long as that document does not offend your own ideas of decency. That should be the only censorship." Although public reaction to these remarks was quite favorable, Eisenhower refused to attack McCarthy further, believing that McCarthy would destroy himself by overreaching. He was convinced, rightly so in this case, that McCarthyism had preceded the senator from Wisconsin and would outlast the man for whom it was named.[47]

In June 1953 McCarthy hired Joseph B. Matthews, a former Methodist minister, as his subcommittee staff director. In July 1953 Matthews wrote an article for *American Mercury* in which he charged that the Protestant clergy were the largest group in America supporting communism. A number of presidential advisers viewed this as an opportunity to strike at McCarthy. Speechwriter Emmet John Hughes, Vice President Nixon, and Assistant Attorney General William Rogers had three clergymen telegraph President Eisenhower protesting Matthews's charge and they prepared a reply to the clergy for the president's signature. Eisenhower's response was to share the clergymen's concern over this attack and to express his conviction that America's clergy were strongly opposed to communism. Timing was important, though, for McCarthy had decided the public reaction to the Matthews article was too great and he was going to discharge him. Eisenhower had not yet signed the response when his advisers discovered McCarthy's plan to hold a press conference and announce the firing. Nixon hurried over to the senator's office and delayed him there until the presidential reply went out on the news wires. Even this petty victory was a source of great cheer for seldom was McCarthy checkmated in this period of the zenith of his power and influence.[48]

McCarthy's political downfall began when the army drafted David Schine. Although military officials granted McCarthy's counsel special privileges, it occurred to the senator that these special considerations were not sufficient. The army, he decided, must be infiltrated with subversives. In January 1954 McCarthy's staff discovered what they thought was a "pink" dentist in the army, Major Irving Peress at Camp Kilmer. Peress had refused to answer questions about his alleged communist activity (he was actually a member of New York's left-wing American Labor party) and, despite this lack of cooperation, had recently received a routine promotion. When army officers discovered that he had not complied with army security regulations, Peress was ordered discharged within ninety days, which was normal procedure.

Sniffing the scent of a possibly real Communist this time, McCarthy pounced. He interrogated Peress and then General Ralph Zwicker and receiving no satisfaction from the general's responses, McCarthy charged that he was "not fit to wear that uniform." When the senator requested Zwicker to reappear for further questioning,

Secretary of the Army Robert Stevens intervened. McCarthy then decided the Army needed investigation. The celebrated Army-McCarthy hearings resulted and were televised for the nation.

Beginning in April 1954, millions of Americans viewed McCarthy for some thirty-five days, and he put on quite a show for them. The hearings were chaired by McCarthy's strong supporter, Senator Karl Mundt, and the Wisconsin senator played the role of chief prosecutor. For the first time, millions of his supporters saw him as he really was, ranting, shouting "point of order," constantly interrupting those who were testifying. His popularity ratings sank dramatically, and he was suddenly vulnerable for the first time.

The Senate then appointed a select committee, chaired by Republican Arthur Watkins of Utah, to consider a motion to censure McCarthy. The committee labored through the summer and autumn and laid its findings before the Senate just before the 1954 congressional elections. The committee recommended he be censured for improper conduct in the army investigation and for showing contempt toward the Senate Committee on Privileges and Elections when it investigated his 1950 campaign activities. McCarthy then publicly abused the Watkins committee, calling it "an unwitting handmaiden of communism" and charging that the Senate was taking part in a "lynching bee."

In the Senate debates that followed, the charges were changed to "condemn," not censure, McCarthy for his attitude toward the Privileges and Elections subcommittee and for his abuse of the Watkins committee. The vote on the former count was sixty-seven to twenty-two to condemn. Senate Minority Leader Lyndon Johnson managed to get all the Democratic senators present to vote against McCarthy, but it was a bipartisan vote, for twenty-two Republicans also supported the motion.[49] From this point on, McCarthy was finished as a political threat. He did not even campaign in 1956; he died the next year of cirrhosis of the liver. Eisenhower was right in his belief that McCarthyism would live on after 1954, but it was not in as virulent a form as it had been at the height of the Wisconsin senator's power. Although probably the only politician popular enough to bring McCarthy to heel when he was running amuck with the Foreign Service and the army, Eisenhower had refused to cross the executive-congressional line and, as a result, McCarthy did untold damage to the United States before his peers subdued him.

INTERNAL SECURITY

The Rosenberg issue, a holdover problem from the Truman administration, awaited Eisenhower when he took office. Julius and Ethel Rosenberg, parents of two small boys, had been convicted of atomic espionage and were sentenced to death—the only United States citizens ever to receive such a penalty for this crime in peacetime. Truman managed to ignore a plea for executive clemency and when Eisenhower became president, he inherited the problem. Many believed, particularly when the Rosenbergs continued to insist on their innocence, that the sentence should at least be commuted to life imprisonment. But Eisenhower was certain of their guilt and insisted that their crime involved "the deliberate betrayal of the entire nation and could very well result in the death of many, many thousands of innocent citizens." He remained adamant and on June 19, 1953 the Rosenbergs were electrocuted.

The Eisenhower administration, meanwhile, was hunting subversives even more diligently than its predecessor. In his first cabinet meeting, Eisenhower issued three guidelines in tightening security regulations: (1) legitimate rights must be protected; (2) uniform standards would be established throughout the national government; and (3) security, not loyalty, would be the test.[50] On April 27, 1953, the president issued an executive order establishing his new program. Significantly, the Truman program of distinction between demanding security checks for eleven sensitive departments and requiring loyalty oaths for the rest was abolished and the test of security applied to the entire government. The Loyalty Review Board and the department loyalty panels established by the Truman administration were canceled and each department head was given final responsibility for reviewing charges. Those who were suspended could have a hearing before a special three-man board selected from a list of names provided by the attorney general, with the stipulation that no one from the department involved could serve on the panel. In this way, homosexuals, those with radical friends or associates, or those with personal habits like excessive drinking or sexual promiscuity which might make them subject to blackmail, could be quietly dismissed. Eisenhower was concerned that this program should work effectively and yet fairly. He suggested to his attorney general that a cutoff date be set after which actions or statements favorable to the Soviet Union would be considered inexcusable. He thought the Berlin blockade in 1948 would be appropriate. This date fairly closely coincided with his own conversion to militant anticommunism.

There now followed what critics called the "numbers game," with administrative officials, including the president, periodically releasing the latest figures on security dismissals. These lists were divided into dismissals and resignations but the question remained whether these terminations were based upon security reasons or some other grounds. Finally, after much criticism, a Senate subcommittee counsel checked the latest list of 3,586 "security dismissals," and found that all but 342 of them were discharged for reasons other than security. The silly business was finally ended.

Abraham Chasanow, employed in the navy's Hydrographic Office for twenty-three years, was one of the innocent victims of this security program. On July 29,

1953, he was summoned to the personnel office where he was notified that he was suspected of being a security risk and was therefore suspended without pay. A review panel then considered the charges. He was alleged to have associated with known Communists and with radicals in his Greenbelt, Maryland, community, and to have been a member of the suspicious Lawyers Guild in 1939. The board found no basis for these complaints. He was the victim of disgruntled neighbors who referred to the family as "communist Jews" for the part Chasanow played in getting the government-built housing community converted to an independent cooperative. Months passed, though, with his continued suspension without pay and he exhausted his savings before a Security Appeal Board cleared him completely. He was then dismissed anyway. A *Washington Daily News* reporter, Anthony Lewis, exposed the sordid mess in a series of articles which finally won reinstatement for Chasanow.[51] The episode revealed what could easily happen under the new security program. The height of ludicrousness in this Red hunting came with the case of Harry Dexter White.

Attorney General Brownell was scheduled to give a luncheon address before the Executive Club in Chicago. He told Eisenhower he was going to use the occasion to expose the strange case of White, and the president agreed he should do this if he believed it to be his duty to do so. White, Brownell told the Club, was a Russian spy who had passed government documents on to Moscow. In 1948, Whittaker Chambers and Elizabeth Bentley had charged him with espionage. In March of that year, a federal grand jury refused to indict him because of lack of evidence, though, and on August 13 he denied being a Communist or an espionage agent before the House Un-American Activities Committee. He died three days later, before the charges could be proven. Most curiously, Brownell told his audience, Truman had appointed White to the International Monetary Fund after he had received an FBI report that White was a spy.

This speech, in effect labeling Truman a traitor, elicited an immediate response from the former president. Truman retorted he did not know White was a spy when he made the appointment and that White was dismissed when his disloyalty became known. But in a later television speech Truman acknowledged that he had received an FBI report on White but had proceeded with the appointment because J. Edgar Hoover had advised him that not to do so would tip off others under FBI surveillance to their danger of exposure. In a subsequent press conference Eisenhower was sharply questioned by reporters on the White case. Was the FBI justified in calling White a spy contrary to the grand jury findings? Should the attorney general have questioned the loyalty of a former president? This questioning evinced one of those rare instances in which Eisenhower publicly displayed his temper.[52]

The uproar over the White incident had not died down when the Oppenheimer case made the headlines. The new security program brought on the development of what became known as "guilt by association" and certainly Dr. J. Robert Oppenheimer, one of the foremost scientists of the atomic age, and supervisor of the Manhattan Project, was its principal victim.

Because of the nature of his work, Oppenheimer had been subjected to a tremendous amount of surveillance and security clearances. In 1947 the Atomic Energy Commission, including Lewis Strauss, reviewed his files and cleared him to become chairman of the General Advisory Committee to the AEC. On November 7, 1953, however, William L. Borden, an executive of Westinghouse, which had government contracts to build nuclear submarine engines, wrote to the chairman of the Joint Congressional Committee on Atomic Energy and to J. Edgar Hoover that he believed Oppenheimer to be a Soviet agent. Borden charged that the physicist had joined leftwing organizations before World War II, that he had associated with Communists and—very serious indeed—he had opposed developing the hydrogen bomb until President Truman had ordered the program begun despite protestations.

When the FBI made the Borden letter public, Eisenhower, fearing the development of another White case under his own administration, immediately ordered a "blank wall" to be placed between Oppenheimer and all classified information until his clearance was assured. Oppenheimer chose to fight the charges and extensive hearings were held in the spring of 1954 by the AEC security board. He admitted to being a "fellow traveler" from 1937 to 1942 and to being a close friend to a French communist intellectual, Haakon Chevalier. He admitted that his brother and sister-in-law were Communists. In the current climate of subversive-hunting hysteria, the administration felt "a fervent need to demonstrate its own purity" and the brilliant physicist was sacrificed.[53] The AEC unanimously affirmed Oppenheimer's loyalty but voted two to one to deny him security clearance and dismissed him from his position. Eisenhower secretly admitted that barring him from atomic secrets was ridiculous but that the scientist's reputation had to be sacrificed to protect the administration from McCarthy and McCarthyism.[54] It was not until 1962 that Oppenheimer was publicly "exonerated" by an invitation to the White House where John F. Kennedy recognized his achievements as a Nobel Prize winner. The following year the AEC awarded him the Enrico Fermi Prize for his contributions to nuclear science.

By 1954, the McCarthyism hysteria had reached the point where a congressional committee was studying as many as twenty-two bills to outlaw the Communist party. Proposals to ban the party had been killed previously because of the opposition of J. Edgar Hoover and the attorney general. Hoover believed such a drastic step could drive the party underground and make his work more difficult. But in August 1954, with congressional elections just weeks away, a group of liberal Democrats, led by Senator Hubert Humphrey of Minnesota, voted to amend a pending bill to outlaw the Communist party, making membership in it a criminal offense. This put Republicans in the embarrasing position of being unable to oppose a measure that would appear to the unenlightened voter as a blow against communism.[55]

During the next several days members of both houses of Congress amended the bill by, among other things, deleting the provision making party membership a felony. The House then passed the measure 305 to 2 and the Senate agreed with only one dissenting vote. The Communist Control Act declared the party to be not a political party but an instrument of a conspiracy to overthrow the government, and it authorized the Subversive Activities Control Board to determine what organizations were communist-infiltrated. The law undoubtedly violated the First and Fifth amendments but it was never intended to be enforced. It was designed to register a formal pronouncement against internal communism and became the only instance where a political party was outlawed in the United States.[56] Similar developments were taking place on the state level. Texas, for instance, penalized membership in the Communist party with a prison sentence of twenty years.

COLD WAR THAW

Development of the hydrogen bomb continued apace and on March 1, 1954, the first thermonuclear device was exploded near Eniwetok in the Marshall Islands. It was even more destructive than its planners expected and the appalling fallout of radioactive particles greatly exceeded their expectations. Twenty-three Japanese fishermen, eighty miles away, were showered with radioactive ashes. One died, and the others were hospitalized for months. The development of the hydrogen bomb led to extensive discussions about having a "summit" conference. The leaders of the great powers should get together and talk, it was argued, before they blew up the world.

Both Eisenhower and Dulles opposed the idea of summit conferences. Obviously, they were concerned about right-wing Republicans who associated summit meetings with "sellouts" to communism. They also believed Russia would utilize such a meeting for propaganda purposes. But, the reason they used most often publicly for their opposition was the lack of sincerity in Soviet motives. Let them do something tangible to show their peaceful intentions, Eisenhower often responded, and then we will see about getting together for discussions. In 1955, Russia made several overtures that seemed to answer this demand.

In April of that year the Soviet Union proposed that the "Big Four" foreign ministers get together and work out a peace treaty with Austria. This was the type of "deed" Eisenhower had been calling for and he later recalled that, with this news, Dulles walked into his office with a grin and said, "Well, I think we've had it."[57] The following month a treaty was concluded—Austria promised to remain neutral in the cold war and was rewarded with the removal of occupying troops. This surprise was quickly followed by another Soviet offer. The Russians announced to the United Nations disarmament subcommittee that they were willing to accept the proposals of the West for nuclear disarmament. The United States then had to backtrack quickly. That September, the American delegate to the disarmament talks, Harold Stassen, notified the subcommittee that the United States was withdrawing its disarmament offer on the grounds that a nuclear stockpile could be hidden from U.S. inspectors by a cheating nation.

In May, a cease-fire was effected in the Formosan Straits. On May 9, Germany became a member of NATO; on May 14, Russia and the East European satellite nations responded to this by signing the Warsaw Pact, the communist counterpart to NATO. On May 19, the Soviet air show exhibited an apparently large long-range bomber fleet. The NATO war games in June demonstrated the probability of 171 atomic bombs being dropped on West European countries in the event the Cold War suddenly became hot. These developments led the European allies, especially Great Britain under Prime Minister Anthony Eden, to insist on a summit conference to try to ease cold war tensions. Eisenhower reluctantly agreed to one in Geneva.

The Big Four leaders, Eisenhower, Eden (who had replaced Churchill as prime minister), Edgar Faure of France, and Nikolai Bulganin and Nikita Khrushchev of Russia, agreed to meet on 18 July 1955. Because Dulles and Eisenhower were certain the Russians would bring up the issue of disarmament, preparations were made for the United States to take the initiative in this. A group composed of Nelson Rockefeller, Harold Stassen, Robert Anderson, and others had been working for some time on a plan for mutual inspectiion of military armaments. Their proposals were ready for the president to present at Geneva.

The discussions opened on a note of cordiality with Bulganin and Khrushchev beaming for photographers and Eisenhower appearing as "coexistence incarnate" by hosting a dinner for the Russian delegates. As Bulganin later recalled, Eisenhower "opened the Martini road" at Geneva.[58] Despite Dulles's admonition to keep a serious countenance during the talks, Eisenhower was unable to suppress his grin when faced with news photographers. The president's old friend Zhukov was there and they were able to reminisce about their days together in Berlin in 1945. On hearing that Zhukov's daughter was about to be married, Eisenhower gave him a pen set and a portable radio to take to her as a wedding present.

All the delegates agreed that the armaments race should be slowed down. But, when Eisenhower's turn came to speak on the stormy afternoon of July 21, he star-

tled his listeners, and apparently the elements, with a
concrete proposal. He began to speak from a text and then
laid down his glasses and presented what became known
as the "Open Skies" proposal: let both sides give the other
their military blueprints and open their skies for aerial
inspection to make certain they were not stockpiling
nuclear weapons. At the precise moment that he finished
talking, a great flash of lightning put out the lights.
When they came back on, Eisenhower chuckled and said,
"Gentlemen, I did not mean to put out the lights." He and
his advisers were certain the Russians would reject his
plan but that it would have wide public appeal throughout the world.[59] They were correct on both counts. Chairman Bulganin replied that the idea seemed to have "real
merit" and they would study it. After adjournment,
Eisenhower went to the cocktail lounge with the Soviet
delegation. He happened to be walking with Party Secretary Khrushchev who said, "I don't agree with the chairman." There was a smile on his face, Eisenhower recalled,
but none in his voice. It was at that point that the American president clearly saw that Khrushchev was the "real
boss of the Soviet delegation" even if the rest of the world
did not yet know it.[60]

Nothing came of the disarmament plans, really, except
a new hope. Reporters began referring to the "Spirit of
Geneva" and the anticipation was expressed with
increasing confidence that the world would not be blown
apart after all. The thaw in the Cold War held the promise that perhaps East and West could coexist. Eisenhower's popularity was never higher. In August 1955, a
Gallup Poll recorded that 79 percent approved his conduct of the presidency. His efforts to achieve peace in the
cold war appeared to be succeeding.

CHAPTER SIX

Pursuing the Middle Road

Eisenhower had always been an early riser, and he continued this practice while in the White House. He was awakened each morning at 6:30, had breakfast along with a quick digest of the news in the *Wall Street Journal* and the *New York Times,* and then proceeded to his office where he read the *New York Herald Tribune* at a more leisurely pace. The word soon spread that the staff could tell his mood for the day by the suit he was wearing; if it was brown, be careful! Eisenhower denied this theory in his memoirs, insisting that each morning he donned whatever suit his valet, Sergeant John Moaney, laid out for him. Sherman Adams found the president's secretary, Ann Whitman, to be a better barometer for the chief executive's mood. He checked with her first every morning for a prediction of what kind of a day it would be in the office.

Eisenhower liked to start his staff meetings early in the morning, for he believed people's thought processes functioned better at that time. He scheduled these discussions, usually running two hours in length, on a regular basis. On Monday mornings he met with Arthur Burns, Gabriel Hauge, Charles Wilson, and the Joint Chiefs of Staff to discuss economics and national defense. Tuesday mornings were devoted to sessions with the legislative leaders from Capitol Hill. On Wednesday mornings he had his famous 10:30 press conferences, preceded by 10:00 briefings with James Hagerty and Sherman Adams on questions to be expected. He met with the National Security Council on Thursday mornings and with the cabinet on Fridays.

Afternoons were devoted to a busy schedule of appointments, and it was usually late in the day when he got to his correspondence. Normally he completed his office work by 6:30 P.M. and went upstairs to the living quarters in the White House where he had a highball, customarily scotch and water, and then dinner at 7:30. Usually once a week, he and Mamie gave a formal state dinner. Much more famous than these were Eisenhower's stag dinners. Early in his presidency he decided to invite fifteen or twenty men from all walks of life for drinks and dinner. The nation's leading businessmen and industrialists dominated the guest lists, but there was a sprinkling of entertainers, professionals, and intellectuals. Cocktails and conversation were followed by dinner, with the main course usually being pheasant. Beside each plate the president liked to leave a souvenir for the guest, ordinarily a small black-handled jackknife and a lucky penny. After dinner the guests had coffee, cordials, cigars, and interesting discussions. Eisenhower was a superb host who could bring out the best in his guests. He used these dinners to try to keep up with the current thinking on leading issues. On other evenings he enjoyed the company of George Allen, Alfred Gruenther, W. Alton "Pete" Jones, William Robinson, and Freeman Gosden (Amos of the Amos and Andy show) and a rubber of bridge, a game at which he was almost professional. Then to bed at 11:00 or 12:00 P.M.

REDEEMING PLEDGES

The Republican party had always opposed government controls of prices, and those imposed during the Korean

War were no exception. Defense Secretary Wilson and Secretary of the Treasury Humphrey wanted all regulations lifted immediately. Experts in the Office of Price Administration, however, were convinced that sudden decontrolling would result in rampant inflation and economic chaos. Arthur Flemming, president of Ohio Wesleyan University and an OPA official during World War II, was brought in to plan the transition. He and Gabriel Hauge were convinced that controls could be lifted rather rapidly, and they, in turn, persuaded the president who was being pressured by Humphrey and Wilson. As a result, in a cabinet meeting on February 6, 1953, Eisenhower decided with a simple "let's go" on lifting all wage and some price rules at once, after Humphrey persuaded him that subsequent rising production would offset the increasing demand for goods and the resultant inflation.[1] The remaining price controls, except on rent, were lifted in April. This was a risky move while the fighting continued in Korea, but it was a success in the short run.

One of the major promises in the Republican platform of 1952—and one that Eisenhower often repeated—was to cut expenditures and balance the budget without endangering national security. The economic and fiscal policies of the Eisenhower administration have often been interpreted "as backward . . . or even antediluvian." This error is made, aside from political reasons, partially because more attention is paid to fiscal talk than to his fiscal policy. Eisenhower and Humphrey continued to talk about balancing the budget but, in actual practice, continued the fiscal revolution begun during the New Deal.[2] Eisenhower was able to accept a record peacetime deficit for fiscal 1958 as inevitable, while at the same time deploring it vehemently. When he took office, he wanted to cut taxes, but not until expenses and inflation were brought under control. Conservative Republicans, however, were convinced a tax cut would force a reduction in government expenditures—if you did not have the money, they reasoned fallaciously, you would not spend it—and they were determined to do just that. H.R. 1, introduced by Daniel A. Reed, a Republican from New York and the new chairman of the House Ways and Means Committee, would advance the date of a 10 percent cut in personal income taxes from January 1, 1954, to July 1, 1953, and Reed indicated he had no intention of yielding to the administration's desire to hold off for the later date. Eisenhower had to throw his personal prestige against the measure. He convinced House Speaker Joe Martin and House Majority Leader Charles Halleck, both conservatives, that the cut, at least $1.5 billion, would be an error. The House Rules Committee then refused to report Reed's bill out to the House.

The president lost, though, in his efforts to raise the debt limit. The ceiling was $272 billion but the nation faced a probable $5 billion deficit for fiscal 1954, Truman's last budget year. There was nothing Eisenhower and Humphrey could do but swallow their fiscal principles and ask for a debt increase. Humphrey wanted an additional $15 billion so he would have a cushion, but Senator Harry Byrd, a Democrat from Virginia and the dominating figure on the Senate Finance Committee, decided that the money was not needed. Byrd, the Democratic high priest of fiscal conservatism, managed to hold the debt ceiling to $275 billion and, as he remarked, "the heavens didn't fall."[3]

But the sky started to fall the next year in the form of a threatening recession which concerned many people, for the Republican administration's reaction to a serious economic downturn was as yet unknown. The cutbacks in military spending, plus a decline in investments in the private sector, caused an economic downturn after mid-1953. With the Crash of 1929 still on the minds of voters, the Republicans feared the image of "the party bringing depression," and Eisenhower was concerned. He began seeing Arthur Burns at least weekly by late 1953, and Burns and Hauge started attending cabinet meetings where they were effective in presenting their views. Eisenhower rejected a laissez-faire philosophy and believed the national government should prevent unemployment. But, he believed a cautious approach was called for and opposed what he termed "slam-bang" measures. In November 1953, the Office of Defense Mobilization began a "set-aside" program, reserving 20 to 30 percent of its contracts for materials for distressed areas, those territories particularly hard hit by recession and unemployment.

Defense Secretary Wilson inadvertently thrust the nation's economic woes into the congressional campaigns of 1954. While speaking at a $100-a-plate dinner in Detroit, an area plagued with high unemployment at the time, Wilson said he had no sympathy for those who would not move to areas where work was available. He assured his audience he had "always liked bird dogs better than kennel-fed dogs . . . one who'll get out and hunt for food rather than sit on his fanny and yell." In the ensuing uproar, the governor of Michigan likened this remark to Marie Antoinette's alleged "let them eat cake." Typically, Wilson offered a somewhat defiant apology, admitting that his "inept remarks" looked terrible in print when they "were distorted by our left-wing opponents." Eisenhower agreed to a tax cut of almost $1 billion in 1954, but he held the line against Democratic urgings for a huge public works program. This "wait and see" approach was successful; the economy was basically sound and by mid-1954 the recession had dissipated. His handling of the recession thus demonstrated that economic conservatism could be joined to welfare liberalism and still not violate the requirements of the Employment Act of 1946.[4] The nation emerged unscathed from the first Republican recession since 1929.

One of Eisenhower's major promises in the 1952 campaign was to turn over the tidelands, or so-called off-shore oil lands, to the states. This issue dated back to at least the 1930s when, in the never-ending search for new supplies of petroleum, the Superior Oil Company and the Pure Oil Company had set up a drilling rig off the coast of Louisiana and struck oil. A rush ensued and geologists soon estimated that there were immense sources of oil in these submerged lands. Ownership immediately became important, for vast sums of money were involved.

In 1946 and again in 1952, lobbyists persuaded Congress to pass legislation giving these lands to the states concerned, but President Truman vetoed the measures in both instances. Then the oil people went to court. But the Supreme Court told California in 1947 and Texas and Louisiana in 1950 that these lands belonged to the national government. The question became a political issue in 1952, with Stevenson opposing giving these lands to the states, although he offered to share the revenue with them, and Eisenhower taking a positive stand that the states should own these deposits. Just before he left office, Truman directly challenged the incoming administration by issuing an executive order making these oil deposits a naval reserve.

A bill was quickly introduced in the Eighty-Third Congress to turn these lands over to the states, and the battle lines were drawn. A coalition of Southern states-rights congressmen, congressmen from the states involved, and conservative Republican congressmen supported the measure, while liberal Northern Democrats and Republicans opposed it. Finding themselves outnumbered, a group of the liberals staged a filibuster in the Senate, not in hopes of winning but to call attention to the "big giveaway," as they called it. Wayne Morse set a speaking record of twenty-two hours and twenty-six minutes on April 24, 1953, but to no avail. The Submerged Lands Act of 1953 granted California, Texas, Louisiana, and Florida rights to oil deposits from the low-tide line three miles out into the ocean and the Gulf of Mexico. It also permitted these states to go to the Supreme Court and assert jurisdiction as far as three leagues (or ten and a half miles) out, which they were claiming as their historical boundaries. The national government retained mineral rights over the continental shelf from the state line out some 100 to 150 miles at sea. The Supreme Court ultimately agreed that Florida and Texas had jurisdiction for three leagues, the other states just for the three miles.[5]

This same coalition of oil congressmen and states-righters combined to pass a bill exempting natural gas from price controls by the Federal Power Commission, letting it revert to state control. The measure passed the House in 1955 by the close vote of 209 to 203. When it reached the Senate in 1956, the lobbyists overplayed their hand. Senator Francis Case, Republican from South Dakota, favored the proposal initially.[6] But, during debate on the bill, he revealed that Mr. John Neff of Lexington, Nebraska, an unregistered lobbyist for Superior Oil Company, had given him an unsolicited $2,500 contribution which he was returning. The Senate set up a select committee to investigate the episode and it was revealed that several senators, including Bourke Hickenlooper, Republican from Iowa, and Barry Goldwater, Republican from Arizona, had received similar gifts. Although Case voted against the bill, it passed by a vote of 53 to 38. President Eisenhower, who favored the measure, believed he had to veto it because of the fuss over the bribe money. He had pledged to clean up the "mess in Washington" and this was an "arrogant" effort that was "in defiance of acceptable standards of propriety," he said.[7]

Eisenhower promised repeatedly in 1952 to curtail national government activities and extend the "partnership" concept to state and local governments and to private enterprise. In other words, the private sector and the state and local governments should increase their activities while Washington played a lesser role, doing just those things that the national government alone could do. The Atomic Energy Act of 1954 was one of these areas where he thought the national monopoly should be terminated. With his approval in August 1954, this law amended the 1946 act to give private power companies and Rural Electrification Association co-ops priority in purchasing surplus electric power from the Atomic Energy Commission (AEC). It further authorized the AEC to license private companies to build atomic reactors and to purchase nuclear materials in order to produce electric power. It also permitted private companies to build atomic reactors and to purchase nuclear materials in order to produce electric power. It also permitted private companies to secure patents on nuclear developments and authorized the sharing of information on peaceful uses of atomic energy with friendly nations.

Also in 1954, Eisenhower approved legislation that every president during the previous thirty years had sought, construction of the St. Lawrence Seaway, a remarkable example of "partnership." This project envisioned a navigation channel deep enough for ocean-going vessels to sail from Montreal to Duluth at the head of Lake Superior and the construction of dams to produce electrical power in the International Rapids section of the St. Lawrence River. Interest in this concept increased after the turn of the twentieth century as industry developed in the Great Lakes area, and finally a treaty was signed with Canada in 1932 to make this a joint endeavor. In 1934, however, the Senate failed to ratify the treaty.

The project was strongly supported by the states of Michigan and Minnesota; cities like Detroit and Duluth; the auto industry; the smaller steel companies and their unions; and farm organizations such as the Grange, the Farm Bureau Federation, and the Farmers' Union. The state of New York was divided on the issue; the electric power was badly needed there, but the seaway would hurt the port of New York City. The opposition was widespread and powerful, combining private utility companies, railroads, inland waterways, coal and big steel companies and their unions, New England states, and port cities of the east coast. When the United States proved reluctant to begin construction, Canadian officials determined to go ahead on their own, for the Province of Ontario badly wanted the project completed. American lobbyists favorable to the plan persuaded Prime Minister Louis St. Laurient to pressure the United States with the threat that if the United States did not agree by July 1954, Canada would build it alone. In addition, the seaway and the power project were separated so the opposition would be divided also. The New York Power Authority applied to the Federal Power Commission and the International Joint Commission, which handles United States-Canadian border problems, for a lease to build power dams.[8]

Eisenhower's conversion to support of the seaway was most important. Henry Cabot Lodge of Massachusetts and Sherman Adams of New Hampshire had earlier persuaded him to oppose it, and the estimated price tag of $2 billion, if the entire seaway was dug to the depth of thirty-five feet, was a sufficient deterrent in itself at a time when the president was trying to reduce expenditures. Then, in 1953, Senator Alexander Wiley, Republican from Wisconsin, and Representative George Dondero, Republican from Michigan, introduced a bill to create the St. Lawrence Seaway Development Corporation. The corporation would be authorized to borrow up to $105 million (a loan guaranteed by the national government) to build the United State's share of the seaway twenty-seven feet deep through the international rapids (the more expensive channel to Duluth was eliminated as well as the greater depth needed for the largest ships) and to charge tolls to recover the costs. Eisenhower then ordered the Commerce Department to study the feasibility of the proposal.

Secretary Sinclair Weeks of Massachusetts approved the project after study and, particularly important, Treasury Secretary Humphrey supported it.[9] Humphrey was concerned over the rapid depletion of iron ore resources in the Great Lakes region. A seaway would make available to the area the huge new deposits being discovered in Labrador. Also, proponents sold Eisenhower on the plan by stressing its importance to national defense. The departments of State and Defense were "strongly favorable" and none of the other departments in the cabinet opposed it.[10] In addition, the National Security Council endorsed it. Now support had to be mustered in Congress.

The opposition of House Majority Leader Halleck was considered important; Wiley, Dondero, and N. R. Danielian of the Great Lakes-St. Lawrence Association, had a discussion of the seaway with the president. When one of them mentioned that Halleck, whom the president was beginning to like a great deal, was in the pay of railroad interests, Eisenhower became extremely angry and began denouncing pressure groups. When Danielian later expressed his concern to Homer Gruenther that the interview might have hurt the chances of the project, Gruenther assured him that Eisenhower had been pulling the temper act on everyone as a way of taking the heat off himself.[11] But the president convinced Halleck of the importance of the proposal and won his crucial support as well as that of House Speaker Martin.

The Senate approved the bill on January 20, 1954, with the impressive vote of 51 to 33. On May 6, 1954, the House passed the measure 241 to 158 and the president signed it into law on May 13. The work was completed and the seaway opened in 1959. Fifteen years later, the channel depth of twenty-seven feet made the seaway obsolete, for the enormous tankers and high-speed containerized freighters that were then being used were too large for the locks. Although its initial purpose—to make the Great Lakes a "fourth seacoast"—was becoming antiquated two decades after the law was passed, the seaway is surely one of Eisenhower's major domestic achievements. If it later becomes necessary to enlarge the channel to accommodate larger ships, the seaway could be modified.

A more lasting monument of the "partnership" concept, the interstate highway system, was one of Eisenhower's pet projects. He never forgot the ghastly experience of his cross-country tour in 1920, and the military importance of the modern German autobahns in World War II had made a powerful impression on him. Recognizing a need for a similar system for the United States, he appointed an advisory committee headed by General Lucius Clay to make a study. The Clay commission recommended a 40,000-mile system of interstate highways that would lower the death toll, prepare for a remarkable increase in the number of motor vehicles that would overload the existing roads, and provide the nation's major cities with good arteries for sudden evacuation of the population in case of an enemy air attack.[12] Clay recommended that a federal corporation build the system and charge tolls to recover the cost.

Democratic opponents disliked this "pay for yourself" plan and proposed, instead, federal financing. For once, Eisenhower was more concerned over getting a program than he was in the manner of financing it.[13] A compromise was easily reached, and on June 29, 1956, he signed into law the Federal Aid Highway Act. This authorized construction of some forty-two thousand miles of four- to eight-lane highways to connect to major cities of the nation. The national government provided 90 percent of the costs, and the states paid 10 percent of the $31 billion project. Also, federal aid on a dollar-matching basis was approved for the improvement of primary and secondary state roads. The costs of all this construction was financed over a sixteen-year period with a national tax on gasoline, tires, diesel fuel, automobiles, trucks, and buses, to be placed in the highway trust fund. Those who used the roads, in other words, would pay for them. This was the greatest peacetime construction project ever undertaken by the United States, and was surely the largest pork-barrel in history. Twenty years later, the interstate system was almost complete, and the highway trust fund was a wealthy one that many people wanted to use for mass transit systems. For better or worse, Eisenhower committed this nation to a greater reliance on motor vehicles, at the expense of public mass transit systems and left an enduring mark on the land.

Public Power Problems

Public power projects were undoubtedly the most controversial aspects of Eisenhower's "partnership" concept and also represented the sharpest break with New Deal philosophy of any of his programs. Eisenhower was particularly concerned with what he viewed as an unwarranted intrusion of the national government into this area. Soon after the 1952 election, he spoke to a gathering of Young Republicans at Custer State Park, South Dakota, and observed that for the previous twenty years there had been "a creeping socialism in the United States." When reporters later asked him for an example of what he meant, he suggested the Tennessee Valley Authority (TVA). This was widely understood to mean that he was opposed to the TVA (he mentioned once that he would like to sell TVA, but that he knew this was politically unfeasible) and there was a flurry of proposals to sell it.

Because many Republicans had for twenty years opposed TVA, people benefitting from the project were concerned over candidate Eisenhower's views on the subject in 1952. When he campaigned through that part of the country, he reassured listeners in Memphis and Knoxville that TVA was a valuable experiment and said there would be no disposition on his part "to impair the effective working out of TVA."[14] But, he disagreed with attempts to expand TVA power production on the grounds that this would mean taxing the entire nation to bring the advantages of cheap power to a local area. Such expansion would be a "vicious circle that has no foreseeable end once set in motion."[15] Eisenhower did not believe that tax-free power should be supplied to any area. Soon after taking office, he was presented with a test of his philosophy, a development that led to the first major scandal of his administration.

The city of Memphis, at the outer edge of the territory TVA supplied with power, needed additional electricity that could not be furnished with existing facilities. Officials decided to build a steam power plant at Fulton, near Memphis, if federal funding was forthcoming. But the government investment in TVA was increasing by about $250 million annually, without further construction, and Eisenhower was dedicated to cutting, not increasing, expenditures. The administration decided, instead, to cut the Atomic Energy Commission's power consumption from TVA, and TVA could then sell this power to Memphis instead of building the Fulton plant. This decision led to a "long series of conflicts known as the Dixon-Yates controversy."[16]

The problem was complicated by the fact that the AEC needed more, not less, power for its own operations, particularly for the atomic energy plant at Oak Ridge, Tennessee. Joseph Dodge, director of the Bureau of the Budget, employed Adolphe Wenzell, a vice president of the First Boston Corporation, to study power needs for the region. Wenzell recommended that private power companies be permitted to supply any additional power requirements, a report that was exactly what Dodge and Eisenhower wanted to hear. At the same time, TVA director Gordon Clapp, who was due to retire soon, stated that if TVA did not receive increased appropriations, it could not supply the AEC with additional power.

At this point Edgar Dixon, president of the Middle South Utilities Company, and Eugene Yates, chairman of the board of directors of the Southern Company, formed a combine for the purpose of supplying required power. They proposed receiving a government contract to build a $107 million steam plant that would furnish electricity to the AEC, which in turn could sell part of it to Memphis. The AEC would in a sense become a power broker. But, from May 1953 to June 1954, Dixon and Yates used Wenzell as a financial consultant, as his company was to finance the construction of the power plant. Unfortunately for Eisenhower, he was not told of Wenzell's dual role.[17] Based on the recommendation of Rowland Hughes, the new director of the Bureau of the Budget, in June 1954, Eisenhower ordered the AEC to negotiate a contract with the Dixon-Yates combine. An offer from a competing syndicate headed by Walter von Tresckow was rejected because of the inexperience of the company. The Dixon-Yates contract was signed in October 1954.

There were immediate outcries from public power advocates. Senator Wayne Morse emphasized that Bobby Jones, an Eisenhower golfing partner, was on the board of directors of the Southern Company. It quickly became a national issue when Senator Lister Hill, Democrat from Alabama, discovered and exposed Wenzell's conflict of interest. At a subsequent press conference, Eisenhower insisted that Wenzell was not consulted on the contract. At his next news conference he described Wenzell as merely a "technical adviser." Obviously, the president could be excused for initially not knowing the details of the rapidly unfolding scandal, but he compounded his problem by continuing to support the contract. Then, on

June 23, 1955, the city of Memphis resolved Eisenhower's dilemma by deciding to build its own plant.

This decision had not been made previously because TVA was extremely popular in Memphis and any attempt to weaken it would be politically inexpedient. But, with the uproar over Dixon-Yates and with von Tresckow assuring the city council his syndicate could raise the necessary $100 million, the city fathers decided to do what the president wanted them to do all along. The contract with Dixon and Yates was cancelled. Work had already been begun on the plant, but the AEC held that the conflict of interest absolved them from financial responsibility. Dixon and Yates sued to recover $3.5 million in expenses, but the Supreme Court ruled in 1961 that the claim was invalid because of conflict of interest. The blame for this major scandal, of course, fell on the president's shoulders.[18] He should have informed himself more thoroughly on the developments and stopped them before they got out of hand. But most people believed him when he said he was unaware of Wenzell's true role and forgave him for not keeping abreast of all the details of activity in the national government.

Meanwhile, Eisenhower's philosophy on public versus private power was undergoing another test. The Truman administration had unsuccessfully sought approval for several regional power authorities, including one on the Missouri River (MVA) and another on the Columbia (CVA). But the issue came to a head in the 1950s on the Snake River. The Idaho Power Company requested a license to build three dams on the river—at Hells Canyon, at Oxbow, and at Brownlee—to provide the electrical power badly needed in the region. The Department of the Interior under Truman blocked this private construction. Public power advocates in the bureaucracy and in Congress wanted, instead, one huge dam to be built by the national government at the Hells Canyon site at an estimated cost of $500 million. Bills to authorize this were killed in the Democratic-controlled Eighty-First and Eighty-Second Congress. Then in 1953, Douglas McKay, former governor of Oregon and a vocal opponent of CVA, became secretary of interior.[19] He reversed the department's previous policy on the Snake River project.

Eisenhower appointed Jerome Kuykendall of Washington, an ardent advocate of state and private, not federal, power, as chairman of the Federal Power Commission (FPC). The FPC then awarded a contract to the Idaho Power Company to build its proposed dams on the Snake River. Public power advocates did not give up, however, and Wayne Morse introduced bills in the Eighty-Fourth and Eighty-Fifth Congress to build the federal project at Hells Canyon. These measures were rejected. When McKay resigned his cabinet post to run for the Senate against Morse in 1956, he was defeated and his loss was widely attributed to his stance on federal power projects. Yet, when Oregon voters were polled, it was evident that they really did not know what "partnership" was; less than half knew what Morse's position was, and only 22 percent knew where McKay stood on the question.[20] Other issues undoubtedly had decided that election.

The Eisenhower power philosophy was also revealed in the Upper Colorado project. This proposed project would dam the Colorado River and its tributaries and use the stored water for irrigation and reclamation purposes. It would benefit Colorado farmers (who would receive about half the water) and the neighboring states of Arizona, New Mexico, Utah, and Wyoming who would use the remainder. It would cost almost $1 billion, far too much for the states involved in terms of the benefits received, so Eisenhower pressed for the national government to finance the program. Californians, fearing the project would reduce the water they received from the Colorado River, unsuccessfully opposed it. Also, preservationists were concerned that the proposed reservoir at Echo Park would ruin Dinosaur Park, and they staged a successful effort to have the site relocated.[21] Finally, it was suggested that the project would endanger Rainbow Bridge National Monument, one of the world's greatest natural bridges, so the law that was enacted in 1955 required the secretary of interior to make certain this monument was protected. Furthermore, Eisenhower asked Congress a number of times to construct a tunnel 5.3 miles long through the continental divide to carry water from the Fryingpan River in the Colorado basin to the arid eastern slopes of the Rockies, but the Fryingpan-Arkansas project was not approved until 1962.

CONTINUING THE NEW DEAL

Conservative Republicans who opposed many of the New Deal-Fair Deal programs were disappointed to find Eisenhower disagreeing with their desire to dismantle them. In fact, under his leadership, most of these programs were strengthened and expanded. The tariff was an outstanding example.

The Republicans, as a party, had long supported a high tariff, in opposition to the Democrats who lowered the tariff rates during the Great Depression by negotiating reciprocal trade agreements. Eisenhower was convinced that extensive trade was fundamental to fighting the cold war and that obtaining markets for American goods was vital. He believed American economic well-being to be as essential in the struggle against communism as national security; in fact, the two went hand in hand. In April 1953 he asked Congress to extend the Reciprocal Trade Agreements Act for one year while the Commission on Foreign Economic Policy, headed by Clarence B. Randall, reexamined this program.

The Randall Commission reported in January 1954, and Eisenhower then asked Congress to extend the Reciprocal Trade Agreements Act for an additional three years. He wanted authority to reduce existing rates on most commodities by 5 percent in each of the three years, to reduce by half the rates on those goods that were imported in negligible amount, and eventually to reduce all rates to at least 50 percent *ad valorum*. He further urged increased American investments abroad, liberalization of the Buy American Act, and stabilization of world prices on raw materials. Finally, he informed Congress he would renegotiate the General Agreement on Tariffs and Trade with friendly nations.

Conservative Republicans and Southern Democrats were cool to these economic proposals, however, and merely extended the Reciprocal Trade Agreements Act for one year. The president had better luck the next year when a Democratic Congress successfully enacted his trade program. Then the Trade Agreement Extension Act of 1958 continued the policy for another four years. Other than raising the rates on watches and bicycles to protect the American industries, Eisenhower generally fought for lower tariff rates and increased foreign trade during his presidency, and in this he received greater support from the Northern Democrats than from members of his own party.[22]

The New Deal farm program of price supports and parity payments came increasingly under fire following the end of the Korean War. Cessation of hostilities meant agricultural surpluses again and, at the same time, the American taxpayer was becoming progressively reluctant to use tax dollars to subsidize products that consumers were having to purchase at higher and higher prices. Then, too, consumer demand had changed and farmers largely ignored these trends. Nylon and margarine, for example, were replacing traditional fibers and table spreads and Commodity Credit Corporation warehouses were being filled with surpluses that were expensive to store. Something needed to be done to align the farm program with reality, and Eisenhower thought he had a secretary of agriculture who could do that. Ezra Taft Benson was convinced that the administration "had to start at least to reverse the twenty-year trend toward socialism in agriculture."[23] He wanted to restore farming to the free enterprise system and found Eisenhower in agreement with him. Lower supports, they believed, would cut production and solve the surplus problems. The difference between the two was that the president was politically astute enough to realize it would have to be done gradually, whereas Benson was ready to reduce controls and supports at once.

During the campaign of 1952, Eisenhower promised to continue price supports at the 90 percent of parity level as provided in the 1949 law. But, as president he began to work for a new concept of parity—a gradual easing into a formula over a two year period that would be based upon the cost-price ratio of the preceding ten years. In January 1954 he presented his farm program to Congress. His call for flexible price supports caused consternation, particularly among Republicans from rural areas, but, "displaying considerable political skill," Eisenhower persuaded Congress to adopt his plan.[24] The act of 1954 established flexible supports of between 82.5 percent and 90 percent of the new parity on wheat, corn, cotton, rice, and peanuts for 1955, and 70 to 90 percent thereafter; dairy products were to be supported from 75 to 90 percent; tobacco supports would remain at 90 percent. In addition, the Agricultural Trade and Development Act of 1954 provided for the use of surplus commodities for school lunch programs, natural disasters, and foreign aid programs.

Farmers responded to the lower supports by using technological improvements to raise more crops to maintain their total income, and the surpluses consequently continued to mount. In the election year of 1956, the farm program became a political football. To reduce surpluses, Eisenhower asked Congress that year to enact a soil bank plan. This would pay farmers to take both marginal and productive land out of cultivation. Congress passed the bill but added several other features such as supports for feed grains, a two-price system for wheat, and other items the president did not want, so he vetoed the bill. Congress then enacted the measure he wanted. Congressmen also met his request for a rural development plan to assist farm families with annual incomes of $1,000 or less, but they never financed it sufficiently, and it never became effective.

The benefits expected of the soil bank program never materialized. Farmers took the poorest land out of production, poured commercial fertilizers on the best and surpluses persisted. Benson continued to be unpopular with farmers and, in 1957, while speaking to a group at Sioux Falls, South Dakota, he was pelted with eggs. But Eisenhower refused to dismiss him even when he offered to resign.[25] In 1959, in an attempt to pacify both sides, Congress passed a measure to cut acreage allotments and raise price supports up to 90 percent. Strong pressure from the White House brought almost every Republican vote in the House to oppose the conference report, however, and the measure died. In 1959 Congress made $1 billion in surplus commodities available to needy families through a food stamp plan which made a tiny dent in the problem. Basically, Republicans were no more successful in solving the recurrent farm problem than the Democrats had been, and the trend of the two previous decades continued through the 1950s—the rich got richer and the poor moved to urban areas to seek work.

The Eisenhower administration added significantly to the Old Age and Survivors Insurance, better known as Social Security. This was one New Deal innovation that Eisenhower believed in wholeheartedly, and when it was proposed to bring more Americans into the system, he emphatically agreed. The president told his cabinet in late 1953, when Social Security changes were being discussed, that Taft once suggested that everyone over age sixty-five should receive a pension. This would make the system easier to administer.[26] Although the cabinet thought this sounded too much like the Townsend plan of the 1930s, it agreed that inflation had brought on a real need to increase benefits, and in January 1954 Eisenhower asked Congress to act. In that year Congress made the most important addition to the program since it was established in 1935. The 1954 amendments added an estimated ten million more Americans to the system, including certain types of farmers and farm workers, teachers, professional people, domestic workers, and state and local government employees. It permitted retired people to earn a maximum of $900 annually without having their pensions reduced and lifted all earnings restrictions from those aged seventy-two and older. It increased benefit payments and to offset the cost, raised the deductions base from $3,600 to $4,200.

In 1956 Congress added still further to the system by including several hundred thousand more farmers and self-employed people, lowering the required benefit age for women to sixty-two and providing for disability payments for workers fifty to sixty-four years of age. Finally, in 1958 Congress voted to increase the amount earnable without penalty to $1,200 annually and to increase the tax base to $4,800 and the rate to 2.5 percent per year. The benefits were again increased significantly. Eisenhower wanted to keep the program self-sufficient, but, because the vote in the House was an overwhelming 375 to 2 and there was no dissenting vote in the Senate, he signed it into law. These changes assured any doubters that the Social Security program was here to stay.

The problem of health costs was closely connected with Social Security, for medical burdens fall heaviest on the elderly. To meet rising costs of health care, Eisenhower proposed a federal "reinsurance" plan. He asked Congress for an initial $25 million to aid insurance companies in extending coverage to the elderly and to those too

poor to afford adequate insurance. This idea was censured on all sides. Labor unions wanted a national health
insurance plan and denounced it as inadequate, while the
American Medical Association decried it as the "opening
wedge" for socialized medicine. Eisenhower observed that
when he was attacked from both sides like this, it made
him feel "pretty good. It makes me more certain I'm on
the right track," he declared.[27] Right course or not, he
received little support for the proposal and it was not
until 1960 that Congress produced a plan he would
approve. In that year the Kerr-Mills bill was enacted
which set up a grants-in-aid system to assist states in
their medicare programs for needy people over age sixty-
five. But the program carried the bitter stipulation that
the recipient had to plead poverty to be eligible—a completely inadequate system that was not improved upon
until Medicare was established in 1966.

Critics stigmatized the administration and the secretary of health, education and welfare, Oveta Culp Hobby,
for the farce made of the polio vaccine program. Ten years
to the day since the death of Franklin Roosevelt, Dr.
Jonas Salk and his associates revealed that they had perfected a vaccine that would prevent infantile paralysis if
three dosages were taken. The subsequent demand for
the Salk vaccine was immediate and overwhelming.
Unfortunately, plans to test the vaccine adequately and
to distribute commercially produced quantities of it to
meet the demand were long in forthcoming.[28] The three
shots cost $4.20—a sum that poor parents could not
afford. Eisenhower was insistent that the national government make funds available for these purposes. No
child should go without the vaccine because of lack of
money, he declared. At a cabinet meeting in April 1955,
Hobby reported that five states had voted funds to inoc-
ulate poor children and thirteen others were planning to
do so. She preferred to wait and see how many states provided such funds before announcing a federal program.

But Eisenhower overrode this and persuaded Congress to appropriate $20 million in grants to states and $4.5 million for grants to individuals for distribution of the vaccine.[29]

Hobby had a meeting with drug manufacturers to discuss production and distribution arrangements. She excluded the press from these discussions because of the problem of discussing trade secrets and potential anti-trust aspects, and she later claimed that the meeting was an entirely satisfactory one. Then the demand for the vaccine overwhelmed the distribution plans. In addition, some of the children contracted polio from defective vaccine. Supplies continually failed to meet the demand, and it took months to straighten out the situation. In July 1955 Hobby resigned her position, pleading her husband's ill health as the reason. One year later the new secretary, Marion Folsom, reported to the president that adequate amounts of the vaccine were then available, although not all those in the priority group (newborns to twenty-year-olds and expectant mothers) could be vaccinated if all of them requested it at once. Even when only one or two doses had been administered, the incidence of polio had declined 75 percent. At last Americans had conquered the crippler of children and young adults.

Another New Deal effort—building federal housing— also received bipartisan support, although there was disagreement over emphasis. Democrats generally promoted public housing, while Republicans stressed federal aid to private builders. Both agreed, however, that national involvement was necessary, and from the beginning of his administration Eisenhower urged an active national role in this area.

In 1954, Eisenhower asked Congress for legislation that would permit construction of 35,000 public houses per year for the next four years, or 140,000 units. These were to be built to replace homes lost through slum clearance and urban renewal. He received approval for 35,000 units, but only for one year's duration. He renewed his appeal the next year and Congress gave him 45,000 units over a two-year period. The argument over numbers and years continued throughout his administration. In 1954, 1955, 1957, and 1958 Congress repeatedly increased the maximum Federal Housing Authority guaranteed mortgages and lowered the required down payments, thus stimulating the housing industry. But the fundamental problem in slum clearance—as in health care, pollution, and other public issues of the decade—was that the longer the solutions were postponed, the more difficult their solution would become.

In many of these programs, Eisenhower received greater support from the Democrats in Congress than from his own party. He had hoped to display Republican unity and progress to the voters, but, instead, he found factionalism and bickering in his party. Then, in the elections of 1954, the Democrats recaptured control of Congress. Actually the Republicans did fairly well here, for in off-year elections the party in the White House normally loses about forty House seats. In 1954 the Democrats gained two seats in the Senate and controlled the House by twenty-nine votes. But Eisenhower was soon to find that these elections helped free him from the restraining influence of right-wing Republicans and he could increasingly become the president "above party."[30] The new Democratic leadership in Congress—Speaker Sam Rayburn in the House and Senate Majority Leader Lyndon Johnson, both from Texas—supported his programs better than his own party leadership. The two Texans believed, and rightly as it turned out, that it was in the best interests of the Democratic party to endorse many of the appeals of this extremely popular president, for when elections came up they could point out to the voters how they had supported Eisenhower better than had their Republican opponents.

As Eisenhower became increasingly frustrated with conservative Republicans, he wondered aloud to Sherman Adams if he really belonged in the Republican party. Had the time come again in American history for a new political realignment? How can there be political responsibility if the White House and Congress, both controlled by the same party, are working at cross purposes? Should he attempt to create a new party—one that agreed with his philosophy of aggressive world leadership and expanding human welfare programs while restricting government spending and controls? Rejecting these alternatives, he tried to reshape his party's thinking on foreign policy and to bring in new blood.[31]

He continued to stress his middle of the road political position by talking about his party appealing to "progressive moderates." Then, in 1955, following the Republican reversals of the year before, he was scheduled to address the Finance Committee of the Republican National Committee. He told Gabriel Hauge he was going to discuss the theme of "conservative dynamism," and Hauge suggested he reverse the terms, which he did, making it "dynamic conservatism." We should conserve our basic system, he then told the Republican leaders, but be dynamic in applying it to serve 165 million Americans.[32] More and more he quoted a Lincoln maxim to express his governmental philosophy: "If something needs to be done for people, other things being equal, let it be done privately. But if it must be done, and it cannot be done privately, and only the government can do it, then let the government do it." This statement soon became synonymous with Eisenhower's concept of modern republicanism.

Increasingly, his actions adhered to the lines he expressed in December, following the 1954 elections, when he said his administration "must be liberal when it was talking about the government and the individual, conservative when talking about the national economy and the individual's pocketbook."[33] After the election of 1956, he defined modern republicanism as:

> The political philosophy that recognizes clearly the responsibility of the federal government to take the lead in making certain that the productivity of our great economic machine is distributed so that no one will suffer disaster, privation, through no fault of his own.

All these expressions were muddled efforts to unify Republican congressmen behind what he considered a responsible political program—a president intent on respecting Congress as a coordinant branch of government but knowing a program had to be enacted to achieve success at the polls.

HEART ATTACK

Three weeks after Eisenhower returned from the Geneva summit meeting he and Mamie went to Denver for an extended vacation. On Friday morning, September 23, 1955, he worked for a while at his office at Lowry Air Force Base. Then he went to Cherry Hills where he played eighteen holes of golf, lunched on a hamburger and huge slices of Bermuda onion, and played nine more holes of golf. About 1:30 A.M. that night, the president was awakened by chest pains. A short time later a searing pain hit his chest. Mamie immediately called the White House physician, Major General Howard Snyder, who suspected a heart attack and administered sedatives. Eisenhower slept for seven hours, walked to a car and was taken to Fitzsimmons army hospital outside Denver. Tests confirmed he had suffered a coronary thrombosis, a blood clot stuck in the artery of an anterior wall of his heart, causing a lesion. Dr. Paul Dudley White, the noted Boston heart specialist, was called in and confirmed that the attack was "moderate"—not serious, not mild.

The news flashed across the nation, stunning everyone. Republicans immediately realized how much they were pinning their hopes on him for 1956, while liberal Democrats considered the fact that their mortal enemy, Richard Nixon, was literally a heartbeat away from the presidency. Millions of Americans of all political persuasions suddenly realized how "their troubled transition from old ways of thinking in public affairs had been eased by its association with this amiable national hero who made all the innovations seem so common sense, so American."[34]

The immediately important question was the presidency, or rather the position of the vice president. The Twenty-Fifth Amendment, providing for cases of presidential disability, lay a decade in the future. The original Constitution merely declared that "In case of [the President's] inability to discharge the powers and duties of the said office, the same shall devolve on the Vice President. . . ." This was a delicate situation for Nixon. He dared not move too overtly and quickly and thus confirm the critics who charged him with being overly aggressive and ambitious; yet if he did nothing he would be criticized for failing to exhibit the necessary leadership required by such a crisis. Immediately he was besieged by supporters like Senator Styles Bridges who wired: "You are the constitutional second-in-command and you ought to assume the leadership. Don't let the White House clique take command."[35] But they were already in the process of doing so.

Fortunately affairs were quiet. The world was still basking in "the spirit of Geneva," and Congress had adjourned. Attorney General Brownell was vacationing in Spain; Sherman Adams was enjoying his first time away from the White House, touring the NATO command; and even Jim Hagerty was on vacation. Hagerty went at once to Denver and took charge. The President had previously told him that in case of such a development, he was to be completely frank with the public. So, with the assistance of the medical staff, Hagerty issued numerous bulletins daily, describing Eisenhower's condition and pace of recovery even, to Eisenhower's horror when he later found out, the rate and amount of his bowel movements.

As soon as Dr. White informed him the odds were good for complete recovery, Hagerty performed two crucial jobs in the next several weeks. One was to keep the public fully informed of the recovery of a sixty-five-year-old man from a moderate heart attack. The other was to tell the world how the president of the United States was gradually resuming the powers of government. In regard to the latter, Hagerty was assisted by the fact that Eisenhower had established an efficient and smoothly operating staff system and also by the interesting governmental phenomenon that what the people think a president is doing is sometimes more important than what he actually does. So, while the people were kept informed as to whether Eisenhower had whole-wheat or white toast for breakfast, they were also informed of the day he signed his full name to a document rather than merely initialing it, as though this were preparatory to assuming the full reins of leadership.[36] Hagerty even missed his son's wedding to serve his president in this crucial period.

Meanwhile, back in Washington, the National Security Council held its usual Thursday meeting with Vice President Nixon presiding as he always did when the president was absent from the capital. A cabinet meeting was called the next day, again with Nixon presiding as customary, and photographers were permitted to record how everything was "business as usual." Dulles informally took charge and saw that everything was done as the president would want it. Brownell proposed that Adams go to Denver and resume his chief of staff duties, determining what Eisenhower should see and hear. Nixon would remain in Washington to preside over NSC and cabinet meetings. Nixon protested this arrangement, but Dulles interjected with arguments favoring Brownell's proposal, leaving the vice president no choice but to endorse the secretary of state's opinions. There would be no delegation of power.[37]

In the next few weeks, the vice president, followed by cabinet members according to rank, made a pilgrimage to Eisenhower's bedside in Denver and reported to newsmen his condition, emphasizing how well the staff system was functioning. Hagerty slipped once, when reporters caught him handing one cabinet member a prepared statement on how well the President looked before the man had actually been admitted to the sickroom. By November 11, 1955, the president had recovered sufficiently to fly to Washington and then drive to Gettysburg for further recuperation. There was nothing that would heal the heart except time, and Eisenhower's new regimen was quite simple; rest one hour before lunch and not lose his temper, the latter being by far the more difficult of the two. While convalescing at Gettysburg he received his first real taste of boredom, and he disliked it. As he recuperated, the nation was also recovering its equilibrium as evidenced by the fact that jokes about his attack were at last beginning to make the rounds. The most recent one in Washington had Nixon greeting the President in front of the Capitol with a slap on the back and a challenge, "I'll race you to the top of the steps."[38] The question now to be determined was the political future.

Eisenhower had contemplated achieving in one term his goals of preserving the Republican party and saving the free world from communism. Mamie was certainly ready to enjoy her own home in Gettysburg. But the heart attack changed all this. The president was terribly bored during his convalescence and repelled by the thought of retirement. Even Mamie changed her mind, agreeing with Dr. Snyder that inactivity for Eisenhower would be fatal. Knowing him better than anyone, she insisted that he listen to trusted advisers and then make his own decision.[39]

In mid-January 1956, he gave a dinner at the White House for his twelve most trusted advisers. The guests were Herbert Brownell, G.O.P. chairman; Leonard Hall; John Foster Dulles; Henry Cabot Lodge; Sherman Adams; Jerry Persons; George Humphrey; Arthur Summerfield; James Hagerty; Howard Pyle; Tom Stephens; and Milton Eisenhower. After dinner they sat on sofas facing each other, and the president made the rounds, listening to each describe why, for the sake of the party, the nation, and world peace, he must win a second term. Then he asked Milton, who believed he had served his country enough and should retire for reasons of health, to summarize the views. After this dinner he went to Walter Reed Hospital for a battery of tests. On February 14, the doctors informed him of the results. If he would continue to lead a normal, active life, he could expect to live another five to ten years. Dr. White announced publicly that, if Eisenhower ran for the presidency again, he would vote for him. On February 29, the president told reporters that if the Republican convention wanted him, his answer would be "positive, that is, affirmative." That evening he addressed the American people on television, explaining completely his condition and his decision. "The work I set out four years ago to do," he said in explaining his determination, "has not yet reached the state of development and fruition that I then hoped would be accomplished within the period of a single term of office." He believed he could run the presidency as well as he ever could, he told the nation, but he would not actively campaign for the job in the usual sense. He would use his energy in the White House, not on the campaign trail.

The Republicans wanted him—desperately. A Gallup Poll taken a few days before his heart attack showed 61 percent voting for him over Stevenson. It also indicated that the Republicans would choose Nixon if the president declined to run. After Eisenhower decided to run for a second term, the important question left was the political future of Richard Nixon.

Even before Eisenhower made public the decision to run again, he had moved to ease Nixon off the ticket. Basically, there were several other men he preferred on the ticket with him, particularly Robert Anderson, the former Democrat from Texas who was soon to be secretary of the treasury. But, Anderson was not interested and refused to take the necessary steps to make his name known and to woo the party leadership. Nixon was the darling of the right wing of the party and had contributed much to the administration's achievements by lining up the support of archconservatives. But, after the fall of McCarthy, the polls continually showed him trailing Stevenson and even other Republicans. Eisenhower described these ratings as "disappointing" and urged Nixon to take a cabinet position where he could get more public exposure. He could have any position he wanted except secretary of state, and the president believed he lacked the necessary administrative experience for attorney general. How about defense? Charles Wilson wanted to quit. Nixon did not take the bait. The vice presidency is a good spot for an ambitious young man when the top spot is occupied by an old man with a heart condition, while cabinet members seldom move up. But Eisenhower persisted; he returned to the subject, pointing out that not since Martin van Buren had a vice president been elected to the presidency.

Nixon thought all this smacked of the treatment he had received following the fund episode. Eisenhower, he observed, was "a far more complex and devious man than most people realized," and he saw what was happening. If he left the vice presidency it would appear as if he had been dumped, and that would end his career. Yet, he had to have Eisenhower's blessing to continue on the ticket, and the president's endorsement was long in coming. As late as March 1956, in response to questioning by reporters, Eisenhower said Nixon would have to "chart his own course." Nixon rightly concluded from this that the president did not want him on the ticket. Finally, Leonard Hall intervened. He was convinced it had to be an "Ike-Dick" ticket for the Republicans to win, and he advised Nixon to unbend and tell the president in no uncertain terms that he wanted the position again. Nixon took this advice and spoke with Eisenhower. The President then had no choice but to accept the incumbent, so he had Hagerty hold a press conference with Nixon to announce the news. Hagerty was authorized to say that Eisenhower was "delighted" with the decision.[40]

A new crisis developed on June 7. Early that morning the president suffered a severe attack of ileitis, an inflammation of the lower intestine, and was rushed to Walter Reed Hospital. From 3:00 to 5:00 A.M. he underwent emergency surgery and the diseased section of the ileum was bypassed with another tube. This was major surgery, especially difficult for a patient his age, but fortunately there was no heart trouble or other complications. With Eisenhower's tremendous constitution, he quickly recovered. To test his stamina, he planned a trip to Panama on July 20 to talk with Latin American leaders. On the day he left, Harold Stassen came to his office for a visit.

Considering Eisenhower's age plus two serious health problems in less than a year, Stassen was worried about the vice presidency. He had taken polls privately which showed Nixon hurting the ticket by as much as 6 percent. He wanted to nominate Christian Herter of Massachusetts who would help the Republican slate. All Eisenhower had to do was say no. Instead, he said that Stassen was free to follow his judgment and gave him a leave of absence from his position to campaign for Herter. It was at this point that the president told Emmet John Hughes, his speech writer, that he had been watching the vice president closely but that Nixon "just hasn't grown. So I haven't honestly been able to believe that he is presidential timber."[41] Leonard Hall and the party leaders squelched Stassen's effort, of course, and Stassen himself seconded Nixon at the convention. It was "Ike and Dick" unanimously.

THE SECOND CAMPAIGN

Eisenhower believed that a Lyndon Johnson-Hubert Humphrey ticket, or a Johnson-John Kennedy combination, would be the strongest the Democrats could name. But, in 1956, Adlai Stevenson really wanted the nomination again. He campaigned hard and won it. The Illinois governor then surprised the convention by throwing open the vice presidential nomination. He noted that seven presidents had been vice presidents and the same qualities should determine the selection of both. If this were done to call attention to the concern over the possibility of Nixon becoming president because of Eisenhower's physical condition, it did not work. In any case, a real fight ensued between Estes Kefauver of Tennessee and Kennedy, with Kefauver emerging victorious. Stevenson then faced the difficult task of convincing the voters that he could run the White House better than Eisenhower. Early in the contest Eisenhower set his strategy. He decided to campaign very little, leaving Nixon to bear the brunt of the attack. He insisted that domestic, not foreign, policy must be the basic issue, thus making himself the focal point and therefore having a beneficial coattail effect for Republican candidates for Congress. The President received a significant endorsement from Adam Clayton Powell, Jr., the congressman from Harlem. When the Negro leader, who had always voted Democratic, was asked why he switched he replied that, because of Eisenhower's actions, he could now register in a first-class hotel in Washington.[42] Both presidential candidates avoided the civil rights issue. Stevenson early in his campaign told a Negro audience in Los Angeles that he would not cut off federal funds or use troops to enforce desegregation; it must come "gradually," he said, and the problem should not be an issue in the presidential race. His equivocation here cost him the support of many influential Negro newspapers.

Rightly or wrongly, Stevenson was known as the "issueless" candidate in this race. He repeatedly called for a halt in the testing of H-bombs and a replacement of the draft with a volunteer army. Here he challenged Eisenhower on grounds where the voters believed their president to be an expert. The Soviet Union had begun a series of H-bomb tests, and Eisenhower thought Stevenson should not try to make this an issue. The president refused to halt the United States tests on the grounds of national security. On September 25, Stevenson made a serious error when he charged that Eisenhower, on the advice of his brother Milton, had loaned the Argentine dictator, Juan Peron, over $100 million. Eisenhower quickly pounced on this. When questioned about the loan two days later, he grinned broadly and said the loans totalled $130 million, but that they were extended in 1950 and 1951 by the Truman administration.[43]

The emergencies in Hungary and Suez, to be discussed later, came just three weeks prior to the election and merely magnified Eisenhower's victory. The people still "liked Ike." When the votes were counted, he had won even more impressively than he had four years earlier. He received a record 35.5 million popular votes to Stevenson's 26 million. Eisenhower carried 41 states with 457 electoral votes to the Democratic candidate's 7 states and 74 votes. Even Virginia, Florida, Texas, and Louisiana went into the Republican column, the latter state for the first time since 1876. Two-thirds of the Negro voters supported Stevenson, but even this represented a Republican gain, for only 20 percent had voted for Eisenhower in 1952. The Negro vote was credited with shifting Tennessee, Kentucky, and Louisiana to the Republican column.[44] Eisenhower carried New York state by 1.5 million votes, a greater margin than any man had ever won in that state to that time, and he became the first Republican to carry Chicago since 1928. He also won a majority of the "youth vote."

For the Democratic party as a whole, however, the Rayburn-Johnson strategy of cooperation rather than opposition had paid off handsomely. Eisenhower became the first president since Zachary Taylor in 1849 to start a new term with his Congress controlled by the opposing party. His popularity did not have the hoped-for coattail effect as the Democrats increased their margin in the House. After the 1956 elections, they controlled the Senate 49 to 47 (Wayne Morse was now a declared Democrat), but had a majority of 235 to 200 in the lower house. "The coattail notion that a good actor can carry a bad play" did not materialize, and the Democratic leadership would continue its positive performance during Eisenhower's last four years in office.[45]

CHAPTER SEVEN

Hazards
of the
Middle Road

The United States Dwight Eisenhower presided over in the 1950s was an interesting society. Television was just coming into general use at the beginning of the decade, but by the end of it there were forty-five million sets in operation, or an average of one per family. The programs offered by the television industry were entertaining, if not educational, with Ed Sullivan's variety show and the "I Love Lucy" comedy series being the most popular. The TV dinner, with each ingredient compartmentalized, frozen, and ready to put in the oven, was perfected in 1954 so that families would not have to talk to each other even at mealtime. Elvis Presley, the gyrating, guitar-playing moaner of "Houn' Dog" and "Blue Suede Shoes," was the teenage rage. Musically, this rock and roll was offset, in part, by Rodgers and Hammerstein's sweetness and light *Sound of Music* in 1960. The nonmusical theatre was represented by writers like William Inge who produced *Bus Stop* in 1955 and Tennessee Williams who wrote *Cat on a Hot Tin Roof* in the same year. When Jack Kerouac published his rambling novel *On the Road* in 1957, he gave a label to an emerging group of young Americans, the "beatniks," who rejected the values of American society. They were the forerunners of the movement of the following decade that erupted in a rebellion of a counterculture.

Quiz shows had a large following, especially "The $64,000 Question." These programs fell into disrepute in 1958 when it was revealed that a big winner on the quiz show "Twenty-One" had been carefully coached not only on his answers but also on his theatrical performances in arriving at the responses. "Payola" entered the language, a term used to describe the bribing of disc jockeys to promote certain music records. People questioned the decline in morals even in higher education when it was learned that certain enterprising New Yorkers were writing Ph.D. dissertations for a nominal fee. But it was also a decade of increased religious fervor. From 1940 to 1960, church membership rose from 43 percent of the population to 63 percent. For those who needed help during the week, a New York City church offered Dial-A-Prayer. In 1954, Congress added the words "under God" to the Pledge of Allegiance, and Billy Graham was saving millions of people with Christianity.

The population was increasing with the postwar baby boom continuing right through the decade. This, in turn, created problems for the already crowded school systems. Americans were becoming increasingly mobile with one-fifth of them changing their addresses annually, and most of them were prosperous as never before. Almost 50 percent were in the $6,000 to $14,999 bracket which, according to national government standards, made them middle class. "Diners Club" and other credit cards were becoming quite popular. The drive-in fad, which began with movies, became so popular it was soon extended to banks, shops, and even churches.

It was an interesting decade. Carl Degler described it as a period of affluence and anxiety. Some called it the Age of Anxiety while others labelled it the Placid Decade. Americans were both anxious and placid, depending upon the issue. Certainly they were apprehensive over the possibility of nuclear annihilation, and they were content with their affluent prosperity and split-level homes. A great majority of Americans, that is, considered themselves happy with their lot. One-fifth of them were not; over fifteen million American Negroes were becoming restive over the long delay in granting them their civil rights. Some of them were growing exceedingly impatient.

THE SUPREME COURT

In his first State of the Union message, Eisenhower pledged "equal opportunity for all," and he proposed to end segregation in the national capital and armed forces. While Army Chief of Staff, he had testified before a congressional committee in 1948, agreeing that black platoons should be used in white companies in the army. But, in keeping with military thinking of the time, he and other leaders saw complete integration as a fifty-year process.[1] The Korean War changed this thinking, and army integration was quickly achieved once it was found successful on the fighting front. President Eisenhower quietly ended segregation in the District of Columbia hotels, theaters, and restaurants, but he ran into trouble with the armed forces. In June 1953, Adam Clayton Powell, Jr., the flamboyant congressman from Harlem, publicly charged that segregation was being practiced on army post schools, in the Veterans Administration facilities, and, especially, in naval bases in the South.

This story rocked the White House and the president ordered action taken immediately. Sherman Adams sent his assistant, Max Rabb, to discuss the situation with Powell. He explained that these matters took time to correct. Give us a chance, he pleaded, and Powell agreed. Eisenhower would write Powell a conciliatory letter if the congressman would respond in kind. Meanwhile, Rabb had called Robert Anderson, the Texas Democrat who was currently secretary of the navy. Anderson immediately solved the problem in the navy without fuss or fanfare. The rest rooms on the naval bases in Charleston and Norfolk were repainted and the segregation signs were not replaced. Mess halls were also desegregated. When civilian Negroes showed up in the cafeterias, they flaunted their new rights, causing some disturbances. The cafeterias were closed, a discussion was held with Negro leaders, and an agreement was reached to avoid further direct confrontations.[2] From here on, Eisenhower kept his eye on the impressive administrator from Texas who would later replace George Humphrey as secretary of the treasury. The president also named a number of Negroes to high government positions, including E. Frederick Morrow, who became the first black White House assistant in history. But, as events unfolded, it was the Supreme Court, rather than the executive or legislative branches, that played the key role in the civil rights movement of the 1950s.

Eisenhower was able to name a number of justices to the Supreme Court and most of his nominees were excellent choices. Taken as a group, they were more liberal, and far more capable, than the Truman and Kennedy appointees. When Chief Justice Fred Vinson died suddenly in September 1953, the president asked Brownell to prepare a list of candidates for the position. There were several who had claims on the administration, including Dewey (who did not want it) and Dulles. The latter was Eisenhower's choice, but the secretary of state had exactly the job he wanted and declined to change. Brownell recommended Earl Warren of California. The attorney general had become well acquainted with Warren when he managed the unsuccessful Dewey-Warren campaign in 1948.

Eisenhower owed Warren no political debt, for the latter had held on to his favorite-son convention support until it was too late for California to make a deciding switch to Eisenhower. The president interviewed Warren early in his administration for a possible appointment and thought he "seemed to reflect high ideals and a great deal of common sense." There were the usual objections to Warren's lack of judicial experience, but he had important experience as an administrator while governor of California and he was strongly recommended by William Knowland, who had just become Senate Majority Leader. Moreover, Warren appeared to be a moderate in his thinking, and this was the direction in which Eisenhower wanted to move the court. Warren received the appointment and, five months later, he was unanimously confirmed by the Senate.[3]

When Justice Robert Jackson died unexpectedly in October 1954, Brownell recommended for the position John Marshall Harlan, grandson of the great, lone dissenter in *Plessy* v. *Ferguson,* the "separate but equal" case of 1896. But the Republicans lost control of the Senate in the elections of 1954, and the new chairman of the Judiciary Committee, James O. Eastland of Mississippi, was searching for judicial selections who would "blunt if not destroy" the desegregation ruling of 1954 in *Brown* v. *Topeka.* The junior senator from Mississippi, John Stennis, introduced a bill in Congress to require all Supreme Court appointees to have a minimum of ten years judicial experience; the bill, fortunately, got nowhere. Eastland was more candid than his colleague. He opposed Harlan's nomination because he feared he would not oppose powerful groups who sought "to declare the United Nations charter, with its taint of communism . . . paramount to the United States Constitution." Harlan's was a political appointment dictated by Dewey, Eastland charged, and Harlan's philosophies were "different" from those of the rest of the country.[4] While he could not block the confirmation, Eastland embarrassed the administration by delaying it four months.

Sherman Minton decided in 1956 to retire and William

J. Brennan, Jr., was named to replace him. Brennan was a Roman Catholic Democrat who satisfied the demand for judicial experience, for he was a justice of the New Jersey state supreme court. But his nomination got caught up in McCarthyism. Although by that time Joe McCarthy was no longer seriously to be feared, the Wisconsin senator denounced Brennan for having described his investigations of subversive activities as "Salem witch hunts" and delayed the confirmation for five months. On the other hand, the confirmation of Charles E. Whittaker of Missouri, to replace Stanley Reed who had resigned in 1957, was secured the same day as Brennan's. Whittaker was to prove to be Eisenhower's weakest appointment to the Court, but he satisfied the conservatives and those who insisted upon prior judicial experience. Eisenhower's fifth, and last, appointment also suffered delay. Justice Harold Burton resigned in 1958, and Potter Stewart of Ohio was named as his successor. Stewart was a federal circuit judge, and senators who disliked the trend of decisions by the Warren Court, especially in desegregation, took out their discontent on him with exhaustive questioning before he was confirmed.[5] The Warren Court managed to antagonize conservatives and southerners to an unprecedented degree with decisions protecting the freedom of the individual and with the segregation cases.

In 1896, the Supreme Court, with John Marshall Harlan dissenting, had handed down the decision that, as long as facilities were equal, separating the races did not violate the Fourteenth Amendment guarantee of equal protection of the laws. North and South then proceeded to segregate blacks from whites in all categories—economic, social, and political. Negroes had to spend the next several generations regaining what had been won in the Civil War and the Reconstruction period. The South particularly had a difficult time in maintaining two separate and equal educational facilities, for the area was so poor that in many instances even one good system could not be offered. As a result, the black institutions were at best weak and occasionally nonexistent. In a series of Supreme Court cases following World War II, segregation in higher education, where it was most costly, was struck down as being unconstitutional. By the end of the Truman administration, Negroes were ready to attack the "separate but equal" doctrine in the entire system of public education, North and South.

In 1952 the Supreme Court heard five cases challenging the "separate but equal" concept. The NAACP, with its counsel, Thurgood Marshall, argued that segregation in the District of Columbia violated the Fifth Amendment due process clause, and that segregated schools in the states of Delaware and South Carolina, a county in Virginia, and a city in Kansas violated the Fourteenth Amendment equal protection clause. They asked that the Plessy decision be overturned. As the Kansas case, *Brown* v. *Topeka,* was first on the list of the five cases, the desegregation decision takes its name from this. The Vinson Court ordered the case argued in 1953, directing counsel on both sides to discuss the intention of the framers of the Fourteenth Amendment in regard to public education, and invited the attorney general to submit his opinion on the question. When the case was reargued before the Warren Court in 1954, Attorney General Herbert Brownell, as amicus curiae, informed the Court that he believed segregation was unconstitutional.

Following oral arguments, the Court was slow in formulating an opinion. Warren was aware of the magnitude of the problem and of the absolute necessity for unanimity in the decision. In addition, he wanted to write an opinion that would withstand the political onslaughts that were certain to come. Finally, on May 17, 1954, speaking for a unanimous Supreme Court, Earl Warren announced the decision. The fundamental question, he observed, was whether segregation in schools on the basis of race deprived the minority group of an equal education. "We believe that it does," he declared, citing a barrage of sociological and psychological studies to prove the thesis. The Court concluded that segregated education generated "a sense of inferiority" that adversely affected the ability to learn.[6] The justices asked the counsel for both sides in the litigation to return a year later with plans for implementing the decision. In 1955 the Court ordered district courts to carry out the opinion and to ensure that the desegregation of the nation's schools proceeded "with all deliberate speed." The decision affected over ten million children, about 40 percent of the school population.

Unfortunately, there was a great deal of deliberation but very little speed. Northern states repealed their laws on segregation, but it continued *de facto,* for the races in the cities were largely separated by neighborhoods, and the children attended their neighborhood schools. The South responded with massive resistance, going to the extreme of closing schools in some cases, rather than integrate them. On the local level, whites formed white citizens councils to resist integration, and in many areas the Ku Klux Klan was revived. Many southerners quickly lumped integrationists and Communists together, viewing the *Brown* decision as a plot hatched in Moscow to mix races and thus weaken America.

The NAACP initiated a massive program of litigation in the courts to force compliance. But it would be a long battle, for in March 1956, 101 of the 128 southern senators and congressmen signed a manifesto declaring political war on the *Brown* decision. Although Eisenhower later stated in his memoirs that he agreed with the *Brown* opinion, at the time he thought the decision was wrong. The adviser to whom he made this observation concluded that the president's views on race relations were "distinctly old fashioned or of another generation, and not a little southern."[7] When reporters asked his reaction to the Court's decision, Eisenhower said it was now the law of the land and would have to be obeyed. But, unfortunately, he added that men's hearts cannot be changed with laws and integration would take a great deal of education. This was taken by some southerners to mean that the president agreed with their opposition. The president ordered an immediate integration of the schools in the District of Columbia, hoping this would serve as a model of compliance for the South, but this was not to be. The South would resist.

CIVIL RIGHTS

In September 1956, Governor Allan Shivers, a Texas "Democrat for Eisenhower," successfully defied a court order to integrate the all-white Texarkana high school. He sent in Texas Rangers to prevent the entrance of Negro students to the white school and to arrest anyone who might provoke violence there.[8] In that same month, John Kasper of New Jersey was active in Clinton, Tennessee. He came to the town, which was in the process of integrating under court orders, to organize a white citizens council in opposition. Addressing white crowds, he asked them to decide if they were Christians or Communists. When he was officially invited to leave town for his efforts, he refused and was jailed for inciting a riot. His supporters then rioted to protest, and state troopers had to be brought in to break up the demonstration. Kasper and six others were found guilty of violating the district court order to integrate the school, and the Clinton difficulty was solved. But the following year a major crisis occurred in Arkansas.

Soon after the *Brown* decision was announced, the school board of Little Rock, Arkansas, announced it would comply with the law and in 1955 worked out plans to begin integrating the high schools in 1957. During early 1957, School Superintendent Virgil Blossom spoke to gatherings, successfully urging support of the program, and it appeared there would be no trouble when September arrived. But Governor Orval Faubus had different ideas. Unexpectedly, on September 2, 1957, the day before the schools were to open, he predicted violence would occur and, without consulting city officials, sent in the National Guard to prevent integration. The action incited the segregationists, who hardly needed encouragement, and disorder erupted. On September 20 the district court enjoined Faubus to remove the National Guard, which he did. The next day, the Negro children were met at the doors of the schools by a howling mob of whites and had to be withdrawn for their own safety. The eyes of the world were now focused on Little Rock and Governor Faubus.

At a press conference six weeks earlier, Eisenhower had stated that he could not "imagine any set of circumstances that would ever induce me to send Federal troops into any area to enforce the orders of a federal court."[9] Being aware of this statement, Faubus telegraphed the president to ask that he help to modify the court order. Eisenhower refused, of course, declaring he would enforce the law. Arkansas congressman Brooks Hays had asked Sherman Adams to persuade the president to talk to the governor; accordingly, Adams drafted a telegram for Faubus to send Eisenhower in which the governor would state his intention to obey the law and request a meeting. When Faubus sent the telegram, however, he changed this to express his desire to obey the law. Despite the less conciliatory wording, Eisenhower invited Faubus to Newport, Rhode Island, where he was vacationing. They met on September 14, and the president became convinced of the governor's sincerity in the situation.

On September 23, Negro students were again attacked as they tried to enter Little Rock's Central High School. Mayor Woodrow Wilson Mann telegraphed the White House, asking for help. The president issued a proclamation calling on Little Rock citizens to obey the law. When the rioting continued, he had no choice but to nationalize the Arkansas National Guard. On September 23 he sent ten thousand guardsmen to Little Rock along with one thousand paratroopers, all under the command of General Edwin A. Walker. The school was then integrated, and over the ensuing months the troops were gradually withdrawn. Eisenhower's reluctant decision to send troops to Little Rock in that crisis was the most vital civil rights decision of the decade, "for it greatly enlarged the federal government's commitment to the revolution in race relations."[10] Significantly, Brownell became determined to increase Justice Department activity in school desegregation issues from then on in order to avoid any further Little Rocks. When he resigned soon after the Little Rock crisis, his successor, William P. Rogers, proved to be equally willing to broaden actions on integration, and, in 1960, his prompt action headed off a similar episode in New Orleans.[11] By the end of the Eisenhower administration, only Alabama, Mississippi, and South Carolina were still refusing token integration.

Meanwhile, the attorney general persuaded Congress to pass the first civil rights legislation since Reconstruction days. A few Republican leaders, including Attorney General Brownell, were beginning to realize that the Negro vote was assuming increasing importance to the Republican party. Particularly when Eisenhower had his heart attack, Brownell thought it even more necessary to woo their votes for Nixon in 1956. Even when the president recovered and decided to run again, Brownell pressed forward with his civil rights proposal. Eisenhower and his staff were difficult to persuade of the necessity for such legislation, however, believing the southern white votes to be more important to the Republican party than northern Negro votes. In March 1956, when Brownell proposed his measure again, he found the cabinet unreceptive. He stuck to his guns, though, and sent two bills to Congress; the administration could only endorse them, although not enthusiastically.[12] The House passed one of the measures, but the Senate refused to consider it. It was not until after the 1956 election, when the importance of the Negro vote became even more obvious, that Eisenhower in 1957 gave his first support to these civil rights proposals.

The civil rights bill again had no difficulty in securing House approval in 1957, but it once again met with southern opposition in the Senate. Southerners were not worried about Section I, which would create a six-member Civil Rights Commission to investigate and report progress on civil rights achievements to the president. Nor did Section II bother them by setting up a Civil Rights Division in the Department of Justice, headed by an additional assistant attorney general. Even Section IV which would help obtain voting rights for Negroes was not particularly disturbing, for it could be easily evaded. Section III, though, caught their attention, for it authorized the attorney general to seek injunctions against violators of civil rights. This conjured up in some southern minds visions of Reconstruction when Negroes and carpetbaggers dominated their region. Yet, Senate Majority Leader Lyndon Johnson knew that if his presidential plans for 1960 were to be realized, he needed to get some type of civil rights legislation enacted. He now put into operation his brilliant parliamentary maneuvering ability.

Johnson persuaded Clinton Anderson, a liberal Democrat from New Mexico, and George Aiken, a liberal Republican from Vermont, to present an amendment to the bill eliminating Section III and all injunctive power from the measure. This was accepted. Then the proposal was further emasculated by an amendment providing for jury trials in criminal cases arising out of violations of voting rights, the reasoning being that all-white southern juries would never vote to convict violators. Labor leaders, pressing for a civil rights law, particularly opposed this section, so Johnson devised an amendment guaranteeing jury trials in all criminal contempt cases, except in states where juries were chosen from registered voter lists. But the House preferred the tougher version it had approved. This presented Speaker Rayburn and Johnson with a serious problem, for they agreed that some compromise measure had to be approved before the elections of 1958.

Johnson met with the southern Senate leaders and found they would accept a thirty-day jail sentence and a $200 fine as the dividing line for judges imposing sentences for injunction violations of the law; any heavier penalty would require a jury trial. Senate Minority Leader William Knowland countered with sixty days and $300 as the dividing line. The two sides reached a compromise when Knowland dropped his demand to forty-five days and Johnson raised his offer to $250. The House agreed to these changes, and so did the Senate, despite a twenty-four hour and eighteen minute one-man filibuster by J. Strom Thurmond of South Carolina (who surpassed Wayne Morse's 1953 record when he opposed the offshore oil bill.)[13] President Eisenhower signed the bill on September 9, 1957, in the middle of the Little Rock crisis.

Experience with the law soon demonstrated its weaknesses, and in the fall of 1959 the Civil Rights Commission recommended several changes. They suggested requiring the preservation of voting records and empowering the president to appoint federal voting registrars in cases where state registrars failed to do their duty. The House approved the record preservation requirement, but, instead of federal registrars, it adopted a plan for court-appointed referees to register voters if a pattern of discrimination could be established.[14] In the Senate, a filibuster temporarily delayed passage, and the Civil Rights Act of 1960 was not signed into law until that

May. Despite these two statutes, the Eisenhower administration filed only six voting rights suits.[15] It was not until the Kennedy administration and the long, hot summers of the 1960s that significant numbers of Negroes were registered and began voting in the South.

The manner in which he handled the civil rights problem was undoubtedly Eisenhower's greatest weakness as president. He was the most popular incumbent in history and could have done much to educate the American people to accept integration. Unfortunately—and even tragically in the light of the violence that characterized the movement in the following decade—he believed that while integration was inevitable, it would take a long time to achieve, and he did little to promote its progress, except in the District of Columbia. It was not until May 1958 that he agreed to speak to an all-Negro group, and at the end of his speech he ad-libbed some remarks, ending with "but you must be patient." This admonition stunned his listeners.[16] They had already waited several generations, and many were becoming increasingly restive. Under more sympathetic presidents in the 1960s, they would become more aggressive in their demands and tactics. At the beginning of the decade, the NAACP under Roy Wilkins and the National Urban League headed by Whitney Young led the civil rights movement. Then, on the evening of December 1, 1955, Mrs. Rosa Parks, a Negro seamstress, boarded a bus in Montgomery, Alabama. Tired and cross, she refused to move to the colored section in the rear when ordered to by the driver. She was arrested for violating the city ordinance. The next night, leaders of the Negro community gathered at the Dexter Avenue Baptist church with its pastor, Martin Luther King, Jr., and decided to boycott the bus line. The boycott was highly effective, and, when company revenues soon dropped by 65 percent, the company begged the city to give up. However, city officials refused to let the bus line integrate until November 1956 when the Supreme Court held this segregation to be unconstitutional.

Meanwhile, Dr. King was convicted of conducting an illegal boycott. He refused to pay his fine and was sentenced to 386 days in jail. This made him a martyr. He then organized the Southern Christian Leadership Conference, adopted Mahatma Gandhi's strategy of passive resistance, and a new charismatic leader of the civil rights movement was born. In January 1960, four Negro college students in Greensboro, North Carolina, followed his example and sat at Woolworth's lunch counter where they were ignored for two and one-half hours. Day after day they returned until they succeeded in breaking the color line and a new tactic was proven successful. Soon tens of thousands of Negroes and white civil rights workers were staging "sit-ins" all over the South. They were cursed, spat upon, and beaten, but they passively endured until the segregation bars were broken in the South.

The construction of school classrooms was closely tied to the civil rights movement, for the problem of segregation defeated passage of much-needed legislation. The postwar population boom soon overcrowded the nation's schools and, because of relatively low salaries—in 1959 the average teacher's salary was $4,940—many teachers were leaving the profession. In 1953, Congress enacted the Federal Impacted Area program, which granted funds to schools where a federal activity like a military installation increased the public school enrollments, but this was only scratching the surface of the problem. There was an estimated shortage of 300,000 classrooms, and it was growing worse yearly. Something had to be done. Again Eisenhower's "partnership" concept was brought into play. In the case of classroom construction, though, Adlai Stevenson came close to a correct analysis of "dynamic conservatism" when he said it meant recommending "the building of a great many schools to accommodate the needs of our children, but not provide the money."[17]

In February 1955, the president asked Congress for

legislation for a $1 billion construction program. The national government would grant $200 million, and the remainder would be raised by the national government purchasing local school district bonds. Liberals opposed this plan, of course, as a "do it yourself" system but, more seriously, the legislation ran into the problem of the "Powell amendment." The House Committee on Labor and Education approved the bill after its chairman, Adam Clayton Powell, added an amendment prohibiting such funds from going to any school district practicing segregation. The House passed this measure but the amendment guaranteed its defeat in the Senate.

That fall, Adlai Stevenson, looking to the 1956 presidential race, denounced the Eisenhower administration before the National Education Association for not solving the "scandalous" classroom situation. Stung by this criticism, the president called a White House conference on education in November 1955. The conference recommended federal aid to education but opposed assistance to parochial schools, noting that an additional $15 billion in new buildings would be needed within five years. Early the next year, the administration tried again. Congress was asked to enact a program of $2 billion over a four year period—$1.25 billion in outright grants and federal purchase of $750 million in local school bonds. The usual Powell amendment was added in Congress and, this time, southerners were joined by Catholics who wanted to extend the aid to parochial schools, to defeat the measure in the House. The administration continued unsuccessfully to request Congress for aid to school construction, the proposals being blocked by Catholics, segregationists, and liberals who wanted the national government to pay the complete costs. Finally, in 1959, the Senate approved a measure granting $20 per school-age child for school construction and teachers' salaries, and in 1960 the House approved a different version, again with the Powell amendment; nothing came of this and the problem continued into the 1960s.

Then there were the original Americans, some three-quarters of a million American Indians living in abject poverty on their desolate, barren reservations. The Dawes Act of 1887 had sought to end tribal ownership of Indian lands and to have the lands taken in severalty, with the Indians becoming citizens. This program did not work well, and the New Deal for Indians restored tribal government and tried to preserve the native culture. Then, after World War II, the Truman administration again tried to achieve "termination" by ending tribal government and tribal ownership of reservation lands.

The Eisenhower administration, in its efforts to cut back government activities, agreed with this concept and attempted to "get the government out of the Indian business." As a result, Congress passed a law in 1953 which made tribes in five states subject to state jurisdiction over criminal and civil cases and provided for similar action in eight other states containing Indians, if the states individually wished to do so. Unfortunately, Congress failed to consult the Indians, and rushed this legislation through in almost indecent haste.[18] The president reluctantly signed the measure. He agreed with the idea but opposed transferring jurisdiction to the eight other states without the consent of the Indians involved. He should have vetoed it, for it is not good practice for a president to accept bad legislation in the hopes that a future Congress will correct it.

The following year Congress enacted six "termination" bills and in 1955 transferred the health program of the Bureau of Indian Affairs to the Public Health Service. "Termination" proved unpopular with the tribes, and by 1956 the push for it began to subside. Continued criticism prompted Secretary of the Interior Fred Seaton to defend the concept publicly in 1958, but he agreed it would be implemented only in those cases where the Indians involved understood "termination" and accepted it.[19] In those tribes where "termination" was carried out, especially among the Menominees of Wisconsin, it was a disaster. The Indians lost control of their lands, and, with heavy tax burdens and improper management, many faced bankruptcy. Moreover, state and federal expenses increased rather than declined under "termination."[20] One of the most lamentable features of "termination" was the effort to make white men out of Indians and thus acculturate them. Fortunately, the Indians and their sympathizers were able to ward off this effort to destroy their culture. Events proved that they needed and wanted economic assistance to maintain their native culture, not "termination" that would destroy their ancient way of life.

The Economy and The Unions

The president had his greatest fiscal problem in preparing the 1958 budget. The budget total, which had been climbing annually, was causing an increasing clamor among conservatives. Eisenhower, who had improvidently pledged in the 1952 campaign to cut the budget to $60 billion, was also concerned over his failure to carry out a prime Republican objective. The Department of Defense was the worst offender, coming back year after year for more money for new programs without eliminating old, obsolete ones. Thus, when the proposed 1958 budget totaled $71.8 billion, a record high for a peacetime budget, everyone in the administration was unhappy. Eisenhower was ready to listen to anyone who had ideas about cuts. He and Humphrey agreed that the latter would hold a press conference to discuss the problem of inflation and increasing government budgets.

At the press conference, Humphrey made his opening statement, which had prior presidential approval, and then added that the nation must economize over a period of time. Economic conditions were getting out of hand, he extemporized, and if the trend continued, "I predict you will have a depression that will curl your hair." The latter statement made good headlines and, at his press conference, the president was asked to respond to his treasury secretary's remarks. He tried to place Humphrey's comments in their proper context but then opened a Pandora's box by adding that if Congress could find places to cut the budget, "it is their duty to do it." Here was the president of the United States asking Congress to slash his own budget requests![21] Out in Tacoma, Edgar Eisenhower, whom his nephew John described as "a little to the right of Ivan the Terrible" and who was currently a director of the conservative Americans for Constitutional Action, wondered publicly "what influence is at work on my brother."

Suddenly the Democrats in Congress became frugal. Harry Byrd of the Senate Finance Committee guessed he could find $6.5 billion in waste; Sam Rayburn was a little more cautious with a $3 billion to $5 billion estimate. The House compounded the president's dilemma by asking him to indicate where substantial cuts could be made. After Eisenhower made two radio and television appeals to save his budget, it emerged from Congress cut by $4 billion; $1 billion of this reduction came out of Eisenhower's precious mutual security funds. At the same time, the economy went into a recession, tax receipts declined, and there was still a $12 billion deficit for fiscal 1958—the largest to that time in peacetime.

Although there was no hair-curling depression, the economy slid into a serious recession in mid-1957. Liquidation of inventories was a prime cause, as was a reduction in defense production which particularly hit the aircraft industry. Unemployment jumped from 3 million in July 1957 to 5.3 million a year later. Again, as in the recession of 1954, Eisenhower refused to panic or to accede to demands for New Deal-type public works. Highway construction was speeded up and defense spending was increased, but the president wanted none of the "pump-priming" schemes being prepared by Democratic congressmen. Surprisingly, farmers did not suffer, but, as in previous recessions, certain depressed areas and "labor surplus" areas where unemployment was over 6 percent were hard hit in 1957and 1958. The president asked Congress to extend unemployment benefits to help these areas, requesting immediate action because this concerned "people—human beings—who need, and should have, the assistance of their government."[22] This was done, but that was all. Many people were pressing for a tax cut to stimulate the economy, but Eisenhower backed his new secretary of the treasury, Robert Anderson, who believed this would add to inflation and would be ill-advised in the long run. So, those Republicans who hoped a recession would force a cut in taxes were disappointed when the president refused to yield to this pressure.

Although the economy recovered in 1958, the depressed areas did not. In April of that year, Democratic Senator Paul Douglas of Illinois introduced a bill to create an Area Redevelopment Administration. This agency would make loans to those areas to help them attract new industry. Both houses passed this measure but the president vetoed it. Although Eisenhower agreed with this type of assistance, he believed this particular measure to be "unsound," for it "would greatly diminish local responsibility." In his 1960 State of the Union message, the president said the coming year promised to be "the most prosperous year in our history," but he was wrong. Another, milder, recession hit, and Congress again passed legislation creating an Area Redevelopment Administration. Again it was vetoed because it would "inhibit" private, state, and local initiative, and because the president believed the problem was a temporary one. The economic conditions in Appalachia and elsewhere were to become a campaign issue in the 1960 presidential race.[23] Despite these setbacks, the gross national product reached $500 billion in 1960, a far cry from the 1945 GNP (in 1960 dollars) of $349 billion.

In spite of these recessions, Americans were prosperous, and labor unions made significant financial gains. In the campaign of 1952, Eisenhower agreed that the Taft-Hartley Act needed changes, and, after the election, he and Taft concurred on several proposals. But, with Secretary of Commerce Weeks adamantly opposed to any alteration, the presidential staff could not agree on specific change recommendations, and in August 1953 Durkin resigned as secretary of labor in protest over what he considered to be a betrayal of promises. The new secretary, James Mitchell, was more successful in securing administrative agreement on changes, and in January 1954 the president asked Congress for some fifteen amendments to the law. Among other changes that were not too far-reaching, he advocated a liberalization of the restrictions on secondary boycotts, a proviso that employers also sign a noncommunist affidavit or drop the requirement that union officials sign one, and permission for striking employees to vote for their bargaining agent.[24] But Congress proved unresponsive to demands to amend the Taft-Hartley Act, and it declined as an issue, especially after the corrupt activities of certain union officials became a national concern.

In 1954, labor won an important victory, though, when Congress broadened the unemployment compensation program to include an additional four million workers and to increase benefits—the most significant single improvement in the system since its enactment in 1935. The next year the minimum wage was raised for the first time since 1949. Eisenhower asked Congress to increase it from seventy-five cents to ninety cents per hour. Liberal congressmen sought to increase it to $1.25 but Congress finally compromised on Paul Douglas's proposal of $1.00, which the president accepted.

The year 1955 also brought two other important events for unions. In that year, the United Auto Workers persuaded the Ford Motor Company and General Motors to accept the guaranteed annual wage concept. This was actually a program of supplementary unemployment benefits which would assure workers of the equivalent of a full year's pay by supplementing their unemployment benefits during periods of seasonal unemployment. That year also saw the merger of the nation's two largest unions. When William Green, president of the AFL, and Philip Murray, president of the CIO, died in 1952, their successors immediately began to work toward merger. Both Green and Murray had opposed this, for their positions of power dated back to the days of the labor split in the 1930s. But the new leaders, George Meany of the AFL and Walter Reuther of the CIO, clearly saw that the advantages of combination far outweighed continuing the old hatreds. The first step was taken when both unions cleaned out corruption from their midst and expelled Communists who opposed the merger. Then, in 1953, they signed a "no raiding" pact, promising not to steal each other's members. Discussions were successfully undertaken, and in 1955 the merger was approved by their annual conventions. The new AFL-CIO contained some fifteen million members.

As early as 1953 it was revealed that the International Longshoremen's Association was dominated by racketeers. Continued revelations of corruption in certain unions led to the establishment in 1957 of a Senate investigating committee, chaired by John McClellan, Democrat from Arkansas. The committee's chief counsel, Robert Kennedy, hit real "pay dirt" while investigating the Teamsters Union, headed by Dave Beck. It was discovered that from 1949 to 1953 Beck had "borrowed" some $320,000 in union treasury funds to invest in the stock market and elsewhere. The Teamsters suspended Beck and elected Jimmy Hoffa as their president in December 1957. The McClellan Committee subsequently found evidence that Hoffa had accepted bribes, and he was convicted of income tax evasion in 1959. These revelations convinced the public that many unions were rife with corruption, and congressmen were persuaded that legislation was needed. The result was two laws controlling unions.

In 1958 Congress easily passed the first of these, the Welfare and Pensions Plans Act, that required public accounting for the use of welfare and pension funds. Passage of the second law was more difficult and involved. The House Committee on Education and Labor worked six months to produce a reform bill, the Landrum-Griffin measure, but in the Senate, John Kennedy was promoting a milder proposal, and the Senate approved his measure by a vote of 90 to 1. Those who supported the Landrum-Griffin bill were afraid they did not have the necessary votes to enact it in the House. The Republican members of the Education and Labor Committee appealed to the president to make a TV appearance and plead for the law.

Eisenhower, who had asked for a labor reform bill in his January 1959 State of the Union message, was happy to comply. He denounced the Kennedy measure and, in strong terms, asked for real labor reform legislation. As a result, the House approved the Landrum-Griffin bill, embodying Eisenhower's requests for amendments to the Taft-Hartley Act, by a vote of 229 to 201. The two proposals then went to a conference committee. The conferees, including Senator Kennedy, "instinctively felt a strong tide running for a stringent bill," and the final compromise measure included both the tough House amendments to the Taft-Hartley Act and the milder Senate regulations of internal union affairs.[25] The Landrum-Griffin Act guaranteed free, secret union elections, and it tightened loopholes in the Taft-Hartley Act by curbing practices like illegal picketing, secondary boycotts, and "hot cargo" contracts, curbs the president had specifically requested.

The Congress also must have sensed a strong public

desire for curbing union activities, because the bill received an overwhelming vote of 95 to 2 in the Senate (only the mavericks Wayne Morse and William Langer of North Dakota opposed it) and 352 to 52 in the House. This measure represented a major victory for the president, for the conservative coalition in Congress of Republicans and southern Democrats, and for large business groups; it was a stunning reversal for unions and liberal northern Democrats, and, as it developed, it hurt small businessmen in their competition against businesses that were organized.

Also, in July 1959, despite a presidential request for further negotiations, a steel strike was called over wage and work rule demands. It became the longest strike in the history of the industry. When the lack of steel production began to affect other industries, Eisenhower held two sessions on September 30—one with the industrialists and the other with the union leaders—to try to get them to agree on terms, but to no avail. Finally the strike was halted by a Taft-Hartley injunction on November 7. On December 3, the president made an appeal on television to both sides. A settlement was reached three weeks before the injunction would expire, giving the workers a sizeable forty-one cents per hour raise, but without modernizing the work rules.

THE SUPREME COURT AGAIN

During Eisenhower's second administration, Congress and the Supreme Court engaged in a confrontation unparalleled since the "court packing plan" of the 1930s.[26] This tension first arose over problems of American troops stationed overseas. When the United States negotiated treaties with foreign nations to help defend them in the cold war, it included in the agreements the principle of extraterritoriality. These status of forces agreements invariably provided that the United States would retain jurisdiction over its military and civilian personnel. This brought up in the 1950s the interesting question—does the Constitution follow the flag overseas? In a series of cases labelled the second "insular cases," the Supreme Court held that these people still retained constitutional guarantees and protection.[27]

The first case, *United States ex rel Toth* v. *Quarles* in 1955, actually involved a congressional statute and represented the first time that the Warren Court declared a national law unconstitutional. Robert Toth had served in the air force in Korea, received an honorable discharge, and returned to the United States to take a civilian job. He was later arrested in Pittsburgh and flown back to Korea where he was charged with murdering a Korean woman while he was in the air force. His subsequent court-martial was conducted under the Uniform Code of Military Justice of 1951, and he appealed to the Supreme Court after he was convicted. The Warren Court freed him, holding that military jurisdiction over civilians under this code was unconstitutional. The Court was determined to maintain the constitutional principle of civilian control over the military, particularly in this period of increasing executive and military power.

Yet the next year, in *Reid* v. *Covert,* the Court found the other way. This case involved a woman who murdered her husband in England while he was in the American armed forces. The Court upheld her conviction of a capital crime by a court-martial because the status of forces agreement with Great Britain provided for military jurisdiction over all American personnel in that country. The decision was six to three, with Justice Felix Frankfurter writing a reservation to the opinion.

The woman appealed again to the Supreme Court in an unusual procedure in 1957 and a change of minds and of personnel brought an abrupt reversal. Justices Frankfurter and Harlan were now converted to the minority view and, with the newly appointed Justice Brennan, joined the 1956 dissenters to free the woman on the same constitutional basis as the *Toth* decision. Eisenhower was astonished at this opinion. He believed a major function of the Supreme Court was to provide stability in a democracy where political expediency sometimes carries the other two branches of government to extremes; yet here it reversed itself in the space of a year.[28] Apparently he waxed indignant over this decision at a Washington social gathering, for a short time later he apologized to the chief justice for the news stories then circulating that he had spoken in angry tones over this opinion. He assured Warren that someone merely overheard him expressing "amazement" and henceforth he would exercise more care in his private conversations.[29]

The case of *Wilson* v. *Girard* in 1957 really exercised many congressmen and much of the general public. William Girard, while on guard duty at a firing range in Japan, shot in the back and killed a Japanese woman who was scavenging for spent shells. The status of forces agreement gave the United States jurisdiction over crimes committed by its personnel while "in the line of duty" and gave Japan jurisdiction over all other cases. Eisenhower found that, over the years, Japan had relinquished jurisdiction in 97 percent of the cases of Americans subject to trial in Japanese courts, and in the other 3 percent, their sentences were quite light.[30] So the United States turned Girard over to the Japanese and the Supreme Court sustained this decision. Public sentiment in the United States was outraged over this, and bills were introduced in Congress to retain all jurisdiction over American personnel under United States authorities. Girard's light sentence, however—three years, suspended—stilled the public clamor and Congress did not seriously consider the legislation.

It was in the category of hunting subversives, though, that Congress and the Court clashed most sharply. In 1951, in *Dennis* v. *United States,* the Supreme Court had followed the tone of McCarthyism and sustained the conviction of high officials in the American Communist party. The majority of the Court determined that the activity of native Communists violated the 1940 Smith Act which made it illegal to advocate the forceful overthrow of any government in the United States. Justices Black and Douglas dissented from the opinion. With the appointments of Warren, Harlan, and Brennan, who joined Hugo Black and William Douglas, there was a new liberal majority on the Court, and the issue was bound to appear again and again as long as the First Amendment was retained. The first test after the *Dennis* case came in 1955, just before Brennan was appointed.

In *Pennsylvania* v. *Nelson,* the Supreme Court overturned the conviction, in a county court, of a communist charged with sedition against the United States. The Supreme Court held, erroneously, that by enacting the Smith Act, Congress intended to preempt the field of hunting for subversives. Normally, this rule-of-thumb on national exclusiveness is correct; when the national government acts, this precludes action by other levels of government. But, the un-American hunters in 1940 welcomed any help they could get, and so, the framers of the Smith law did not intend to preempt the activity of discovering subversion. But, ignoring congressional intent, the *Nelson* decision held that the national government had exclusive jurisdiction unless and until legislation was passed specifically permitting states to enter this field.

Then, in 1957 in *Jencks* v. *United States,* the Court supposedly opened FBI files to defendants. Clinton Jencks was a New Mexico union official who had signed a noncommunist affidavit as required by the Taft-Hartley Act. The national government, in an attempt to prove that the signature was given under false pretense, used the testimony of an admitted perjurer, Harvey Matusow. Defense counsel demanded to see the files, but the request was refused, so Jencks appealed to the Supreme Court. Justice Brennan, speaking for the majority, threw the case out on the basis that the accused had the right to see this material in order to build a defense. He failed to make clear, however, the limits that should be imposed on the accused's rights of access to classified information.[31] If the government did not want to produce the evidence, Brennan said, it would have to drop the prosecution. Justice Tom Clark was the only dissenter, declaring this opinion would give criminals "a Roman holiday for rummaging through confidential information as well as vital national secrets." The administration and many congressmen were shocked by the decision, and a bill was speedily introduced in Congress to circumscribe it. The "Jencks Act" which easily passed Congress, provided, in similar cases, for the trial judge to review the file and determine what should be released to the defendant.

Two weeks after the *Jencks* decision, the Supreme Court handed down several opinions on the day that critics of the Court labelled "Red Monday." The first of these, *Watkins* v. *United States*, was a direct challenge to Congress and its power to investigate. John Watkins had testified before the House Un-American Activities Committee (HUAC) and had been most cooperative in discussing his communist past. When questioned about friends who had left the Communist party, however, he refused to answer, arguing that this went beyond the scope of the committee's authority. Dividing six to one, the Supreme Court justices agreed with him. Following World War II, Earl Warren observed for the majority, "there appeared a new kind of congressional inquiry unknown in prior periods of American history . . . [that] involved a broad-scale intrusion into the lives and affairs of private citizens." The power of Congress to investigate, he warned, was "not unlimited." In this instance, the mandate of the House of Representatives to the committee was too vague, he asserted, for "who can define the meaning of un-American?" The questions the committee members posed to the witness also suffered from vagueness, so he could not be held in contempt of Congress.[32]

Immediately following the delivery of the *Watkins* decision, Justice Harlan began reading the opinion in *Yates* v. *United States*. This case involved the conviction of a number of "second string" Communists under the Smith Act. The basic question here, Harlan argued, was whether or not the Smith Act forbade advocacy of violent overthrow of government "as an abstract principle, divorced from any effort to instigate action to that end." The Court held that it did not. Organizing the Communist party was one thing, but the day-to-day activities of keeping it running did not constitute incitement to direct action to overthrow the government. The Court thus moved from its "bad tendency" interpretation in the *Dennis* case of 1951 back to a more liberal view of the "clear and present danger" doctrine of the First Amendment. But the Supreme Court had more to say on this.

The case of *Service* v. *Dulles* involved the refusal of the state department to reinstate John Service, who had been discharged as a security risk. Although he had been cleared five times by a departmental review board and twice by the Loyalty Review Board, the departmental board had, in its third action, found "reasonable doubt" about him, and the secretary of state had terminated him without reviewing the entire record. This action, Harlan held, violated the department's own rules of procedure and was therefore invalid. The Court was not yet finished that day. In *Sweezy* v. *New Hampshire,* the Supreme Court placed the same restrictions on state investigations of subversives that it had placed on the national HUAC in the *Watkins* case.

After having angered conservative cold warriors in Congress, the White House, and the state governments with these decisions, the Court then took on the legal profession and law enforcement officers. In *Schware* v.

New Mexico, the Supreme Court found that the appellant had been denied due process of law by the state board of bar examiners in refusing him admission to the bar because he had been a Communist. In *Konigsberg* v. *California,* Ralph Konigsberg had refused to tell the California examining committee whether or not he was a Communist, and he was refused certification to the state bar. The Court sustained his refusal to answer on the grounds that to force him to do so would violate his First Amendment rights. In *Mallory* v. *United States,* a forerunner of the 1966 *Miranda* decision, the Court found a man's rights had been violated by police. Mallory, a slow-witted Negro boy, had been arrested in Washington D.C., on charges of rape. He had been questioned for several hours, given a lie detector test, and signed a confession before he was told of his constitutional rights. The Supreme Court held this was an"unnecessary delay" in informing him of his rights.

Typically, Eisenhower was not critical of the Court when asked his opinion of these decisions. He did agree, though, that anyone who did not have legal training would have "very great trouble understanding" some of them. But the outrage of ultraconservatives over these decisions knew no bounds. Senator William Jenner was particularly harsh in his criticism. He charged that the opinions represented "a successful blow at key points of the legislative structure erected . . . for the protection of the internal security of the United States," and he introduced a bill to overturn them. The proposed Jenner bill represented the most drastic attack on the Supreme Court since Congress removed its jurisdiction over habeas corpus during Reconstruction. His measure would have removed jurisdiction over review of cases involving contempt of Congress, the loyalty-security programs, state antisubversives statutes, and rules governing admission to practice law. It was so extreme that Attorney General William Rogers thought it represented "the retaliatory approach of the same character as the court packing plan of 1937."[33]

The conservative coalition of Republicans and southern Democrats in Congress now found real common cause. Both groups were enraged at the Court for "coddling" Communists, as some described recent opinions, and southerners by this time were becoming particularly incensed over court enforcement of the desegregation decision. The Senate Majority Leader, Lyndon Johnson, a southerner, now really had his leadership ability put to the test, for the coalition was determined to curb the Supreme Court's power.

During hearings on the Jenner bill, Senator John Butler, Republican from Maryland, decided it would never pass in its original form, and offered several amendments in committee. The Jenner-Butler bill, as reported to the Senate, proposed removing Court jurisdiction only on bar examiners. It would reinstitute state sedition statutes, and make each house of Congress the final determinant of the pertinency of the activities of their investigating committees. It would also make it a crime to teach the violent overthrow of government, in addition to making illegal the organizing and continuing activities of subversive parties. The House, more conservative than the Senate, had already approved several measures overturning these Court opinions, including H.R. 3 which would reverse *Pennsylvania* v. *Nelson*. The real question was whether or not the Senate would act. Most observers agreed that the Jenner-Butler bill could easily pass the House of Representatives, but there were several barriers to its passage in the upper house: the Justice Department opposed it even in its amended form, the liberals in the Senate would be harder to stampede into hasty acceptance of the measure than those in the House, and Lyndon Johnson opposed it.[34]

The Senate majority leader would have refuted the Jenner-Butler measure even if he had liked its provisions, for it had the potential of splitting the Democrats badly. He did not want that happening, particularly just before the elections of 1958. Furthermore, such a division would be damaging to his prestige and his presidential ambitions. But, how to hold his party together? The southern wing was demanding that the legislation be brought to a vote. Finally, Johnson became convinced he had the necessary votes against it and allowed the proposal to be debated on August 20, 1958. As Johnson had hoped, the Jenner-Butler bill was tabled 49 to 41. Then Paul Douglas almost undid everything Johnson had worked for on the Court bills. After the tabling, Douglas immediately offered an amendment to a bill then being considered, that Congress approve the Supreme Court decision holding segregation to be unconstitutional. The damage was quickly shown when a motion to table H.R. 3 lost 39 to 46. The conservative coalition could smell blood and demanded a vote on the measure, but Johnson managed to get the Senate recessed.

There was consternation among the liberals now, as well as in the administration. The cabinet was badly split. Attorney General Rogers, the vice president, and the president opposed H.R. 3. There were rumors, though, that Postmaster General Summerfield, Commerce Secretary Weeks, and Robert Anderson of Treasury would resign if H.R. 3 were passed and then vetoed. The answer was to defeat it in the Senate. But how? Johnson did not have the votes. Finally, believing he was within one vote of victory, he talked to Everett Dirksen, Republican from Illinois, who was to become minority leader upon the retirement of Knowland later that year. Johnson pointed out that if it came to a tie vote, Vice President Nixon would vote against H.R. 3. That would be ruinous to Nixon's presidential race in 1960 as well as to Republican chances in general. Johnson suggested instead that Dirksen talk Wallace Bennett of Utah into changing his mind. Although Bennett was a co-sponsor of the bill, he was becoming convinced it would not pass the Senate; he would also want to help the party. As the roll was being called, Bennett came on the floor. The tally stood 40 to 40 when the clerk called his name again. He voted "aye" to commit and H.R. 3 went down to defeat.[35]

The effort to obtain passage of these anti-Court bills ceased. The administration opposed them, and there were a number of new liberal faces in the Senate the next year. In addition, some of the conservatives, like Knowland and Jenner, retired in 1958, and Bricker was defeated in his race for reelection. Then, too, the Supreme Court seemed to be coming back in line. In 1959, by a five to four vote, the Court sustained the contempt conviction of a college professor; in *Barenblatt* v. *United States,* the majority seemed to indicate the Court had gone too far in the *Watkins* decision and they upheld the HUAC.[36] The right to root out subversives was more important than the "preferred position" of the First Amendment. Perhaps, conservatives reasoned, the liberals on the Court would not be able to deliver the country to the Communists after all.

FURTHER SETBACKS

On October 5, 1957, American newspapers carried a startling story. The Soviet news agency, Tass, announced that Russia had successfully launched the first artificial earth satellite. Called Sputnik, meaning a "traveler with a traveler," it was moving around the earth every hour and thirty-five minutes at a height of 560 miles. The official tone of the United States was calm. When asked about the president's reaction, Press Secretary Hagerty said the development was "of great scientific interest." Then on November 3 came an even more impressive achievement. The Soviet Union launched Sputnik II, weighing 1,120 pounds and orbiting over 1,000 miles away with a live dog in it.

Americans were stunned. They had always considered themselves to be superior to everyone in science and technology in the postwar period. Now, the Russian Bear was doing something the United States could not do. What was wrong? Part of the problem lay in the interservice rivalry of the 1950s. Each military branch wanted its own rockets, and the result was that the navy had the satellite programs while the army and air force were concentrating on ballistic missiles. The army's Jupiter and the air force's Atlas were both rockets large enough to put a satellite in orbit. After Sputnik, Eisenhower ordered the army to launch a satellite immediately with a Jupiter. The launch date was set for December 4 at Cape Canaveral, Florida, but problems developed. Launching was postponed until December 6. After further technical problems were dealt with, the rocket was finally launched. It rose a short height and crashed. The foreign press had a field day. "Flopnik," they called it, and "Stay-putnik." Finally, on January 31, 1958, a satellite weighing thirty pounds was successfully launched and the space race was on.[37]

This contest prodded the president into appointing Dr. James Killian, president of the Massachusetts Institute of Technology, as a special White House adviser on science and technology. In the Senate, Lyndon Johnson took the lead in establishing the National Aeronautics and Space Administration (NASA) under the Department of Defense, which would coordinate all American space efforts and put the United States in front once more.

Leakage of the Gaither Report just before the Sputnik launch added to the public furor. In April 1957 Eisenhower had appointed a special panel headed by H. Rowan Gaither, Jr., of the Ford Foundation, to investigate the problem of civil defense against nuclear attack. The Gaither group presented a gloomy picture. The Russians were superior to the Americans in weapons technology,

they decided, and civil defense provisions were completely inadequate. By 1959 the Soviet Union might be
able to launch a number of Inter-Continental Ballistics
Missiles (ICBMs) armed with nuclear warheads. The
report further noted that the United States must begin at
once a massive program of building fallout shelters. As
these choice items were leaked to the press, the administration tried to remain calm. The president had obtained
detailed knowledge of Soviet capabilities from the reports
by high-flying reconnaissance planes, and he knew that
the Gaither panel was in error. But the more he ignored
the clamor over the Gaither report, the louder became the
criticism of his administration for losing the missile race
to Russia, and thus the Cold War. The launching of Sputnik, following leakage of the report, seemed to confirm
public fears of military inferiority.[38] Eisenhower failed,
in this situation, to gauge the impact of Sputnik on the
American people's sense of security or to reassure them
adequately that the country was not lagging behind
Soviet technology.

Fallout shelters were quickly dug and built all over the
nation, and Americans began laying in supplies of food
and water to last the necessary waiting period after a
nuclear attack. More importantly, American education
was almost turned around. Curricula in public schools
and colleges were revised to put much greater emphasis
on mathematics and sciences, to the neglect of the social
sciences and humanities. In 1958 Congress enacted the
presidentially endorsed National Defense Education Act
(NDEA). This program set up a loan fund permitting college students to borrow up to $10,000 for educational
expenses, repayable over a ten-year period at 3 percent
interest. Half the loan would be forgiven if the student
taught in a primary or secondary school for five years
after graduation. In addition, NDEA set up a $280 mil-
lion fund-matching program for public schools to provide
money for laboratories, equipment, and textbooks to

teach modern languages, mathematics, and sciences. The law also contained a loyalty oath requirement, one of the last remnants of McCarthyism. The oath requirement was removed in 1962.

In addition, Congress appropriated $137 million in 1958 for the mass production of the Nike Zeus antimissile missile. Eisenhower believed the missile should not be produced until it had been tested, however, and refused to spend the money. A big campaign was waged by the producing companies in newspaper advertisements and in Congress to promote the project. The house majority leader, John McCormack, Democrat from Massachusetts, pleaded for the United States to "close the gap in our missile posture, muzzle the mad dog missile threat of the Soviet Union, and loose the Zeus through America's magnificent production line."[39] To no avail; Eisenhower still refused to buy the missiles until they were proven satisfactory.

One afternoon some three weeks after Sputnik I, the president was working at his desk when the words on the page he was reading appeared to roll off the top of the paper. He felt dizzy and could not hold a pen. He could not speak. Finally he was able to buzz for his secretary, Ann Whitman, who contacted Dr. Snyder immediately. The president had suffered a minor cerebral stroke. Again the nation worried. Would the president resign? Would he be able to complete his term? Once again his amazing vitality stood him in good stead. Within two weeks his memory had returned along with his speech and he was almost completely recovered. Thereafter he suffered a slight speech impediment, as if he were groping for the right word, but no other permanent damage resulted. After this scare Eisenhower wrote out an agreement with Richard Nixon; if a future disability occurred, Eisenhower would personally inform the vice president who would then take over as acting president until the crisis ended; if Eisenhower should be incapable of communication with him personally, Nixon would consult with appropriate people like Dulles and Adams before taking over. In either case, the president would determine when he was capable of resuming his powers.[40] The Twenty-fifth Amendment, of course, which was ratified in 1967, makes formal provision for such contingencies.

The year 1958 was not a good one for Eisenhower. He had a recession to worry about, and he was receiving low ratings in the polls after Sputnik. Now he was no longer immune to common jokes. Early in 1958 he went to Mile-stone, the Humphrey plantation in Georgia, for a hunting and golf vacation. Jokesters began insisting that Bobby Jones, the famous professional golfer, should take over the White House, for if the president was going to be a golfer, the nation deserved the best. When reporters learned the president was going to fly back to Washington via Phoenix so that Mamie could visit the Elizabeth Arden beauty resort there, the event, which would have gone unnoticed previously, now made headlines. In March a Gallup Poll announced that support for Eisenhower had dropped to 57 percent, the lowest popularity rating of his presidency.[41] Then to cap off the year, he lost his chief of staff, and the Republicans suffered further losses in the elections of 1958.

The very nature of Sherman Adams's duties made him a target of criticism. His abrasive personality and the diligence he brought to his tasks exacerbated the situation. Critics could not easily strike at the popular president, but they could at his granite-faced assistant if the opportunity arose, and it did in 1958. In order to build up Nixon's image for the race in 1960, it was decided he would not conduct his biennial excursion against Democrats. Someone needed to do it, though, and Adams was selected. Although he was not as efficient in this as the vice president, he managed to make a number of additional personal enemies, who were ready to pounce.

In February 1958 the House Committee on Legislative

Oversight began investigating the activities of Bernard Goldfine, a wealthy Massachusetts textile manufacturer. It was revealed that Adams had accepted the gifts of an expensive Oriental rug and a vicuna coat from Goldfine, and the textiler had paid for some of Adams's hotel bills. The two had been friends for years, and when Goldfine had problems in Washington, he naturally called on Adams. On one occasion he was charged with mislabeling his fabrics. Adams called the Federal Trade Commission and asked for a report on the matter. The charge was dropped, but a year later a new one was filed, and Adams again obliged Goldfine by setting up an appointment for him with the FTC chairman. Shortly thereafter, following a complaint by the Securities Exchange Commission about Goldfine's company, Adams had a presidential assistant officially check on the investigation.

Adams was called by the congressional committee to explain all this. The rug, he claimed, was a loan, although he admitted the coat was a gift. Furthermore, he saw nothing wrong in staying at his friend's hotel suite when he was in Boston. He had sought no special favors for anyone. He had, he argued, merely done what was routine in official Washington. What he would not acknowledge was that his influence was so powerful that his mere expression of interest in a situation was enough to bring him a favorable response. He did admit he had made a mistake in the affair and had not been sufficiently discreet. The committee cleared him of wrongdoing.[42]

Eisenhower himself had received many gifts, as do all popular presidents. Instead of disposing of them quietly, however, as was normally done, he kept many of them for his Gettysburg farm. He explained that he did this to build up the value of the farm and that there was no conflict of interest for he intended to leave it to the nation as a monument. Many expensive gifts also ended up at the Eisenhower Museum in Abilene. It was estimated that, by 1960, gifts to his farm in the form of livestock and

machinery totalled over $300,000 in value.[43] Most jour-
nalists, with the exception of Drew Pearson, tended to
overlook these indiscretions of a popular president; no
one could really conceive of Eisenhower as personally and
deceitfully profiting from these gifts. It was a different
matter for Adams, though, especially in this election
year.

As the November elections drew closer, Republicans
began demanding Adams's scalp. Eisenhower stood firm;
he would not part with his right-hand man. He defended
Adams vigorously in a public statement, saying plain-
tively, "I need him." This, of course, confirmed the opinions of those who saw the president as an incapable non-
entity whose every action was directed by Adams. When
the Democrats, headed by Edmund Muskie, swept the
Maine primary in September in a foreshadowing of what
would happen two months later, Republican demands to
fire Adams grew increasingly shrill. The president had
Nixon and Meade Alcorn, the new national secretary of
the Republican party, sound out Republican leaders.
Their advice was clearly that Adams had to go. Bowing to
the inevitable, Eisenhower, typically, sent Gerald Morgan, a White House assistant, to request that Adams
submit his resignation. Adams was replaced by Jerry
Persons. By waiting this long to get rid of Adams, it certainly appeared that the president had acted at the wrong
time for precisely the wrong reason.

The recession was also an issue in these elections, as
was the Republican effort in many states to enact the
so-called right to work laws provided for in section 14 (b)
of the Taft-Hartley Act. The elections were a disaster for
the Republican party. The Democrats gained forty-eight
seats in the House and fifteen in the Senate, giving them
their greatest control of Congress since 1936. New York
was about the only Republican bright spot, for here Nelson Rockefeller smashed Averell Harriman's attempt to
win the governorship with a half-million plurality vote,

automatically making Rockefeller a leading national figure.

In May 1959 Eisenhower suffered another severe blow when John Foster Dulles died of cancer. Dulles's place was taken by the undersecretary of state, Christian Herter, and from here on the president began playing a larger role in personal diplomacy. A month after Dulles's death, Eisenhower endured the most severe personal rebuke of his administration when the Senate refused to confirm Lewis Strauss as secretary of commerce. Strauss had made many enemies during his long public career, alienating liberals during the Dixon-Yates and Oppenheimer disputes especially. Most importantly, he had incurred the wrath of Senator Clinton Anderson, Democrat from New Mexico and a member of the Joint Atomic Energy Committee. Anderson accused Strauss of defects in his character and of lying in the confirmation hearings.[44] The final vote was 46 to 49, making this the first time since 1925 and the eighth time in history that the Senate rejected a cabinet appointee. Two Republicans, Margaret Chase Smith of Maine and William Langer of North Dakota, were held responsible for the defeat. Eisenhower described this as "one of the most depressing official disappointments" he had while in the White House.[45]

With the Democrats having even greater congressional control in his last two years, President Eisenhower finally relented and allowed his good friend Charles Halleck of Indiana to challenge Joe Martin for the House minority leadership. Halleck won and proved to be a more effective leader than Martin, working well with his Senate counterpart Everett Dirksen. But, about the only victory the Republicans won in 1959 was the admission of Hawaii to the Union. Ever since the days of martial law in World War II, Hawaii had worked to become a state. But because the Republican party predominated on the islands, the Democrats had held them out. At the same time, the Democrats wanted to bring in Alaska where they had a majority. The Alaskans finally pulled the "Tennessee maneuver," whereby they formed a state government and elected delegates to Congress without specific authorization. They were then admitted in 1959. That same year, the opposition of racists and southerners was overcome and Hawaii entered the Union as the fiftieth state. Also, in 1959 Congress overrode an Eisenhower veto for the first time, passing over his objections a public works bill which he thought contained more "pork barrel" features than the situation justified. All in all, Eisenhower's second administration was not noted for as many significant domestic achievements as his first four years, but he was certainly not the lame duck president many had predicted in 1957.[46]

CHAPTER EIGHT

Working
for
Peace

Although soldiering was his lifelong profession, Dwight Eisenhower was basically a man of peace. His mother and her pacifist teachings, he often admitted, had a great deal of influence on him. During World War II he saw the horrible agonies of war firsthand; he knew the useless tragedy of conflict and this made him a more effective general. By the same token, European allies welcomed him to build and command NATO as they would have no other general, for he seemed to them a true "civilian" soldier—made to order for the new military situation.

But Eisenhower was a product of his times and, as the cold war enveloped the world, he increasingly took up the cudgels for the West. By the time he was elected president in 1952, there were few cold warriors more fervid then he in their opposition to monolithic communism. Four years in the White House modified his views somewhat. Near the end of his first term he was willing to meet at the summit with the Soviet leaders if it would advance the cause of world peace. Détente might not be possible, but he realized that the two camps could not continue the armaments race unabated without ending in nuclear holocaust. Something must be done to slow down. In addition, the arms race was doing unhealthful things to the American economy and society.

During his second term, Eisenhower constantly warned against alarmists who would have turned the United States into a garrison state. He also began paying increasing attention to broad foreign problems. This resulted in neglect both to domestic concerns and to day-to-day diplomacy, for his goal became that of reaching agreement with the Soviet Union on the great issues of the Cold War.[1] Part of this concentrated attention was due to the loss of Dulles as secretary of state, but the president had always kept a tight rein on foreign policy. Some of the change was due to advancing age and his realization that his chances for making a lasting contribution to world peace were rapidly waning. Much of it was due to his desire to utilize his vast reservoir of worldwide popularity and enormous personal prestige to promote the cause of world peace. That he failed in his ultimate goal—détente and peaceful coexistence with communism—is less a commentary on his capabilities as a leader than a tribute to his vision, which was broader than the simplistic concept of a world of good versus evil that appeared intent on destroying itself. But his efforts to achieve world peace came in his later presidential years. He had been reelected in 1956 because the voters believed his leadership was necessary in the Cold War crises, and he was at that time still a willing cold warrior.

SUEZ AND HUNGARY

Trouble erupted in the Mideast just at the end of the 1956 campaign. This came, in part, because of Dulles's "pactomania." NATO had the Communists flanked in Europe and the nebulous SEATO supposedly hemmed them in (at least on paper) in the Far East. This left a 3,000 mile gap between Pakistan and Turkey that worried Dulles, who liked to create these parchment barriers. Yet he had to move carefully in the Middle East, for here was the diplomatic tightrope of Arab versus Jew. Dulles was relieved when Iraq signed an agreement in Bagdad with Turkey in early 1955 and invited others to join. In a short time, to Dulles's great pleasure, Pakistan, England, and France joined the Bagdad Pact. The United States did not join so as not to anger Egypt and Syria, Iraq's traditional enemies.

The Bagdad Pact, though, had unforeseen repercussions, for the Soviet Union now increased its interest in the Middle East. Also, Gamal Abdel Nasser, who became president of Egypt following the overthrow of King Farouk in 1952, was seeking to become the leader of the Arab world. He viewed the Bagdad Pact as a threat to his leadership. At this time he was seriously threatened by Israel. On February 28, 1955, on orders from Defense Minister David Ben Gurion, Israeli paratroopers attacked Egypt in the Gaza Strip, touching off an Arab-Israeli conflict that dates back to Genesis and has yet to be resolved.[2] Alarmed by Israel's large arsenal of French-supplied arms, Nasser sought protection by trying to buy armaments in the United States. When the United States equivocated over such a sale, he turned to Russia. The Soviet Union was agreeable and, partly as a cover, brought Czechoslovakia into the deal. In late 1955 Nasser announced an agreement to exchange Egyptian cotton for Czech armaments. He now had arms for fedayeen raids—guerrilla warfare—against the Israelis in the Gaza Strip.

Meanwhile, Nasser was trying to finance his great dream, construction of the Aswan Dam. To be located eight hundred miles upstream from Cairo, this would be the world's largest earthen dam; it would bring some two million acres of land under irrigation and provide electric power for industry. In December 1955 the United States offered to help finance the dam, but the implementation

of this offer was frustrated by American domestic politics.
As Khrushchev had suggested cooling off the Middle East
by a U.N.-imposed arms embargo, Nasser turned further
east for insurance. In May 1956 he recognized the People's Republic of China and sold surplus cotton to the Chinese. To many Americans, especially southerners who
failed to understand why they should help Nasser grow
more cotton with his High Dam (thus offering both competition in the world cotton market and support for a
deadly enemy), this was the last straw. Support for assist-
ing Egypt rapidly dissipated. The climax came when
rumors began circulating of a Russian offer to build the
Aswan Dam. In July 1956 the United States abruptly
cancelled its offer of aid. Eisenhower approved the can-
cellation, although he later admitted Dulles did it in an
"undiplomatic" manner.[3] Nasser's response to this was
the announcement that he was going to nationalize the
Suez Canal. The owners—the British government owned
about 45 percent of the stock and French citizens about 50
percent—would be reimbursed, and he would use the $25
million in annual tolls to pay for the dam.

The French, and especially the British, were conster-
nated. They did not believe Nasser would keep his promise to leave the canal open to all countries for he had
already closed it to Israel. In addition, they believed the
Egyptians were technically unable to operate the canal.
To the British, the Suez Canal was a lifeline to India and
to the oil of the Middle East. To Eisenhower, the situation
was critical, for without this Arab oil the NATO allies
would be prostrate. Prime Minister Eden and his French
allies were ready to force Nasser to give up the canal,
while Eisenhower urged them not to use coercion, except
as a last resort.[4] They could not believe that when the test
came, Eisenhower's personal abhorrence of war would
outweigh his hatred of communism. Dulles and Eisenhower spent that busy summer trying to find a peaceful
solution to the Mideast crisis, while Nixon carried the
brunt of the political campaigning.

At the same time Eastern Europe was in turmoil. Khrushchev had consolidated his position in the Soviet Union, and he used the occasion of the Twentieth Party Congress in February 1956 to denounce Stalin for his crimes and cruelty. He further announced that Stalin had been in error for insisting that there was only one route to communism. This "de-Stalinization" swept swiftly through the satellite nations. That summer there were bread riots in Poznan, Poland, and an industrial strike that brought into power Wladyslav Gomulka, who had once been jailed in a Stalin purge. Clashes between Polish and Soviet troops followed. Then Khrushchev unexpectedly backed down and withdrew his forces. Gomulka's Poland, though still dominated by Moscow, soon became the most independent satellite in East Europe, following the Tito line of communism. The Polish success served as an example to restless Hungarians.

The Hungarian communist regime was the most repressive of the satellite countries; the people were restive, and they were frequently reminded of Republican promises of liberation by Radio Free Europe. On October 23, three days after Soviet troops left Poland, a revolt broke out in Budapest. It soon got out of hand and Imre Nagy was installed in power. Nagy's predecessor had summoned Soviet troops and clashes soon occurred between the soldiers and the rioters. Then the USSR decided to negotiate as had been done with Poland. On October 30, Moscow announced that the troops would be removed. Flushed with this success, the Hungarian "freedom fighters" then went too far, particularly as the CIA-financed Radio Free Europe continued to exhort them to take further steps. What started out as a Titoist movement now became an effort for complete independence. The Hungarians informed the Soviets that they were withdrawing from the Warsaw Pact and, urged on by Radio Free Europe, the revolution spread even against Nagy. The Soviet Union could not allow this to happen and began pouring troops and tanks into Hungary on

October 31, crushing the rebellion in one week. As Eisenhower noted, Hungary was inaccessible to the United States by land or by sea and to send help would undoubtedly turn the Cold War into a hot one. The right-wing rhetoric of liberation by force was exposed for the sham it was.[5] In any case, the United States was far more concerned at this point over the Middle East, for the crisis there was rapidly getting out of hand.

Dulles had tried to ease the Suez situation by having the United Nations sponsor a Suez Canal Users Association, but the Soviet Union vetoed this in the Security Council. Israel and France, with the blessing of Great Britain, made plans to take care of Egypt without American help. United States Ambassador to France Douglas Dillon reported in mid-October that he had been unofficially told of British-French-Israeli plans for war against Egypt to be implemented immediately after the elections in the United States. American high-flying U-2 reconnaissance planes noted a military buildup on Cyprus and in Israel. The conspirators decided to accelerate their plans and strike before the American presidential election on the grounds that, presented with an accomplished fact, Eisenhower would not jeopardize his chances for reelection by intervening. In the period before they acted, Eisenhower cabled Ben Gurion repeatedly, pleading with him not to use force. But on October 24, with French air assistance, Israeli paratroopers dropped into the Sinai peninsula forty miles east of the Suez Canal.

Fearing a widening of the war and disgusted with his closest allies for not informing him fully of their plans, Eisenhower was both angry and apprehensive. He appeared on television before the American people on October 31, saying, "there can be no peace without law. And there can be no law—if we were to invoke one code of international conduct for those who oppose us—and another for our friends."[6] His friends, France and Britain, had just sent Nasser an ultimatium—he must withdraw his forces from the Suez Canal and permit them to occupy it; also, both sides must cease firing. When Nasser rejected this, Britain and France launched an air attack against Cairo while Israeli forces moved rapidly across Sinai, capturing many prisoners and much equipment. Nasser sank ships in the canal to block it and, in sympathy, other Arab nations cut pipelines and took other steps to keep oil from reaching France and Britain.

United States Ambassador to the U.N. Henry Cabot Lodge introduced a resolution in the Security Council for a cease-fire and withdrawal of all forces. Britain and France vetoed this, Britain using a veto for the first time in the Security Council, so Dulles introduced the motion in the General Assembly. The vote there was sixty-four to five against the attackers, with only New Zealand and Australia supporting them. The next day Dulles entered Walter Reed Hospital for major abdominal surgery. The Soviet Union, correctly believing that the United States would not interfere in the Hungarian situation, proposed to the United States that the two superpowers jointly intercede in the Middle East—an offer that was icily rejected by the administration with a warning that the Soviets had better not intervene unilaterally. The Soviet Union then issued an ultimatum to France and England—cease firing and withdraw or face bombardment with rockets. After Eisenhower made numerous phone calls to 10 Downing Street and pressure grew on the pound sterling, Great Britain and her allies reluctantly accepted a cease-fire and pullback on November 5; the next day Americans voted for their president. Thus ended the most serious crisis since the Korean War.

Several lessons were learned by all concerned in the Suez crisis and the Hungarian uprising. The British and French discovered that they were second-rate powers and could not operate successfully on their own; the Russians learned how powerful nationalism was in their satellites; American politicians stopped insisting on liberation by force; the Israelis learned they were on their own in their struggle with the Arabs, following French and British decline in the Middle East; and Nasser now looked increasingly to Russia for help, for he erroneously believed it was the Soviet Union that had saved him rather than United States action in the U.N.[7] Finally, the dark-skinned peoples of the world, the former colonies, believed the Suez intervention was far worse than the blood-letting in Hungary.

The Suez crisis ended British and French dominance in the Middle East; it also increased Soviet interest in the area. Something had to be done quickly to fill this political void. On New Year's Day 1957, less than two months after the canal crisis, Eisenhower met with the congressional leaders of both parties. "The existing vacuum in the Middle East," he warned them, "must be filled by the United States before it is filled by Russia." Then on January 5, he addressed Congress, asking for authority to assist Middle East countries to maintain their independence. He wanted specific power to use American armed forces in the area to help any nation that requested such aid "against overt armed aggression from any country controlled by international communism."[8]

The Democratic-controlled Congress was reluctant to take such an unprecedented step, which would give the president a blanket authority that could lead to war without congressional consent. In addition, others argued, the Soviet Union did not usually move overtly, preferring to achieve its goals through infiltration. The House rather quickly passed the resolution, though, on January 30, by voting 355 to 61. An attempt in the Senate to eliminate funds for economic and military assistance was beaten back and the Upper House approved the measure 72 to 19. The president signed the resolution that became known as the Eisenhower Doctrine on March 9. Three weeks later the first convoy of ships went through the Suez Canal since its blocking during the 1956 invasion.

The Mideast crisis was temporarily over. The United States was now the protector of the world's greatest known reservoir of oil. Yet, the problem of Israel remained.

The Eisenhower Doctrine was soon put to tests. The president wined and dined King Saud of Saudi Arabia and won him over, When, in April 1957, pro-Nasser military officers tried to remove King Hussein of Jordan, Eisenhower moved the Sixth Fleet to the eastern Mediterranean area and sent Hussein some $20 million in military hardware. Now Saudi Arabia, Turkey, Lebanon, Jordan, and Iraq were firmly in the camp of the West. Syria was in Nasser's orbit, and early in 1958 Syria and Yemen joined Egypt to form the United Arab Republic. Stability in the area was endangered in July 1957 when King Faisal of Iraq was assassinated and a pro-Nasser government was established under General Abdul Karim Kassim. The Iraqis soon put pressure on neighboring Jordan and Lebanon.

The Lebanese population was rather evenly divided between Moslems and Maronite Catholics. President Camille Chamoun maintained an uneasy truce between the two, a balance that shifted in April 1958 when Chamoun announced he wanted to amend the constitution to permit himself an unprecedented third term as president. The Moslems began to rebel, and Dulles and Eisenhower were convinced that the Communists were behind this nationalistic ferment. The day after the coup in Iraq, Chamoun of Lebanon and Hussein of Jordan appealed to the United States for help. Eisenhower promptly sent thirty-five hundred marines to Lebanon, and two days later Prime Minister Harold Macmillan notified Hussein he was sending British paratroopers to Jordan.

Once Eisenhower decided to commit troops to Lebanon, he went all the way. The initial movement of marines to the area was quickly augmented by some eleven thousand American soldiers, shipped from their posts in West

Germany. The Joint Chiefs of Staff wanted to occupy all of Lebanon.[9] President Eisenhower, though, decided to occupy only the airfield and the capital. If the Lebanese army could not subdue the rebels with this help, he reasoned, the United States was backing the wrong government and should pull out.[10] This major display of force was sufficient. The rebellion was put down and the troops were withdrawn three months later, in October 1958. The Eisenhower Doctrine survived its first real test. In 1959 the Bagdad Pact was replaced by the Central Treaty Organization (CENTO), signed by Turkey, Iran, Pakistan, Great Britain, and the United States. CENTO had its headquarters in Ankara and was designed to fill the gap between NATO and SEATO.

By this time, North Africa was assuming increasing importance to the United States. In 1956, France finally gave Morocco and Tunisia their independence. Both of these countries were vital to the United States and NATO because of the American air bases there. After the air base network in Spain was completed in 1960 and that country had become a NATO ally, the North African nations played a lesser role in the West's defense system. Between Morocco and Tunisia lay Algiers, a country that France was exceedingly reluctant to grant independence, for it had belonged to France since 1830. Finally, in 1954, a Moslem rebellion broke out against French rule. The civil war became increasingly bitter and hurt France badly, both in terms of heavy expenses and also because of strong feelings of anticolonialism in the Third World. The long, costly civil war did not end until 1962 when President Charles de Gaulle granted Algeria its independence.

Several countries in southern Africa were in ferment, illustrating the problems that came with granting a colonial people their independence too quickly without adequate preparation. The most serious problem here came in July 1960 when Belgium granted the Congo its independence. Black troops soon revolted against their white officers and went on a rampage of terror in Leopoldville. The Belgians rushed in paratroopers to protect their citizens, and President Joseph Kasavubu and Premier Patrice Lumumba asked the United Nations to intervene. A U.N. army composed of Africans was hastily sent in, and order was restored. But the rich province of Katanga wanted its independence from the Congo, and Moishe Tshombe, leader of the secessionists, persuaded the Belgian troops to remain there. Lumumba, backed by the Soviet Union, called on the U.N. to halt the attempted secession and to force the Belgians out of the province. A resolution from the Security Council ordered the Belgians out and U.N. troops into Katanga, but postponed the decision on its independence.

Meanwhile Lumumba had begun moving farther to the left, and on September 5, 1960, Kasavubu ousted him from office. Backed by Soviet interest, however, he refused to step aside, and a week later the army chief of staff, Joseph Mobuto, suddenly seized power. Mobuto supported Kasavubu's demands that the Communists go home. Finally, in December 1960, Lumumba was arrested; in January he was flown to Katanga and given over to Tshombe, who is believed to have ordered him murdered.[11] The new Congolese premier, Cyrille Adoula, was able to maintain order although he was unable to unify the country, and Katanga seceded. The Congo situation also indirectly caused the death of U.N. Secretary General Dag Hammerskjold in September 1961 when his plane crashed in northern Rhodesia while on a peacekeeping flight to the area.

It was also becoming increasingly obvious by this time that the United States had been seriously neglecting its Latin American neighbors. Many of these countries, in the grip of dictatorships, were suffering from abject poverty and exploitation of the masses by the landholders; they had the highest birth rates in the world and were ripe for communist penetration. Political ferment was everywhere. In 1955 Argentinians voted Juan Peron out of office; in 1957 the dictator Gustavo Rojas was overthrown in Colombia; in 1957 Venezuelans ousted their dictator Perez Jiminez and replaced him with an ex-Communist, Romulo Betancourt. The United States viewed many of these uprisings, if not as communist inspired, at least as situations that needed to be watched for potential communist penetration, as in Guatemala in 1954. Latin Americans, on the other hand, saw American mutual security funds going everywhere in the free world with only an occasional dribble coming to South America, and at the same time they resented the Yankee interference in their internal affairs.

Because of the unrest, Eisenhower decided to send Vice President Nixon on a goodwill tour of Latin America in 1958. Nixon quickly discovered how widespread was the resentment against the United States. A mob in Lima, Peru, booed, stoned, and even spat upon the vice president and his wife. A huge anti-American demonstration was staged upon his arrival in Bogota, Colombia. From there Nixon went to Caracas, Venezuela, where a mob smashed the car in which the Nixons were riding and threatened to drag them from it. That same day the United States was being blamed for French troubles in Algeria, Burmese mobs were demonstrating against the United States, and there was rioting in Lebanon prior to American troops landing there. "Maybe I should be digging out my uniforms," Eisenhower told Mamie that evening, "to see if they still fit." The president ordered troops in Gantanamo Bay in Cuba and Puerto Rico to be alerted, ready to move in and rescue the Nixons if necessary.[12] On his return, Nixon recommended that Latin America receive much more attention and economic assistance.

In the last two years of Eisenhower's administration, $2 billion in foreign aid went to Latin America. Through American influence, the World Bank and the Export-

Import Bank increased their loans to these countries. The results of these efforts were indicated when Eisenhower, in February 1960, made a goodwill trip to South America and was warmly received everywhere. Then in September 1960 the Act of Bogota was signed by the United States and all the Latin American nations except Cuba; the act pledged a cooperative movement to improve Latin American economic, health, and education facilities and to achieve land reform. To assist in this, the Inter-American Development Bank was established with the United States contributing the bulk of its assets. Eisenhower's "good partnership" policy in Latin America enjoyed success everywhere except in Cuba.

Cubans had suffered since 1953 under the iron dictatorship of Fulgencio Batista, who, by strong-arm tactics and corrupt government practices, had managed to alienate almost all his countrymen. The wealthy commercial classes were angered when he ruined the Cuban economy by looting some $200 million in government funds and depositing the money in Swiss banks; the peasants were disillusioned by his failure to bring about land reform. A few hundred guerrillas, led by a group of visionaries under Fidel Castro, the son of a wealthy planter and a graduate of Havana Law School, began making successful raids from the Sierra Maestra mountains. Castro and his followers continued to gain support from the populace, and, finally, the Cuban army turned against Batista. The dictator fled to the Dominican Republic, and in January 1959 Castro and his supporters made a triumphal entry into Havana.

As early as November 1958, the U.S. ambassador to Cuba had informed the state department that the Castro movement was infiltrated and controlled by Communists. This was not true. Castro was not a Communist, although his brother Raul and Che Guevara, two leading figures in the revolution, were Marxists. But some Communists did receive important government posts.[13]

Americans, and particularly the press, early welcomed

the revolution for they were certain Castro would establish constitutional government and institute land reform as he was promising. Castro visited the United States in April 1959, where he received a tremendous welcome, promising he would hold elections in four years. But he and the United States were soon on a collision course. As he began to socialize the Cuban economy, to break up the huge plantations, and to expropriate property, more and more upper- and middle-class Cubans began fleeing to Florida. These refugees insisted that Castro was communizing Cuba and he would soon export his communist revolution to other Latin American countries. Already predisposed to thinking of this as a Kremlin-inspired movement, many Washington officials found these developments to be intolerable, and as a result, relations between the two countries rapidly deteriorated.

The question of Cuban sugar exports became crucial (sugar accounted for about 80 percent of Cuban exports and 30 percent of the national income). By American law the United States had to buy half the Cuban crop at premium prices. Castro wanted to increase exports to the United States but the Eisenhower administration remained adamant on this, believing economic leverage would force Castro to become more conciliatory. Instead, he began searching for other markets and soon found one in Russia. Khrushchev, anxious for a foothold in the western hemisphere, pronounced the Monroe Doctrine to be dead and welcomed Castro as a new Latin American force. In February 1960 the USSR and Cuba signed a trade agreement exchanging Cuban sugar for oil and machinery.[14] The following month President Eisenhower authorized the CIA to begin training Cuban refugees in Guatemala for an invasion. The fruits of this undertaking would be realized by Eisenhower's successor in the Bay of Pigs episode.

With assurance of Soviet aid, Castro became more bold. In July 1960 he seized several American oil refineries because they refused to refine Russian oil. This provocation was too much, and the administration asked Congress for authority to adjust the Cuban sugar quota. Congress responded affirmatively. Although experts warned that this would merely drive Castro closer to the Soviets, the president cut the quota by 700,000 tons, a severe blow to the Cuban economy. Castro responded to this by seizing more property. When Khrushchev promised Castro Soviet missiles to prevent any American invasion of Cuba, Eisenhower warned the Kremlin not to meddle in the western hemisphere.[15] In October the United States announced a ban on all exports to Cuba except for food and medicine—the most severe blockade Americans had imposed on any country except mainland China. Castro seized more American property. On January 2, 1961, Castro decided that the U.S. embassy in Havana was overstaffed and ordered all but eleven persons home. Eisenhower immediately severed all diplomatic relations with Cuba. It was then up to his successor to seek a liberal alternative to Castro.

MORE PERSONAL DIPLOMACY

The volatile Quemoy-Matsu crisis erupted once more in 1958. Chiang steadily reinforced his outposts and the Chinese Communists responded to this provocation by increased shelling of the islands in September. Alarmists were certain this was preparatory to a communist Chinese invasion. Dulles, in Eisenhower's name, protested the shelling and warned against any invasion attempts. The British allies were unresponsive to this crisis, though, and the American people appeared reluctant to get tough in the situation. Eisenhower exhorted the nation via radio and TV. Comparing the situation to another Munich, he promised there would be no appeasement in this case. But as the White House mail continued strongly against intervention, it was decided instead to attempt to ease the tension. The president promised the British he would not use tactical atomic weapons for deterrence, and Dulles told reporters he thought Chiang's deployment of troops to be "rather foolish." The American military were satisfied, for the crisis presented the opportunity to test the Sidewinder, a new air-to-air missile, and it had performed well. The tests were made preparatory to using it in the Formosan Straits. Fortunately, the mainland Chinese were content with the results of their warning. The shelling ceased, but the issue would arise again in the campaign of 1960.[16]

Berlin, which had been quiet as a cold war problem since the suppression of the East Berlin uprising in 1953, was again becoming a thorn in East-West relations. Divided Berlin was a problem for Khrushchev, for some 300,000 East Berliners—mostly young, educated, professional people—annually defected to West Berlin. Also, West Berlin had the "largest combination of espionage agencies ever assembled as well as radio stations constantly broadcasting propaganda into the satellite nations." At the same time, West Berlin was becoming a Western showcase in West Germany's spectacular economic rehabilitation.[17] In November 1958 Khrushchev suddenly announced that East Germany would be given control of access rights to West Berlin unless the West evacuated and made Berlin a free city; he set a deadline of six months. This was viewed as a crude attempt to force the West to recognize the German Democratic Republic (East Germany), and Eisenhower responded that the West would never abandon Berlin.

By early January 1959 the administration concluded that Moscow was sincere in its determination to turn access rights over to East Germany. Plans were made to use force if Allied convoys were halted on their way to Berlin. The basic question concerned the number of troops to be used. The Joint Chiefs of Staff wanted to utilize a complete division, but Dulles objected, believing world opinion would repudiate such a sizeable force.

Eisenhower agreed with the secretary of state on the grounds that one division was too small to fight its way into Berlin but too large to be called a "show of force" to indicate Western determination. The following tactics were finally decided upon: withdrawal of any halted convoys; evacuation of dependents from West Berlin; presentation of the issue to the United Naions; and the undertaking of large-scale military preparations.[18]

Neither Paris nor London were as concerned over access rights control by East Germany as were the United States and West Germany. Macmillan decided to go to Moscow and talk sense to Khrushchev. The Soviet premier was conciliatory, assuring the British prime minister that the May 27 deadline on Berlin was certainly not an absolute ultimatum. Macmillan found that Khrushchev wanted another summit conference and that this accounted for much of his belligerency. To get this, Khrushchev agreed to hold a conference of foreign ministers in Geneva to discuss the Berlin problem. At this conference, the Western ministers tried to persuade Soviet Foreign Minister Andrei Gromyko to unify Germany and to ratify an all-Europe security treaty. Gromyko continued to insist that the Berlin issue was a separate and distinct one, but the fact that the conference was held at all meant that Khrushchev was allowing his six-month deadline to pass without direct action. Meanwhile, Macmillan came to Washington to persuade Eisenhower of the necessity of a summit conference.

Eisenhower did not want another hollow "spirit of Geneva." Again, he insisted that the Communists demonstrate their good intentions by concrete actions, not promises. The best way of showing this, he said, was to permit successful negotiations at the foreign ministers conference going on at Geneva. In July 1959 Khrushchev told a visiting delegation of American state governors that discussions between himself and the American president would be helpful to world peace. President Eisenhower was noncommital about this overture. Then, Trol

Krozlov, the Soviet first deputy premier, came to New York City to open the Soviet trade exhibit followed by a tour around the country to inspect American industries. Vice President Nixon was scheduled to go to the Soviet Union for a similar mission. Just before Nixon arrived in Moscow on July 23, the president signed a routine congressional resolution proclaiming the annual Captive Nations Week, and Khrushchev was furious. In this belligerent mood, Khrushchev and Nixon had several arguments, the bitterest one taking place in the kitchen of the model home display of the American exhibit. Khrushchev ridiculed the idea that the average worker in the United States could have such a home and Nixon, never one to back down before strong words from a Communist, took the offensive, shouting and shaking his finger at the Soviet premier. While his words were not recorded, pictures were taken and Nixon's political stock rose rapidly when Americans saw him standing up to Khrushchev.[19]

Despite this exchange, Khrushchev continued to hint that he would enjoy visiting the United States, and Eisenhower finally acceded. He had Undersecretary of State Robert Murphy issue an invitation to the Soviet premier to visit the United States, provided the foreign ministers at Geneva could make sufficient progress to justify a meeting of the heads of state. Murphy misunderstood his instructions, though, and failed to pass along the proviso. Eisenhower was dumbfounded when Khrushchev immediately and happily accepted his invitation and reciprocated by inviting the president to visit the Soviet Union. It was the president's own fault that he was stuck with an unwelcome guest (a "most unpleasant experience," he called it), without having achieved anything of substance in the Geneva talks.

De Gaulle and West German Chancellor Konrad Adenauer were disturbed over the impending exchange of visits—Khrushchev's U.S. tour in late 1959 and Eisenhower's trip to the Soviet Union in late 1960. So the president traveled to London, Bonn, and Paris to reassure his allies he would not give away the free world to Moscow. Then he took a brief vacation at Culzean Castle (which Scotland had given him for life) and hurried home to prepare for Khrushchev's visit.

Not all segments of the American public were pleased with the premier's impending trip. Conservative congressmen were aghast at this display of friendliness toward a Soviet leader, unmatched since the war days of 1945. The bishop of Philadelphia said a mass and sent the president a telegram deploring the coming occasion. Eisenhower felt impelled to make a personal call to Francis Cardinal Spellman, explaining the difficult situation in which he found himself.

Three days before the Soviet premier arrived in the United States, the USSR successfully launched a rocket to the moon, a noteworthy feat, but the president did not miss the timing of it. Khrushchev presented him with a model of the rocket and they had a brief, private conversation before admitting reporters. President Eisenhower used the occasion to try to persuade the Soviet premier that he could go down in history as a great leader if he would use his power and position to promote peace. Khrushchev seemed impressed with Eisenhower's sincerity. Following the meeting with the press, they went for a helicopter ride over the city of Washington, followed by a state dinner that evening.[20]

Khushchev and his entourage took a ten-day tour of the country. Eisenhower assigned Henry Cabot Lodge, instead of Richard Nixon, to accompany him, a choice that was not lost on some people, for Lodge got a good deal of publicity in the next few days. At Hollywood, the party visited the movie set of the musical *Can Can* where Khrushchev was scandalized by the "indecent" dancing and costumes of the female cast members. He was further shocked by Mayor Norris Poulson at a dinner in Los Angeles. Seemingly determined to prove he was more anticommunist than other mayors, Poulson grandly threw Khrushchev's boast, "we shall bury you," back at him, declaring that, if challenged, Americans would fight to the death. The Soviet premier, quite affronted, replied that he had referred to the inevitabilities of history and not to military capabilities and then suggested he might cut short his visit. The mayor rather bluntly explained to the president later that Khrushchev "wanted to know about the people and the country and I told him."[21] Khrushchev was more politely received in his tour of the farming areas of Iowa, though, and by the time he reached Camp David, he was ready to talk.

At Camp David the two leaders agreed to increase cultural exchanges, and Khrushchev cancelled deadlines on Berlin while Eisenhower acceded to a summit conference. This agreement to attempt to coexist peacefully was welcomed by almost everyone and the "spirit of Camp David" promised a new era. But the summit conference, to be held in Paris, was postponed until May 1960 at the insistence of de Gaulle, who wanted France to be a nuclear power before the talks began. To increase their prestige for the conference, Khrushchev toured India and Indonesia and Eisenhower visited the Middle East and India where an estimated one and a half million Indians welcomed him to New Delhi.

The basic problem hovering over the impending summit was that both Khrushchev and Eisenhower had gone too far towards peaceful coexistence to please the cold warriors in their own countries. The Democrats were shouting about the "missile gap" and demanding more armaments, while conservative Republicans wanted more talk about liberation. Khrushchev had hardliners pushing him in Moscow. Also, Mao was presenting Khrushchev with much the same trouble that Chiang was bestowing on the United States, because the Kremlin would not support the Chinese demand for wars of national liberation—a basic factor in the growing Sino-

Soviet split.[22] Both Khrushchev and Eisenhower were saved from the headaches of summitry by the U-2 incident.

The U-2 was, in effect, a motorized glider; it had a thin shell, no armaments, and was designed to fly at altitudes of eighty thousand feet. This last characteristic put it out of the range both of Soviet aircraft and antiaircraft missiles, and it was used for reconnaissance purposes. The planes, if hit, would crash and from that altitude it was believed they would be destroyed along with their camera equipment. The pilots were given cyanide capsules to take in the unlikely event they survived the crash and were captured, but they knew the risks, and the CIA paid them the then handsome salary of $30,000 per year.

Beginning in 1956, after Khrushchev's boast that "we shall bury you," regular flights over the Soviet Union were undertaken by these planes, equipped with the most sensitive electronic surveillance equipment available. Khrushchev knew of these flights but could do nothing, for if he called attention to them he would be admitting to his people that he was powerless to prevent American planes from penetrating Soviet air space. On the other hand, the excellent photographs taken of Soviet military installations on these flights gave Eisenhower proof that the United States was ahead of the Soviet Union in missile development and military capabilities. Thus he kept his counsel while Democratic politicians, hopefully eyeing the White House, loudly complained about loss of American prestige and Russian military superiority and missile gaps.

In order to avoid embarrassing incidents, the U-2 flights were suspended during Khrushchev's visit to the United States and then were resumed until the Samos spy satellite could be ready for operation. By May 1960 the Samos had made the U-2 flights obsolete, but for some unexplained reason, it was decided to make one more U-2 flight just prior to the Paris conference. This was done without the president's approval. The result was a disaster made worse by the manner in which the Eisenhower administration bungled the aftermath.

On May Day 1960, Francis Gary Powers took off in his U-2 from Pakistan on a seventeen hundred mile flight over Soviet territory, planning to land in Norway. As he neared Sverdlovsk, where a previous flight had taken some good pictures indicating a possible ICBM base, a rocket exploded, causing his plane to crash. Powers bailed out, landed safely, and was taken prisoner immediately. When he failed to land in Norway as scheduled, NASA released a cover story on May 3 that it had a weatherplane missing. Then, on May 5, Khrushchev undermined the veracity of this story when he announced that an American plane had violated Soviet air space. The next day the State Department assured reporters that the United States had never, never deliberately violated Soviet air space, which was exactly what the Soviet premier wanted to hear.

On May 7, Khrushchev revealed to the Supreme Soviet that the plane and equipment had been recovered and the pilot captured alive. He then displayed blown-up pictures he claimed came from the captured camera that showed Soviet air bases and missile sites. He expressed the hope that the American president was being tricked by his military officers and knew nothing of these flights. Then the state department pulled a real boner. An announcement was made justifying the U-2 flights for security reasons, but insisting that Washington had not authorized this particular one. The president had second thoughts about this statement, though, for it now appeared as if he did not have control of his government. Thus, on May 9 Christian Herter released another announcement in which Eisenhower assumed full responsibility for the U-2 flights and implied that they would continue in the future.[23] The United States had gotten caught in espionage, lied about it, and then compounded the error by reversing policy statements. Khrushchev, in turn, was in trouble with the central committee of the Communist party and "to regain support, perhaps even to survive," he was forced to scuttle the summit conference he had worked so hard to get.[24] The Paris meeting was due to open on May 16.

President Eisenhower arrived in Paris on May 15 to confer with his allies prior to the talks. The next day Secretary of Defense Thomas Gates compounded the tense situation by ordering a worldwide alert of American forces, which was cancelled some ten hours later after the damage was done. Khrushchev boycotted the first day's meeting. On the second day, de Gaulle recognized Eisenhower to speak, and at that point Khrushchev demanded the floor. He delivered a long harangue against the violation of Soviet air space by the United States and ended up cancelling the invitation for Eisenhower to visit the USSR later that year. The Soviet premier insisted he would not attend another summit for six or eight months, that is, until after a change in American presidents. Eisenhower endured this abuse in silence, admitting that, for the first time since he quit smoking, he wanted a cigarette "just to give myself something to do."[25] Then he quietly answered that if he were unwelcome in the Soviet Union, a simple statement to that effect would suffice. He refused to apologize for the U-2 flights, but he did announce that they would not be resumed. This ended the conference and any hopes for a solution to the Berlin problem or the easing of the Cold War.

Eisenhower then decided to take a goodwill tour of the Far East, including a three-day visit to Japan, to refurbish his image as a world leader seeking peace. While he was visiting Manila and Formosa, communist-led students in Tokyo rioted, attacking the car in which advance man Jim Hagerty was riding. The demonstrations got out of hand, and the Japanese prime minister was forced to cancel the visit because he could not guarantee the president's safety.

In September 1960 Khrushchev made an extended

visit to the United Nations. For security reasons, he was confined to Manhattan Island. The Soviet premier addressed the U.N. delegates with a fiery attack on the United States, describing the country as "a disgrace to civilization." When Harold Macmillan rose to reply to this attack, Khrushchev heckled him. The Soviet leader shocked the world when he removed his shoe and began pounding his desk during a speech by a Filipino delegate. All in all, he had an interesting twenty-five day stay. The Third World was also scandalized by his use of the United Nations for such blatant political purposes.[26] His visit coincided with the U.S. presidential race that was beginning to heat up at that time.

The Last Campaign

Few people disputed the probability that Dwight D. Eisenhower could have been reelected president in 1960 and, indeed, could have had the presidency for as long as he lived. But the Twenty-Second Amendment prevented this. That amendment had been sponsored by Republicans as soon as they had captured control of Congress in 1946. Directed at the deceased Franklin Roosevelt, it prohibited any person from being elected for more than two terms, or for more than one full term if the person had completed over two years of another president's term. It was ratified in 1951 and the Republicans were immediately sorry, for they had found an unbeatable candidate. But, in 1960, Eisenhower could select a successor who he believed would continue his policies.

Nelson Rockefeller gained a great deal of influence in the Republican party with his impressive victory in New York in 1958. He immediately put this prestige, and his immense wealth, to work to secure the presidential nomination. Hiring a large staff of aides and researchers, he began speaking out on a number of issues, trying to present himself as the candidate of the liberal wing of the party. But Richard Nixon had many political IOUs to call in and his kitchen debate with Khrushchev had increased his prestige a great deal. Also, by 1960, he had moved closer to the middle, thereby gaining the support of the center of the Republican party, in addition to his old right-wing support. So, at the convention, the Californian won the nomination without dispute. For balance on the ticket, he chose Henry Cabot Lodge of Massachusetts as his running mate.

Nixon made a serious mistake in constructing the party platform that year. The platform had originally been outlined by Charles Percy, a rising young politician from Illinois. Its philosophy conflicted with Rockefeller's, for it was naturally laudatory toward the Eisenhower administration, which was basically conservative; this conflicted with Rockefeller, who sided with the alarmists who thought the nation was in peril. Knowing he needed the support of the liberal elements of the party in order to win, Nixon flew to New York City to confer with the governor. Rockefeller forced him to accept his far more liberal ideas in return for his important support.

A party does not successfully criticize the accomplishments of its incumbent president, particularly if that man is one of the most popular in history. Conservatives were affronted at this "Treaty of Fifth Avenue," as they labelled it, and so were the numerous Eisenhower supporters. At the convention, the platform that Percy had outlined was redrafted so that the final document was a combination of his proposals, modified by the more liberal positions of Rockefeller. Basically it satisfied no one. What mattered was that Eisenhower was outraged. He was particularly incensed at the plank calling for increased defense appropriations, which was practically a repudiation of his eight years of leadership.[27] The president used his invitation to address the convention to defend his defense policies and his supporters were not completely placated when Nixon informed the delegates in his acceptance speech that America was the strongest nation in the world, militarily, economically, and ideologically.

The Democrats had a number of likely candidates and two senators, John Kennedy and Hubert Humphrey, slugged it out on the primary trail. After losing West Virginia, Humphrey sorrowfully withdrew, leaving Kennedy to face Senate Majority Leader Lyndon Johnson and the party pros at the convention. But the team of young political experts that Kennedy had brought together was unbeatable, and, as the convention voted, the results were exactly what they had predicted. Their man won easily on the first ballot. To the surprise of many, and over the objections of his brother Robert, John Kennedy asked Lyndon Johnson to take the second spot. This gave the ticket great support in the South and was to have tremendous implications in 1964 and 1968.

When the conventions were over and the candidates selected, a Gallup Poll showed 50 percent for Nixon, 44 percent for Kennedy and 6 percent undecided. Both candidates knew it was going to be a tough campaign. The Nixon strategy was really simple. The Republican candidate must project himself as the mature administrator, capable of filling the shoes of the popular incumbent and of carrying out the foreign policies of the Eisenhower Administration. Eisenhower early agreed that Nixon should take command and run his own campaign, and Nixon, too, was eager to show that he could run his own show. As one of Nixon's close advisers put it, "All we want out of Ike is for him to handle Khrushchev at the UN and not let things blow up there. That's *all*."[28] In other words, Nixon would run on Eisenhower's program, but the president must stay in the background so as not to outshine his protege.

Early in the campaign, Eisenhower hurt the image Nixon was trying so hard to project. At a press conference in August, a reporter asked him what big decisions the vice president had made that the president had accepted. No one can make a decision for the president, Eisenhower testily responded. The reporter agreed but pressed him to suggest a major idea of Nixon's that he had used. "If you give me a week, I might think of one," the president snapped. "I don't remember."[29] This delighted the Democrats, of course, and embarrassed the Republican candidate. Nixon admitted this remark hurt him for the rest of the campaign because it denigrated his principal theme—experience and maturity.

Kennedy ran under two serious handicaps. He was young, and he was the first Catholic to try seriously for the presidency since Alfred Smith in 1928. His victory in the West Virginia primary, a state that was billed (misleadingly) as 95 percent Protestant, indicated his religion should be no handicap, and Nixon carefully and correctly refrained from using it as an issue. Kennedy purposefully met the question head-on in an address to a group of Protestant ministers in Houston, in which he announced in strong terms his belief in the separation of church and state. But while Nixon wisely ignored the issue because it might backfire on him, many rank-and-file Republicans staged a whispering campaign similar to that of 1928 about the pope moving into the White House.

Nixon was less wise in attempting to juxtapose his own maturity against Kennedy's youthful image, which he hoped to accomplish by accepting Kennedy's challenge to debate. Kennedy had issued his challenge early in the campaign. Eisenhower opposed the debates because they could only help Kennedy by giving him additional exposure, but the vice president, a champion debater since high school and college days, believed he would appear to be a coward if he refused, and so he accepted.[30] The first encounter was seen by some eighty million TV viewers, an estimated seventy million of them adults. Kennedy carefully did his homework in preparation, cramming facts and rehearsing answers. Nixon, on the other hand, had just spent two weeks in the hospital with a bad knee and had tried to make up for the loss of time by extra campaigning. Thus he came to the debate tired and with no time to prepare. In addition, he had a heavy beard that no amount of makeup could cover under the bright TV lights. Kennedy, on the other hand, was most handsome and photogenic. He appeared quite at ease, in control of himself, and sure of his responses. By contrast, Nixon, tired and haggard-looking, seemed uncertain and unsure of himself. So while neither candidate "won" the debate, Nixon lost it. He turned in a bad performance while Kennedy, who needed the exposure, appeared cool, capable, and mature—the image Nixon was supposed to project.[31]

It was generally agreed that the two debaters broke even in the remaining three debates, but as meaningful ways of exploring the candidates' positions on issues, the debates were ridiculous. Issues could not be covered adequately in the time allotted, and the performances certainly did not enlighten the electorate in the manner intended. In the third debate, Kennedy raised the question of Quemoy and Matsu, insisting that the United States should not go to war to defend them for they historically belonged to the mainland. Nixon argued that not an inch of soil should be yielded to communism. The issue could have become a serious one. Eisenhower was disturbed that this delicate, inflammatory problem had been inserted into the campaign, and he discussed it with Nixon. An announcement was made that the president and vice president were in agreement on policy; the United States would fight for Quemoy and Matsu only in the sense of defending Formosa, not for the sake of the islands themselves. Kennedy said he agreed with this and the issue then dropped out of the campaign.[32]

Kennedy's basic theme was the necessity to get the nation moving again. The economy was slumping badly, and he declared he wanted to inject new life into it, promising to accelerate economic growth. On the foreign scene, he stressed the bugaboo Democrats had hit for two years and which had worried the public since Sputnik— potential Russian military superiority. He insisted there was a serious "missile gap." From the U-2 flights, the administration knew that the United States still held military superiority over the Soviet Union, but Kennedy did not have this information and, unfortunately for the success of his campaign, Nixon could not reveal it. The Democratic candidate tried to convince the voters that the country was in crisis—both domestically and in foreign policy.

As the November election approached, the news media were forecasting a Democratic victory, and Republicans became increasingly concerned. Why was Nixon not taking advantage of the Republicans' greatest asset—Eisenhower's popularity? Kennedy realized in what esteem the public held the president and he carefully refrained from mentioning him by name. Republican policies, not Eisenhower, were at fault, he insisted. Nixon, by contrast, constantly invoked the name of his mentor while seldom mentioning Republican policies.

Eisenhower, meanwhile, was chafing at being unable to respond to Kennedy's attacks on his policies. When he finally got the green light from Nixon, he was ready to go. On October 26 he gave his first major address in Philadelphia, accusing Kennedy of demonstrating "amazing irresponsibility" by distorting the nation's image. Nixon was impressed with the response to this speech and asked the president to campaign actively in the last week. Eisenhower agreed with alacrity and hammered away at Kennedy's immaturity, drawing tremendous ovations everywhere he went. His efforts, although too late to turn the tide, gave Nixon's campaign a badly needed lift.

Despite this last minute effort, Nixon lost the race. Kennedy won the electoral college vote by 303 to 219, but he popular vote was the closest in history. Kennedy

received 34,227,096 votes (49.7 percent) to Nixon's
34,108,546 (49.6 percent), or a plurality of slightly over
100,000. A switch of 33,000 votes in Texas and Illinois
would have given the electoral college vote to the Republican. Many agreed that if Nixon had asked the president
to campaign for him earlier, he would have won the election. Eisenhower took the defeat hard. He was frustrated
by not being asked earlier to campaign. A fortnight
before the election he lamented to a Republican leader
that Nixon "just seems like a loser to me. I look at those
slumping shoulders and those drooping eyes, and I can
tell you he'd never get a promotion in any army of mine."
When Nixon called him the day after the election, he
reported he had never heard the president sound so
depressed.[33] To the president, the voters had repudiated
his policies, and it seemed that the last eight years were
wasted. One of the principal reasons for his running in
1952—reinvigoration of the Republican party—had not
been achieved.

But there were still two months to serve, and he kept
busy. There were details to wrap up, and he had to provide for an orderly transition of administrations. Kennedy came to the White House on December 6 to discuss
these arrangements. Eisenhower impressed Kennedy at
this meeting. The younger man admitted the president
was "better than I had prepared for. . . . Takes a simpli-
fied view of things, but . . . better than I had thought."[34]
Then there was the address to the nation to prepare. Like
George Washington, Eisenhower wanted to leave his
people some useful advice. On January 17, 1961, he gave
his farewell address. His theme was a warning against a
significant, if not irrepressible, phenomenon that had
emerged since World War II. It was dangerous and must
be watched. "In the councils of government," he warned,
"we must guard against the acquisition of unwarranted
influence, whether sought or unsought, by the military-
industrial complex. The potential for the disastrous rise

of misplaced power exists and will persist." What American was better qualified to issue the warning about the military-industrial complex? On January 20 the oldest president in history escorted the youngest man ever elected to that office to his inauguration. Then he left Washington for Gettysburg and retirement. At last he could play his precious game of golf without being criticized. He had become the first Republican since Grant to complete two full terms in the White House.

A SUMMING UP

Eisenhower believed, of course, that historians would evaluate his presidential achievements highly, and he was aware that historical judgments are altered "by the events that followed upon the life of the subject . . . whether or not these events were directly related to the person under scrutiny."[35] Nowhere is this observation better illustrated than the change made in evaluations of his foreign policy after the American experience in Vietnam in the 1960s. The greatest achievement of his eight years in the White House was to keep America at peace while under conditions of greater provocation than those of his three successors. "The United States never lost a soldier or a foot of ground in my administration," he later bragged, "We kept the peace. People asked how it happened—by God, it didn't just happen, I'll tell you that."[36] Part of his success here came from his experience in saying "no" to generals, something his predecessor and his successors had trouble in doing, for they were more in awe of the brass than was Eisenhower.

He was far more successful in foreign policy than in internal matters, undoubtedly, because he had no experience prior to the presidency in domestic concerns that were unrelated to the military. He responded to these problems with deeply held conservative convictions developed in turn-of-the-century Kansas and a lifetime in the army. This explains why Attorney General Brownell could get his support for a civil rights bill or Secretary Marion Folsum could get him to endorse a school construction bill, "but when the showdown came, he would 'snap back' to his former position" and refuse to pressure congressmen into supporting the administration's measures.[37]

But there were certain great successes at home. Eisenhower demonstrated that one could successfully be a fiscal conservative and a welfare liberal at the same time. He contributed much to the development of the staff system that permitted a more efficient functioning of the White House staff. Certainly the St. Lawrence Seaway and the interstate highway network would remain as monuments to his administration long after achievements of less capable presidents were forgotten. His Supreme Court appointments were excellent for the most part, outstanding in the case of the chief justice of the United States (even though he later described the choice as "the biggest damfool mistake I ever made"), and the Warren Court left an indelible mark on American history. The civil rights decisions of the 1950s and the opinions of the 1960s protecting the rights of accused people make this libertarian court one of the most important in history. Eisenhower also succeeded in getting the right wing of the Republican party to abandon isolationism and in getting conservatives to tolerate the New Deal programs—no mean achievements in themselves.

Liberals complained that the eight years of his administration were spent in standing still, during a period of crisis when progress was urgent. The joke went around and around during his presidency about the Eisenhower doll: You wind it up and it does nothing for eight years. Others complained that this was the "placid decade," forgetting the deep concern over the stridency and hysteria of McCarthyism at the start of the period. Eisenhower calmed that frenzy, and that was a significant achievement. His refusal to take on McCarthy possibly hurt America; conceivably he was correct in believing that, given enough rope, McCarthy would hang himself without presidential assistance. This happened. Was the method worth the hurt? Certainly Eisenhower failed in providing the necessary leadership in the civil rights movement. This beloved president could have done much to alleviate the stresses and strains and violence of the movement in the following decade if he had tried to change the hearts of his countrymen by persuasion and example. Yet, in fairness to him, it should be noted that Congress, the people's representatives, did even less than he to achieve integration.

Eisenhower was a reflection of his times. He was what the public wanted in the 1950s. He, like they, wanted to have his cake and eat it too. They, like he, wanted to keep America strong and increase social services while at the same time balancing the budget and cutting taxes. He and his people suffered from the delusion that the United States could accomplish the miracle of policing the world against atheistic communism while remaining untouched by the evils inherent in such an undertaking. The huge defense expenditures meant neglect of problems at home such as education, ghettos, and water and air pollution. By the end of the decade, he and many Americans were beginning to wonder about this commitment to the "Free World" and what it was doing to American society. They would find out in a few short years in the jungles of Vietnam.

The Eisenhower administration can be summed up like all previous and future ones; much was achieved and much was left undone. Issues were resolved, and solutions to other problems were postponed, only to grow worse with time. Eisenhower made spectacular achievements, both at home and in promoting peace abroad. It is lamentable that he failed to use his great popularity to achieve more in bringing equality to all Americans. But, he probably took the American people as far as they wanted to go in this direction. Like all great leaders, Eisenhower was a product of his era. Still, he left an enduring mark on his times. As a general he led the allied armies to victory over fascism, and as president he guided his nation through eight turbulent years of the cold war. For twenty years his story was, in a large sense, the history of his country.

Gettysburg at Last

On January 20, 1961, for the first time in almost forty-five years of married life, Dwight and Mamie Eisenhower went to a home they could call their own. They had built a beautiful house near Gettysburg during the White House years and had improved and stocked the farm. Now they could enjoy these fruits for which they had spent their lives working. There were many adjustments to be made after a lifetime in the public limelight. Dwight Eisenhower had to relearn to dial a telephone and drive a modern automobile, for instance, and to undertake for himself many other activities that had been done for him for twenty years. But, even in retirement there was work to be done, and he labored as hard in the final years as many men do in their prime. Usually, he was in his office by 8:15 A.M. and did not return home until 6:00 P.M.

The president of Gettysburg College generously loaned him the use of the presidential house, and Eisenhower set up an office there. His son, John, retired from the army and became his chief assistant in writing his presidential memoirs. Doubleday Publishing Company sent an editor to Gettysburg, and a researcher was employed. The editor and John provided rough drafts of episodes and chapters which Eisenhower would then revise and rewrite until they were scarcely recognizable to John.[38] In 1963 the first volume, *Mandate for Change*, covering the first administration, came off the press. The second volume,

Waging Peace, appeared two years later. These two books are quite detailed in description of events but totally lacking in reflection or philosophical background. Eisenhower comes through as an honest, sincere president who is reluctant to admit to being wrong. In addition, Eisenhower found time to write *At Ease* (subtitled, perhaps significantly, *Stories I Tell to Friends*) in 1967, stories of his boyhood and years in the military service. This is one of the most entertaining and revealing memoirs any president has ever written. In contrast to his presidential memoirs, Eisenhower is frank and open in this book, and it is pleasurable reading.

Unlike Ulysses S. Grant, Eisenhower did not have to write these books for the income of the royalties. Besides his substantial investments, he received a $25,000-a-year pension as a former president, plus $50,000 annually for expenses. Congress restored his five-star rank which entitled him and Mamie to free transportation and medical care. There were no financial worries. Golf continued to be Eisenhower's favorite relaxation, and in 1968 he realized a golfer's dream at Palm Springs—a hole-in-one. During his later years, lumbago and arthritis gradually curtailed his game until he could play no more.

Besides writing and trying to handle the importunities of callers who made all kinds of demands on him, Eisenhower was busy as head of his party. He kept tabs on the new administration and was particularly aroused by what he considered exorbitant Democratic spending. The vast and profound changes in the air in the 1960s disturbed him. When he came to Abilene to dedicate his library, he deplored the current decline in morals and the increasing vulgarity in literature, the theater, and modern art. Even the new dance, the Twist, he thought represented "some kind of change in our standards."[39]

Soon it was time to think of the election of 1964. Nixon was out of the running, for his defeat in 1960 had left both wings of his party embittered. If Nixon had listened to advice, both the left and the right argued, he would not have suffered that loss. Who could replace him? Eisenhower still favored Bob Anderson, but the Texan was not interested. In fact, Anderson supported his fellow Texan, Lyndon Johnson, in 1964. Eisenhower's only other favorites were Generals Lucius Clay and Alfred Gruenther, or his brother Milton. But they were not politically viable candidates. He considered Barry Goldwater, one of the front-runners, "nuts." "He's got everything but brains," Eisenhower complained.[40] Nelson Rockefeller, the other major candidate, had thrown cold water on his political appeal by divorcing his wife of many years and marrying another woman whose husband had named the New York governor as co-respondent in his divorce suit.

On November 21, 1963, Eisenhower traveled to New York City for a political strategy session with Clay and Brownell. The next day, tragedy struck. John Kennedy was gunned down by an assassin, and Lyndon Johnson became president. The strategy meeting never took place. Instead, Eisenhower journeyed to Washington to consult with the new president. The split in the Republican party now widened as Goldwater and his forces began the primary route, and Rockefeller staged a campaign to block him. Then, in late 1963, a new—truly new—face appeared in the picture. William Scranton, elected governor of Pennsylvania in 1962, was young and handsome and had proven himself both a vote-getter and an outstanding administrator. While on the way to winter quarters in Palm Springs, California, in December 1963, Eisenhower stopped at Harrisburg for a visit to the governor's mansion. The party chief advised Scranton to get in there and fight for the nomination. When Goldwater won the California primary and eliminated Rockefeller, the liberal wing of the party immediately began pinning its hopes on the Pennsylvania governor.

Soon after the California primary, Eisenhower again met with Scranton. The governor came out of this meeting convinced that, if he made a bid for the nomination, Eisenhower would openly endorse him, and the former president's blessing was necessary in order to stop Goldwater. The annual governors' conference met that year in Cleveland. Most of the Republicans there hoped mightily for a Scranton announcement and an Eisenhower endorsement. But Eisenhower had read the news stories of his meeting with Scranton the previous day. He called Scranton and expressed the hope that the governor had not misunderstood their conversation. Eisenhower would not be part of a "cabal" to block Goldwater. So, no announcement was made and no endorsement was issued. Brother Milton and Malcolm Moos informed Eisenhower that "in his well-meaning meddling, he had muddled."[41]

Goldwater, in accepting his party's nomination, declared that "extremism in the defense of liberty is no vice! ... Moderation in the pursuit of justice is no virtue!" This was anathema to Eisenhower, but the party's chief finally endorsed Goldwater in August and they taped a half-hour TV show in which they exchanged banalities. In November, the Republican candidate suffered the worst defeat in a presidential race to that time. At this point Eisenhower retired from politics.

Lyndon Johnson phenomenally escalated the fighting in Vietnam. In July 1967, as the nation became more and more agonizingly divided over Vietnam, Eisenhower denounced the "war of gradualism." Congress, he said, should declare war on North Vietnam. If war had been declared earlier, the nation might not be rending itself apart; now it was too late. As the protest mounted, Eisenhower publicly supported President Johnson's policies. His endorsement was "purely Eisenhoweresque" for he believed support for foreign policy should be bipartisan. More importantly, he considered the Gulf of Tonkin resolution to be a declaration of war; once a nation was at war, its full resources should be used to bring the conflict to an end as soon as possible.[42] He invited Omar Bradley to Gettysburg in November 1967 and the two old warriors taped a TV "news" program. Both agreed emphatically the war must be won. In April 1968 Eisenhower soundly denounced the war dissenters in a magazine article. The current confrontation, he said, "is rebellion, and it verges on treason."[43] But the dissent mounted, and Lyndon Johnson was forced to concede that his policy of escalation had made him too unpopular to enter the race for the presidency in 1968.

Eisenhower was completely out of the 1968 campaign, for in April of that year he suffered his fourth heart attack. In 1965, he had suffered a second heart attack that was quickly followed by a third. Knowing the next one could be his last, he began cutting back on activities and disposing of his herd of Angus cattle. The fourth attack was severe, and he was old. Each attack took that much more of his heart's reserve. He showed slow improvement until August 1968 when he had another attack. Again he improved and on October 14, his seventy-eighth birthday, he had visitors and the Army band serenaded him outside his hospital window. In late February 1969 he had to have surgery to correct complications from the old ileitis operation. On March 28, 1969, he quietly died in bed. To the end he remained alert and full of his usual ardor for life.

The army put his body in an eighty-dollar coffin, dressed in the "Eisenhower jacket" he had made so famous in World War II, and a train took him back across the country to Abilene for its final resting place. On the day he died, Dwight D. Eisenhower spoke perhaps his own best eulogy when he murmured, "I've always loved my wife, I've always loved my children. I've always loved my grandchildren. I've always loved my country." The soldier had devoted his entire life to his nation.

CHAPTER 9

Verdict
of
History

The place of Dwight D. Eisenhower in military history
is assured; he was one of the greatest of American generals. Stephen Ambrose's definitive biography of his
exploits in World War II rates him as outstanding, not
only for coordinating the Allied war effort, but also for his
military ability.[1] The studied verdict of his achievements
as president is only beginning to come in, and undoubtedly the assessment of his political ability is the point
most at issue. Here the debate will probably rage for as
long as historians study him.

William V. Shannon, in a 1958 magazine article, set
the tone of interpretation of the Eisenhower administration that was to dominate for years when he described the
period as "the time of the great postponement"—when
"Eisenhower's Fabian tactics carried through successfully [a] defensive holding action. . . ."[2] Historians and
political scientists subsequently characterized him as a
puppet president, humane and well-meaning, but manip-
ulated by slick, powerful personages behind the throne,
such as Sherman Adams and John Foster Dulles. He was
portrayed as being "above politics," as being indifferent
to and disliking politics and politicians, and as being politically naive; many described him as a modern-day

Ulysses S. Grant. Thus Clinton Rossiter in 1956 had
called him a "gifted amateur" in politics, although he
thought labelling him another Grant was "absurd."[3] In
1960, Walter Johnson asserted that "Eisenhower created
an aura of moral sanctity over his refusal to commit himself to party leadership."[4] In that some year Norman A.
Graebner noted that Eisenhower "had little taste for politics."[5] In 1964 Wilfred E. Binkley described him as "an
amateur politician."[6] In 1966 Thomas A. Bailey wrote
that Eisenhower gave the appearance of being "above the
battle" of politics but conceded that "he gradually developed into a fairly sophisticated politician" and thought
that historians ranked him too low in the presidential
polls.[7] As late as 1970, George E. Reedy insisted that he
was "uninterested" in politics.[8] In that same year John E.
Mueller noted that Eisenhower was the only post-World
War II president whose popularity did not "inexorably"
decline during a four-year term and noted his "amateur
status" as a politician as one of the reasons for this
phenomenon.[9]

One of the basic factors in early assessments of Eisenhower and his administration was his handling of the
press. He and Hagerty became adept at using the press
conference for political purposes, and he was accessible to
reporters through this medium. But his problem came
with the upper levels of the journalistic hierarchy. Knowing he was extremely popular, and believing that columnists could do little to harm that popularity he ignored
the nation's top journalists. This a president does at grave
risks to his image. Columnists such as Walter Lippmann,
James Reston, Joseph Alsop, Marquis Childs, Drew Pearson, Richard Rovere, and Walter Krock can help the reputation of a president a great deal in return for the favor
of an exclusive interview or periodic news leaks, or they
can hurt that image if they feel slighted. These journalists, notes Patrick Anderson, "have done much to lower
the nation's opinion of his presidency."[10] Historians writ-

ing "instant history" were subsequently much influenced by these writers.

In recent years historians have begun to modify the early interpretations of the Eisenhower presidency. In the famous Arthur Schlesinger, Sr., poll of 1962, historians rated Eisenhower at the lower range of "average" presidents—he and Chester Arthur tied for twenty-first and twenty-second out of thirty-one presidents. In 1968, historians were again polled on their ranking of the presidents and this time he place slightly higher. The 1962 poll had asked only for a single judgment of the presidents; the 1968 poll was far more sophisticated in asking for a rating on seven dimensions. The later poll ranked Eisenhower nineteen out of thirty-five in "general prestige." But while he ranked only twenty out of thirty-five for the accomplishments of his administration, he ranked fifth in terms of flexibility (a major attribute of a politician).[11]

Recently (primarily, one suspects, as a result of the reaction against the war in Vietnam), Eisenhower has been evaluated by some scholars as a "political genius." Samuel Lubell was one of the first to discern the political capabilities that President Eisenhower kept so carefully hidden. As early as 1956, Lubell believed him to be "as compleat a political angler as ever fished in the White House."[12] In 1967, Murray Kempton became the first liberal to announce his conversion to this thesis. In a most enjoyable short essay, Kempton concludes that Eisenhower was a superb actor who concealed his intelligence, that even his garbled syntax was an instrument used for that purpose, and that it was years before he looked at Eisenhower's picture "and realized that the smile was always a grin."[13] In 1969, Garry Wills wrote that Eisenhower was "a political genius," as proven by the manner in which he handled Nixon.[14] In 1970, Richard Rhodes saw Eisenhower as "An Artist in Iron," a "brilliant man"; although not an intellectual, a practical man with a "phenomenal memory" and an "ability to reason of the highest caliber."[15] In 1971, William L. O'Neill described him as "a man of drive, intelligence, ambition, and ruthlessness."[16]

In a brief article in 1972, Robert L. Branyan attempted to modify the "myth" of Eisenhower's political ineptness and called attention to several significant achievements of the Eisenhower administration, using as illustrations Eisenhower's approval of the St. Lawrence Seaway and the Bricker Amendment.[17] In 1973, a "tactical" revisionist, Barton J. Bernstein, argued that Eisenhower displayed "shrewdness" and "skill" in his handling of the problems of foreign affairs.[18]

Those who rate Eisenhower a political genius might consider Kempton's warning, which he himself apparently forgot, that "there is always the danger of going overboard in moments when the watcher thinks he has found Eisenhower out." Richard Rovere evidently thought this was sound advice in 1973 when he considered the revisionist thinking. The revisionist phenomenon came about, Rovere says, primarily because Eisenhower kept the nation out of war for eight years. While Eisenhower was "no slouch politically," Rovere regards as "silly" the idea that he was a political genius.[19] Herbert S. Parmet, in his 1972 history of the Eisenhower administration, agrees that he was not a political genius but notes that he had "a remarkable political instinct."[20] In a 1974 biography, Peter Lyon presents Eisenhower as "canny and precise in his mental processes, observant, retentive, with a puissant will to win."[21] In a 1975 history of Eisenhower's presidential years, Charles C. Alexander notes a change in his own attitude which consists of "rejecting or at least softening a number of opinions" he had previously held about Eisenhower, whom he is coming to view "more favorably."[22] In a study of Eisenhower and the Eighty-third Congress, also written in 1975, Gary W. Reichard presents conclusive evidence that Eisenhower was quite concerned over his role as party leader and that, from the beginning of his presidency, he exerted effective political leadership although he did not attempt, as political myth has it, to revamp his party's ideology.[23] In a 1977 monograph, Douglas Kinnard concludes that in "the making and management of strategic policy he was a strong, active, and effective president" and corroborates the view that Eisenhower kept firm control over the Pentagon and his chiefs of staff.[24] Journalist Theodore White remembered in 1978 that Eisenhower's mind was "tough" and he had "a shrewdness of manipulation."[25] The latest examination of his presidency, by Elmo Richardson in 1979 in the Kansas series on the presidents, agrees with the recent assessments of Eisenhower as being in control of his administration.[26] Unfortunately, this excellent study was published too late for use in the present work. Further investigations by historians will undoubtedly reveal greater insights into the political processes and thought patterns of this complicated man. Probably, they will also demonstrate that he accomplished a great deal more in those eight years of his presidency than has hitherto been believed.

The historiography of Eisenhower achievements in domestic affairs has not really begun, for little has been written in this area. By contrast, there is a growing body of literature that analyzes his foreign policy. Norman Graebner laid down the first major interpretation in this area with *The New Isolationism,* published in 1956. Graebner emphasized the lessons Dulles had learned from watching what happened to his predecessor, Secretary of State Dean Acheson. This led him to decide to remain politically popular at home. To achieve this, Dulles took a hard stance as a determined cold warrior and espoused the policies, popular in many quarters, of "liberation" and "massive retaliation" in order to appease the "new" brand of isolationists.[27] Louis J. Halle and Adam Ulam continued this theme in their studies of the cold war.[28] Revisionists, however, following William A. William's "open door" interpretation of American foreign policy, began to reassess this traditional interpretation and also to cast more blame on the United States for creating Cold War tensions than did the liberal historians. Thus Walter LaFeber views American foreign policy in the postwar years as an effort primarily to establish hegemony over the Third World and its natural resources.[29] Joyce and Gabriel Kolko agree with LaFeber, stressing the continuity of the Truman and Eisenhower foreign policies.[30] Richard Aliano, in a recent study of the transition of foreign policy from Eisenhower to Kennedy, concludes that developments in the 1950s led to decisions made by the Kennedy administration in the 1960s.[31]

Revisionists, however, have been most active recently in reassessing the Eisenhower-Dulles relationship. Marquis Childs was one of the first writers to emphasize that Dulles completely dominated the Eisenhower foreign policy.[32] His thesis is pursued further by the Englishman, Richard Goold-Adams, and by Herbert Finer, who see the secretary of state as pulling the strings of a puppet president.[33] Even Louis Gerson, writing for the secretaries of state series, accepts this view, as does the famous political scientist Hans J. Morgenthau, and to a lesser extent, Stephen Ambrose.[34] The latest writer in this school of thought, Townshend Hoopes, strongly laments the dominance of Dulles over foreign affairs during the 1950s.[35]

David B. Capitanchik was the first to attempt to attribute more credit to the president for conducting foreign policy.[36] Moreover, his most recent biographer, Peter Lyon, views Eisenhower as dominating foreign policy, using Dulles as a lightning rod to attract criticism.[37] The New Left historians have come to view Eisenhower in the same light as the voting public did two decades ago—as a great hero who was well-versed in international affairs, a man dedicated to world peace.[38] Increasingly, as more research and further studies are made available, historians are coming full circle by evaluating Eisenhower as favorably as did his contemporary American public.

Notes

CHAPTER ONE

1. Dwight D. Eisenhower, *At Ease: Stories I Tell to Friends* (Garden City, N.Y.: Doubleday, 1967), pp. 29–30.
2. Kenneth S. Davis, *Soldier of Democracy* (Garden City, N.Y.: Doubleday, 1945), p. 10.
3. Oral History Interview with Reverend Ray I. Witter, August 28, 1964, Transcript at Dwight D. Eisenhower Library, Abilene, Kansas (hereafter cited as DDEL).
4. Eisenhower, *At Ease*, p. 62.
5. Davis, *Soldier of Democracy*, pp. 32–33.
6. Ibid., pp. 43–44.
7. Eisenhower, *At Ease*, pp. 68–69.
8. Ibid., p. 31.
9. John McCallum, *Six Roads from Abilene: Some Personal Recollections of Edgar Eisenhower* (Seattle: Wood and Reber, 1960), p. 33.
10. Oral History Interview with Orin Snyder, October 6, 1964, Transcript at DDEL.
11. Davis, *Soldier of Democracy*, p. 65.
12. Eisenhower, *At Ease*, pp. 52–53.
13. Davis, *Soldier of Democracy*, p. 68.
14. R. G. Tonkin, "I Grew Up with Eisenhower," *Saturday Evening Post* 224 (May 3, 1952), pp. 19; 46.
15. Eisenhower, *At Ease*, p. 95.
16. Ibid., pp. 96–97; McCallum, *Six Roads from Abilene*, pp. 72–74.

17. Tonkin, "I Grew Up with Eisenhower," p. 49.

18. Davis, *Soldier of Democracy,* pp. 56–58.

19. Eisenhower, *At Ease,* pp. 89–90.

20. Dwight D. Eisenhower, "What I Have Learned," *Saturday Review* 49 (September 10, 1966), p. 31.

21. Davis, *Soldier of Democracy,* pp. 84–85.

22. Ibid, p. 82.

23. Ibid, p. 84.

24. *The Helianthus,* 1909, Abilene High School Yearbook, DDEL.

25. Davis, *Soldier of Democracy,* p. 92.

26. Eisenhower, *At Ease,* p. 102.

27. E. E. Hazlett to Dwight D. Eisenhower, May 23, 1944, Principal Files, 1916–1952, Eisenhower Papers, DDEL.

28. Relman Morin, *Dwight D. Eisenhower: A Gauge of Greatness* (New York: Associated Press, 1969), p. 19.

29. Swede Hazlett told the story of Dwight's appointment to two early biographers, Alden Hatch and Kenneth Davis. See E. E. Hazlett to Dwight D. Eisenhower, May 23, 1944, Principal Files, 1916–1952, Eisenhower Papers, DDEL.

30. Eisenhower, *At Ease,* p. 107.

CHAPTER TWO

1. Dwight D. Eisenhower, *At Ease: Stories I Tell to Friends* (Garden City, N.Y.: Doubleday, 1967), pp. 3–4.

2. Ibid., pp. 4–5.

3. Peter Lyon, *Eisenhower: Portrait of the Hero* (Boston: Little, Brown, 1974), p. 43.

4. P.A. often discussed his roommate in the letters he wrote home. See Edward M. Coffman, "My Roommate Is Dwight D. Eisenhower," *American Heritage* 24 (April, 1973), pp. 102–3.

5. *Official Register of the Officers and Cadets of the United States Military Academy, 1911,* copy in Dwight D. Eisenhower Library, Abilene, Kansas. Hereafter cited as DDEL.

6. Allison Danzig, *Oh, How They Played the Game* (New York: Macmillan, 1917), pp. 291–92.

7. Paul A. Hodgson, Excerpts of His Letters, Principal Files, 1916–1952, Eisenhower Papers, DDEL.

8. Ibid.

9. These stories are told in Eisenhower, *At Ease,* pp. 7–10.

10. Paul A. Hodgson, Excerpts of His Letters, Principal Files, 1916–1952, Eisenhower Papers, DDEL.

11. Eisenhower, *At Ease,* p. 22.

12. Quoted in Kevin McCann, *Man from Abilene* (Garden City, N.Y.: Doubleday, 1952), p. 62.

13. William F. Longgood and Simone Gossner, *Ike: A Pictorial Biography* (New York: Time-Life Books, 1969), p. 25.

14. Eisenhower, *At Ease,* pp. 23–26.

15. Ibid., pp. 115–16.

16. See especially her picture in Longgood and Goosner, *Ike: A Pictorial Biography,* p. 27, or Relman Morin, *Dwight D. Eisenhower: A Gauge of Greatness* (New York: Associated Press, 1969), p. 30.

17. Eisenhower, *At Ease,* pp. 117–18.

18. Mamie Doud Eisenhower, "Introduction" to Don Ramsey (ed.) *Ike: A Great American* (Kansas City, Mo.: Hallmark Cards, 1972), p. 8.

19. Kenneth S. Davis, *Soldier of Democracy* (Garden City, N.Y.: Doubleday, 1945), pp. 165–66. See also Charles A. Case to Dwight D. Eisenhower, August 10, 1943, Principal Files, 1916–1952, Eisenhower Papers, DDEL, in which Case described the poker incident and almost chortled that Mamie "about had a fit" when Ike got home.

20. Mamie Eisenhower, "Introduction" to Ramsey (ed.) *Ike: A Great American,* pp. 6, 10.

21. Eisenhower, *At Ease,* pp. 127–28.

22. Alden Hatch, *General Ike* (Chicago: Consolidated Books, 1944), p. 61.

23. Davis, *Soldier of Democracy,* p. 177.

24. McCann, *Man From Abilene,* p. 71.

25. Eisenhower, *At Ease,* pp. 157–67.

26. Ibid, pp. 169–73.

27. Ibid., p. 178.

28. Ibid., pp. 180–82. Mamie wrote that with Icky's death, "for a time it was as if a shining light had gone out of Dwight's life," in "Introduction" to Ramsey (ed.), *Ike: A Great American,* p. 10.

29. Lyon, *Eisenhower,* p. 57–59.

30. Davis, *Soldier of Democracy,* pp. 192–93.

31. Eisenhower, *At Ease,* pp. 185–87.

32. Morin, *Dwight D. Eisenhower*, pp. 20–41.

33. Quoted in Davis, *Soldier of Democracy*, p. 197.

34. Eisenhower, *At Ease*, p. 187.

35. Ibid., pp. 199–200.

36. Ibid., pp. 202–3.

37. Morin, *Dwight D. Eisenhower*, p. 44.

38. Quoted in Ibid., pp. 220–21.

39. Hatch, *General Ike*, p. 82.

40. Eisenhower, *At Ease*, pp. 210–11.

41. John Gunther, *Eisenhower* (New York: Harper, 1951), p. 27.

42. Quoted in Lyon, *Eisenhower*, p. 69.

43. Eisenhower, *At Ease*, p. 213.

44. Eisenhower discussed this episode at some length in an interview with Raymond Henle for the Hoover Library Oral History Project, July 13, 1967, Transcript at DDEL.

45. Davis, *Soldier of Democracy*, p. 240.

46. Quoted in McCann, *Man from Abilene*, pp. 94–95.

47. Hatch, *General Ike*, pp. 92–93.

48. Eisenhower, *At Ease*, pp. 229–30.

49. Davis, *Soldier of Democracy*, pp. 271–74.

CHAPTER THREE

1. See Dwight D. Eisenhower, *Crusade in Europe* (Garden City, N.Y.: Doubleday, 1948), p. 5.

2. Stephen E. Ambrose, *The Supreme Commander* (Garden City, N.Y.: Doubleday, 1970), pp. 12–13.

3. Maurice Matloff (ed.), *American Military History* (Washington, D.C.: Department of the Army, 1969), p. 421.

4. Eisenhower, *Crusade*, pp. 18–22.

5. Ambrose, *Supreme Commander*, p. 9.

6. Ibid., p. 21.

7. Eisenhower, *At Ease: Stories I Tell to Friends* (Garden City, N.Y.: Doubleday, 1967), pp. 248–49.

8. Ambrose, *Supreme Commander*, p. 22.

9. Forrest C. Pogue, *George C. Marshall: Ordeal and Hope* (New York: Viking Press, 1966), p. 339; see also Winston S. Churchill, *The Hinge of Fate* (Boston: Houghton Mifflin, 1950), pp. 384–85.

10. Eisenhower, *Crusade*, p. 50.

11. Kenneth S. Davis, *Soldier of Democracy* (Garden City, N.Y.: Doubleday, 1945), pp. 302–3.

12. Ambrose, *Supreme Commander,* pp. 80–81.

13. Eisenhower, *Crusade,* p. 62.

14. Ambrose, *Supreme Commander,* p. 59.

15. Steve Neal, *The Eisenhowers Reluctant Dynasty* (Garden City, N.Y.: Doubleday, 1978), pp. 175–79. For the story of Mamie contemplating divorce, see Eban Ayers' Diary, May 25, 1953, Box 27, p. 174, in Harry Truman Library, Independence, Missouri.

16. Martin Blumenson, *Eisenhower* (New York: Ballantine Books, 1972), p. 22.

17. Eisenhower, *Crusade,* p. 95.

18. Captain Harry C. Butcher, *My Three Years with Eisenhower* (New York: Simon and Schuster, 1946), pp. 170–72.

19. Ambrose, *Supreme Commander,* p. 119.

20. Davis, *Soldier of Democracy,* p. 393.

21. Arthur Bryant, *The Turn of the Tide* (New York: Doubleday, 1957), p. 455.

22. Churchill, *Hinge of Fate,* pp. 685–91.

23. Ambrose, *Supreme Commander,* p. 159.

24. Blumenson, *Eisenhower,* pp. 40–43.

25. John Gunther, *Eisenhower,* (New York: Harper, 1951) pp. 19–24.

26. Davis, *Soldier of Democracy,* pp. 425–26; Eisenhower, *Crusade,* pp. 164–66.

27. Eisenhower, *Crusade,* pp. 163–64.

28. Ibid., pp. 179–83.

29. Ambrose, *Supreme Commander,* pp. 226–28; 231–32.

30. *The War Reports of General George C. Marshall, General H. H. Arnold and Admiral Ernest King* (Philadelphia: J. B. Lippincott, 1947), pp. 160–62.

31. Blumenson, *Eisenhower,* pp. 75–76.

32. Eisenhower, *Crusade,* p. 197.

33. Winston S. Churchill, *Closing the Ring* (Boston: Houghton Mifflin, 1951), p. 418.

34. Robert E. Sherwood, *Roosevelt and Hopkins* (New York: Universal Library, 1950), p. 803.

35. Alden Hatch, *General Ike* (Chicago: Consolidated Books, 1944), p. 208.

36. Ambrose. *Supreme Commander,* pp. 335–38.
37. Davis, *Soldier of Democracy,* pp. 461–62.
38. Eisenhower, *Crusade,* pp. 224–25.
39. Ambrose, *Supreme Commander,* pp. 370–76.
40. Eisenhower, *Crusade,* pp. 245–56.
41. Ibid., pp. 242–45; Churchill, *Closing the Ring,* pp. 590, 615.
42. Stephen E. Ambrose, *Ike: Abilene to Berlin* (New York: Harper and Row, 1973), p. 9.
43. Blumenson, *Eisenhower,* p. 93.
44. Ambrose, *Supreme Commander,* p. 426.
45. Butcher, *My Three Years,* p. 617.
46. Eisenhower, *Crusade,* pp. 297–98.
47. B. H. Liddell Hart, *History of the Second World War* (New York: G. P. Putnam's Sons, 1970), pp. 557–67.
48. *The Memoirs of Field Marshal the Viscount Montgomery of Alamein* (New York: World Publishing Co., 1958), p. 243.
49. Peter Lyon, *Eisenhower: Portrait of the Hero* (Boston: Little, Brown, 1974), p. 310.
50. Chester Wilmot, *The Struggle for Europe* (New York: Harper, 1952), pp. 573–74.
51. Blumenson, *Eisenhower,* p. 127.
52. Ambrose, *Ike,* p. 184.
53. Omar N. Bradley, *A Soldier's Story* (New York: Henry Holt, 1951), pp. 486–88.
54. Eisenhower, *Crusade,* pp. 366–67.
55. Walter Bedell Smith, *Eisenhower's Six Great Decisions* (New York: Longmans, Green, 1956), p. 155.
56. Eisenhower, *Crusade,* p. 218.
57. See especially Stephen E. Ambrose, *Eisenhower and Berlin, 1945: The Decision to Halt at the Elbe* (New York: W. W. Norton, 1967).
58. Winston S. Churchill, *Triumph and Tragedy* (Boston: Houghton Mifflin, 1953), pp. 459–60.
59. Quoted in Forrest C. Pogue, *George C. Marshall: Organizer of Victory* (New York: Viking Press, 1973), pp. 583–84.
60. Quoted in Davis, *Soldier of Democracy,* pp. 551–52.

CHAPTER FOUR
1. Dwight D. Eisenhower, *Crusade in Europe* (Garden City, N.Y.: Doubleday, 1948), chap. 24.

2. Ibid., pp. 441–42.

3. Quoted in Barton J. Bernstein, "The Quest for Security: American Foreign Policy and International Control of Atomic Energy, 1942–1946," *Journal of American History* 61 (March 1974), p. 1004.

4. Harry S Truman, *Memoirs*, (Garden City, N.Y.: Doubleday, 1955–1956), vol. 1, p. 416.

5. See, for instance, Martin J. Sherwin, "The Atomic Bomb and the Origins of the Cold War: U.S. Atomic Energy Policy and Diplomacy, 1941–45," *American Historical Review* 78 (October 1973), p. 966. For Ike's views, see Eisenhower, *Crusade*, p. 443.

6. R. Alton Lee, "The Army 'Mutiny' of 1946," *Journal of American History* 53 (December 1966), pp. 555–71.

7. Quoted in Stephen A. Ambrose, *Rise to Globalism* (Baltimore: Pelican, 1971), p. 134.

8. *New York Times*, June 16, 1945, p. 1.

9. Kevin McCann, *Man From Abilene* (Garden City, N.Y.: Doubleday, 1952), pp. 123, 125; Alfred D. Sandler, "Truman and the National Security Council, 1945–1947," *Journal of American History* 59 (September 1972), p. 370.

10. U.S., Senate, 1947, *Hearings on S. 758*, Pt. 1, 80 Cong., 1 Sess., pp. 89–115.

11. See Peter Lyon, *Eisenhower: Portrait of the Hero* (Boston: Little, Brown, 1974), 400 ff.

12. Quoted in Ibid., 348.

13. Eisenhower, *Crusade*, p. 444.

14. See, for example, Cabell Phillips, *The Truman Presidency* (New York: Macmillan, 1966), chap. 5.

15. Quoted in Editors of American Heritage and United Press International, *Eisenhower: American Hero* (New York: McGraw-Hill, 1969), p. 88.

16. Pre-Press Conference Notes, Ann Whitman File, September 11, 1956, The Papers of Dwight D. Eisenhower as President of the United States, 1953–1961, Dwight D. Eisenhower Library, Abilene Kansas (hereafter cited as DDEL); Robert A. Divine, *Foreign Policy and U.S. Presidential Elections, 1940–1948* (New York: New Viewpoints, 1974), p. 190.

17. Memo, Frank McNaughton to Don Bermingham, June 4, 1948, McNaughton Papers, Harry S Truman Library, Independence, Missouri.

18. Dwight D. Eisenhower to Leonard V. Finder, January 23, 1948, Principal Files, 1916–1952, Eisenhower Papers, DDEL.

19. Winston S. Churchill to General Dwight D. Eisenhower, July 27, 1948, Ibid.

20. Dwight D. Eisenhower to E. E. Hazlett, Jr., July 19, 1947, Ibid.

21. Relman Morin, *Dwight D. Eisenhower: A Gauge of Greatness* (New York: Associated Press, 1969), p. 135.

22. Dwight D. Eisenhower, *At Ease: Stories I Tell to Friends* (Garden City, N.Y.: Doubleday, 1967), pp. 354–55.

23. Quoted in Herbert S. Parmet, *Eisenhower and the American Crusades* (New York: Macmillan, 1972), p. 36.

24. Eisenhower, *At Ease,* pp. 376–77.

25. See especially Eric F. Goldman, *The Crucial Decade—And After* (New York: Vintage Books, 1960), chap. 4.

26. Richard F. Haynes, *The Awesome Power: Harry S Truman as Commander in Chief* (Baton Rouge: Louisiana State University Press, 1973), pp. 152–53.

27. McCarthy's story is best told in Richard Rovere, *Senator Joe McCarthy* (New York: Meridian Books, 1960).

28. Haynes, *The Awesome Power,* chap. 10. For Eisenhower's views, see Dwight D. Eisenhower, *The White House Years: Mandate for Change* (New York: Doubleday, 1963), pp. 82–83.

29. For the dismissal, see Trumbull Higgins, *Korea and the Fall of MacArthur* (New York: Oxford University Press, 1960), chap. 8.

30. James T. Patterson, *Mr. Republican* (Boston: Houghton Mifflin, 1972), pp. 484–93.

31. Eisenhower, *At Ease,* pp. 371–72; Averell Harriman to Dwight D. Eisenhower, September 14, 1951, Principal Files, 1916–1952, Eisenhower Papers, DDEL.

32. Lord Moran, *Churchill* (Boston: Houghton Mifflin, 1966), p. 381.

33. Krock got the story from Supreme Court Justice William O. Douglas, who heard it from Truman the day of the interview. Douglas later refused to retract the story. Arthur Krock, *Memoirs* (New York: Funk and Wagnalls, 1968), pp. 267–69.

34. Eisenhower, *Mandate,* pp. 16–18.

35. Barton J. Bernstein, "The Election of 1952," in Arthur

Schlesinger, Jr. (ed.), *The Coming to Power* (New York: Chelsea House, 1972), pp. 396–97.

36. C. L. Sulzberger, *A Long Row of Candles* (New York: Macmillan, 1969), pp. 735–36, 747.

37. Kirk H. Porter and Donald Bruce Johnson (comps.), *National Party Platforms, 1840–1960* (Urbana: University of Illinois Press, 1966), pp. 496–505.

38. Robert A. Divine, *Foreign Policy and U.S. Presidential Elections, 1952–1960* (New York: New Viewpoints, 1974), pp. 23–27.

39. Bernstein, "The Election of 1952," pp. 404–10.

40. Truman, *Memoirs,* vol. 2, pp. 512–13.

41. Emmet John Hughes, *The Ordeal of Power* (New York: Dell Publishing Co., 1962), p. 26.

42. Eisenhower, *Mandate,* pp. 52–55.

43. Divine, *Foreign Policy, 1952–1960,* pp. 50–54.

44. Nixon's version is in Richard M. Nixon, *Six Crises* (New York: Pyramid Communications, 1962), chap. 2.

45. Garry Wills, *Nixon Agonistes* (New York: New American Library, 1969), chap. 5.

46. Bruce Mazlish, *In Search of Nixon* (Baltimore: Penguin Books, 1973), p. 101.

47. Parmet, *Eisenhower,* pp. 127–28; 131–32.

48. Divine, *Foreign Policy, 1952–1960,* pp. 69–74.

49. Angus Campbell, et al., *The Voter Decides* (White Plains, N.Y.: Row, Peterson, 1954), p. 16.

50. Divine, *Foreign Policy, 1952–1960,* p. 85.

CHAPTER FIVE

1. Richard Rhodes, "Ike: An Artist in Iron," *Harper's Magazine* 241 (July 1970), p. 76.

2. For an overview of Eisenhower's political maneuvering while in the presidency, see Robert L. Branyan, "Eisenhower the Politician," *American Chronicle* 1 (January 1972), pp. 43–47.

3. George H. Mayer, *The Republican Party 1854–1966* (New York: Oxford University Press, 1967), p. 495.

4. Merriam Smith, *Meet Mister Eisenhower* (New York: Harper, 1955), pp. 75, 194.

5. Dwight D. Eisenhower, *The White House Years: Mandate for Change* (Garden City, N.Y.: Doubleday, 1963), p. 95.

6. Eliot Janeway, *The Economics of Crisis* (New York: Weybright and Talley, 1968), p. 243.

7. Herbert S. Parmet, *Eisenhower and the American Crusades* (New York: Macmillan, 1972), p. 176.

8. Eisenhower, *Mandate*, pp. 198–99. For the failure to amend the Taft-Hartley Act, see Gerald Pomper, "Labor Legislation: The Revision of Taft-Hartley in 1953–1954," *Labor History* 6 (Spring 1965).

9. Patrick Anderson, *The President's Men* (New York: Anchor Books, 1969), p. 165.

10. Sherman Adams, *Firsthand Report* (New York: Popular Library, 1962), pp. 56–67.

11. Richard E. Neustadt, *Presidential Power* (New York: Science Editions, 1960), p. 159.

12. Robert Keith Gray, *Eighteen Acres Under Glass* (Garden City, N.Y.: Doubleday, 1962), pp. 32, 46.

13. Milton S. Eisenhower, *The President Is Calling* (Garden City, N.Y.: Doubleday, 1974), pp. 308–16.

14. Adams, *Firsthand Report,* p. 78.

15. Eisenhower, *Mandate,* p. 478.

16. Quoted in Parmet, *Eisenhower,* p. 176.

17. Walter Johnson, *1600 Pennsylvania Avenue* (Boston: Little, Brown, 1963), p.322.

18. Douglas Kinnard, *President Eisenhower and Strategy Management* (Lexington: University Press of Kentucky, 1977), p. 14.

19. James T. Patterson, *Mr. Republican* (Boston: Houghton Mifflin, 1972), p. 600.

20. Adams, *Firsthand Report,* p. 94.

21. Emmet John Hughes, *Ordeal of Power* (New York: Dell Publishing Co., 1962), p. 218.

22. David B. Capitanchik, *The Eisenhower Presidency and American Foreign Policy* (New York: Humanities Press, 1969), pp. 40–44.

23. Richard A. Aliano, *American Defense from Eisenhower to Kennedy* (Athens: Ohio University Press, 1975), p. 37.

24. Peter Lyon, *Eisenhower: Portrait of the Hero* (Boston: Little, Brown, 1974), pp. 535–36.

25. Ambrose, *Rise to Globalism,* p. 227; Eisenhower quote in Hughes, *Ordeal of Power,* p. 119.

26. Eisenhower, *Mandate*, p. 254.

27. Lyon, *Eisenhower,* pp. 489–90.

28. David Wise and Thomas B. Ross, *The Invisible Government* (New York: Random House, 1964), pp. 110–13.

29. Eisenhower, *Mandate,* p. 166.

30. Neil Sheehan, *The Pentagon Papers* (New York: Bantam Books, 1971), p. 8.

31. Eisenhower, *Mandate,* p. 351.

32. Capitanchik, *The Eisenhower Presidency,* p. 53.

33. David Halberstam, *The Best and the Brightest* (Greenwich, Conn.: Fawcett, 1973), pp. 169–79.

34. Eisenhower, *Mandate,* p. 341; Dwight D. Eisenhower to J. E. Shaeffer, April 23, 1968, Papers of J. Earl Shaeffer, Dwight D. Eisenhower Library, Abilene, Kansas. Hereafter cited as DDEL.

35. Ambrose, *Rise to Globalism,* p. 233.

36. Sheehan, *Pentagon Papers,* pp. 13–25.

37. Ambrose, *Rise to Globalism,* p. 239.

38. Lyon, *Eisenhower,* pp. 589–91.

39. Wise and Ross, *Invisible Government,* pp. 172–78.

40. Eisenhower, *Mandate,* pp. 425–27.

41. Athan G. Theoharis, *The Yalta Myths* (Columbia: University of Missouri Press, 1970), p. 160.

42. Gary W. Reichard, "Eisenhower and the Bricker Amendment," *Prologue* 6 (Summer 1974), pp. 91–92; Dwight D. Eisenhower to J. Earl Schaeffer, January 22, 1954, J. Earl Schaeffer Papers, DDEL.

43. Reichard, "Eisenhower and the Bricker Amendment," p. 98.

44. Patterson, *Mr. Republican,* pp. 595–96.

45. Ibid., p. 589.

46. Robert Griffith, *The Politics of Fear: Joseph R. McCarthy and the Senate* (Lexington: University Press of Kentucky, 1970), pp. 207–16.

47. Eisenhower, *Mandate,* pp. 320–21.

48. Griffith, *The Politics of Fear,* pp. 254–59.

49. Robert L. Branyan and R. Alton Lee, "Lyndon B. Johnson and the Art of the Possible," *Southwestern Social Science Quarterly* 45 (December 1964), pp. 215–17.

50. Eisenhower, *Mandate,* pp. 308–09.

51. Robert J. Donovan, *Eisenhower: The Inside Story* (New York: Harper, 1956), pp. 287–88.

52. Lyon, *Eisenhower*, pp. 567–69.

53. Parmet, *Eisenhower*, pp. 342–44.

54. Lyon, *Eisenhower*, p. 573.

55. Richard Rovere, *Affairs of State: The Eisenhower Years* (New York: Farrar, Straus and Cudahy, 1956), p. 216.

56. Donald G. Morgan, *Congress and the Constitution* (Cambridge, Mass.: Harvard University Press, 1966), p. 254.

57. Lyon, *Eisenhower*, p. 649.

58. Eric F. Goldman, *The Crucial Decade—And After* (New York: Vintage Books, 1960), p. 287.

59. Lyon, *Eisenhower*, p. 653.

60. Eisenhower, *Mandate*, p. 521.

CHAPTER SIX

1. Charles J. V. Murphy, "The Eisenhower Shift," in Dean Albertson (ed.), *Eisenhower as President* (New York: Hill and Wang, 1963), pp. 53–54.

2. Herbert Stein, *The Fiscal Revolution in America* (Chicago: University of Chicago Press, 1969), pp. 282–83.

3. Murphy, "The Eisenhower Shift," pp. 63–64.

4. For the Wilson fiasco, see R. Alton Lee, "Federal Assistance to Depressed Areas in the Postwar Recessions," *Western Economic Journal* 2 (Fall 1963), pp. 14–17; for the link between economic conservatism and welfare liberalism, see Edward S. Flash, Jr., *Economic Advice and Presidential Leadership* (New York: Columbia University Press, 1965), p. 162.

5. Herbert S. Parmet, *Eisenhower and the American Crusades* (New York: Macmillan, 1972), pp. 222–24.

6. Francis Case to E. J. Kahler, December 14, 1955, Natural Gas—For, South Dakota Letters, Francis Case Papers, Dakota Wesleyan University, Mitchell, S.D.

7. Dwight D. Eisenhower, *The White House Years: Mandate for Change* (Garden City, N.Y.: Doubleday, 1963), pp. 555–56.

8. See William R. Willoughby, *The St. Lawrence Seaway* (Madison: University of Wisconsin Press, 1961) for these earlier developments.

9. Dr. N. R. Danielian, Interview with John Lutter, August 28, 1972, Washington, D.C., Columbia Oral History Project, transcript at Dwight D. Eisenhower Library, Abilene, Kansas. Hereafter cited as DDEL, pp. 16–17.

10. Memo for Director, Bureau of the Budget, March 12, 1953, OF 155—D-1, DDEL.

11. Danielian interview, pp. 25–26.

12. Merle J. Pusey, *Eisenhower the President* (New York: Macmillan, 1956), p. 233.

13. Eisenhower, *Mandate,* p. 548.

14. Dwight D. Eisenhower to John Jennings, Jr., October 22, 1952, OF 50, DDEL.

15. Homer E. Greunther to Joe L. Evins, August 21, 1953, OF 50, DDEL.

16. Aaron Wildavsky, *Dixon-Yates: A Study in Power Politics* (New Haven, Conn.: Yale University Press, 1962), p. 44.

17. Ibid., pp. 301–2.

18. David A. Frier, *Conflict of Interest in the Eisenhower Administration* (Baltimore: Pelican Books, 1970), pp. 76–77.

19. Elmo Richardson, *Dams, Parks and Politics* (Lexington: University Press of Kentucky, 1973), p. 83.

20. Ibid., p. 185.

21. Ibid., pp. 129–52.

22. Pusey, *Eisenhower,* pp. 245–48.

23. Ezra Taft Benson, *Cross Fire: The Eight Years with Eisenhower* (New York: Doubleday, 1962), pp. 254–55.

24. Edward L. Schapsmeier and Frederick H. Schapsmeier, "Eisenhower and Ezra Taft Benson: Farm Policy in the 1950s," *Agricultural History* 44 (October 1970), p. 373.

25. Sherman Adams, *Firsthand Report* (New York: Popular Library, 1962), pp. 205–11. See also Edward L. Schapsmeier and Frederick H. Schapsmeier, *Ezra Taft Benson and the Politics of Agriculture* (Danville, Ill.: Interstate Printers and Publishers, 1975), chap. 9.

26. Robert J. Donovan, *Eisenhower: The Inside Story* (New York: Harper, 1956), p. 172.

27. Ibid., p. 229.

28. Robert L. Branyan and Lawrence H. Larsen (eds.), *The Eisenhower Administration 1953–1961: A Documentary History,* 2 vols. (New York: Random House, 1971), vol. 1, p. 575.

29. Donovan, *Eisenhower,* p. 323.

30. Gary W. Reichard, *The Reaffirmation of Republicanism* (Knoxville, Tenn.: University of Tennessee Press, 1975), p. 217.

31. Adams, *Firsthand Report,* pp. 36–37.

32. Donovan, *Eisenhower,* p. 152.

33. Eric F. Goldman, *The Crucial Decade—And After* (New York: Vintage Books, 1960), p. 282.

34. Ibid., pp. 295–96.

35. Richard M. Nixon, *Six Crises* (New York: Pyramid Communications, 1962), p. 159.

36. Patrick Anderson, *The President's Men* (New York: Anchor Books, 1969), pp. 223–25.

37. Parmet, *Eisenhower,* pp. 415–16.

38. Peter Lyon, *Eisenhower: Portrait of the Hero* (Boston: Little, Brown, 1974), p. 671.

39. John S. D. Eisenhower, *Strictly Personal* (New York: Doubleday, 1974), pp. 183–85; Eisenhower, *Mandate,* p. 571.

40. Ann Whitman Diary, February 9, 1956, The Papers of Dwight D. Eisenhower as President, 1953–1961, DDEL; Nixon, *Six Crises,* pp. 169–77; Adams, *Firsthand Report,* pp. 229–33.

41. Emmet John Hughes, *The Ordeal of Power* (New York: Dell Publishing Co., 1962), p. 152.

42. Malcolm Moos, "Election of 1956," in Arthur Schlesinger, Jr. (ed.), *History of American Presidential Elections,* 4 vols. (New York: Chelsea House, 1972), vol. 4, p. 3352.

43. Divine, *Foreign Policy, 1952–1960,* pp. 136–43.

44. Samuel Lubell, *Black and White: Test of a Nation* (New York: Harper and Row, 1964), p. 71; Charles A. H. Thomson and Frances M. Shattuck, *The 1956 Presidential Election* (Washington, D.C.: The Brookings Institution, 1960), p. 353.

45. Moos, "Election of 1956," pp. 3353–54.

CHAPTER SEVEN

1. Richard Dalfiume, *Desegregation in the U.S. Armed Forces: Fighting on Two Fronts, 1939–1953* (Columbia, Mo.: University of Missouri Press, 1969), p. 201.

2. Robert J. Donovan, *Eisenhower: The Inside Story* (New York: Harper, 1956), pp. 155–59.

3. William F. Swindler, *Court and Constitution in the Twentieth Century: The New Legality, 1932–1968,* 2 vols. (Indianapolis: Bobbs-Merrill, 1970), vol. 2, pp. 22–23.

4. Ibid., pp. 223–25.

5. Ibid., pp. 225–27.

6. *Brown* v. *Board of Education of Topeka,* 349 U.S. 294 (1954).

7. Arthur Larson, *Eisenhower: The President Nobody Knew* (New York: Charles Scribner's Sons, 1968), pp. 124–27. See also Emmet John Hughes, *Ordeal of Power* (New York: Dell Publishing Co., 1962), p. 176.

8. Ronald Schlundt, "Civil Rights in the Eisenhower Years," unpublished Ph.D. dissertation (Houston: Rice University, 1973), p. 138.

9. *Public Papers of the Presidents of the United States, 1957* (Washington, D.C.: Government Printing Office, 1960), p. 546. Hereafter cited as *Public Papers* with the appropriate year.

10. Anthony Lewis (ed.), *Portrait of a Decade* (New York: Bantam, 1964), p. 93.

11. Schlundt, "Civil Rights Policies," pp. 129–31; 162–63; 172.

12. J. W. Anderson, *Eisenhower, Brownell and Congress: The Tangled Origins of the Civil Rights Bill of 1956–1957* (University, Ala.: University of Alabama Press, 1964), pp. 60–62.

13. Robert L. Branyan and R. Alton Lee, "Lyndon B. Johnson and the Art of the Possible," *Southwestern Social Sciences Quarterly* 45 (December 1964), pp. 218–21.

14. Daniel M. Berman, *A Bill Becomes a Law—The Civil Rights Act of 1960* (New York: Macmillan, 1962), pp. 89–91.

15. Alexander M. Bickel, *Politics and the Warren Court* (New York: Harper and Row, 1965), p. 59.

16. *Public Papers, 1958,* p. 394.

17. Quoted in Eric F. Goldman, *The Crucial Decade—And After* (New York: Vintage Books, 1960), p. 282.

18. Jan Dykshorn, "Public Law 83-280 and the Reasons for its Failure," unpublished M.A. thesis (Vermillion, S.D.: University of South Dakota, 1970), p. 46.

19. William T. Hagan, *American Indians* (Chicago: University of Chicago Press, 1961), p. 163.

20. Richard N. Ellis (ed.), *The Western American Indian* (Lincoln, Neb.: University of Nebraska Press, 1972), p. 189.

21. Herbert S. Parmet, *Eisenhower and the American Crusades* (New York: Macmillan, 1972), pp. 497–500.

22. *Public Papers, 1958,* p. 306; Dwight D. Eisenhower to Joseph W. Martin, Jr., March 8, 1958, OF 114, Dwight D. Eisenhower Library, Abilene, Kansas (hereafter cited as DDEL).

23. R. Alton Lee, "Federal Assistance to Depressed Areas in the Postwar Recessions," *Western Economic Journal* 2 (Fall 1963), pp. 20–22.

24. Dwight D. Eisenhower, *The White House Years: Mandate for Change* (Garden City, N.Y.: Doubleday, 1963), pp. 291–92.

25. Eight Congressmen to the President, July 31, 1959, OF 124-1959, DDEL; Edward B. Shils, "Impact of Landrum-Griffin on the Small Employer," *The Annals of the American Academy of Political and Social Sciences* 333 (January 1961), pp. 143–44.

26. Swindler, *Court and Constitution,* vol. 2, p. 235.

27. Alfred H. Kelly and Winfred A. Harbison, *The American Constitution,* 4th ed. (New York: W. W. Norton, 1970), p. 869.

28. Dwight D. Eisenhower to Edward F. Hutton, July 10, 1957, OF 100-A, DDEL.

29. Dwight D. Eisenhower to Earl Warren, June 21, 1957, Ibid.

30. Dwight D. Eisenhower, *The White House Years: Waging Peace* (Garden City, N.Y.: Doubleday, 1965), pp. 140–41.

31. Paul L. Murphy, *The Constitution in Crisis Times, 1918–1969* (New York: Harper and Row, 1972), p. 327.

32. 354 U.S. 178.

33. Attorney General to the President, May 27, 1958, Rogers Papers, D-Misc.-2, DDEL.

34. Walter F. Murphy, *Congress and the Court* (Chicago: University of Chicago Press, 1962), pp. 170–71.

35. Ibid., pp. 200–17.

36. Anthony Lewis, "Earl Warren," in Leon Friedman and Fred L. Israel (eds.), *The Justices of the United States Supreme Court 1789–1969,* 4 vols. (New York: Chelsea House, 1969), vol. 4, p. 2734.

37. Goldman, *The Crucial Decade,* pp. 307–11.

38. Peter Lyon, *Eisenhower: Portrait of the Hero* (Boston: Little, Brown, 1974), pp. 756–57.

39. Quoted in Blanche Weisen Cook, "Dwight David Eisenhower: Antimilitarist in the White House," *Forums in History* (St. Charles, Mo.: Forum Press, 1974), p. 11.

40. Eisenhower, *Waging Peace,* pp. 233–34.

41. Marquis Childs, *Eisenhower: Captive Hero* (New York: Harcourt, Brace and World, 1958), pp. 261, 275, 284.

42. Parmet, *Eisenhower,* pp. 518–20.

43. David A. Frier, *Conflict of Interest in the Eisenhower Administration* (Baltimore: Pelican Books, 1970), pp. 209–10.

44. Parmet, *Eisenhower,* pp. 542–43.

45. Eisenhower, *Waging Peace,* p. 396.

46. See especially Rowland Evans and Robert Novak, *Lyndon B. Johnson: The Exercise of Power* (New York: New American Library, 1966), chap. 10, "Too Many Democrats."

CHAPTER EIGHT

1. David B. Capitanchik, *The Eisenhower Presidency and American Foreign Policy* (New York: Humanities Press, 1969), p. 63.

2. Peter Lyon, *Eisenhower: Portrait of a Hero:* (Boston: Little, Brown, 1974), pp. 682–84.

3. Dwight D. Eisenhower, *The White House Years: Waging Peace* (New York: Doubleday, 1965), pp. 32–33.

4. Robert A. Divine, *Foreign Policy and U.S. Presidential Elections, 1952–1960* (New York: New Viewpoints, 1974), pp. 117–21.

5. Lyon, *Eisenhower,* pp. 707–10.

6. *Public Papers of the Presidents of the United States, 1956* (Washington, D.C.: Government Printing Office, 1960), pp. 1064–66. Hereafter cited as *Public Papers,* followed by the appropriate year.

7. Stephen E. Ambrose, *Rise to Globalism* (Baltimore: Pelican Books, 1971), p. 253.

8. Eisenhower, *Waging Peace,* pp. 178–80.

9. Ambrose, *Rise to Globalism,* pp. 254–55.

10. Eisenhower, *Waging Peace,* p. 275n.

11. Divine, *Foreign Policy, 1952–1960,* pp. 219, 238, 246.

12. Richard M. Nixon, *Six Crises* (New York: Pyramid Communications, 1962), Section 4; Eisenhower, *Waging Peace,* p. 519.

13. Hugh Thomas, *The Cuban Revolution* (New York: Harper and Row, 1977), pp. 273, 300.

14. Ambrose, *Rise to Globalism,* pp. 269–70.

15. Divine, *Foreign Policy, 1952–1960,* pp. 213–14.

16. Lyon, *Eisenhower,* pp. 781–86.

17. Ambrose, *Rise to Globalism,* p. 258.

18. Eisenhower, *Waging Peace,* pp. 340–41.

19. Divine, *Foreign Policy, 1952–1960,* pp. 194–95.

20. Eisenhower, *Waging Peace,* pp. 434–39.

21. Norris Poulson to the President, September 21, 1959, OF 225-E, Dwight D. Eisenhower Library, Abilene, Kansas. Hereafter cited as DDEL.

22. Ambrose, *Rise to Globalism,* pp. 263–64.

23. Divine, *Foreign Policy, 1952–1960,* pp. 201–3.

24. Lyon, *Eisenhower,* pp. 810–11.

25. Emmet John Hughes, *The Ordeal of Power* (New York: Dell Publishing Co., 1962), p. 264.

26. Divine, *Foreign Policy, 1952–1960,* pp. 249–50.

27. Theodore H. White, *The Making of the President 1960* (New York: Pocket Books, 1961), pp. 229, 240.

28. Ibid., p. 370. Emphasis in the original.

29. *Public Papers, 1960,* pp. 652–53.

30. Milton S. Eisenhower, *The President Is Calling* (Garden City, N.Y.: Doubleday, 1974), p. 368.

31. Theodore C. Sorensen, "Election of 1960," in Arthur M. Schlesinger, Jr., and F. L. Israel (eds.), *History of American Presidential Elections,* 4 vols. (New York: Chelsea House, 1971), vol. 4, p. 3463.

32. Divine, *Foreign Policy, 1952–1960,* pp. 263–64.

33. Lisenhower quote in Emmet John Hughes, "The Politics of the Sixties—From the New Frontier to the New Revolution," *New York Times Magazine* (April 4, 1971), p. 70; Nixon, *Six Crises,* p. 426.

34. Hughes, *Ordeal of Power,* p. 10.

35. Eisenhower, *Waging Peace,* pp. 653–54.

36. Cited in Patrick Anderson, *The President's Men* (New York: Anchor Books, 1969), p. 215.

37. James L. Sundquist, *Politics and Policy: The Eisenhower, Kennedy and Johnson Years* (Washington, D.C.: The Brookings Institution, 1968), pp. 419–21.

38. Herbert S. Parmet, *Eisenhower and the American Crusades* (New York: Macmillan, 1972), p. 578.

39. John S. D. Eisenhower, *Strictly Personal* (Garden City, N.Y.: Doubleday, 1974), pp. 304–7.

40. Arthur Larson, *Eisenhower: The President Nobody Knew* (New York: Charles Scribner's Sons, 1968), p. 6.

41. Theodore H. White, *The Making of the President 1964* (New York: Pocket Books, 1965), pp. 175–88.

42. Milton Eisenhower, *The President Is Calling,* pp. 425–26.

43. Dwight D. Eisenhower, "Let's Close Ranks on the Home Front," *Reader's Digest* 92 (April 1968), p. 51.

CHAPTER NINE

1. Stephen E. Ambrose, *The Supreme Commander* (Garden City, N.Y.: Doubleday, 1970). See also the evaluation in Martin Blumenson, *Eisenhower* (New York: Ballatine Books, 1972), p. 159.

2. William V. Shannon, "Eisenhower as President," *Commentary* 26 (November 1958), pp. 390, 394.

3. Clinton Rossiter, *The American Presidency* (New York: New American Library, 1956), pp. 21, 128.

4. Walter Johnson, *1600 Pennsylvania Avenue* (Boston: Little, Brown, 1960), p. 325.

5. Norman A. Graebner, "Eisenhower's Popular Leadership," *Current History* 39 (October 1960), p. 233.

6. Wilfred E. Binkley, *The Man in the White House* (New York: Colophon Books, 1964), p. 114.

7. Thomas A. Bailey, *Presidential Greatness* (New York: Appleton-Century-Crofts, 1966), pp. 325–28.

8. George E. Reedy, *The Twilight of the Presidency* (New York: New American Library, 1970), p. 64.

9. John E. Mueller, "Presidential Popularity from Truman to Johnson," *American Political Science Review* 64 (March 1970), p. 31.

10. Patrick Anderson, *The President's Men* (New York: Anchor Books, 1969), p. 230.

11. Gary M. Maranell, "The Evaluation of Presidents: An Extension of the Schlesinger Polls," *Journal of American History* 57 (June 1970), pp. 104–13.

12. Samuel Lubell, *Revolt of the Moderates* (New York: Harper, 1956), p. 25.

13. Murray Kempton, "The Underestimation of Dwight D. Eisenhower," *Esquire* 68 (September 1967), pp. 108–9, 156.

14. Garry Wills, *Nixon Agonistes: The Crisis of the Self Made Man* (New York: New American Library, 1969), p. 117.

15. Richard Rhodes, "Ike: Artist in Iron," *Harper's Magazine* 241 (July 1970), pp. 70–77.

16. William L. O'Neill, *Coming Apart: An Informal History of the 1960s* (Chicago: Quadrangle Books, 1971), p. 5.

17. Robert L. Branyan, "Eisenhower the Politician," *American Chronicle* 1 (January 1972), pp. 43–47.

18. Barton J. Bernstein, "Foreign Policy in the Eisenhower Administration," *Foreign Service Journal* 50 (May 1973), pp. 17–20, 29–30, 38.

19. Richard Rovere, "Eisenhower Revisited—A Political Genius? A Brilliant Man?," *New York Times Magazine* (February 7, 1971), pp. 14–15, 54, 58–59, 62.

20. Herbert S. Parmet, *Eisenhower and the American Crusades* (New York: Macmillan, 1972), p. 577.

21. Peter Lyon, *Eisenhower: Portrait of the Hero* (Boston: Little, Brown, 1974), p. 474.

22. Charles C. Alexander, *Holding the Line: The Eisenhower Era 1952–1961* (Bloomington: Indiana University Press, 1975), p. xvi.

23. Gary W. Reichard, *The Reaffirmation of Republicanism: Eisenhower and the Eighty-third Congress* (Knoxville: University of Tennessee Press, 1975), pp. 218–37.

24. Douglas Kinnard, *President Eisenhower and Strategy Management* (Lexington: University Press of Kentucky, 1977), p. 136.

25. Theodore H. White, *In Search of History* (New York: Harper and Row, 1978), pp. 347, 350.

26. Elmo Richardson, *The Presidency of Dwight D. Eisenhower* (Lawrence: The Regents Press of Kansas, 1979).

27. Norman A. Graebner, *The New Isolationism* (New York: Ronald Press, 1956).

28. Louis J. Halle, *The Cold War as History* (New York: Harper Colophon Books, 1967); Adam Ulam, *The Rivals* (New York: Viking Press, 1971).

29. Walter LaFeber, *America, Russia and the Cold War 1945–1966* (New York: John Wiley and Sons, 1971).

30. Joyce and Gabriel Kolko, *The Limits of Power* (New York: Harper and Row, 1972).

31. Richard A. Aliano, *American Defense Policy from Eisenhower to Kennedy* (Athens, Ohio: Ohio University Press, 1975).

32. Marquis Childs, *Eisenhower: Captive Hero* (New York: Harcourt, Brace and World, 1958).

33. Richard Goold-Adams, *The Time of Power* (London: Weidenfeld and Nicolson, 1962); Herbert Finer, *Dulles over Suez* (Chicago: Quadrangle, 1967).

34. Louis Gerson, *John Foster Dulles* (New York: Cooper Square Publishers, 1967); Hans A. Morgenthau, *Truth and Power* (New York: Praeger, 1971); Stephen E. Ambrose, *Rise to Globalism* (Baltimore: Pelican Books, 1971).

35. Townshend Hoopes, *The Devil and John Foster Dulles* (Boston: Little, Brown, 1973).

36. David B. Capitanchik, *The Eisenhower Presidency and American Foreign Policy* (New York: Humanities Press, 1969).

37. Lyon, *Eisenhower.*

38. See especially Blanche Wiesen Cook, "Dwight David Eisenhower: Antimilitarist in the White House," in *Forums in History* (St. Charles, Mo.: Forum Press, 1974).

Selected
Bibliography

I. BOOKS

Acheson, Dean. *Present at the Creation.* New York: W.W. Norton and Company, 1969.

Adams, Sherman. *Firsthand Report.* New York: Harper and Row, 1961.

Albertson, Dean, ed. *Eisenhower as President.* New York: Hill and Wang, 1963.

Alexander, Charles C. *Holding the Line: The Eisenhower Era 1952–1961.* Bloomington: Indiana University Press, 1975.

Aliano, Richard A. *American Defense Policy from Eisenhower to Kennedy.* Athens: Ohio University Press, 1975.

Ambrose, Stephen E. *Eisenhower and Berlin, 1945: The Decision to Halt at the Elbe.* New York: W.W. Norton and Company, 1967.

————. *Ike: Abilene to Berlin.* New York: Harper and Row, 1973.

————. *Rise to Globalism.* Baltimore, Md.: Pelican Books, 1971.

————. *The Supreme Commander.* Garden City, N.Y.: Doubleday and Co., 1970.

Anderson, J. W. *Eisenhower, Brownell and Congress: The Tangled Origins of the Civil Rights Bill of 1956–1957.* University: University of Alabama Press, 1964.

Anderson, Patrick. *The President's Men.* Garden City, N.Y.: Doubleday and Co., 1969.

Bailey, Thomas A. *Presidential Greatness.* New York: Appleton-Century-Crofts, 1966.

Barck, Oscar T., Jr. *A History of the United States Since 1945.* New York: Dell Publishing Co., 1965.

Bartley, Nunan V. *The Rise of Massive Retaliation.* Baton Rouge: Louisiana State University Press, 1969.

Benson, Ezra Taft. *Cross Fire: The Eight Years with Eisenhower.* Garden City, N.Y.: Doubleday and Co., 1962.

Berman, Daniel M. *A Bill Becomes a Law: The Civil Rights Act of 1960.* New York: Macmillan, 1962.

Bernstein, Barton J., ed. *Politics and Policies of the Truman Administration.* New York: Quadrangle Books, 1970.

Bickel, Alexander M. *Politics and the Warren Court.* New York: Harper and Row, 1965.

Blaustein, Albert P., and Ferguson, Clarence Clyde, Jr. *Desegregation and the Law.* Rutgers, N.J.: Rutgers University Press, 1957.

Blumenson, Martin. *Eisenhower.* New York: Ballantine Books, 1972.

Bradley, Omar N. *A Soldier's Story.* New York: Henry Holt, 1951.

Branyan, Robert L., and Larsen, Lawrence H., eds. *The Eisenhower Administration 1953–1961: A Documentary History.* 2 vols. New York: Random House, 1971.

Brooks, John. *The Great Leap.* New York: Harper and Row, 1966.

Bryant, Arthur. *The Turn of the Tide.* Garden City, N.Y.: Doubleday and Co., 1957.

Butcher, Captain Harry C. *My Three Years with Eisenhower.* New York: Simon and Schuster, 1946.

Campbell, Angus; Gurin, Gerald; and Miller, Warren E. *The Voter Decides.* White Plains, N.Y.: Row, Peterson and Co., 1954.

Capitanchik, David B. *The Eisenhower Presidency and American Foreign Policy.* New York: Humanities Press, 1969.

Childs, Marquis. *Eisenhower: Captive Hero.* New York: Harcourt, Brace and World, 1958.

Churchill, Winston S. *Closing the Ring.* Boston: Houghton Mifflin Co., 1957.

―――. *The Hinge of Fate.* Boston: Houghton Mifflin Co., 1950.

———. *Triumph and Tragedy*. Boston: Houghton Mifflin Co., 1953.

Cook, Fred J. *The Nightmare Decade*. New York: Random House, 1971.

Cornwell, Elmer E., Jr. *Presidential Leadership of Public Opinion*. Bloomington: Indiana University Press, 1965.

Cox, Archibald. *The Warren Court: Constitutional Decision as an Instrument of Power*. Cambridge: Harvard University Press, 1968.

Dalfiume, Richard. *Desegregation in the U.S. Armed Forces: Fighting on Two Fronts, 1939–1953*. Columbia: University of Missouri Press, 1969.

David, Paul T., ed. *The Presidential Election and Transition 1960–1961*. Washington, D.C.: The Brookings Institution, 1961.

Davis, Kenneth S. *Soldier of Democracy*. Garden City, N.Y.: Doubleday and Co., 1945.

———. *The Politics of Honor: A Biography of Adlai E. Stevenson*. New York: G. P. Putnam's Sons, 1967.

Degler, Carl. *Affluence and Anxiety*. Glenview, Ill.: Scott, Foresman and Co., 1968.

Divine, Robert A. *Foreign Policy and U.S. Presidential Elections 1940–1948*. New York: New Viewpoints, 1974.

———. *Foreign Policy and U.S. Presidential Elections 1952–1960*. New York: New Viewpoints, 1974.

Donovan, Robert J. *Eisenhower: The Inside Story*. New York: Harper and Row, 1956.

Ealau, Heinz. *Class and Party in the Eisenhower Years*. New York: The Free Press, 1962.

Eisenhower, Dwight D. *At Ease: Stories I Tell to Friends*. Garden City, N.Y.: Doubleday and Co., 1967.

———. *Crusade in Europe*. Garden City, N.Y.: Doubleday and Co., 1948.

———. *The White House Years: Mandate for Change*. Garden City, N.Y.: Doubleday and Co., 1963.

———. *The White House Years: Waging Peace*. Garden City, N.Y.: Doubleday and Co., 1965.

Eisenhower, John S. D. *Strictly Personal*. Garden City, N.Y.: Doubleday and Co., 1974.

Eisenhower, Milton S. *The President Is Calling*. Garden City, N.Y.: Doubleday and Co., 1974.

————. *The Wine Is Bitter.* Garden City, N.Y.: Doubleday and Co., 1963.

Engler, Robert. *The Politics of Oil.* Chicago: University of Chicago Press, 1961.

Evans, Rowland, and Novak, Robert. *Lyndon B. Johnson: The Exercise of Power.* New York: New American Library, 1966.

Finer, Herman. *Dulles Over Suez.* New York: Quadrangle Books, 1964.

Flash, Edward S., Jr. *Economic Advice and Presidential Leadership.* New York: Columbia University Press, 1969.

Fox, William T. R., and Fox, Annette B. *NATO and the Range of American Choice.* New York: Columbia University Press, 1967.

Fried, Richard M. *Men Against McCarthy.* New York: Columbia University Press, 1976.

Friedman, Leon, and Israel, Fred L., eds. *The Justices of the United States Supreme Court 1789–1969.* New York: Chelsea House, 1969.

Frier, David A. *Conflict of Interest in the Eisenhower Administration.* Ames: Iowa State University Press, 1969.

Gaddis, John Lewis. *The United States and the Origins of the Cold War, 1941–1947.* New York: Columbia University Press, 1972.

Gerson, Louis L. *John Foster Dulles.* New York: Cooper Square Publishers, 1968.

Goldberg, Arthur J. *AFL-CIO Labor United.* New York: McGraw-Hill, 1956.

Goldman, Eric F. *The Crucial Decade—And After.* New York: Vintage Books, 1960.

Gray, Robert Keith. *Eighteen Acres Under Glass.* Garden City, N.Y.: Doubleday and Co., 1962.

Griffith, Robert. *The Politics of Fear: Joseph R. McCarthy and the Senate.* Lexington: University Press of Kentucky, 1970.

Griffith, Robert, and Theoharis, Athan, eds. *The Specter.* New York: New Viewpoints, 1974.

Gunther, John. *Eisenhower.* New York: Harper and Row, 1951.

Halberstam, David. *The Best and the Brightest.* New York: Random House, 1969.

Harper, Alan D. *The Politics of Loyalty.* Westport, Conn.: Greenwood Press, 1969.

Hatch, Alden. *General Ike.* Chicago: Consolidated Books, 1944.

Haynes, Richard F. *The Awesome Power: Harry S Truman as Commander in Chief.* Baton Rouge: Louisiana State University Press, 1973.

Hughes, Emmet John. *The Ordeal of Power.* New York: Atheneum, 1962.

Huthmacher, J. Joseph, and Susman, Warren I., eds. *The Origins of the Cold War.* Waltham, Mass.: Ginn and Co., 1970.

Jameson, Henry B. *They Still Call Him Ike.* New York: Vantage, 1972.

Janeway, Eliot, *The Economics of Crisis.* New York: Weybright and Talley, 1968.

Johnson, Walter. *1600 Pennsylvania Avenue.* Boston: Little, Brown and Co., 1963.

Kemper, Donald K. *Decade of Fear.* Columbia: University of Missouri Press, 1965.

Kinnard, Douglas. *President Eisenhower and Strategy Management.* Lexington: University Press of Kentucky, 1977.

Kistiakowski, George B. *A Scientist at the White House: The Private Diary of President Eisenhower's Special Assistant for Science and Technology.* Cambridge: Harvard University Press, 1976.

Krock, Arthur. *Memoirs.* New York: Funk and Wagnalls, 1968.

Larson, Arthur. *A Republican Looks at His Party.* New York: Harper and Row, 1956.

———. *Eisenhower: The President Nobody Knew.* New York: Charles Scribner's Sons, 1968.

Latham, Earl. *The Communist Controversy in Washington.* Cambridge, Mass.: Harvard University Press, 1966.

Lewis, Anthony, ed. *Portrait of a Decade.* New York: Random House, 1964.

Lewis, Wilfred, Jr. *Federal Fiscal Policy in the Postwar Recessions.* Washington, D.C.: The Brookings Institution, 1962.

Liddell, Hart B. H. *History of the Second World War.* New York: G. P. Putnam's Sons, 1970.

Longgood, William F., and Gossner, Simone. *Ike: A Pictorial Biography*. New York: Time-Life Books, 1969.

Lubell, Samuel. *Black and White: Test of a Nation*. New York: Harper and Row, 1964.

——. *The Future of American Politics*. Garden City, N.Y.: Doubleday and Co., 1951.

——. *Revolt of the Moderates*. New York: Harper and Row, 1956.

Lyon, Peter. *Eisenhower: Portrait of the Hero*. Boston: Little, Brown, 1974.

Martin, John Bartlow. *Adlai Stevenson of Illinois*. Garden City, N.Y.: Doubleday and Co., 1976.

——. *Adlai Stevenson and the World*. Garden City, N.Y.: Doubleday and Co., 1977.

Matloff, Maurice, ed. *American Military History*. Washington, D.C.: Department of the Army, 1969.

Mayer, George H. *The Republican Party 1854–1966*. 2d ed. New York: Oxford University Press, 1967.

Mazlish, Bruce. *In Search of Nixon*. Baltimore: Penquin Books, 1973.

McCallum, John. *Six Roads from Abilene: Some Personal Recollections of Edgar Eisenhower*. Seattle: Wood and Reber, 1960.

McCann, Kevin. *Man from Abilene*. Garden City, N.Y.: Doubleday and Co., 1952.

Miller, Douglas T. and Nowak, Marion. *The Fifties: The Way We Really Were*. New York: Doubleday and Co., 1977.

Millis, Walter, ed. *The Forrestal Diaries*. New York: Viking Press, 1951.

Mitau, G. Theodore. *Decade of Decision: The Supreme Court and the Constitutional Revolution*. New York: Charles Scribner's Sons, 1967.

Moran, Lord. *Churchill*. Boston: Houghton Mifflin, 1966.

Morgan, Donald G. *Congress and the Constitution*. Cambridge, Mass.: Harvard University Press, 1966.

Morin, Relman. *Dwight D. Eisenhower: A Gauge of Greatness*. New York: Associated Press, 1969.

Morrow, E. Frederic. *Black Man in the White House*. New York: Coward-McCann, 1963.

Murphy, Paul L. *The Constitution in Crisis Times, 1918–1969*. New York: Harper and Row, 1972.

Murphy, Robert. *Diplomat Among Warriors*. Garden City, N.Y.: Doubleday and Co., 1964.

Murphy, Walter F. *Congress and the Court*. Chicago: University of Chicago Press, 1962.

Neal, Steve. *The Eisenhowers Reluctant Dynasty*. Garden City, N.Y.: Doubleday and Company, 1977.

Neustadt, Richard E. *Presidential Power*. New York: John Wiley and Sons, 1960.

Nixon, Richard M. *Six Crises*. Garden City, N.Y.: Doubleday and Co., 1962.

O'Neill, William L. *Coming Apart: An Informal History of the 1960s*. New York: Quadrangle, 1971.

Parmet, Herbert S. *Eisenhower and the American Crusades*. New York: Macmillan, 1972.

Patterson, James T. *Mr. Republican*. Boston: Houghton Mifflin, 1972.

Pogue, Forrest C. *George C. Marshall: Ordeal and Hope*. New York: King Press, 1966.

———. *George C. Marshall: Organizer of Victory*. New York: Viking Press, 1973.

Pollack, Jack Harrison. *Earl Warren, The Judge Who Changed America*. Englewood Cliffs, N.J.: Prentice-Hall, 1979.

Porter, Kirk H., and Johnson, Donald Bruce, comps. *National Party Platforms, 1840–1960*. Urbana: University of Illinois Press, 1966.

Pusey, Merle J. *Eisenhower the President*. New York: Macmillan, 1956.

Ramsey, Don, ed. *Ike: A Great American*. Kansas City, Mo.: Hallmark Cards, 1972.

Reedy, George E. *The Twilight of the Presidency*. New York: New American Library, 1970.

Reichard, Gary W. *The Reaffirmation of Republicanism: Eisenhower and the Eighty-third Congress*. Knoxville: University of Tennessee Press, 1975.

Richardson, Elmo. *Dams, Parks and Politics*. Lexington: University Press of Kentucky, 1973.

———. *The Presidency of Dwight D. Eisenhower*. Lawrence: The Regents Press of Kansas, 1979.

Rogin, Michael Paul. *The Intellectuals and McCarthy: The Radical Spectre*. Cambridge, Mass.: The Massachusetts Institute of Technology Press, 1967.

Rossiter, Clinton. *The American Presidency.* New York: Harcourt, Brace and World, 1956.

Rovere, Richard. *Affairs of State: The Eisenhower Years.* New York: Farrar, Straus and Cudahy, 1956.

———. *Senator Joe McCarthy.* New York: Harcourt, Brace and World, 1959.

Schapsmeier, Edward L., and Schapsmeier, Frederick H. *Ezra Taft Benson and the Politics of Agriculture: The Eisenhower Years, 1953–1961.* Danville, Ill.: Interstate Printers and Publishers, 1975.

Schlesinger, Arthur, Jr., ed. *The Coming to Power.* New York: Chelsea House, 1972.

Sheehan, Neil. *The Pentagon Papers.* New York: Bantam Books, 1971.

Sherwood, Robert. *Roosevelt and Hopkins.* New York: Universal Library, 1950.

Smith, Merriam. *Meet Mister Eisenhower.* New York: Harper and Row, 1955.

Smith, Walter Bedell. *Eisenhower's Six Great Decisions.* New York: Longmans, Green, 1956.

Snyder, Marty. *My Friend Ike.* New York: Frederick Fell Publishers, 1956.

Solberg, Carl. *Riding High: America in the Cold War.* New York: Mason and Lipscomb, 1973.

Stapleton, Margaret L. *The Truman and Eisenhower Years: A Selective Bibliography.* Metuchen, N.J.: Scarecrow Press, 1973.

Stein, Herbert. *The Fiscal Revolution in America.* Chicago: University of Chicago Press, 1969.

Stone, I. F. *The Haunted Fifties.* New York: Random House, 1963.

Sulzberger, C. L., *A Long Row of Candles.* New York: Macmillan, 1969.

Summersby, Kay. *Eisenhower Was My Boss.* Englewood Cliffs, N.J.: Prentice-Hall, 1948.

———. *Past Forgetting: My Love Affair with Dwight D. Eisenhower.* New York: Simon and Schuster, 1977.

Sundquist, James L. *Politics and Policy: The Eisenhower, Kennedy and Johnson Years.* Washington, D.C.: The Brookings Institution, 1968.

Swindler, William F. *Court and Constitution in the Twentieth Century.* 2 vols. Indianapolis: Bobbs-Merrill, 1969–1970.

Theoharis, Athan G. *The Yalta Myths.* Columbia: University of Missouri Press, 1970.

Thomson, Charles A. H., and Shattuck, Frances M. *The 1956 Presidential Campaign.* Washington, D.C.: The Brookings Institution, 1960.

Truman, Harry S. *Memoirs.* 2 vols. Garden City, N.Y.: Doubleday and Co., 1955–1956.

Vatter, Harold G. *The U.S. Economy in the 1950s.* New York: W. W. Norton, 1963.

West, J. B. *Upstairs at the White House.* New York: Coward, McCann and Geoghegan, 1973.

White, Theodore H. *The Making of the President 1960.* New York: Atheneum, 1961.

———. *The Making of the President 1964.* New York: Atheneum, 1965.

———. *In Search of History.* New York: Harper and Row, 1978.

Wildavsky, Aaron. *Dixon-Yates: A Study in Power Politics.* New Haven: Yale University Press, 1962.

Willoughby, William R. *The St. Lawrence Seaway.* Madison: University of Wisconsin, 1961.

Wills, Garry. *Nixon Agonistes: The Crisis of the Self Made Man.* Boston: Houghton Mifflin, 1969.

Wilmot, Chester. *The Struggle for Europe.* New York: Harper and Row, 1952.

Wise, David, and Ross, Thomas B. *The Invisible Government.* New York: Random House, 1964.

———. *The U-2 Affair.* New York: Random House, 1962.

Yarmolinsky, Adam. *The Military Establishment.* New York: Harper and Row, 1971.

II. ARTICLES

Aaron, Benjamin. "Amending the Taft-Hartley Act: A Decade of Frustration," *Industrial and Labor Relations Review* 11 (April 1958): 327–38.

Bernstein, Barton J. "Foreign Policy in the Eisenhower Administration," *Foreign Service Journal* 50 (May 1963): 17–20, 29–30, 38.

———. "The Quest for Security: American Foreign Policy and International Control of Atomic Energy, 1942–1946," *Journal of American History* 60 (March 1974): 1003–44.

————. "Election of 1952," in *History of American Presidential Elections*, 4 vols., edited by Arthur M. Schlesinger, Jr., and Fred L. Israel. New York: McGraw-Hill, 1971. Vol. 4, pp. 3215–66.

Bernstein, Irving. "The Growth of American Unions, 1945–1960" *Labor History* 2 (September 1961): 131–57.

Branyan, Robert L. "Eisenhower the Politician," *American Chronicle* 1 (January 1972): 43–47.

Branyan, Robert L., and Lee, R. Alton. "Lyndon B. Johnson and the Art of the Possible," *Southwestern Social Science Quarterly* 45 (December 1964): 213–25.

Coffman, Edward M. "My Roommate Is Dwight D. Eisenhower," *American Heritage* 24 (April 1973): 102–3.

Cook, Blanche Weisen. "Dwight David Eisenhower: Antimilitarist in the White House." In *Forums in History*. St. Charles, Mo.: Forum Press, 1974. Pp. 1–14.

Cook, Don. "General of the Army Dwight D. Eisenhower," in Field Marshall Sir Michael Carver (ed.) *The War Lords: Military Commanders of the Twentieth Century*. Boston: Little, Brown and Co., 1976. Pp. 509–37.

DeSantis, Vincent. "Eisenhower Revisionism," *The Review of Politics* 38 (April 1976): 190–207.

Dibacco, Thomas V. "American Business and Foreign Aid: The Eisenhower Years," *Business History Review* 41 (1967): 21–35.

Eisenhower, Dwight D. "Ike on Ike," *Newsweek* 62 (November 11, 1963): 107–10.

————. "Let's Close Ranks on the Home Front," *Reader's Digest* 92 (April 1968): 49–53.

————. "What I Have Learned," *Saturday Review* 49 (September 10, 1966): 29–33.

Graebner, Norman A. "Eisenhower's Popular Leadership," *Current History* 39 (October 1960): 230–36.

Handlin, Oscar. "The Eisenhower Administration: A Self-Portrait," *Atlantic Monthly* 212 (November 1963): 67–72.

Huston, James A. "The Eisenhower Era," *Current History* 57 (July 1969): 24–30.

Kempton, Murray. "The Underestimation of Dwight D. Eisenhower," *Esquire* 68 (September 1970): 108–9; 156.

Lee, R. Alton. "Federal Assistance to Depressed Areas in the Postwar Recessions," *Western Economic Journal* 2 (Fall 1963): 1–23.

———. "The Army Mutiny of 1946," *Journal of American History* 53 (December 1966): 555–71.

Maranell, Gary M. "The Evaluation of Presidents: An Extension of the Schlesinger Polls," *Journal of American History* 57 (June 1970): 104–13.

Mueller, John E. "Presidential Popularity from Truman to Johnson," *American Political Science Review* 64 (March 1970): 18–34.

Moos, Malcolm. "Election of 1956," in *History of American Presidential Elections,* 4 vols., edited by Arthur M. Schlesinger, Jr. and Fred L. Israel. New York: McGraw-Hill, 1971. Vol. 4, pp. 3341–54.

Murphy, Charles J. V. "The Eisenhower Shift," *Fortune* 53 (January, February, March, April 1956): 83–87, 110–13, 113–16.

Parrish, Michael E. "Cold War Justice: The Supreme Court and the Rosenbergs," *American Historical Review* 82 (October 1977): 805–42.

Pomper, Gerald F. "Labor Legislation: The Revision of Taft-Hartley in 1953–1954," *Labor History* 6 (Spring 1965): 143–58.

Reichard, Gary W. "Eisenhower and the Bricker Amendment," *Prologue* 6 (Summer 1974): 88–99.

Rhodes, Richard. "Ike: Artist in Iron," *Harpers* 241 (July 1970): 70–77.

Rovere, Richard. "Eisenhower Revisited—A Political Genius? A Brilliant Man?" *New York Times Magazine* (February 7, 1971): 14–15, 54, 58–59, 62.

———. "Eisenhower over the Shoulder," *American Scholar* 31 (Spring 1962): 176–79.

Sandler, Alfred D. "Truman and the National Security Council, 1945–1947," *Journal of American History* 29 (September 1972): 369–88.

Schapsmeier, Edward L., and Schapsmeier, Frederick H. "Eisenhower and Ezra Taft Benson: Farm Policy in the 1950s," *Agricultural History* 44 (October 1970): 369–78.

————. "Western Livestock Policy During the 1950s," *Journal of the West* 14 (July 1975): 25–31.

Shannon, William V. "Eisenhower as President," *Commentary* 26 (November 1958): 390–98.

Sherwin, Martin J. "The Atomic Bomb and the Origins of the Cold War: U.S. Atomic Energy Policy and Diplomacy, 1941–1945," *American Historical Review* 78 (October 1973): 945–68.

Shils, Edward B. "Impact of Landrum-Griffin on the Small Employer," *The Annals of the American Academy of Political and Social Sciences* 333 (January 1961): 141–52.

Sorensen, Theodore C. "Election of 1960," in *History of American Presidential Elections,* 4 vols., edited by Arthur M. Schlesinger, Jr., and F. L. Israel. Vol. 4, pp. 3449–69. New York: McGraw-Hill, 1971.

Taft, Philip. "The Impact of Landrum-Griffin on Union Government," *The Annals of the American Academy of Political and Social Sciences* 333 (January 1961): 130–40.

Tonkin, R. G. "I Grew Up with Eisenhower," *Saturday Evening Post* 224 (May 3, 1952): 18–19, 46, 48–49, 51, 53.

Index

Abilene, Kansas, 115, 148–49
Acheson, Dean, 123, 139–40, 141
Act of Bogota, 305
Adams, Sherman: appointment as assistant to the president, 177–78; and Eisenhower campaign (1952), 147; and Eisenhower's heart attack, 241; and Goldfine scandal, 288–89; and Little Rock crisis, 260; resignation, 289; and St. Lawrence Seaway, 223
Adoula, Cyrille, 303
Aiken, George, 262
Alaskan statehood, 291
Alcorn, Meade, 289
Alexander, Charles C., 334
Alexander, Sir Harold, 82, 88
Aliano, Richard, 336
Allen, George, 216
Allen, Henry J., 20
Ambrose, Stephen, 331, 336
Anderson, Clinton, 262, 290
Anderson, Gen. Sir Kenneth, 84
Anderson, Patrick, 332
Anderson, Robert: and desegregation, 253–54; and Jenner bill, 282; tax cut, opposition to, 270
Antwerp, 105, 106
ANVIL invasion, 96, 105
Anzio landing, 96
Area Redevelopment Administration, 270
Armas, Col. Carlos Castillo, 196–97

Arnhem, Allied arrival in, 107
Arnold, Gen. H. H., 109
Aswan Dam, 295–96
Atkins, Tommy, 32
Attlee, Clement, 118
Atomic Energy Acts: (1946), 124; (1954), 222

Badoglio, Pietro, 92
Bagdad Pact, 295
Bailey, Thomas A., 332
Barenblatt v. United States, 283
Barkley, Alben, 160
Baruch, Bernard, 57, 123
Batista, Fulgencio, 305
Beck, Dave, 272
Belle Springs Creamery, Eisenhower's employment at, 7, 17, 21
Ben Gurion, David, 295, 298
Bennett, Wallace, 282–83
Benson, Ezra Taft, 176, 233–34
Bentley, Elizabeth, 208
Bernstein, Barton J., 334
Betancourt, Romulo, 304
Bidault, Georges, 188
Binkley, Wilfred E., 332
Black, Douglas, 128
Blossom, Virgil, 259–60
Bohlen, Charles E. (Chip), 201
Bradley, Gen. Omar: as commander of II Corps in Africa, 85; as Eisenhower's classmate at West

Point, 35–36; MacArthur's Korean strategy, opposition to, 143; World War II career, 104, 107–10

Branyan, Robert L., 334

Brennan, William J., Jr., 255–56

Bricker, John, 199–200

Bridges, Styles, 201, 241

Bristow, Joseph L., 23–24

Brooke, Sir Alan, 83

Brownell, Herbert: as attorney general, 175; and Civil Rights Act (1957), 261–62; desegregation, views on, 257; Eisenhower cabinet, selection of, 174; and Eisenhower's heart attack, 242; and Little Rock crisis, 261; Supreme Court recommendations, 254–55; and White, Harry Dexter, 208–9

Brown v. Topeka, 255, 257–58

Bulganin, Nikolai, 213, 214

Burns, Dr. Arthur, 179

Burton, Harold, 256

Butcher, Harry, 57, 73, 128

Butler, John, 281

Byrd, Harry, 218, 269

Byrnes, James, 119

Camp Colt, 44–45

Camp Meade, 44, 46–47, 52

Camp Wilson, 43–44

Capitanchik, David B., 336

Carlson, Frank, 147

Carroll, Paul, 139

Case, Francis, 221

Castro, Fidel, 305–7

Central Intelligence Agency: establishment, 126; in Guatemala, 196–97; in Iran, 190–91

Chambers, Whittaker, 208

Chasanow, Abraham, 207–8

Chevalier, Haakon, 210

Childs, Marquis, 332, 336

Chotiner, Murray, 165

Churchill, Winston: Eisenhower, meetings with, 75, 82, 94, 188; and Eisenhower's candidacy, 132, 145; OVERLORD, support of, 100; "Rainbow Five," affirmation of, 72; re-election defeat, 118

Civil Rights Acts: (1957), 261–64; (1960), 263–64

Clark, Tom, 278

Clark, Gen. Wayne Mark: Darlan, meeting with, 80; and Italian invasion, 93; Korean briefings with Eisenhower, 173; and Louisiana maneuvers, 65

Clay, Gen. Lucius: and Dulles, 158; Eisenhower cabinet, selection of, 174; as Eisenhower's intermediary, 147; and highway advisory commission, 225; Moscow visit, 117

Cochran, Jacqueline, 148

Cohn, Roy, 202

Conner, Gen. Fox: Camp Gaillard, command of, 49; and Eisenhower's admission to Command School, 53; as Eisenhower's tutor, 50–51

Coplon, Judith, 140

Cunningham, Sir Andrew, 79

Cutler, Robert, 177

Dai, Bao, 194

Danielian, N. R., 224

Darlan, Adm. Jean Francois: Algiers, capture in, 80; assassination, 81; as head of North African government, 80

Davis, Bob, 16–17

Defense Early Warning System, 186

de Gaulle, Charles: and Algerian independence, 302; as Free French leader, 77; French Africa, domination of, 81; Paris conference, 312, 315; Paris liberation, 105

Degler, Carl, 252

Demobilization after World War II, 121

Dennis v. United States, 276–77

Dewey, Thomas E., 131, 146

Diem, Ngo Dinh, 194

Dien Bien Phu, 192

Dillon, Clarence, 127

Dillon, Douglas, 298

Dirksen, Everett, 159, 290

Dixon, Edgar, 228

Dodge, Joseph, 227

Dondero, George, 223

Doud, John Sheldon (Mamie's father), 39

Douglas, Paul: amendment to 1958 court bill, 282; and Area Rede-

velopment Administration, 270; and 1954 minimum wage, 271
Duff, James, 147
Dulles, Allen: as CIA director, 190; and Guatemala, 196; and United Fruit Company, 196
Dulles, John Foster: and Austrian peace treaty, 212; death, 290; as Eisenhower's secretary of state, 177, 184, 188, 193, 242, 294; and Geneva accords, 193; 1952 campaign, 162; 1952 Republican platform, 157; and Suez crisis, 296; and United Fruit Company, 196
Durken, Martin, 176, 271

Eastland, James O., 255
Eden, Anthony, 188, 213
Eisenhower, Arthur (brother of Dwight D.): 6, 17, 55, 268
Eisenhower, David (father of Dwight D.), 4, 6, 10–11, 71
Eisenhower, Doud Dwight (first son of Dwight D.), 44, 49
Eisenhower, Dwight David: PRE-PRESIDENCY: ancestry and birth, 2–6; Antwerp error, 106–7; at Army War College, 56; and Battle Monuments Commission, 55–57; Battle of the Bulge, 107–9; Berlin decision, 110–12; at Camp Gaillard, 49; at Camp Meade, 46–47; childhood in Abilene, 1–17; Columbia University presidency, 132–33; at Command School, 54; Conner, Gen. Fox, and, 48–53; *Crusade in Europe* (World War II memoir) authorship, 133–34; Darlan, Adm. Jean Francois, agreement with, 80–81; D-Day decision, 101–2; family reunion (1926), 55; father's death, 71–72; as football coach, 40–41, 49, 52, 55; at Fort Louis, 65; at Fort Sam Houston, 38; and GOODWOOD, 104; Hazlett, "Swede," friendship with, 22–24, 26; high school career, 17–21; homecoming to Abilene (1945), 115; Italy, invasion of, 92–93; Japanese bombings, disapproval of, 120; Korean intervention, approval of, 142, 167–68; and

Louisiana maneuvers, 65–66; MacArthur, Gen. Douglas, employment under, 58–69; Mamie Doud, introduction to, 39; marriage to Mamie, 41–43; and Marshall, Gen. George C., 68–72, 114; and military reorganization after World War II, 125–26; Moscow visit, 117–18; in North Africa, 79–86; NATO leadership, 138; Operations Division, leadership of, 71; and OVERLORD operation, 94–95, 98, 100, 102; in Panama Canal Zone, 49–52; and Paris, liberation of, 105; Paris, move to, 138–39; Patton, George S., Jr., introduction to, 47–48; in the Philippines, 62–64; as a pilot, 63; political aspirations, 128–32, 145–47; presidential campaign (1952), 161–69; presidential primaries (1952), 148, 158; presidential victory, 168; promotion to chief of staff of the army, 120; promotion to five-star rank, 109; promotion to rank of general, 66; and "Rainbow Five," 69; Republican presidential nomination (1952), 159; and "Secret Nixon Fund," 163–65; Sicily, invasion of, 87–89; Summersby, Kay, rumors of love affair with, 75–76; War Plans Division, work in, 68–71; West Point career, 25–37; World War II career, 43–45; and World War II demobilization, 122 PRESIDENCY: achievements as president, summary, 323–26; and Adams, Sherman, 287–89; and American Indian affairs, 267–68; Atomic Energy Act (1954), 222; "Atoms for Peace" speech to U. N. delegates, 189; Bermuda summit meeting (1953), 188; Bricker amendment, opposition to, 199–201; and *Brown* decision, 258–59; budgetary policy, 217, 268–69; cabinet sessions, 177–79; cerebral stroke (1958), 286; Civil Rights Act (1957), 262–64; Cuban problems, 305–7; desegregation of armed forces, 253; and Dien Bien Phu, 194; and Dixon-Yates controversy, 227–29; economic recessions: (1954), 218–19, (1957), 269–70; Eisenhower Doctrine, 300; farm policy, 233–34; Federal Aid Highway Act, 225–26; federal intervention, proposal for reducing, 221–22; foreign policy precepts, 185; and Formosan Straits crisis, 194–95; and Gaither report, 284–85; Geneva conference, 213; Guatemala, policy in, 195–97; health care plan, 235–36; heart attack (1955), 240–44; and Ho Chi Minh, 191–92; housing program, 237–38; and Hungarian revolution, 297–98; ileitis operation, 246; and Iranian revolution, 187–91; Korea, visit to, 173–74; Korean truce talks, 187–88; Krushchev visit, 310–12; labor policy, 271–74; and Landrum-Griffin Act, 273; Latin America, aid to, 304–5; Lebanon, U. S. occupation of, 301–2; and Little Rock crisis, 259–61; McCarthy library purge, opposition to, 202–3; and military-industrial complex, 322–23; military, "New Look" of, 185; natural gas controls, 221, "Open Skies" proposal, 214; and Oppenheimer case, 209–10; at Paris Conference, 315; political philosophy, 239–40; presidential reelection campaign and victory (1956), 247–49; and presidential candidates Nixon and Kennedy (1960), 318–21; price controls, removal of, 217; and public power plants, 229–31; and Quemoy-Matsu crisis, 307; and Rosenberg trial, 206; St. Lawrence Seaway construction, approval of, 222–25; and school construction, 265–66; security program, 206–7; and social security, 234–35; and Sputnik, 284; and Suez crisis, 295–96; summit conferences, 212; Supreme Court appointments, 254–56; tariff policy, 231–32; television image, 180–81; and Tennessee Valley Authority, 226–27; tidelands oil policy, 219–21; and U-2 incident with Russia, 314; and White, Harry Dexter, 208–9; White House daily routine, 215–16 POST-PRESIDENCY: death, 330; five-star rank, restoration to, 327; library dedication, 327; memoirs, 326–27; presidential campaign involvement (1964), 328–29; retirement to Gettysburg, 326; and Vietnam War, 329–30

Eisenhower, Dwight David II (grandson of Dwight D.) , 135, 172

Eisenhower, Earl (brother of Dwight D.), 7, 55

Eisenhower, Edgar (brother of Dwight D.), 6, 12–13, 21, 55

Eisenhower, Frederick (Dwight's great-grandfather), 3

Eisenhower, Ida (mother of Dwight D.), 4–6, 11–12, 95

Eisenhower, Jacob (grandfather of Dwight D.), 3–5, 7

Eisenhower, John Sheldon Doud (second son of Dwight D.), birth, 50; marriage and children, 135; Moscow visit, 117; presidential memoirs, assistance with, 326; West Point career, 95

Eisenhower, Mamie (Doud): courtship and marriage to Dwight, 39–42; and Dwight's 1955 heart attack, 243–44; and presidential campaign (1952), 148; retirement to Gettysburg, 236; reunion with Ike (1944), 95; White House sleeping arrangements, change in, 171–72

Eisenhower, Milton: birth, 7; and Department of Agriculture, 55–56; as presidential advisor, 180; scarlet fever, 16; as university president, 55

Eisenhower, Paul, 7

Eisenhower, Roy, 7, 55, 95

En-lai, Chou, 193

Faubus, Orval, 260

Faure, Edgar, 213

Finer, Herbert, 336

Flemming, Arthur, 217

Folsum, Marion, 237

Forrestal, James, 126–27; 136

Fort Lewis, 65

Fort Oglethorpe, 44
Fredendall, Gen. Lloyd, 76, 85
Fuchs, Karl, 140

Gaither Report, 284–85
Galbraith, John Kenneth, 160
Gates, Thomas, 315
Gault, Col. James, 139
Gerow, Gen. Leonard T., 54, 68
Gerson, Louis, 336
Giraud, Henri, 77, 80
Goldfine, Bernard, 288
Goldwater, Barry, 221, 329
Gomulka, Wladyslav, 297
Good, Milton, 5–6
Goold-Adams, Richard, 336
Gosden, Freeman, 216
Graebner, Norman, 332, 335
Graham, Billy, 252
Green, William, 272
Groves, Leslie, 119
Gruenther, Gen. Alfred, 139, 216, 224
Guaranteed annual wage, 271–72

Hagerty, James, 180–82, 241–43
Hall, Leonard, 246, 247
Halle, Louis J., 335
Halleck, Charles: as House Majority Leader, 218; as House Minority Leader, 290; and St. Lawrence Seaway, 224
Hammerskjold, Dag, 303
Harlan, John Marshall, 255
Harmon, Gen. Ernest, 85
Harriman, W. Averell, 145
Hauge, Gabriel: as economic adviser to Eisenhower, 182; and Eisenhower's political philosophy, 239; price controls, opposition to, 217; rewriting of Eisenhower's 1952 campaign speeches, 161
Hawaii, 290–91
Hays, Brooks, 260
Hazlett, Everett E., Jr. (Swede), 22, 24, 35
Herter, Christian, 246, 290
Hickenlooper, Bourke, 221
Hiss, Alger, 140
Hitler, Adolf: and Battle of the Bulge, 107; French conquest, 64; and National Redoubt, 111, 113; rise to power, 64; suicide, 113
Hobby, Oveta Culp, 177, 236–37

Hodges, Courtney, 110
Hodgson, Paul, 29–30
Hoffa, Jimmy, 272
Hoffman, Paul, 128
Hoopes, Townshend, 336
Hoover, J. Edgar, 209–10
Howe, Joe, 20
Hughes, Emmet John, 161, 203
Humphrey, George: and federal budget (1958), 268–69; price controls, opposition to, 217; St. Lawrence Seaway, approval of, 224; as secretary of the treasury, 174
Humphrey, Hubert H., 211, 318
HUSKY (invasion of Sicily), 87

Insular cases, 274–76

Jackson, C. D., 161
Jackson, Robert, 255
Jencks v. United States, 277–78
Jenner, William: and 1957 court bill, 280–83; and presidential campaign (1952), 166; in Subcommittee on Internal Security, 202
Jiminez, Perez, 304
Jodl, Alfred, 113
Johnson, Lyndon B.: and Civil Rights Act (1957), 262–63; Jenner-Butler bill, opposition to, 281–82; and McCarthy, Senate move to censure, 205; as majority leader, Senate, 238; as NASA sponsor, 284; as president, 328; and Vietnam, 329–30
Johnson, Walter, 332
Jones, W. Alton (Pete), 190, 216

Kaghan, Theodore, 202
Kai-shek, Chiang, 120, 139–40
Kasavubu, Joseph, 303
Kasper, John, 259
Kefauver, Estes, 160, 247
Kempton, Murray, 333
Kennedy, John F.: assassination, 328; and Landrum-Griffin Act, 273; and Oppenheimer, Robert, 210; presidential campaigns (1956), 247; (1960) 318–21
Kennedy, Robert, 202, 272
Kerouc, Jack, 251
Kerr-Mills bill, 236
Khrushchev, Nikita: and Berlin

issue, 308; "de-Stalinization" speech, 297; and Geneva conference, 213–14; and Hungarian revolution, 297–98; Nixon, debate with, 310; and Paris Conference, 315; United Nations, visit to, 315–16; United States, 1959 visit to, 311–12; and U-2 incident, 314
Killian, James, 284
King, Martin Luther, Jr., 264–65
Kinnard, Douglas, 335
Knowland, William, 198, 200, 263
Kohler, Walter, 166
Konigsberg v. California, 280
Korean War, 142, 167–68
Kreuger, Lt. Gen. Walter, 65
Krock, Walter, 332
Ku Klux Klan, 258
Kurusu, Saburo, 68
Kuykendall, Jerome, 230

LaFeber, Walter, 336
Landrum-Griffin Act, 273–74
Langer, William, 274
Lansdale, Edward, 194
Lear, Lt. Gen. Ben, 65
Leclerc, Philippe, 105
Leigh-Mallory, Trafford, 98, 100
Lend-Lease Act, 67
Lewis, Anthony, 208
Lippman, Walter, 332
Little Rock crisis, 259–61
Lodge, Henry Cabot: Eisenhower, Paris visit with, 147; and "Fair Play" rule, 159; as Khrushchev's tour guide, 311; as Nixon's running mate, 317; and St. Lawrence Seaway, 223; and Suez crisis, 299; as U. N. ambassador, 179
Lubell, Samuel, 333
Lumumba, Patrice, 303
Lyon, Peter, 334, 336

MacArthur, Gen. Douglas: as army chief of staff, 58; and Bonus Army March, 59–60; dismissal, 143–44; Eisenhower, praise for, 61–62; in Korea, 142–43; in the Philippines, 61; promotion to five-star rank, 109; and Wake Island conference, 142
McCann, Kevin, 139
McCarran, Pat, 201

McCarthy, Joseph: and book-burning, 202; Brennan, William J., Jr., denunciation of, 256; Committee on Government Operations, chairmanship of, 202; death, 205–6; and Eisenhower, 166–67, 206; Marshall, attack on, 166; and Matthews, Joseph B., 203–4; and Peress, Maj. Irving, 204; Red Scare, exploitation of, 140–41; Senate censure, 205
McClellan, John, 272
McCloy, John J., 203
McCormack, John, 286
McKay, Douglas, 175, 230
Macmillan, Harold, 301, 309, 316
Mallory v. United States, 280
Mann, Woodrow Wilson, 260
Marshall, Gen. George C.: China mission, 120; and demobilization, 120–21; and Eisenhower, 52, 66, 94, 114; and HUSKY, 88–89; and Louisiana maneuvers, 65–66; McCarthy, attack by, 141; and military reorganization, 125; Normandy front, visit to, 102; promotion to five-star rank, 109; as secretary of defense, 127; World War II success, 116
Martin, Joe, 198, 218, 224, 290
Martin, John Bartlow, 160
Matthews, Joseph B., 203–4
Matusow, Harvey, 277
Meany, George, 272
Merle, Miller, 75
Merrifield, Wesley, 14
Messina, 89
Minh, Ho Chi, 191–92
Minton, Sherman, 255
Mitchell, James, 177
Moaney, John, 215
Mobuto, Joseph, 303
Monnet, Jean, 139
Montgomery, Gen. Bernard: Arnhem failure, 107; and Battle of the Bulge, 108–9; field marshal appointment, 105; and GOODWOOD, 104; and HUSKY involvement, 103–4; and MARKET-GARDEN, 106; in North Africa, 76; and NATO, 139
Moos, Malcolm, 329
Morgan, Gerald, 289

Morgenthau, Hans J., 336
Morrow, E. Frederick, 254
Morse, Wayne: and Dixon-Yates controversy, 228; and Hells Canyon federal power plant proposal, 230; Landrum-Griffin Act, opposition to, 274; party affiliation, 197, 249; and tidelands oil filibuster, 220
Mossadegh, Mohammed, 190
Mueller, John E., 332
Mundt, Karl, 163, 204–5
Murphy, Robert, 77
Murray, Philip, 272
Muskie, Edmund, 289
Musser, Chris, 7
Mussolini, Benito, 64, 92

Nagy, Imre, 297
Nasser, Gamal Abdel: and Aswan Dam, 295–96; and Bagdad Pact, 295; Suez Canal nationalization, 296
National Defense Education Act, 285–86
National Security Council, 126, 182
NATO, 137–38
Neff, John, 221
Nehru, Jawaharlal, 187
Nixon, Richard M.: "Checkers" speech, 164; and court bill (1958), 282; and Eisenhower's heart attack, 240–43; Latin America, visit to, 304; and Matthews, Joseph B., 203–4; presidential campaigns: (1956), 245–46, (1960), 317–21; and presidential disability agreement, 286–87; Russia, visit to, 310; vice presidential candidacy, 159

O'Neill, William L., 333
Oppenheimer, Robert, 209–10

Pahlavi, Mohammed Reza, 190–91
Pannikkar, K. M., 187
Pantelleria, 88, 125
Parks, Rosa, 264
Parmet, Herbert S., 334
Patch, Alexander, 105
Patton, Gen. George S., Jr.: Avranches, capture of, 104; and Bastogne, 108; and Eisenhower, 54; and HUSKY invasion, 89;

incident with shell-shocked soldier, 89–90; and Louisiana maneuvers, 66; negative publicity, 89–90, 97; North Africa, U. S. invasion of, 76; Rhine, crossing of, 110; and tank experiments, 47–48
Pearl Harbor, 66
Pearson, Drew, 332
Pennsylvania v. Nelson, 277
Percy, Charles, 317
Peress, Maj. Irving, 204
Peron, Juan, 304
Pershing, Gen. John J., 53, 55
Persons, Lester, 202
Persons, Gen. Wilton B. (Jerry), 139, 179, 289
Petain, Marshal Henri Philippe, 77
Poulson, Norris, 311–12
Powell, Adam Clayton, Jr., 247–48, 253, 266
Powers, Gary, 314
Presley, Elvis, 251
Proskauer, Joseph, 202

Queen Mary, 70
Quemoy and Matsu, 195, 307, 320
Quezon, Manuel, 61, 63–64

Rabb, Max, 253
Radford, Arthur, 186, 192
Rainbow Five, 69
Randall, Clarence B., 231
Rayburn, Sam, 238, 263, 269
Reed, David A., 218
Reed, Stanley, 256
Reedy, George, 332
Reichard, Gary W., 334
Reston, James, 332
Rhee, Syngman, 173, 187–88
Rhodes, Richard, 333
Richardson, Elmo, 335
Richardson, Sid, 128
Ridgeway, Matthew, 144, 186, 192–93
Roberts, Clifford, 128
Roberts, Roy, 128
Robinson, William, 216
Rockefeller, Nelson, 287–90, 316–17
Rogers, William P., 203, 261, 280–82
Rojas, Gustavo, 304
Rommel, Erwin, 73, 84
Roosevelt, Franklin D.: Churchill,

meetings with, 72, 82, 94; death, 118; and OVERLORD, 94–95; vacations, 172
Roosevelt, Kermit (Kim), 190
Rosenberg, Julius and Ethel, 140, 206
Rossiter, Clinton, 332
ROUNDUP, postponement of, 73
Rovere, Richard, 332, 334
Ryder, Gen. Charles, 76

Saigon military mission, 194
St. Lawrence Seaway, 222–25
Salk, Jonas, 236
Schine, David, 202, 204
Schlesinger, Arthur, Jr., 160
Schlesinger, Arthur, Sr., 333
Schware v. New Mexico, 279–80
Scranton, William, 328–29
SEATO, 194
Seaton, Fred, 175, 267
Service v. Dulles, 279
Shannon, William V., 331
Shivers, Allan, 259
"Sit-ins," 265
Smith, Walter Bedell (Beetle): as CIA leader, 160; as Eisenhower's chief of staff, 74, 177; and Geneva Accords, 193; as undersecretary of state, 180; and United Fruit Company, 196
Snyder, Gen. Howard, 240
Soil Bank, 233–34
Spaatz, Carl, 98
Sparkman, John, 160, 201
Sputnik, 283
Stalin, Josef, 72, 94, 117–18, 136–37, 186
Stassen, Harold, 148, 246–47
Steelman, John R., 178
Stennis, John, 255
Stevenson, Adlai, 160–61, 247–48, 265–66
Stewart, Potter, 256
St. Lawrence Seaway, 222–25
Strategic Air Command, 186
Strauss, Lewis, 209, 290
Summerfield, Arthur, 175
Summersby, Kay, 75–76
Sweezy v. New Hampshire, 279

Taft, Sen. Robert A.: and Bohlen, Charles (Chip), 201; conservative political views, 144–45; death,

183; Eisenhower, meeting with, 145; and presidential campaign (1952), 148, 158–59, 163; and Republican platform (1952), 198–99; as Senate majority leader, 197; Social Security, views on, 234–35
Taylor, Maxwell, 92, 186
Tedder, Sir Arthur, 82–83
Thurmond, J. Strom, 132, 263
Tidelands oil issue, 219–21
Tojo, Hideki, 67–68
TORCH, 76
Tribal termination bills, 267–68
Truman, Harry S: and atomic bomb, 119; and Eisenhower's marital problems, 75; and Eisenhower's presidential candidacy, 129, 167; and Ho Chi Minh, 191; and hydrogen bomb, 140; Korean involvement, 142; loyalty program, 207; MacArthur, dismissal of, 143–44; Potsdam meeting and Japan ultimatum, 118–20; presidential victory (1948), 132; reconversion problems, 129; tidelands oil issue, 220; and Wake Island conference, 142; and White, Harry Dexter, 208–9
Tse-tung, Mao, 120, 139
Twining, Nathan, 193

Ubeco, Jorge, 196
Ulam, Adam, 335
U-2 incident, 313–14

Vandenberg, Arthur, 141
Vaughan, Harry, 146
von Armin, Gen. Juergen, 84
V-1 rockets, 102–3

Walker, Edwin A., 261
Wallace, Henry A., 132
Waltz, Milland, 38
Warren, Earl, 159, 255, 257–58
Watkins, Arthur, 205
Watkins v. United States, 278–79
Watson, Thomas, Jr., 127
Weeks, Sinclair, 176, 224
Wenzell, Adolphe, 227–28
White citizens councils, 258
White, Harry Dexter, 208–9
White, Paul Dudley, 240–41, 244
White, Theodore H., 335

Whitman, Ann, 196, 215
Whitney, John Hay, 128
Whittaker, Charles, E., 256
Wiley, Alexander, 223
Wilkins, Roy, 264
Williams, William A., 335–36
Wills, Gary, 333
Wilson, Charles E., 175, 186, 217, 219

Yates, Eugene, 228
Yates v. United States, 279
Young, Whitney, 264

Zahedi, Fazollah, 190–91
Zhukov, Georgi, 117, 213
Zwicker, Ralph, 204